APOCALYPSE, PROPHECY, AND PSEUDEPIGRAPHY

Apocalypse, Prophecy, and Pseudepigraphy

On Jewish Apocalyptic Literature

John J. Collins

WILLIAM B. EERDMANS PUBLISHING COMPANY
GRAND RAPIDS, MICHIGAN / CAMBRIDGE, U.K.

Published 2015 by
Wm. B. Eerdmans Publishing Co.
2140 Oak Industrial Drive N.E., Grand Rapids, Michigan 49505 /
P.O. Box 163, Cambridge CB3 9PU U.K.

Printed in the United States of America

21 20 19 18 17 16 15   7 6 5 4 3 2 1

Library of Congress Cataloging-in-Publication Data

Collins, John J. (John Joseph), 1946–
[Essays. Selections]
Apocalypse, prophecy, and pseudepigraphy:
essays on Jewish Apocalyptic literature / John J. Collins.
pages   cm
Includes bibliographical references.
ISBN 978-0-8028-7285-2 (pbk.: alk. paper)
1. Apocalyptic literature — History and criticism.
2. Bible. Old Testament — Criticism, interpretation, etc.   I. Title.
BS646.C649   2015
220′.046 — dc23
                    2015024172

www.eerdmans.com

Contents

v

Preface

The essays in this volume have been written over the last fifteen years. Two of them have not been published previously.

The introductory essay revisits the problem of defining Apocalypse as a literary genre, in light of developments in literary theory over the last few decades.

The remaining essays are grouped into five parts. In the first part, three essays deal with the relationship between apocalypse and prophecy. The second part contains five essays on different apocalyptic texts, each of which represents a distinctive variation on the genre. The third part considers three important themes in apocalyptic literature. The fourth deals with pseudepigraphy, by considering three different examples. The final section, on Ethics and Politics, contains four essays, and discusses some of the troubling ethical issues raised by apocalyptic texts.

These essays complement my book *The Apocalyptic Imagination* (3rd ed.; Grand Rapids: Eerdmans, 2016), which discusses the various apocalyptic writings in their historical contexts, by studies that are primarily thematic. Readers should also note my edited volume, *The Oxford Handbook of Apocalyptic Literature* (New York: Oxford, 2014), which offers a wider range of thematic essays by multiple authors.

My thanks are due to Michael Thomson, who acquired the volume for Eerdmans and guided it through production, to James Nati, who compiled the bibliography, and to Laura Carlson, who compiled the indices.

Acknowledgments

My thanks are due to the following publishers for permission to re-publish the essays listed:

E. J. Brill of Leiden for
"Enochic Judaism: An Assessment," in Adolfo D. Roitman, Lawrence H. Schiffman, and Shani Tzoref, eds., *The Dead Sea Scrolls and Contemporary Culture: Proceedings of the International Conference Held at the Israel Museum, Jerusalem* (July 6-8, 2008) (STDJ 93; Leiden: Brill, 2011) 219-34.

"The Genre of the Book of Jubilees," in Eric F. Mason et al., eds., *A Teacher for All Generations: Essays in Honor of James C. VanderKam* (JSJSup 153/2; Leiden: Brill, 2011) 737-55.

"The Sibyl and the Apocalypses," in David E. Aune and Frederick E. Brenk, eds., *Greco-Roman Culture and the New Testament* (Leiden: Brill, 2012) 185-202.

"The Afterlife in Apocalyptic Literature," in A. J. Avery Peck and J. Neusner, eds., *Judaism in Late Antiquity, Part 4: Death, Life-After-Death, Resurrection and the World-to-Come in the Judaisms of Antiquity* (Handbuch der Orientalistik; Leiden: Brill, 2000) 119-39.

"Pseudepigraphy and Group Formation in Second Temple Judaism," in E. G. Chazon and M. Stone, eds., *Pseudepigraphic Perspectives: The Apocrypha and Pseudepigrapha in Light of the Dead Sea Scrolls* (Leiden: Brill, 1999) 43-58.

"Enoch and Ezra," in Matthias Henze and Gabriele Boccaccini, eds., *Fourth Ezra and Second Baruch: Reconstruction after the Fall* (Leiden: Brill, 2013) 83-97.

Acknowledgments

Bloomsbury Publishing Plc for
"The Eschatology of Zechariah," in L. L. Grabbe and R. D. Haak, eds., *Knowing the End from the Beginning: The Prophetic, the Apocalyptic, and Their Relationship* (New York: T&T Clark International, 2003) 74-84.
"The Beginning of the End of the World," in John Ahn and Stephen Cook, eds., *Thus Says the Lord: Essays on the Former and Latter Prophets in Honor of Robert R. Wilson* (New York: Continuum, 2009) 137-55.

The Rennert Center, Bar Ilan University, for
"Jerusalem and the Temple in Jewish Apocalyptic Literature of the Second Temple Period." *International Rennert Guest Lecture Series* 1 (Bar Ilan University, 1998) 31pp.

Mohr Siebeck, Tübingen, for
"The Idea of Election in 4 Ezra," *Jewish Studies Quarterly* 16 (2009) 83-96.
"Cognitive Dissonance and Eschatological Violence: Fantasized Solutions to a Theological Dilemma in Second Temple Judaism," in Nathan MacDonald and Ken Brown, eds., *Monotheism in Late Prophetic and Early Apocalyptic Literature* (Tübingen: Mohr Siebeck, 2014) 201-17.

Oxford University Press for
"Radical Religion and the Ethical Dilemmas of Apocalyptic Millenarianism," in Zoe Bennett and David B. Gowler, eds., *Radical Christian Voices and Practice: Essays in Honour of Christopher Rowland* (Oxford: Oxford University Press, 2012) 87-102.

Peeters Publishers of Leuven for
"Sibylline Discourse," in Eibert Tigchelaar, ed., *Old Testament Pseudepigrapha and the Scriptures* (BETL 270; Leuven: Peeters, 2014) 195-210.

The Society of Biblical Literature for
"Gabriel and David: Some Reflections on an Enigmatic Text," in Matthias Henze, ed., *Hazon Gabriel: New Readings of the Gabriel Revelation* (SBLEJL; Atlanta: SBL, 2011) 99-112.

Svensk Exegetisk Årsbok for
"Apocalypse and Empire," which appeared in the *Svensk Exegetisk Årsbok* 76 (2011) 1-19.

Schöningh Publishers, Munich, for
"Ethos and Identity in Jewish Apocalyptic Literature," in Matthias Konradt and Ulrike Steinert, eds., *Ethos und Identität. Einheit und Vielfalt des Judentums im hellenistisch-römischer Zeit* (Munich: Schöningh, 2002) 51-65.

In addition,
Chapter 1, Introduction, "The Genre Apocalypse Reconsidered," was presented at a symposium on *Forms of Ancient Jewish Literature in Its Graeco-Roman and Ancient Near Eastern Setting,* University of Manchester, January 19-21, 2009.
Chapter 4, "Apocalypticism and the Transformation of Prophecy," was delivered as the Johannes Munck Lecture: "Apocalypticism and the Transformation of Prophecy in the Second Temple Period," University of Aarhus, October 10, 2013.
Chapter 11, "Journeys to the World Beyond in Ancient Judaism," was published in Martin McNamara, ed., *Apocalyptic and Eschatological Heritage: The Middle East and Celtic Realms* (Dublin: Four Courts, 2003) 20-36. Four Courts Press no longer exists.

CHAPTER 1

Introduction:
The Genre Apocalypse Reconsidered

In 1979 an attempt to define and outline the genre apocalypse was published in the journal *Semeia,* number 14.[1] (The actual analysis had been completed about two years before that.) The attempt had been undertaken as part of a "Forms and Genres" project in the Society of Biblical Literature, conceived by the late Robert W. Funk. The larger project was not very cohesive. Other working groups were devoted to parables, pronouncement stories, miracle stories, and letters.[2] The project was conceived in the context of New Testament studies, in the tradition of form criticism. But there was no attempt to co-ordinate the work of these groups in any way, or to impose a common understanding of genre. Each group dealt with its own material as it saw fit. In the case of the apocalypse group, the immediate context was provided not so much by New Testament form criticism as by the discussion of "apocalyptic" in Old Testament and Ancient Judaism, which had been revitalized by such scholars as Klaus Koch, Paul Hanson, and Michael Stone.[3] At the time, there was less prior agreement as to what constituted an apocalypse than was the case with some of the other genres. Accordingly, our initial objective was a rather modest one: to reach agreement as to what body of texts we were talking about.

1. John J. Collins, ed., *Apocalypse: The Morphology of a Genre* (*Semeia* 14; Chico, CA: Scholars Press, 1979).

2. Publications relating to the other working groups can be found in *Semeia* 11 (1978), 20 (1981), 22 (1981), and 29 (1983).

3. Klaus Koch, *The Rediscovery of Apocalyptic* (Naperville, IL: Allenson, 1972); Paul D. Hanson, "Apocalypse, Genre," "Apocalypticism," *IDBSup* (1976) 27-34; Michael E. Stone, "Lists of Revealed Things in Apocalyptic Literature," in F. M. Cross et al., eds., *Magnalia Dei: The Mighty Acts of God* (Garden City: Doubleday, 1976) 414-54.

The primary focus of the project was on Jewish and Christian texts composed between 250 BCE and 250 CE, approximately. The volume on apocalypses included essays on Greco-Roman, Gnostic, rabbinic (mainly Hekaloth), and Persian material, much of which (apart from the Greco-Roman material) was arguably later.[4] I think there was value in including this material, but it was not the primary focus of the analysis. The definition and typology were worked out with reference to the Jewish and Christian material,[5] and we then looked for analogous material in the other areas. An analysis of the Hekaloth or of the Middle Persian literature in its own right would probably have used different categories. Our definition lent itself more readily to the accounts of otherworldly journeys in Greek and Roman literature, and the Gnostic apocalypses (with some significant qualification). For purposes of this discussion, however, I will leave aside the broader comparative aspect of the project and focus on the problems of identifying and describing the genre in ancient pre-rabbinic Judaism.

We did not engage in discussions of literary theory, in the belief that discussions of genre in the abstract were likely to be at least as intractable as the discussion of a particular genre. Nonetheless, we inevitably took positions that have also been adopted, and disputed, in literary criticism. If I were to organize another such project thirty-five years on, I would certainly try to be more explicit about the theoretical underpinnings of the approach. That would not necessarily lead to very different results, but it would, I think, be helpful to locate both our approach and some of the objections it encountered in the broader context of literary study.

Etic/Emic

It should be noted at the outset that we viewed the genre as an etic category: "It is important to note that the classification 'apocalyptic' or 'apocalypse' is a modern one. Some ancient Jewish, Christian and Gnostic works are entitled *Apokalypsis* in the manuscripts. . . . However, the title is not a reliable guide to the genre."[6] Accordingly, we took the modern usage of

---

4. The essay on Greek and Roman apocalypses was contributed by Harold Attridge, the one on Gnosticism by Francis T. Fallon, the one on rabbinic literature by Anthony J. Saldarini, and the survey of Persian material by the author.

5. The analyses of the Jewish and Christian material were written by the author and Adela Yarbro Collins, respectively.

6. J. J. Collins, "Introduction: Towards the Morphology of a Genre," *Semeia* 14 (1979) 2.

"apocalypse" and "apocalyptic" as our starting point and set out to make it more consistent.[7] We took the self-presentation of the texts into account (we looked for any texts that might be described as revelations), but our definition was at a higher level of abstraction than the self-presentation of individual texts. A revelation might be introduced as a vision, or a dream of the night, or a "word," or just by a verb, such as "I saw." For our purposes, all of these counted as "revelations." It is possible to object to such an etic approach. Crispin Fletcher-Louis finds our approach "unhelpfully circular" and lacking in historiographic objectivity.[8] "The starting point for a robustly historical search for an ancient genre," he writes, "should be the conventions, expectations and intentions of ancient authors, not the twentieth century judgments of modern scholars who may, in fact, inhabit an entirely different worldview and be guilty of their own back-projections on the ancient texts."[9] The conventions, expectations, and intentions of ancient authors are certainly a worthy subject of investigation, but there was no systematic reflection on literary genre in ancient Judaism. Such genre labels as we find are quite inconsistent. In all likelihood, the *Similitudes of Enoch,* despite their patent debt to Daniel, were called *meshalim* (or its Aramaic equivalent), like the Book of Proverbs, with which it has little in common. Moreover, genres often take time to crystallize. The word *apokalypsis* as a genre label becomes common only in the second century CE,[10] but similar works were certainly being produced for some centuries before that. So, while I do not dispute the value of emic analysis of the self-presentation of texts, this does not invalidate the use of analytic categories, based on the commonalities we now perceive between ancient texts, whether their authors perceived them or not. I think it is very likely that

---

7. Pace Gregory L. Linton, "Reading the Apocalypse as Apocalypse: The Limits of Genre," in David L. Barr, ed., *The Reality of Apocalypse: Rhetoric and Politics in the Book of Revelation* (SBL Symposium Series 39; Atlanta: SBL/Leiden: Brill, 2006) 9-41 (34), we did NOT decide from the outset which works were apocalypses. Rather, we decided which works we would examine. In several cases we rejected current scholarly usage (e.g., the so-called "Apocalypse of Isaiah" and the "little apocalypse" in Mark 13).

8. C. Fletcher-Louis, "Jewish Apocalyptic and Apocalypticism," in S. E. Porter and T. Holmén, eds., *The Handbook of the Study of the Historical Jesus* (4 vols.; Leiden: Brill, 2011) 2.1569-1607 (here 1582).

9. Fletcher-Louis, "Jewish Apocalyptic and Apocalypticism," 1582.

10. Morton Smith, "On the History of *Apokalypto* and *Apokalypsis,*" in D. Hellholm, ed., *Apocalypticism in the Mediterranean World and the Near East: Proceedings of the International Colloquium on Apocalypticism, Uppsala, August 12-17, 1979* (Tübingen: Mohr-Siebeck, 1983) 9-20.

the authors of later apocalypses (including the Book of Revelation) were consciously participating in a literary tradition, but some of the earlier apocalypses, such as Daniel and the *Book of the Watchers,* are perceived as belonging to the genre only in retrospect, because of their affinities with works that were written later.

Definition and Classification

We defined a genre as "a group of texts marked by distinctive recurring characteristics which constitute a recognizable and coherent type of writing."[11] We then proceeded to make a list of features that occur frequently in texts that are commonly regarded as apocalyptic, and formed grids to show which texts attested these features and which did not. The grid, or master paradigm, consisted on the one hand of framing elements (form) and on the other of patterned content. The narrative framework described the manner in which the revelation was allegedly received (vision, epiphany, discourse, otherworldly journey, etc.). We also noted the disposition and reaction of the recipient. Many apocalypses also have a narrative conclusion. In the content, we distinguished between a temporal axis, describing the course of history, and a spatial axis, describing otherworldly places and beings.[12] The temporal axis could begin with creation or primordial events, and often divided history into periods. It invariably included eschatological predictions, sometimes including cosmic upheavals, but invariably including individual judgment after death. We also recognized paraenesis as an important component in these texts that could not be assigned to either the temporal or the spatial axis.

No text contains all the features in question, but some features appear consistently in several texts. On the basis of this analysis, we defined "apocalypse" as *"a genre of revelatory literature with a narrative framework, in which a revelation is mediated by an otherworldly being to a human recipient, disclosing a transcendent reality which is both temporal, insofar as it envisages eschatological salvation, and spatial insofar as it involves another,*

11. Collins, "Introduction," 1.

12. Interestingly enough, Michael E. Vines, "The Apocalyptic Chronotope," in Roland Boer, ed., *Bakhtin and Genre Theory in Biblical Studies* (Semeia Studies 63; Atlanta: Society of Biblical Literature, 2007) 109-17, argues that, from a Bakhtinian perspective, "the peculiar way in which time and space is constructed within apocalypse is one of the genre's most distinctive features" (112).

supernatural world."[13] We also distinguished broadly between two types of apocalypse, one of which is characterized by an extended review of history (the "historical" type) and the other by the motif of otherworldly journey.[14] We also proposed further sub-types of each of these types, largely on the basis of their eschatology (cosmic or individual).[15] We also acknowledged related types and genres, which met many of the criteria, but not all.

Critiques

Carol Newsom, who has written the most intelligent and helpful critique of the project that I have seen, characterizes this approach as "one of definition and classification," which was "characteristic of genre studies of the time."[16]

Critics might differ as to the criteria for classification. R. S. Crane focused on formal or structural characteristics.[17] For Wellek and Warren: "Genre should be conceived, we think, as a grouping of literary works based, theoretically, upon both outer form (specific metre or structure) and also upon inner form (attitude, tone, purpose — more crudely, subject and audience)."[18] More recently, however, the whole idea of classification and definition has encountered resistance.

13. Collins, "Introduction," 9.

14. Vines, "The Apocalyptic Chronotope," 116, misidentifies the first type as "mystical visions." He argues that since the two types construe space and time in the same way the difference is only formal and not essential. We also concluded that the two should be considered as types of one genre rather than as two different genres.

15. These sub-types are: (Ia) "historical" apocalypses with no otherworldly journey; (Ib) apocalypses with cosmic and/or political eschatology; (Ic) apocalypses with only personal eschatology (and no otherworldly journey); (IIa) "historical" apocalypses with an otherworldly journey; (IIb) otherworldly journeys with cosmic and/or political eschatology; (IIc) otherworldly journeys with only personal eschatology.

16. Carol A. Newsom, "Spying Out the Land: A Report from Genology," in R. L. Troxel, K. G. Friebel, and D. R. Magary, eds., *Seeking Out the Wisdom of the Ancients* (Winona Lake, IN: Eisenbrauns, 2005) 437-50 (438). For a useful review of genre studies in the 1970s, with an eye to their applicability to biblical studies, see William G. Doty, "The Concept of Genre in Literary Analysis," in Lane C. McGaughey, ed., *Society of Biblical Literature Proceedings* 2 (1972) 413-48.

17. R. S. Crane, *Critical and Historical Principles of Literary Criticism* (Chicago: University of Chicago Press, 1971) 38.

18. René Wellek and Austin Warren, *Theory of Literature* (New York: Harcourt, Brace and World, 1956) 231.

The resistance is of various kinds. One objection arises from acute appreciation of the individuality of every text and the fear that this individuality will be lost if a work is viewed as a member of a genre. Jacques Derrida allows that "a text cannot belong to no genre," but would prefer to "speak of a sort of participation without belonging — a taking part in without being part of, without having membership in a set."[19] Newsom comments that this kind of approach "accommodates better not only the multigeneric nature of many apocalypses but also their irreducible particularity." She notes that recent defenders of classification often do so "in a way that quite changes the nature and purposes of classification from a descriptive enterprise to that of a critical category devised by the critic for the purposes of the critic."[20] For example: "Adena Rosmarin, in *The Power of Genre,* argues that genre can be seen as a kind of intentional category error in which two things that are not the same are brought together 'as if' they were the same."[21] A similar skepticism about generic classification underlies the recent Manchester-Durham project led by Alexander Samely, which attempts to profile all ancient Jewish literature.[22] Samely and his colleagues avoid specific genre labels until the end of their analysis, and focus on smaller literary features. While they do not exclude the possibility of identifying genres, they hold that "speaking in genre terms . . . is by necessity a selection and emphasis, and also a simplification," and so they favor a modular approach to the study of ancient texts rather than attempt to categorize whole works.[23]

I would agree, and have always agreed, that classification is something devised by critics for their purposes. The objections of people like Derrida seem to me to apply, not to classification as such, which I think is simply unavoidable, but to rigidity in its application. To say that a text is an apocalypse is not to exclude the possibility that it may be simultaneously something else; or to put it another way, the fact that a text can

19. Jacques Derrida, "The Law of Genre," in *Modern Genre Theory,* ed. David Duff (Harlow, Essex: Longman, 2000) 219-31 (230).

20. Newsom, "Spying Out the Land," 439.

21. Newsom, "Spying Out the Land," 439. Cf. Adena Rosmarin, *The Power of Genre* (Minneapolis: University of Minnesota Press, 1985) 21-22; also Ralph Cohen, "History and Genre," *New Literary History* 17 (1986) 203-18.

22. Alexander Samely, in collaboration with Philip Alexander, Rocco Bernasconi, and Robert Hayward, *Profiling Jewish Literature in Antiquity: An Inventory from Second Temple Texts to the Talmud* (Oxford: Oxford University Press, 2013).

23. Samely et al., *Profiling Jewish Literature in Antiquity,* part III, chapter 11, 343-48.

be profitably grouped with apocalypses does not exclude the possibility that it may be also profitably grouped with other texts for different purposes.[24] It is also true that every text has an individual character and conveys its meaning in large part through the ways in which it modifies generic conventions.[25]

Some scholars object to classification on the basis of a list of characteristics, which they see as simply a list of things that happen to be found in apocalypses. This objection was often brought against older treatments of "apocalyptic" such as that of Philipp Vielhauer.[26] Newsom invokes George Lakoff's idea of an "idealized cognitive model": " 'elements' alone are not what trigger recognition of a genre; instead, what triggers it is the way in which they are related to one another in a *Gestalt* structure that serves as an idealized cognitive model. Thus the elements only make sense in relation to a whole. Because the *Gestalt* structure contains default and optional components, as well as necessary ones, individual exemplars can depart from the prototypical exemplars with respect to default and optional elements and still be recognizable as an extended case of 'that sort of text.' "[27]

But as she also notes, the analysis of the genre apocalypse in *Semeia* 14 was not based just on a list of elements, but on something like a *Gestalt* notion of the way these elements related to each other. Many elements in the grid against which the texts are measured are optional, but some bear structural weight, as they shape an implied view of the world. These were the elements singled out in the definition, by reference to the manner of revelation and to the transcendent reality, both spatial and temporal. The content of the genre implies a distinctive worldview. In this respect, our analysis is quite similar to the Bakhtinian approach proposed by Michael

24. See now my essay, "The Genre of the Book of *Jubilees*," in Eric F. Mason et al., eds., *A Teacher for All Generations: Essays in Honor of James C. VanderKam* (JSJSup 153/2; Leiden: Brill, 2011) 737-55.

25. Alastair Fowler, *Kinds of Literature: An Introduction to the Theory of Genres and Modes* (Cambridge, MA: Harvard University Press, 1982) 24: "genres are actually in a continual state of transmutation. It is by their modification, primarily, that individual works convey literary meaning."

26. Philipp Vielhauer, "Apocalypses and Related Subjects," in E. Hennecke and W. Schneemelcher, eds., *New Testament Apocrypha II* (trans. and ed. R. McL. Wilson; Philadelphia: Westminster, 1965) 581-607. See E. P. Sanders, "The Genre of Palestinian Jewish Apocalypses," in Hellholm, ed., *Apocalypticism in the Mediterranean World*, 447-59 (448-50).

27. Newsom, "Spying Out the Land," 444; cf. George Lakoff, *Women, Fire, and Dangerous Things: What Categories Reveal about the Mind* (Chicago: University of Chicago Press, 1987) 68.

Vines, who emphasizes the "temporal and spatial unboundedness of apocalypse," which "affords a divine perspective on human activity."[28] We differ from Vines, however, insofar as we hold that this worldview can also find expression in other genres. According to Vines, "A Bakhtinian approach to the problem of genre suggests that this cannot be the case. The particular way in which a literary work construes the world is essential to its genre."[29] Vines, in effect, equates genre with worldview. In our approach, the literary form of revelation remains essential to the genre, while the worldview can be expressed in other ways.

This point is also relevant to the recurring debate as to whether eschatology is an essential ingredient in apocalypses. Fletcher-Louis objects that "there remain swathes of revelatory material in the apocalypses which have nothing to do with eschatology."[30] The *Book of the Watchers* is a case in point, where he finds eschatology in only a fraction of the material, in 1:3-9 and parts of chapters 22 and 25–26. In fact, much more material that Enoch sees on his guided tour is relevant to the final judgment: the place of punishment of the disobedient stars and fallen angels in chapter 21, the mountain of God and the tree of life in chapter 24, the vision of paradise in chapter 32, which can hardly be separated from the geographical context described in chapters 28–31. I would argue that the divine judgment is in fact the focal point of Enoch's journeys, and that much of the cosmological detail is supplied to establish the reality of the places of judgment, reward, and punishment. In any case, it is not enough to establish that a given element is present in the text, or to calculate the amount of space it occupies; one must also consider the way it functions in the text.

It is, of course, possible to define apocalypse simply by formal criteria. The late Jean Carmignac defined it as "Genre littéraire qui décrit des révélatons célestes à travers des symboles."[31] He then proceeded to argue, on the basis of this definition, that prophetic visions, such as those of Amos, were "apocalypses," as indeed they are by his definition. Similarly, Christopher Rowland writes that "to speak of apocalyptic . . . is to concentrate on the theme of the direct communication of the heavenly mysteries

28. Vines, "The Apocalyptic Chronotope," 113.

29. Vines, "The Apocalyptic Chronotope," 116.

30. Fletcher-Louis, "Jewish Apocalyptic and Apocalypticism," 1578-79.

31. Jean Carmignac, "Description du phénomène de l'Apocalyptique," in Hellholm, ed., *Apocalypticism in the Mediterranean World,* 163-70 (165). Carmignac would accept the formal part of the definition in *Semeia* 14, but not the reference to the content of the revelation.

in all their diversity."[32] These definitions "work" just as well as the one in *Semeia* 14, in the sense that one can find a corpus of texts that fit them, but that corpus is much broader than what has traditionally been called "apocalyptic." Conversely, one might argue, with Martha Himmelfarb, that heavenly journeys are really a different genre from that of the "historical apocalypses," although one would have to grant that the two are related in many ways.[33] For the present, however, my concern is with the possibility of defining a genre at all.

Family Resemblance

Perhaps the most widespread objection to the kind of definition offered in *Semeia* 14 rests on the assumption that genres cannot actually be defined, although we may know one when we see it. At the end of the Uppsala conference on apocalypticism, a resolution *contra definitionem, pro descriptione* was carried.[34] This was not, however, the outcome of systematic discussion; it was simply a diplomatic evasion of the issue at the end of a stimulating but exhausting conference.[35] There is, however, resistance to definitions in literary criticism on more principled grounds. Appeal is often made to Wittgenstein's idea of family resemblance, although the philosopher did not have literary genres specifically in mind. In a celebrated passage in the *Philosophical Investigations,* he writes:

> 66. Consider for example the proceedings we call 'games.' I mean board games, card games, ball games, Olympic games, and so on. What is common to them all? — Don't say: 'There *must* be something common, or they would not be called 'games' — but *look* and *see* whether

---

32. Christopher Rowland, *The Open Heaven: A Study of Apocalyptic in Judaism and Early Christianity* (New York: Crossroad, 1982) 14. Cf. also Hartmut Stegemann, "Die Bedeutung der Qumranfund für die Erforschung der Apokalyptik," in Hellholm, ed., *Apocalypticism in the Mediterranean World,* 495-530.

33. Martha Himmelfarb, *Tours of Hell: An Apocalyptic Form in Jewish and Christian Literature* (Philadelphia: University of Pennsylvania Press, 1983) 6.

34. Hellholm, ed., *Apocalypticism in the Mediterranean World,* 2.

35. See my comments in my essay, "Genre, Ideology and Social Movements in Jewish Apocalypticism," in J. J. Collins and J. H. Charlesworth, eds., *Mysteries and Revelations: Apocalyptic Studies since the Uppsala Colloquium* (Sheffield: Sheffield Academic Press, 1991) 11-32 (12).

there is anything common to all. — For if you look at them you will not see something that is common to *all*, but similarities, relationships, and a whole series of them at that. Look for example at board games, with their multifarious relationships. Now pass to card games; here you find many correspondences with the first group, but many common features drop out, and others appear. When we pass next to ball games, much that is common is retained, but much is lost — Are they all 'amusing'? Compare chess with noughts and crosses. Or is there always winning and losing, or competition between players? Think of patience. In ball games there is winning and losing; but when a child throws his ball at the wall and catches it again, this feature has disappeared. . . . Think now of games like ring-a-ring-a-roses; here is the element of amusement, but how many other characteristic features have disappeared! . . .

And the result of this examination is; we see a complicated network of similarities overlapping and criss-crossing: sometimes overall similarities, sometimes similarities of detail.

67. I can think of no better expression to characterize these similarities than 'family resemblances'; for the various resemblances between members of a family: build, features, colour of eyes, gait, temperament, etc., etc. overlap and criss-cross in the same way. — And I shall say: 'games' form a family.[36]

The "family-resemblance" approach was adapted to the study of genre and popularized by Alastair Fowler:

Literary genre seems to be just the sort of concept with blurred edges that is suited to such an approach. Representatives of a genre may then be regarded as making up a possible class whose septs [clans or classes] and individual members are related in various ways, without necessarily having any single feature shared in common by all.[37]

Moreover, on this approach two texts that have no distinctive features in common may be assigned to the same genre.

Many critics have found this approach unsatisfactory. In the words of David Fishelov, "Wittgenstein's concept, at least in one of its interpreta-

---

36. Ludwig Wittgenstein, *Philosophical Investigations* (Oxford: Blackwell, 1958) 31-32.
37. Fowler, *Kinds of Literature,* 41-42.

tions, has perhaps become too fashionable, too little scrutinized. Instead of being a methodology of last resort, it has become the first and immediate refuge in the wake of disappointment with one or other rigid definition made up of a confined list of characteristics."[38] John Swales comments that "a family resemblance theory can make anything resemble anything."[39] Moreover, Wittgenstein's formulation, which did not have literary genres in mind, has its own problems. Dictionaries have no great problem in providing serviceable definitions of "game." The one provided by Webster's *New World Dictionary of the American Language,* "any form of play, or way of playing," may perhaps only defer the problem, as playing admits of several definitions. The *Oxford Dictionary* proposes a narrower definition: "A diversion of the nature of a contest, played according to rules, and decided by superior strength, skill or good fortune." In fact, this definition fits the vast majority of games quite well. It is not invalidated by Wittgenstein's example of patience, since, as John Swayles reminds us, the contest can be against the game itself. Swales concedes that "we are left with an unaccounted-for residue as represented by such children's games as 'ring-a-ring-a-roses,' "[40] although even this would fit under the broader definition of Webster's dictionary. The crucial point to note here is that any definition is an abstraction, and the higher the level of abstraction the more material will fit. Of course, a definition may be so abstract as to be useless, and that is a matter of judgment. But it is not the case that genres or categories cannot be defined on the basis of shared features. It is rather the case that most definitions of genres, and of categories, admit of some problematic border-line cases. This is certainly true of the genre apocalypse as we defined it. There is a difference, however, between saying that a genre admits of borderline cases and denying that it is possible to define a genre at all.

"Family resemblance" is too vague to be satisfactory as a basis for genre recognition, but the discussion highlights a persistent problem with attempts at classification: the difficulty of drawing a clean line between a genre and closely related works.

38. David Fishelov, *Metaphors of Genre: The Role of Analogies in Genre Theory* (University Park: Pennsylvania State University Press, 1993) 54.

39. John Swales, *Genre Analysis: English in Academic and Research Settings* (Cambridge: Cambridge University Press, 1990) 51.

40. Swales, *Genre Analysis,* 51.

Prototype Theory

The most successful attempt to address this problem, insofar as I am aware, is "prototype theory" developed in cognitive psychology.[41] As described by John Frow:

> the postulate is that we understand categories (such as *bird*) through a very concrete logic of typicality. We take a robin or a sparrow to be more central to that category than an ostrich, and a kitchen chair to be more typical of the class of chairs than a throne or a piano stool. Rather than having clear boundaries, essential components, and shared and uniform properties, classes defined by prototypes have a common core and then fade into fuzziness at the edges. This is to say that we classify easily at the level of prototypes, and with more difficulty — extending features of the prototype by metaphor and analogy to take account of non-typical features — as we diverge from them.[42]

Membership in a category may be a matter of degree. It should be noted that prototypical exemplars of a genre are not necessarily historical archetypes: classic works that became models for later writers. Late exemplars may also be prototypical, if they exemplify especially well the typical features of the genre.

This approach to genre has considerable appeal. In the words of Swales: "It allows the genre analyst to find a course between trying to produce unassailable definitions of a particular genre and relaxing into the irresponsibility of family resemblances."[43] Or, as Carol Newsom puts it:

> One of the advantages of prototype theory is that it provides a way for bringing together what seems so commonsensical in classificatory approaches, while avoiding their rigidity. At the same time it gives more discipline to the family-resemblance approach, because not every resemblance or deviation is of equal significance. As applied to genre categories, prototype theory would require an identification of

---

41. Eleanor Rosch, "Cognitive Representations of Semantic Categories," *Journal of Experimental Psychology (General)* 104 (1975) 192-233; "Principles of Categorization," in E. Rosch and B. Lloyd, eds., *Cognition and Categorization* (Hillsdale, NJ: Erlbaum, 1978) 27-48.

42. John Frow, *Genre* (London: Routledge, 2006) 54.

43. Swales, *Genre Analysis*, 52.

exemplars that are prototypical and an analysis of the privileged prop-
erties that establish the sense of typicality.[44]

As Newsom recognizes, the analysis of the genre apocalypse in *Semeia* 14 has much in common with the prototype model. It started from a
list of apocalypses that were regarded as prototypical, and distinguished
between central and peripheral characteristics.[45] The main difference is
that prototype theory would refuse to establish a strict boundary between
texts that are members of the genre and those that are not. It rather distinguishes between texts that are highly typical and those that are less typical.
And this, I think, is an improvement that might have saved us some agoniz-
ing about boundary cases. I will return below to some of these boundary
cases that might be accommodated more easily by prototype theory than
by the classificatory approach applied in *Semeia* 14.

The Question of Function

The aspect of *Semeia* 14 that was most controversial at the time was our
failure to specify a function for the genre. As David Hellholm asked: "Why
were apocalypses ever written?"[46] The omission was intentional.[47] Our
conviction was that function was best discussed at the level of individual
texts, in their specific contexts, and the commonly accepted idea that apocalypses were intended to comfort and exhort a group in crisis[48] did not
necessarily hold true in all cases. A follow-up volume on early Christian
apocalypticism, in *Semeia* 36 (1986), emended the definition by adding that
an apocalypse is *"intended to interpret present, earthly circumstances in light
of the supernatural world of the future, and to influence both the understand-*

---

44. Newsom, "Spying Out the Land," 443.

45. The statement of Linton, "Reading the Apocalypse as Apocalypse," 34, that "the
Apocalypse Group of the SBL Genres Project followed the procedure of constructing the
genre apocalypse by analogy with the Apocalypse of John" is, again, incorrect. The Apocalypse of John was only one of several apocalypses that made up the core group.

46. David Hellholm, "The Problem of Apocalyptic Genre," in Adela Yarbro Collins,
ed., *Early Christian Apocalypticism: Genre and Social Setting = Semeia* 36 (1986) 13-64 (26).

47. The Manchester-Durham project of Samely et al. also refrains from speculating
about social function.

48. As suggested by Hellholm, "The Problem of Apocalyptic Genre," 27, but reflecting
a widespread assumption.

ing and the behavior of the audience by means of divine authority."[49] This formulation is considerably more abstract than the idea that an apocalypse is addressed to a group in crisis, which is true of some apocalypses but not all. Here again, the level of abstraction makes a difference, and one has to decide what level of abstraction is most helpful for one's purpose.[50]

The question of function has also figured in theoretical discussions of literary genre. John Swales contends that "the principal criterial feature that turns a collection of communicative events into a genre is some shared set of communicative purposes."[51] He rejects the obvious objection that purpose is less overt and demonstrable than other features, such as form, on the grounds that one ought to study each text in detail before assigning it to a genre. But the real issue here is whether there is a simple correlation between form and function, and I would argue that there is not. An obvious consideration here is the possibility of parody or ironic usage: think for example of the parodies of Lucian, or of the *Testament of Abraham,* which includes a heavenly journey that is formally similar to the journeys of Enoch but serves a very different purpose. More fundamentally, literary forms are adaptable. While many of the Jewish and Christian apocalypses are subversive and revolutionary, there is also what Bernard McGinn has called an imperial apocalypticism.[52] This appears especially in the Middle Ages, but the journey of Aeneas to the Netherworld in the sixth book of the *Aeneid* may perhaps qualify as an early example. This is not to deny that genres may have shared functions at some level of abstraction, but that level may be considerably higher than what most people think about when they talk about function.

Neither is it to deny that some genres may be identified on the basis of setting or function. The (fictional) setting in a gentile court is essential to the recognition of court tales in ancient Judaism, although these tales also often have a typical literary form. Genres may be of different kinds. But it seems to me that those features that are explicitly present in the texts, rather than communicative purposes that have to be inferred, provide the safest starting point for genre recognition.

---

49. Adela Yarbro Collins, "Introduction," *Semeia* 36 (1986) 7. Cf. David Aune, "The Apocalypse of John and the Problem of Genre," *Semeia* 36 (1986) 87. Compare Vines, "The Apocalyptic Chronotope," 113: "The purpose of apocalypse would therefore seem to be to gain a God's-eye view on human history and activity."

50. As noted helpfully by Hellholm, "The Problem of Apocalyptic Genre," 27.

51. Swales, *Genre Analysis,* 46.

52. B. McGinn, *Visions of the End* (New York: Columbia University Press, 1979) 33-36.

Diachronic Considerations

Definitions are by nature synchronic and static. Genres, in contrast, evolve and are constantly changing. In this sense, genre definitions are somewhat like ideal types in sociology, models that indicate what is typical but do not correspond exactly to any historical exemplar. The historical nature of genres is something that has come to be appreciated only in modern times, but it now seems almost self-evident, especially in the case of a genre such as apocalypse, which made its appearance, at least in Jewish literature, at a relatively late point. Alastair Fowler distinguishes three phases in the life of a genre. In the first, "the genre complex assembles, until a formal type emerges." In the second phase, the form is used, developed, and adapted consciously. A third phase involves the secondary use of the form, by ironic inversion or by subordinating it to a new context. In historical reality these phases inevitably overlap, and the lines between them are often blurred.[53] Fowler claimed that these phases were "organic and inevitable." He has been criticized for succumbing to "the organistic fallacy."[54] But whether or not this kind of organic development can be posited in all genres, it seems to me quite useful in the case of apocalypses. Early apocalypses such as Daniel and the *Book of the Watchers* seem experimental, mixing a range of forms from biblical and Near Eastern tradition. Some of the later apocalypses, especially those involving otherworldly journeys, seem much more predictable and reflect a deliberate adherence to a generic model. And eventually, people stopped producing such texts, although the death of the genre, I think, can be placed no earlier than the Middle Ages. (Arguably, the genre is still alive and well, although not in high literary repute.) Long before that, one sees evidence of Fowler's tertiary phase in the rise of commentary, at least on the canonical apocalypses.

While this kind of historical development is not adumbrated in the kind of generic analysis offered in *Semeia* 14, diachronic and synchronic analyses must be seen as complementary rather than as mutually exclusive. It was always my intention to follow the analysis of the genre with a historical study that tried to address the function of particular texts in their historical contexts, and I attempted this in my book *The Apocalyptic Imag-*

---

53. A. Fowler, "The Life and Death of Literary Forms," *New Literary History* 2 (1971) 199-216. Compare his discussion of the transformations of genre in *Kinds of Literature*, 170-90.

54. Fishelov, *Metaphors of Genre*, 28.

ination.[55] We still lack such a study of the Christian, Gnostic, or Greco-Roman apocalypses. I think such studies are still desirable. It remains true, as Michael Sinding has argued, that one can read prototypical texts out of historical order and without being aware of historical influences and still get a good sense of the genre.[56] But one can obviously get a much better sense by taking historical relationships into account.

The task attempted in *Semeia* 14, however, was never meant to be more than the first stage of a study of the genre, focused on definition and recognition and on establishing a typology. I still think that this is a necessary step toward the understanding of a genre, but it was never intended to be seen as the whole story.

Some Problematic Cases

By way of conclusion, I would like to consider two texts that have posed problems for the analysis of the apocalyptic genre: *Jubilees* and *Joseph and Aseneth.*

Jubilees

The problematic character of *Jubilees* is readily apparent.[57] In the opening chapter, the angel of the presence is bidden to write for Moses the account from the beginning of creation until "the time when my sanctuary shall be built among them for all eternity, and the Lord appear in the sight of all, and all know that I am the God of Israel." In short, we have here a revelation that is mediated to Moses by an angel, in prototypical apocalyptic form. Moreover, the content is supposed to cover the whole of history, and it has at least an eschatological horizon, in the time when the Lord will appear in the sight of all. Angels and demonic figures, notably Mastema, play an important role throughout, and there is a further

---

55. New York: Crossroad, 1984. Revised edition: Grand Rapids: Eerdmans, 1998.

56. Michael Sinding, "After Definitions: Genre, Categories, and Cognitive Science," *Genre* 35 (2002) 181-220.

57. See Collins, *The Apocalyptic Imagination* (revised ed.) 79-84. See now also Todd R. Hanneken, *The Subversion of the Apocalypses in the Book of Jubilees* (SBL Early Judaism and Its Literature 34; Atlanta: SBL, 2012). See now my essay, "The Genre of the Book of *Jubilees*" (cited in n. 24 above).

discourse on the eschatological future in chapter 23, which includes a promise of beatific afterlife for the righteous. Nonetheless, the great bulk of the book is quite atypical of apocalypses, and is rather a rewriting of the narrative of Genesis and to a lesser extent of Exodus, and so it is often classified with another genre, even more problematic than apocalypses, that of "rewritten Bible."

In *Semeia* 14, I classified *Jubilees* 23 as an apocalypse, but this is clearly unsatisfactory. While it is certainly possible to have an apocalypse as a sub-unit within a larger composition, *Jubilees* 23 is not a distinct unit in itself, and it cannot be regarded as an apocalypse in isolation from *Jubilees* 1. In *The Apocalyptic Imagination* I abandoned that position and said that the *Rahmengattung*, or generic framework, of *Jubilees* is an apocalypse, although the book as a whole is atypical of the genre and might equally well be grouped with other texts. I would still defend that view, although it could be more fully articulated.

Armin Lange has argued against the classification of *Jubilees* as an apocalyptic writing because of its avoidance of symbolic dreams, even in its re-telling of the Joseph story.[58] Lange's observation is certainly significant for our understanding of *Jubilees,* but it alone cannot determine the literary genre of the work. Lange, in fact, is less than clear as to whether he is addressing the question of literary genre: he writes of *Apokalyptik,* as a movement *(Bewegung),* much as scholars of an earlier generation had spoken of "apocalyptic" before the whole discussion of the 1970s. Yet the question whether *Jubilees* is "an apocalyptic writing" is surely a question of genre. But while symbolic dreams are an important medium in many apocalypses, they are by no means a constant feature of the genre.[59] We scarcely find them at all in the otherworldly journeys that make up one major sub-type of the genre, and we do not find them in the *Apocalypse of Weeks,* an apocalypse that was probably known to the author of *Jubilees.* Even in Daniel, the symbolic dream is only one of several media of revelation. Daniel 10–12 presents a verbal angelic revelation, just as *Jubilees* does. The avoidance of symbolic dreams in *Jubilees* is significant, but it must be

58. Armin Lange, "Divinatorische Träume und Apokalyptik im Jubiläenbuch," in M. Albani, J. Frey, and A. Lange, eds., *Studies in the Book of Jubilees* (Tübingen: Mohr Siebeck, 1997) 25-38.

59. See the excellent study of Bennie H. Reynolds III (Lange's student!), *Between Symbolism and Realism: The Use of Symbolic and Non-Symbolic Language in Ancient Jewish Apocalypses 333-63 b.c.e.* (JAJ Sup 8; Göttingen: Vandenhoeck & Ruprecht, 2011) especially 225-374 ("Non-Symbolic Apocalypses").

weighed against other features of the book that align it with the apocalyptic genre. The study of the genre apocalypse was largely inspired by frustration with the tendency of scholars to identify what is "apocalyptic" with a motif of their choice, without regard to the role that motif played in the bigger picture. To argue that *Jubilees* is excluded from the apocalyptic genre by its avoidance of symbolic dreams is, I think, to relapse into that older tendency. Symbolic dreams are an optional component of apocalyptic revelations, not a necessary one.

It now seems to me that the relation of *Jubilees* to the apocalypses can be clarified by the use of prototype theory, as Carol Newsom has suggested. *Jubilees* is an apocalypse, but it is not a prototypical one and in fact is rather atypical.[60] It belongs on the fuzzy fringes of the genre, and this is quite compatible with its affinity with other genres, such as the quasi-genre of "rewritten Bible." It is also helpful, I think, to consider it in light of Fowler's understanding of the life and death of literary forms. *Jubilees* presupposes some familiarity with the apocalyptic mode of revelation. The authority of a work can be established by presenting it as revelation, given to an ancient worthy by an angel, and its message can be reinforced by reference to an impending eschatological judgment. But neither presentation as revelation nor validation by an eschatological judgment is peculiar to one kind of message. The author of *Jubilees* was certainly familiar with the early Enoch literature, and probably also with Daniel. But he used the form of an apocalypse to present a message that was quite different from that of the earlier apocalypses, not only in his evaluation of symbolic dreams but especially in the centrality of the Mosaic law.[61] This would not be the only time that an author would use the form of an apocalypse to argue against the viewpoint of another apocalypse. Regardless of how one decides priority between *4 Ezra* and *2 Baruch,* there is clearly a running dispute between them on the question of theodicy and the sufficiency of the Torah. Exemplars of a genre can take issue with each other in various ways. As Fowler put it, they can relate to each other "by conformity, variation, innovation, or antagonism."[62] In the case of *Jubilees,* the author's use of Enochic traditions is complex. He draws on these traditions to formulate

60. Hanneken, *The Subversion of the Apocalypses,* argues that *Jubilees* has the form of an apocalypse but uses that form ironically to subvert the apocalyptic worldview. I am not persuaded that the use of the genre in *Jubilees* is ironic.

61. See now Gabriele Boccaccini and Giovanni Ibba, eds., *Enoch and the Mosaic Torah: The Evidence of Jubilees* (Grand Rapids: Eerdmans, 2009).

62. Fowler, *Kinds of Literature,* 23.

his own understanding of the world, but he is far from reproducing them uncritically.

Joseph and Aseneth

In the case of *Joseph and Aseneth,* it is not the genre of the work as a whole that is at issue, but only the sub-section relating the apparition to Aseneth of a man from heaven, in chapters 14–17. This text has not usually been included in discussions of apocalyptic literature, but Edith Humphrey made an interesting case that it should be regarded as an apocalypse, on the definition proposed in *Semeia* 14.[63] More recently, Fletcher-Louis finds "a pointed irony" in our failure to include this text in *Semeia* 14, and seems to assume that it was excluded because of the lack of a futurist eschatology. On his reading, "the angel reveals to Aseneth a transcendent reality: the world of Jewish piety, mystically conceived, in which the life of paradise, an angelomorphic existence and immortality belong to all the faithful." It is not clear to me that this reading is fully justified, but I agree that the angel discloses to Aseneth a transcendent reality. From that day on she is given new life and will eat the bread of life and drink the cup of immortality (chapter 15). The honeycomb that he gives her is made by the bees of Paradise. The angels eat of it, and no one who eats of it ever dies.

In fact, the omission of this text from *Semeia* 14 was only an oversight. The eschatology implied is different from what we find in Daniel or *Enoch,* but not so far removed from an apocalypse like *3 Baruch,* which has a purely personal eschatology. If *Joseph and Aseneth* allows for eternal life as a present reality, its relevance to the genre remains no less than that of the Gnostic apocalypses. Here again I think prototype theory is helpful. The angel's revelation here is an apocalypse, but a somewhat exceptional one. Again, it is helpful to see this as a secondary appropriation of the genre. (The account of the angel's apparition is modeled to some degree on Daniel chapter 10.) The author makes use of an established form, but does so with a twist, to present a view of eschatology that is somewhat different from that of the source text.

63. E. M. Humphrey, *The Ladies and the Cities: Transformation and Apocalyptic Identity in Joseph and Aseneth, 4 Ezra, and the Apocalypse of the Shepherd of Hermas* (Sheffield: Sheffield Academic Press, 1995) 35-40; *Joseph and Aseneth* (Sheffield: Sheffield Academic Press, 2000) 41.

Conclusion

The analysis of the genre apocalypse attempted thirty-five years ago would have benefited from more theoretical discussion even then, and would have been significantly facilitated by prototype theory, which was being developed around the time when the analysis was under way. I think that theory would have refined the analysis significantly, but I do not think it would have changed it substantially.

I should emphasize, however, that genre analysis may be undertaken for various reasons, and that these reasons may call for different approaches. In the case of *Semeia* 14, the goal was to identify and define, and this was never supposed to be more than the first stage of a more comprehensive study. There were certainly aspects of the genre that we did not address, such as the rhetorical dimensions of apocalyptic discourse, or questions of mode and tone.[64] These aspects are not so easy to mark off on a grid, or to quantify, and for that reason were less conducive to the kind of analysis we were doing, but they are surely important aspects of a genre. A full literary analysis of a genre should include these aspects. Similarly, the attention in the Manchester-Durham project to such matters as governing voice is an important contribution to a full literary analysis. But I think it is still true that the first stage in the analysis of any genre is to identify it. This stage requires definition, at least of the prototypical core, even if there are also fuzzy fringes. Without such definition, or without clarity about a prototypical core, there can only be confusion as to what it is that we are talking about.

---

64. See the interesting volume edited by Greg Carey and L. Gregory Bloomquist, *Vision and Persuasion: Rhetorical Dimensions of Apocalyptic Discourse* (St. Louis: Chalice, 1999). I comment on some aspects of apocalyptic language in *The Apocalyptic Imagination*, 14-19.

PART I

Apocalypse and Prophecy

CHAPTER 2

The Eschatology of Zechariah

The genre apocalypse in ancient Judaism is recognized by the combination of a number of distinctive features.[1] Apocalyptic revelations are typically mediated to the human recipient by an angelic figure, who functions either as an interpreter or as a heavenly guide. These revelations typically disclose a supernatural world, either by reporting actions of angelic or demonic beings or by describing otherworldly places. While they often give an overview of history, they invariably refer to an eschatological judgment. In many cases this involves a new creation, or a radical break with the present order. It invariably involves a judgment of the dead. In the Hebrew Bible, the only book that exhibits all these features is the Book of Daniel. Other examples of the genre are found in the Pseudepigrapha and in the New Testament Book of Revelation.

Apocalyptic Eschatology

There are, however, several writings in the later part of the prophetic corpus that exhibit some of the features of apocalyptic literature.[2] The prophe-

---

1. John J. Collins, *Apocalypse: The Morphology of a Genre* (Semeia 14; Chico, CA: Scholars Press, 1979); *The Apocalyptic Imagination* (2nd ed.; Grand Rapids: Eerdmans, 1998) 1-42.

2. Paul D. Hanson, *The Dawn of Apocalyptic* (Philadelphia: Fortress, 1975); idem, *Old Testament Apocalyptic* (Nashville: Abingdon, 1987); S. L. Cook, *Prophecy and Apocalypticism: The Postexilic Social Setting* (Minneapolis: Fortress, 1995). See now also Antonios Finitsis, *Visions and Eschatology: A Socio-Historical Analysis of Zechariah 1–6* (Library of Second Temple Studies; London: T&T Clark, 2011); S. L. Cook, "Apocalyptic Prophecy,"

cies of Zechariah, as found in Zechariah 1–8, have long been recognized as a boundary case in the development of the genre apocalypse.[3] Zechariah's visions are explained to him by an interpreting angel. They disclose a supernatural world, peopled by angelic figures and a satanic adversary. They do not envision a judgment of the dead, and at least in this respect they are clearly distinguished from later apocalypses such as Daniel. But the degree to which they envision a radical break between present and future is a matter of dispute. In the classic view of Wellhausen, all that Zechariah aimed for was the restoration of the temple, and perhaps the elevation of Zerubbabel to the throne of David.[4] Stephen Cook, in contrast, has claimed that "the text clearly evidences the same millennial worldview observable in the comparative anthropological evidence."[5] Specifically, he argues that Zechariah's eschatology is radical.

> In his view, historical processes are going nowhere and will accomplish nothing . . . the eradication of the perpetrators of evil . . . the overthrow of all the enemies of Israel . . . the anticipated blazing physical presence of God in the city . . . and the turning of the many nations to YHWH . . . are all inconceivable without direct apocalyptic divine intervention from beyond history. Although this intervention is imminent, it is still a future hope.[6]

Cook's understanding of apocalyptic eschatology is, I believe, essentially in harmony with that of Paul Hanson, who defined prophetic eschatology as a perspective in which the divine plan is translated "into the terms of plain history, real politics and human instrumentality," while apocalyp-

---

in John J. Collins, ed., *The Oxford Handbook of Apocalyptic Literature* (New York: Oxford University Press, 2014) 19-35.

3. S. Amsler, *Zacharie et l'origine de l'apocalyptique* (VTSup 22; Leiden: Brill, 1972) 227-31; H. Gese, "Anfang und Ende der Apokalyptik dargestellt am Sacharjabuch," *ZTK* 70 (1973) 20-49; E. J. Tigchelaar, *Prophets of Old and the Day of the End: Zechariah, the Book of the Watchers and Apocalyptic* (Leiden: Brill, 1997).

4. J. Wellhausen, "Zechariah, Book of," in T. Cheyne, ed., *Encyclopaedia Biblica* (New York: Macmillan, 1903) 5390-95.

5. Cook, *Prophecy and Apocalypticism*, 133. The use of anthropological models is also advocated by L. L. Grabbe, "The Social Setting of Early Jewish Apocalypticism," *JSP* 4 (1999) 27-47. Note the cautions expressed by D. C. Sim, "The Social Setting of Ancient Apocalypticism: A Question of Method," *JSP* 13 (1995) 5-16.

6. Cook, *Prophecy and Apocalypticism*, 128-29.

tic visions focus on the cosmic vision which is not so translated.[7] Cook's book is largely a critique of Hanson's understanding of the social setting and function of apocalyptic literature, but Cook seems to accept Hanson's understanding of apocalyptic eschatology.[8]

But the prospect of direct divine intervention is not necessarily apocalyptic. Amos surely envisioned direct divine intervention on "the day of the Lord," when God would wipe a sinful people off the face of the earth. Whether Amos anticipated that the Assyrians would be the rod of YHWH's anger may be debated, but there is little doubt that the Assyrian destruction of northern Israel was accepted by many as fulfillment of those prophecies. Divine intervention is not necessarily "beyond history" and is not incompatible with human instrumentality. The point can be nicely illustrated by the "oracular insertion" in Zechariah 4:6-10:

> This is the word of the Lord to Zerubbabel: Not by might, nor by power, but by my spirit says the Lord of hosts. What are you, O great mountain? Before Zerubbabel you shall become a plain; and he shall bring out the top stone amid shouts of "Grace, grace to it!" Moreover, the word of the Lord came to me, saying: The hands of Zerubbabel have laid the foundation of this house; his hands shall also complete it. Then you will know that the Lord of hosts has sent me to you. For whoever has despised the day of small things shall rejoice, and shall see the plummet in the hand of Zerubbabel.

There is no doubt here about the agency of Zerubbabel, or about the historicity of the foundation of the Second Temple. Yet we are told that this does not happen by human power, but by the spirit of the Lord. All biblical eschatology posits divine intervention. If apocalyptic, or proto-apocalyptic, eschatology is at all distinctive, it must be distinguished by something more than this.

Rather than try to base distinctions on divine intervention or human

---

7. Hanson, *The Dawn of Apocalyptic*, 11.

8. Hanson's definition, proposed more than a quarter of a century ago, has played little part in the discussion of apocalypticism in the Hellenistic period, but continues to appear in studies of the Persian period. It should be noted, however, that the literature of the Persian period (Haggai, Zechariah, Third Isaiah, Isaiah 24–27) is at most "proto-apocalyptic" and is significantly different from what we find in the apocalypses of Daniel and the Pseudepigrapha.

instrumentality, it may be more helpful to revert to the older distinction offered by Sigmund Mowinckel, between "national, political, this-worldly" eschatology on the one hand, and "super-terrestrial, otherworldly" eschatology on the other.[9] The first kind is usually restorative, in the sense that it aims at a restoration of a former state, albeit in idealized form. The classic messianic prophecies of the Hebrew Bible seem to me to be of this type. For example, Isaiah 11 is a prophecy of the restoration of the Davidic monarchy to its full glory. Never mind that the wolf did not lie down with the lamb in the time of David or Solomon. This is an idealized description of a this-worldly kingdom. Even Isaiah 65:17, which speaks of a new heaven and a new earth, still proposes a condition that differs from human life as we know it in degree rather than in kind. People will live to fantastic ages, but they will still plant vineyards, build houses, and die. In contrast, the new heaven and new earth in the Book of Revelation bespeak a radically different world, where death will be no more.

Of course Mowinckel's distinction will not resolve all problems. Kingship is described in mythological language from hoary antiquity, and it is often difficult to know just how such language should be understood. Language that seems to posit a radical break in history, such as Ezekiel's vision of the valley full of dry bones, may be understood as metaphorical, with reference to a historical, this-worldly, development (the restoration of Israel from the Exile). Some texts, such as Isaiah 24–27, are especially difficult to interpret in this regard. In the case of Zechariah, however, this distinction seems to fit quite well the rival interpretations that have been proposed. On the one hand, there is the position of Wellhausen, that Zechariah's goals were quite this-worldly: the rebuilding of the temple and, perhaps, the restoration of the monarchy in the person of Zerubbabel. On the other hand are the views of those who think that the prophet's hopes were not vested in his contemporary leaders and that they envisioned a radically new order. My primary goal in this chapter is simply to try to determine what it was that Zechariah expected, regardless of how we label those expectations. A test case is provided by the expectations centering on the historical figures of Zerubbabel and Joshua.

9. S. Mowinckel, *He That Cometh* (Nashville: Abingdon, 1954) 281.

The צמח or Shoot

A key passage for this issue is found in Zechariah 6:9-14. Here the prophet is told to take gold and silver and make עטרות and to crown Joshua the High Priest, and say to him:

> Here is a man whose name is צמח, for he shall sprout in his place, and he shall build the temple of the Lord . . . he shall bear royal honor, and he shall build the temple of the Lord . . . there shall be a priest by his throne, with peaceful understanding between the two of them. (Zech. 6:12-13)

There are two glaring anomalies in this passage. First, עטרות is most easily taken as a plural form; yet only one figure is crowned. This anomaly has been explained in various ways. Some scholars argue that only one crown is involved. Either the word should be emended to a singular form עטרת, or עטרות should be accepted as a singular form.[10] Wellhausen argued that the original passage envisioned one crown and that it was intended for Zerubbabel and only secondarily transferred to Joshua.[11] More recent scholars who see only one crown assume that it was meant for Joshua.[12] Other scholars hold that the passage envisions two crowns.[13] In this case there is still a division of opinion between those who suppose that the second crown was meant for Zerubbabel[14] and those who think it was reserved for a future messianic king.[15]

The suspicion that a royal figure was originally crowned in this passage, either instead of Joshua or in addition to him, arises from the speech addressed to Joshua in Zechariah 6:12: "This is the man whose name is צמח." The word צמח is an allusion to a pair of oracles in Jere-

10. W. Rose, *Zemah and Zerubbabel: Messianic Expectations in the Early Postexilic Period* (JSOTSup 34; Sheffield: Sheffield Academic Press, 2000) 50-56, 84-86.

11. J. Wellhausen, *Die kleinen Propheten* (Berlin: Reimer, 1893) 185; P. L. Redditt, "Zerubbabel, Joshua, and the Night Visions of Zechariah," *CBQ* 54 (1992) 249-59; idem, *Haggai, Zechariah, Malachi* (NCB; Grand Rapids: Eerdmans, 1995) 66.

12. Rose, *Zemah and Zerubbabel*, 58-59.

13. D. L. Petersen, *Haggai and Zechariah 1–8* (OTL; Philadelphia: Westminster, 1984) 275; C. L. and E. M. Meyers, *Haggai, Zechariah 1–8* (AB 25B; New York: Doubleday, 1987) 350-51.

14. Petersen, *Haggai, Zechariah 1–8*, 276-77.

15. Meyers and Meyers, *Haggai, Zechariah 1–8*, 355; Rose, *Zemah and Zerubbabel*, 248; Cook, *Prophecy and Apocalypticism*, 135.

miah 23:5 and 33:15. According to the first of these passages: "The days are surely coming, says the Lord, when I will raise up for David a righteous Branch (צמח צדיק), and he shall reign as king and deal wisely, and shall execute justice and righteousness in the land." Accordingly, most scholars recognize here an allusion to a messianic figure who would restore the Davidic line, whether this figure is identified with Zerubbabel or not.[16]

In a recent monograph that originated as an Oxford dissertation, Wolter Rose has tried to argue that the word צמח precludes identification with a historical figure such as Zerubbabel.[17] The preceding chapter in Jeremiah had announced that none of the offspring of Jehoiakin would succeed in sitting on the throne of David and ruling again in Jerusalem (Jer. 22:30). Rose infers that there must be a contrast between the צמח and the term used in the Jehoiakin oracle (זרע). He concludes that the clause in Jeremiah 23 "is used to express the idea that no simple historical development, but only an intervention by God can provide a future for the monarchy," and that "'David' is not the origin or source of a new sprout or the like, as in Isa. 11.1, but only the recipient of the צמח."[18] But divine intervention is not incompatible with continuity on the human level. On Rose's reading, it is unclear in what sense the צמח can be said to be raised up for David. If we read the prophetic books historically rather than canonically, then there is no need to reconcile Jeremiah 23:5 with the prophecy on Jeconiah. The צמח oracle is inserted to correct the earlier oracle and insist that God will honor the promise to David, Jeremiah's prophecy notwithstanding. We find a further qualification of the צמח oracle in Jeremiah 33:14-22, which reaffirms the prophecy despite delay in its fulfillment.[19] The passage in Jeremiah 33 is also relevant to Zechariah 6 because it affirms not only the covenant with David but also the covenant with the Levites and the future of the priesthood.

Even though there is no reference to David in Zechariah, the allusion

---

16. W. M. Schniedewind, *Society and the Promise to David: The Reception History of 2 Samuel 1–17* (New York: Oxford University Press, 1999) 134-35. K. E. Pomykala, *The Davidic Dynasty Tradition in Early Judaism* (SBLEJL 7; Atlanta: Scholars Press, 1995) 53-60, is exceptional in doubting the Davidic overtones of the צמח.

17. Rose, *Zemah and Zerubbabel*, 91-120.

18. Rose, *Zemah and Zerubbabel*, 118-19; cf. Pomykala, *The Davidic Dynasty Tradition*, 55.

19. M. Fishbane, *Biblical Interpretation in Ancient Israel* (Oxford: Oxford University Press, 1985) 471-74.

to Jeremiah strongly suggests that the צמח is a figure who would restore the Davidic line. The צמח is also mentioned in Zechariah 3:8, which says only "I am going to bring my servant, the צמח." Servant is not necessarily a royal title, but it is certainly compatible with royal status. (It is used more than forty times with reference to David.)[20] Perhaps the most interesting aspect of this reference is its context: Joshua, the High Priest, and his colleagues are told that they are "men of portent" (אנשי מופת), for "behold I am bringing my servant צמח" (Zech. 3:8). The presence of Joshua and his supporters (who are not necessarily all priests) is a sign that the monarchy will be restored. Since the "men of portent" are already present, it is reasonable to infer that the restoration must be close at hand. The oracle clearly indicates that Joshua is not meant to be the supreme ruler of restored Judah.

The passage in Zechariah 6 also associates Joshua with the צמח, while making clear that they are not identical. In this case we are given a little more information about the צמח. He will sprout "in his place" (מתחתיו) and he will build the temple of the Lord. He will rule on this throne, and he will work in harmony with a priest. The temple in question can only be the Second Temple, which was built in the Persian period. According to Ezra 5:1-2, Zechariah played an active role in having this temple built, and the work was carried out under the leadership of Joshua and Zerubbabel, the governor, a grandson of king Jehoiakin. Haggai 1:14 also testifies to his involvement. It is gratuitous to suppose that Zechariah has a different, eschatological, temple in mind in chapter 6.[21] Moreover, Zerubbabel is explicitly identified as the one who would build the temple in Zechariah 4:6b-10a. This passage is universally recognized as an insertion, since it interrupts the question-and-answer format of the chapter. But it must be a very early insertion, since it presupposes that the temple has not yet been completed. Eric and Carol Meyers, in their Anchor Bible commentary, allow that Zechariah himself, or less probably a disciple, may be responsible for the insertion.[22] Moreover, they consider this passage to be one of three major oracular additions in Zechariah 1–8. The others are the two passages that refer to the coming of the צמח. Whether these other passages are regarded as secondary or not, the association with the building of the temple makes it difficult to suppose that the צמח was anybody

20. Rose, *Zemah and Zerubbabel*, 122.
21. Pace Meyers and Meyers, *Haggai, Zechariah 1–8*, 356.
22. Meyers and Meyers, *Haggai, Zechariah 1–8*, 242.

other than Zerubbabel.[23] Since the building took place in the time when Zechariah was active, the reference cannot be to an eschatological figure in the distant future.

The Meyerses object to the identification of Zerubbabel with the צמח on the grounds that the restoration of the kingship was not in the realm of possibility under Persian rule.[24] But such considerations would hardly have carried much weight with a prophet who relied not on power or might but on the spirit of the Lord. The objections raised by Rose are weaker still.[25] The oracles consistently refer to the צמח as future, while Zerubbabel was already present in Judah when Zechariah prophesied. But the point of the oracles is not the arrival of the Davidide in Judah, but his assumption of the monarchy. The name Zerubbabel is not used in these passages, but was it necessary? (Lemaire points out that צמח is attested as a proper name and suggests that it was the Hebrew name of Zerubbabel.)[26] In Zechariah 6, at least, the צמח is assumed to be present when the crown is placed on the head of Joshua. The question of the crown or crowns remains problematic. It may be that Rose is right that there was only one crown and that it was placed on Joshua as a portent of the coming monarchy, just as Joshua and his companions were said to be men of portent in chapter 3. In that case, the sign would surely suggest that the assumption of monarchy was imminent, not in the indefinite future. I rather suspect, however, with Wellhausen and others, that the text has been altered. The form עטרות is most naturally read as plural. We should expect then that the prophet would place one on the head of Joshua, and say something to him, and then place the other on the head of Zerubbabel, and say, "This is the man whose name is צמח." The reason for the alteration of the text is all too clear. The coronation of Zerubbabel never took place. The governor may have been more pragmatic than the prophet, or perhaps the Persians intervened. We do not know. But the hypothesis that the text was altered to avoid the implication of rebellion seems to me much more plausible than the supposition that the prophet wanted to crown a priest as a way of indicating that the monarchy would be restored at some indefinite future time.

---

23. Petersen, *Haggai and Zechariah 1–8*, 276.
24. Meyers and Meyers, *Haggai, Zechariah 1–8*, 203.
25. Rose, *Zemah and Zerubbabel*, 131.
26. A. Lemaire, "Zorobabel et la Judée à la lumière de l'épigraphie (fin du VIe S. av. J.-C.)," *RB* 103 (1996) 48-57.

A Dyarchy?

The relation between priest and king raises another question about the kind of future governance envisioned by Zechariah. This is often called a dyarchy, and, despite some recent objections,[27] the designation seems to me to be apt. We have seen that the High Priest is juxtaposed with the צמח in chapters 3 and 6. Their cooperative relationship is expressed well in chapter 6: the royal figure will sit on his throne and the priest will be על כסאו, which can be interpreted either to mean that the priest will be by the throne of the king, or, taking the preposition in its more usual sense, that he will have a throne of his own. In any case there will be עצת שלום between them, which I take to mean that they will take counsel together for the welfare of the state. The duality of leadership is also at issue in chapter 4, where the two olive trees beside the lampstand are interpreted as "the two sons of oil (יצהר) that stand beside the Lord of the whole earth." The familiar translation, "the two anointed ones," has been rejected by several recent commentators on the grounds that the word יצהר is not used for the oil of anointing (שמן).[28] Rather, in the words of David Petersen, "to speak of a person using the image of the olive tree is . . . to view him or her as beautiful, productive, and important."[29] In view of the fact that there are two such figures, the only plausible candidates are Joshua and Zerubbabel, or rather the offices that they initially fill. In the words of Petersen again, "the polity of the new community is to be diarchic rather than monarchic."[30] Rose's suggestion that these figures "who stand before the Lord" are angelic cannot explain the duality, as he himself admits.[31] Boda suggests that the reference is to two prophetic figures, Haggai and Zechariah, but there is no clear reference to a pair of prophets anywhere in Zechariah 1–8, whereas the priestly and royal pair are well attested.[32] Anointed or not, these two figures are the channels of God's blessing for their community. But granted that this is the primary meaning of the symbolism, I wonder whether the connotation of anointing can be completely

---

27. Rose, *Zemah and Zerubbabel*, 251.

28. Meyers and Meyers, *Haggai, Zechariah 1–8*, 258; Tigchelaar, *Prophets of Old*, 40.

29. Petersen, *Haggai and Zechariah 1–8*, 230.

30. Petersen, *Haggai and Zechariah 1–8*, 234; Meyers and Meyers, *Haggai, Zechariah 1–8*, 275.

31. Rose, *Zemah and Zerubbabel*, 206.

32. M. J. Boda, "Oil, Crowns and Thrones: Prophet, Priest and King in Zechariah 1:7–6:15," *JHS* 3 (2001) article 10.

excluded. After all, Joshua was certainly anointed as High Priest. If, as I have argued, Zerubbabel was the צמח who was expected to assume the kingship, he would be anointed, too, even if that anointing never actually took place. It seems to me then that the idea of anointing is not so wide of the mark here as some recent commentators have claimed.

Was Zerubbabel Seen as a Messiah?

This brings me to my final question. Did Zechariah view Zerubbabel as a messiah? The answer, naturally, depends on what we mean by messiah. I use the term to refer to "an eschatological figure who sometimes, but not necessarily always, is designated as משיח in the ancient sources."[33] As we know from the Dead Sea Scrolls, messiahs in this sense could be priests or prophets as well as kings. In the case of Zerubbabel, the question is obviously whether he was a royal messiah. The expectation of a kingly messiah was rooted in the promise to David in 2 Samuel 7, which promised that a descendant of David would always sit on the throne in Jerusalem. This promise seemed to be broken when the last kings of Judah were deported by the Babylonians. In this context, a messianic king was one who would restore the Davidic kingship in a definitive way. The צמח of Jeremiah 23 was a messiah in this sense. The expectation was not simply for a restoration of the kingship, but for a definitive restoration that would live up to the full ideals of the kingship. This did not, however, imply that the king was a superhuman figure or that one king would reign forever. Rather, he would restore the dynasty in an ideal form.

It seems to me that such a king can reasonably be called a messiah. The צמח in Jeremiah and the shoot from the stump of Jesse in Isaiah 11 are messianic in this sense. The צמח in Zechariah, whom I take to be Zerubbabel, may also be regarded as a messiah. The expectation is eschatological, as it involves a definitive, lasting, future state. Such expectations can also be found in apocalyptic writings, but they are not distinctively apocalyptic. There is no messianic expectation in the early Jewish apocalypses of Daniel or *Enoch*. (The משיח נגיד of Daniel 9 is a historical figure who did not bring about a definitive change.) In the later apocalypse of *4 Ezra*, the messiah is a pre-existent figure who is revealed at the end of history, but he still

33. John J. Collins, *The Scepter and the Star: Messianism in Light of the Dead Sea Scrolls* (2nd ed.; Grand Rapids: Eerdmans, 2010) 17-18.

dies after 400 years (2 Esd. 7:29). The new creation and resurrection that follow the death of the messiah in *4 Ezra* are the trademarks of apocalyptic eschatology. Apocalyptic eschatology could accommodate messianic expectation, but only as part of a larger, cosmic transformation. This is also the case in the Dead Sea Scrolls.[34]

Conclusion

In conclusion, then, I would argue that the future expectations of Zechariah were eschatological, in the prophetic sense, and messianic, but not apocalyptic, in any plausible sense of the word. Wellhausen may have understated the matter when he said that Zechariah was only interested in Joshua and Zerubbabel, but Cook surely overstates the radical nature of his expectation when he says that history was going nowhere. On the contrary, it seems to me that Zechariah, like his contemporary Haggai, thought that the fulfillment of history was imminent. That fulfillment was itself historical. It involved the restoration of the Judean monarchy and its integration into a new political order. The power of the king would be balanced by that of the High Priest, and they would together engage in counsels of peace and well-being.

34. J. J. Collins, *Apocalypticism in the Dead Sea Scrolls* (London: Routledge, 1997) 71-90.

CHAPTER 3

The Beginning of the End of the World in the Hebrew Bible

"Heaven and earth will pass away," Jesus is reported to have said, "but my words will not pass away" (Mark 13:31). The psalmist in Psalm 102:26-27 says that heaven and earth will wear out like a garment and pass away, in contrast to the permanence of the Lord. But in fact such ideas are rather exceptional, at least in the Hebrew Bible. The weary comment of Qoheleth, "A generation goes, and a generation comes, but the earth remains forever" (Qoh. 1:4), rests, like many of his skeptical observations, on commonplace assumptions.[1] As late as the first century of the Common Era, Philo, while allowing that since the world has come into being it is destructible, holds that it may be made immortal by divine providence.[2] When we find speculation about the end of the world in the biblical tradition, it is seldom a matter of cosmological necessity, or of the world growing old, although that motif does occur.[3] Rather, it is a matter of divine judgment, and the idiom is mythological.

The end of the world is associated especially with apocalyptic literature, and even there it does not occur consistently. It is not explicit in the book of Daniel, and is only mentioned briefly in the writings that make up *1 Enoch*.[4] In the Dead Sea Scrolls, the destruction of the world is only

1. C. L. Seow, *Ecclesiastes* (AB 18C; New York: Doubleday, 1997) 106, suggests that the Hebrew of Qoheleth 1:4 may mean that the earth remains unchanged, but to remain unchanged it must also endure.

2. Philo, *Decal.* 58. In *Haer.* 2.4.6, he refers to the views of some who maintain that while the world is by nature destructible, it will never be destroyed, by the will of its Maker. The authenticity of the treatise *On the Eternity of the World* is disputed.

3. E.g., 2 Esdras 5:50-55; 14:10.

4. In the *Apocalypse of Weeks*, the world is written down for destruction in the ninth

evoked in a poetic passage in the Hodayot (1QHa 11:28–36). It is only at the end of the first century CE that the end of this world appears regularly in such works as *4 Ezra*, *2 Baruch*, Revelation, and *Sibylline Oracles* 4 and 5. Some of the formulations in these books may be influenced by Greek or Persian conceptions.[5] But the expectation that the world would be destroyed also had a biblical genealogy. In this study, I want to reflect on how the idea developed in the biblical tradition.

The Destruction of Nature

The great Akkadian and Ugaritic myths that articulate the conceptual context of ancient Near Eastern cosmology typically deal with the construction of the world, not with its dissolution. Even the Ugaritic Baal myth, which does not explicitly describe creation, is recognized as cosmogonic, insofar as it describes how the kingship of Baal is secured, and so right order prevails.[6] Right order in the cosmos has direct repercussions for the earth. When Baal is not in power, there is "no dew, no showers, no surging of the two seas, no benefit of Baal's voice,"[7] and so the furrows of the field are dry. When Baal lives, the heavens rain down oil and wadis run with honey.

In one episode in the Baal myth, Baal is swallowed up by Death. But his death is not final. He is rescued by his sister Anat, who splits Death with a sword. Baal returns to life, and the wadis run again. It seems clear that this myth reflects the cycle of nature, with its succession of dry and rainy seasons.[8]

The desolation of the earth through drought could also be invoked as a curse, to be inflicted by gods quite apart from the cycle of nature. So, for example, the Assyrian king Esarhaddon threatens the vassal that if he should not abide by the terms of the treaty:

---

week. In the tenth, the first heaven will vanish (*1 En.* 91:16). The *Astronomical Book* refers to a new creation in *1 Enoch* 72:1.

5. See J. J. Collins, *The Sibylline Oracles of Egyptian Judaism* (SBLDS 13; Missoula, MT: Scholars Press, 1974) 101-10.

6. F. M. Cross, *Canaanite Myth and Hebrew Epic* (Cambridge, MA: Harvard University Press, 1973) 120.

7. From the story of Aqhat, trans. M. D. Coogan, *Stories from Ancient Canaan* (Philadelphia: Westminster, 1978) 41.

8. See the comments of J. Day, "Baal (Deity)," *ABD* 1.546.

May Adad, the canal inspector of heaven and earth put an end [to vegetation] in your land, may he avoid your meadows and hit your land with a severe destructive downpour, may locusts, which diminish the (produce) of the land, [devour] your crops. . . (*ANET*, 538)

Similar curses are invoked in the Bible, should the Israelites violate their covenant with Yahweh.[9]

Imagery of cosmic destruction in the Hebrew Bible is typically associated not with the cycle of nature but with the punitive action of the deity. In part, the destruction was entailed by any theophany, which was typically described in the language of earthquake and thunderstorm.[10] Habakkuk 3:3-6 reads:

> God came from Teman,
> > the Holy One from Mount Paran. . .
> Before him went pestilence,
> > and plague followed close behind.
> He stopped and shook the earth;
> > he looked and made the nations tremble.
> The eternal mountains were shattered. . .
> > The everlasting hills sank low.[11]

This is a theophany of the divine warrior, coming to the rescue of his people:

> In fury you trod the earth,
> > in anger you trampled nations.
> You came forth to save your people,
> > to save your anointed. (Hab. 3:12-13)

Several psalms celebrate the kingship of Yahweh by describing the disruption of nature: "The mountains melt like wax before the Lord, before the Lord of all the earth" (Ps. 97:5). It is likely that the universal kingship of Yahweh was proclaimed in such terms in the Jerusalem cult, most proba-

---

9. Leviticus 26:16, 20; Deuteronomy 28:22-24, 38-42.

10. Cross, *Canaanite Myth*, 147-77.

11. Theodore Hiebert, *God of My Victory: The Ancient Hymn in Habakkuk 3* (HSM 38; Atlanta: Scholars Press, 1986).

bly in connection with the Festival of Tabernacles or Sukkoth.[12] There is no implication in the Psalms that God will destroy the whole world: the destruction does not extend to Judah and Jerusalem. When the mountains melt like wax, "Zion hears and is glad, and the towns of Judah rejoice" (Ps. 97:8). The destruction of the rest of the world is the corollary of the exaltation of Zion.

One of the great innovations of the Hebrew prophets was the idea that the wrath of Yahweh could be directed against Israel as well as against other nations. Amos famously warned the people of the northern kingdom of Israel that the Day of the Lord would be darkness and not light (Amos 5:18). It is in this context that the Hebrew prophets first speak of an "end" that is coming. This is not the end of the world, but the end of Israel. The Day of the Lord was originally the festival day when the kingship of Yahweh would be celebrated. The originality of Amos lay in suggesting that the appearance of Yahweh would be destructive for Israel, too. Thereafter, the Day of the Lord became synonymous with the Day of Judgment.[13] The judgment could be against Judah (Zephaniah 1) or a foreign nation (Babylon, in Isaiah 13). It could be executed by invading armies or even by a plague of locusts (Joel 2). It typically involves cosmic imagery and involves some destruction of nature. Even while his wrath is primarily directed against human pride, Isaiah 2:12-14 speaks of Yahweh's anger being directed towards the natural environment:

> The Lord of hosts has a day
> > against all that is proud and lofty. . .
> against all the cedars of Lebanon,
> > lofty and lifted up;
> > and against all the oaks of Bashan;
> against all the high mountains
> > and against all the lofty hills. . .

12. For the classic theory of S. Mowinckel that these psalms pertain to a supposed "Enthronement Festival" of Yahweh see Mowinckel, *The Psalms in Israel's Worship* (Oxford: Blackwell, 1962; repr. Grand Rapids: Eerdmans, 2004) 106-92. On the reception of this theory, see J. L. Crenshaw, comments in his "Foreword," to the reprint of Mowinckel's work (pp. xxviii-xxix). Mowinckel's theory that the festival celebrated the enthronement of Yahweh, rather than his permanent kingship, has not been widely accepted.

13. Hans-Peter Müller, *Ursprünge und Strukturen Alttestamentlicher Eschatologie* (BZAW 109; Berlin: Töpelmann, 1969) 69-85; R. H. Hiers, "Day of the Lord," *ABD* 2.82-83.

Isaiah 13:10-13 reads:

> the stars of heaven and their constellations will not give their light; the
> sun will be dark at its rising, and the moon will not shed its light. I will
> punish the world for its evil and the wicked for their iniquity. . . . There-
> fore I will make the heavens tremble, and the earth will be shaken out
> of its place, at the wrath of the Lord of hosts, in the day of his fierce
> anger.[14]

Despite the cosmic imagery, it is clear that the prophet is speaking about
the destruction of Babylon, not of the whole world. The cosmic imagery
provides hyperbolic language to underline the significance of a specific
historical and geographical situation.

Perhaps the most sweeping judgment associated with the Day of the
Lord is that spoken by Zephaniah, in the reign of King Josiah, in the late
seventh century BCE, in the context of a judgment oracle against Judah
and Jerusalem:

> I will utterly sweep away everything
>   from the face of the earth, says the Lord,
> I will sweep away humans and animals;
>   I will sweep away the birds of the air
>   and the fish of the sea.
> I will make the wicked stumble.
>   I will cut off humanity
>   from the face of the earth. (Zeph. 1:2-3)

As Jimmy Roberts has observed, this destruction is even more comprehensive than the flood, since it does not even spare the fish.[15] If Zephaniah
is aware of God's covenant with Noah, as reported in Genesis 8:21, he
abrogates it.[16] In any case, the threatened destruction represents a very different view of God's relation to creation from what we find in the Priestly
tradition.

This oracle concludes with an even more sweeping pronouncement:

---

14. Cf. Isaiah 34:4, where the heavens will be rolled up like a scroll.

15. J. J. M. Roberts, *Nahum, Habakkuk, and Zephaniah* (OTL; Louisville: Westminster, 1991) 170.

16. So Adele Berlin, *Zephaniah* (AB 25A; New York: Doubleday, 1994) 82.

> in the fire of his passion
>> the whole earth will be consumed;
> for a full, a terrible end
>> he will make of all the inhabitants of the earth. (Zeph. 1:18b)

And yet the destruction prophesied by Zephaniah is not final. Even though "all the inhabitants of Jerusalem" are threatened with destruction in chapter 1, in chapter 3 Jerusalem is told to rejoice, because the Lord has taken away the judgments against her. Perhaps we should read the pronouncement of universal destruction as a threat that is later revoked. (Cf. Amos 7:1-6, where threatened punishments are revoked.) Or perhaps this too should be read as hyperbolic, on the understanding that the prophet was not literally predicting the end of life on earth.[17] This is poetic language, which cannot be pressed for logical consistency.

Jeremiah

A little later than Zephaniah, Jeremiah evoked cosmic destruction to convey his foreboding about the coming destruction of Jerusalem:

> I looked on the earth, and lo, it was waste and void;
>> and to the heavens, and they had no light.
> I looked on the mountains, and lo they were quaking
>> and all the hills moved to and fro.
> I looked, and lo there was no one at all,
>> and all the birds of the air had fled.
> I looked, and lo, the fruitful land was a desert,
>> and all its cities were laid in ruins
>> before the Lord, before his fierce anger. (Jer. 4:23-26)

Jeremiah was not predicting the end of the world. He was describing a vision of destruction. Waste and void, תהו ובהו was the condition of the earth before creation (Gen. 1:2). The imagery does not imply that the

---

17. So Roberts, *Nahum, Habakkuk and Zephaniah*, 185. The hyperbolic character of eschatological language is emphasized by G. B. Caird, *The Language and Imagery of the Bible* (Philadelphia: Westminster, 1980) 243-71, even in the case of the New Testament, where his argument is strained.

world will cease to exist. Rather, it is returned to its primeval state before creation. If there is a prediction here, it is a prediction of the destruction of Jerusalem. But, in fact, Jeremiah's evocation of cosmic destruction is different in character from that of Zephaniah. Where Zephaniah uttered a threat, Jeremiah's oracle is expressive, articulating the desolation caused by the Babylonian invasion and the impending destruction of Jerusalem. Again, a quite specific historical and geographical instance is endowed with cosmic significance.

The So-called Apocalypse of Isaiah

The most elaborate symbolism of cosmic destruction in the Hebrew Bible is found in Isaiah 24–27, especially in 24:1-20:

> Now the Lord is about to lay waste the earth and make it desolate,
>> and he will twist its surface and scatter its inhabitants,
> and it shall be, as with the people, so with the priest. . . .
> The earth shall be utterly laid waste and utterly despoiled;
>> for the Lord has spoken this word. (24:1-3)

The passage continues by describing how the earth dries up and withers, and identifies a reason:

> The earth dries up and withers,
>> the world languishes and withers;
>> the heavens languish together with the earth.
> The earth lies polluted
>> under its inhabitants;
> for they have transgressed its laws,
>> violated the statutes,
>> broken the everlasting covenant.
> Therefore a curse devours the earth. . . (Isa. 24:4-6a)

Therefore the vine withers; there is no wine and no merry-making. The effect is felt especially in "the city of chaos," קרית־תהו. The term תהו recalls the vision of Jeremiah, and the state of the world before creation. It is not immediately clear whether the city is one that causes desolation or that now suffers desolation because of the cosmic destruction.

The passage concludes even more forcefully:

> For the windows of heaven are opened,
>   and the foundations of the earth tremble.
> The earth is utterly broken,
>   the earth is torn asunder,
>   the earth is violently shaken.
> The earth staggers like a drunkard,
>   it sways like a hut;
> its transgression lies heavy upon it,
>   and it falls, and will not rise again. (Isa. 24:18b-20)

Since the time of Bernhard Duhm, it has been generally accepted that Isaiah of Jerusalem did not utter these lines.[18] In language and tone, Isaiah 24–27 belongs rather with the exilic and postexilic additions to the book of Isaiah, or with other Second Temple compositions such as the later chapters of Zechariah.[19] Despite the common designation as "the Apocalypse of Isaiah," these chapters do not constitute an apocalypse.[20] There is no heavenly revelation such as we find in Daniel or Enoch. Rather, this is a cluster of prophetic oracles, similar in kind to other oracles that were added anonymously to prophetic books in the Second Temple period. In the book of Isaiah, they are placed after the oracles against the nations in chapters 13–23, and provide a fitting conclusion to that section of the book by expanding the horizon from particular nations to the whole earth.[21]

The extent of the literary unit is a matter of dispute. It has been de-

---

18. Bernhard Duhm, *Das Buch Jesaia* (5th ed.; Göttingen: Vandenhoeck & Ruprecht, 1968, first published in 1892) 172: "In der Tat könnte Jes. ebenso gut das Buch Daniel geschrieben haben wie diese Schrift." Duhm's dating of these chapters to the second century BCE is now universally rejected. For the history of scholarship see Brian Doyle, *The Apocalypse of Isaiah, Metaphorically Speaking* (BETL 151; Leuven: Peeters, 2000) 11-45.

19. Hans Wildberger, *Isaiah 13–27* (trans. T. H. Trapp; CC; Minneapolis: Fortress, 1997) 464: "the language used in the apocalypse belongs in the Persian period, and generally fits better into the earlier rather than the later part of the Persian era." See further D. C. Polaski, *Authorizing an End: The Isaiah Apocalypse and Intertextuality* (BibInt 50; Leiden: Brill, 2001) 58-70.

20. John J. Collins, "The Jewish Apocalypses," *Semeia* 14 (1979): 21-59 (29); idem, *The Apocalyptic Imagination* (2nd ed.; Grand Rapids: Eerdmans, 1998) 24-25; Polaski, *Authorizing an End*, 49-51.

21. Marvin A. Sweeney, *Isaiah 1–39, with an Introduction to Prophetic Literature* (FOTL XVI; Grand Rapids: Eerdmans, 1996) 316.

scribed as "a compendium of mostly eschatological logia, addresses and psalms, with no very obvious internal arrangement or logical sequence,"[22] and as "a maddeningly frustrating text that rapidly shifts its focus."[23] Many scholars see these chapters as a collection of fragments that have grown into their present form over the course of centuries.[24] Marvin Sweeney, however, finds "a high degree of unity and purpose." According to Sweeney,

> Not only do chs. 24–27 display a coherent literary structure and ge-
> neric character as a prophetic announcement of salvation, but their
> worldview is consistently universal insofar as it focuses on YHWH's
> plans for the "land" or "earth" in general, including the nations and
> Israel. Furthermore, the entire work presupposes the overthrow of the
> anonymous "city of chaos" (24:10). . . . In addition, chs. 24–27 employ
> a relatively consistent mythological pattern employing motifs of death,
> life, and agricultural fertility to express its concern with the overthrow
> of the oppressive ruling city and the renewal of the oppressed.[25]

Sweeney allows that "there are some indications that 27:1-13 may have a different origin than that of 24:1 to 26:21," since chapter 27 has a narrower focus on Israel.[26] I would modify this and say that the narrower focus is found in 27:2-13, since 27:1 manifestly refers to the same complex of mythic motifs as are prominent in the preceding chapters.[27]

We do not know whether these chapters ever circulated independently. It is unlikely that these chapters were composed for purely literary reasons, to provide a conclusion to the oracles against the nations. The preoccupation with the "city of chaos," and a reference in 25:8 to "the disgrace of his people" bespeak an existential situation that gave rise to these oracles.

---

22. Joseph Blenkinsopp, *A History of Prophecy in Israel* (rev. ed.; Louisville: West-minster, 1996) 237.

23. Donald C. Polaski, "Destruction, Construction, Argumentation. A Rhetorical Reading of Isaiah 24–27," in G. Carey and L. G. Bloomquist, eds., *Vision and Persuasion: Rhetorical Dimensions of Apocalyptic Discourse* (St. Louis: Chalice, 1999) 19-39 (21).

24. E.g., J. Vermeylen, "La composition littéraire de l'apocalypse d'Isaïe (Is. XXIV–XXVII)," *ETL* 50 (1974) 5-38; idem, *Du prophète Isaïe à l'apocalyptique* (Paris: Gabalda, 1977) 349-81.

25. Sweeney, *Isaiah 1–39*, 316-17.

26. Sweeney, *Isaiah 1–39*, 317.

27. Dan G. Johnson, *From Chaos to Restoration: An Integrative Reading of Isaiah 24–27* (JSOTSup 61; Sheffield: JSOT Press, 1988) 84: "Isa 27.1 brings to a conclusion the section celebrating the imminent victory of Yahweh over the enemy."

But there is no agreement as to the precise setting. Proposals range from the eighth century to the second, although the later extreme is shown to be untenable by discovery of the scrolls of Isaiah at Qumran.[28] As Dan Johnson has pointed out, the language of cosmic destruction is exceptional in its degree. The closest parallel in the Hebrew Bible is found in Jeremiah 4:23-28. "But this," writes Johnson, "is Jeremiah's way of describing the destruction of Jerusalem and the ensuing exile which he perceived as imminent." It is "an example of cosmic imagery applied to a specific geographical situation."[29] Johnson infers that Isaiah 24:1-20, too, "was written on the eve of the destruction of Jerusalem in 587," although the other chapters were written later. Most commentators date all these chapters somewhat later, in the Persian period.[30]

The City of Chaos

It is quite likely that the cosmic imagery of Isaiah 24 was also originally applied to a specific situation. Attempts to identify that situation depend inevitably on the identification of the "city of chaos" mentioned in Isaiah 24:10: "The city of chaos is broken down." There are further references to a city in 25:2; 26:5-6; and 27:10. Chapter 25 begins:

> O LORD, you are my God,
>   I will exalt you, I will praise your name;
> for you have done wonderful things,
>   plans formed of old, faithful and sure.
> For you have made the city a heap,
>   the fortified city a ruin;
> the palace of aliens is a city no more,
>   it will never be rebuilt.

The reference in 26:5-6 likewise praises God for bringing the lofty city low. At least in chapters 25 and 26, the city described as "the palace of aliens" can hardly be other than Babylon.[31]

---

28. For an overview see Doyle, *The Apocalypse of Isaiah*, 31-37.

29. Johnson, *From Chaos to Restoration*, 28.

30. Sweeney, *Isaiah 1–39*, 319, opts for the late sixth century BCE.

31. Sweeney, *Isaiah 1–39*, 318. For a survey of suggestions, see Doyle, *The Apocalypse of Isaiah*, 37-43. The identification with Babylon was championed by W. Rudolph, *Jesaja 24–27*

Nonetheless, some scholars have argued that 24:1-20 is a separate composition and that the "city of chaos" in chapter 24 is Jerusalem.[32] Dan Johnson argues that "the tone and mood were those of a lament," and that the prophet had employed the funeral dirge in a politicized fashion to describe the death of the city."[33] He reasons that the prophet would not have mourned the destruction of an enemy city. He further argues that the Hebrew word הארץ throughout this poem should be translated "land" rather than earth, that the reference is to the land of Israel, and that the broken covenant is that of Sinai.[34] ארץ, however, is parallel to תבל, which unambiguously means "world," in 24:4, and the Sinai covenant is never called "the eternal covenant." Most scholars take the "eternal covenant" as the covenant with Noah (Gen. 9:8-17), which applies to Gentiles as well as Jews.[35] No specific violations of the Sinai covenant are mentioned. It is more likely, then, that the reference is to the destruction of the whole earth, rather than a judgment on Judah. Moreover, the destruction of the city is an occasion for giving glory to the Lord in vv. 14-15, and this would hardly be the case if the city were Jerusalem. In view of the clear references to an alien city in chapters 25 and 26, it is safer to take the "city of chaos" in 24:10 also as a reference to Babylon. Sweeney claims that "The 'city of chaos' in 24:10 is designed as a deliberate pun to call to mind Tiamat and to question the self-proclaimed role of Babylon as the center of world order."[36] Even if we do not see a pun here, the designation is telling, since the Babylonian creation epic, the *Enuma Elish*, celebrated the role of Marduk, god of Babylon, as creator of the earth. It is a repudiation of the Babylonian view of the world, wherein Babylon was the very symbol of the triumph of Marduk over chaos.

Johannes Lindblom argued that the oracles of destruction were a reaction to the destruction of Babylon by Xerxes in 485 BCE.[37] This is pos-

---

(BWANT 4/10; Stuttgart: Kohlhammer, 1933) 62; J. Lindblom, *Die Jesaja Apokalypse. Jesaja 24–27* (Lund: Gleerup, 1938) 72-84; Vermeylen, *Du prophète Isaïe*, 355.

32. Johnson, *From Chaos to Restoration*, 29-35. W. R. Millar, *Isaiah 24–27 and the Origin of Apocalyptic* (HSM 11; Cambridge, MA: Harvard University Press, 1976) 118-19, even identifies the "city of aliens" in Isaiah 25 and 26 as Jerusalem. See further Doyle, *The Apocalypse of Isaiah*, 41-42.

33. Johnson, *From Chaos to Restoration*, 29-35.

34. So also Polaski, *Authorizing an End*, 96.

35. Wildberger, *Isaiah 13–27*, 479.

36. Sweeney, *Isaiah 1–39*, 318.

37. Lindblom, *Die Jesaja-Apokalypse*, 72-84.

sible, but it is also possible that the passage is entirely predictive. I do not mean that it should be read as purely eschatological, without any historical moorings.[38] Sweeney has noticed that the enigmatic statement in 24:16, "for the treacherous deal treacherously," is a citation of Isaiah 21:2, which refers to the rebellion of Elam (Persia) and Media against Babylon. He infers that "this reference hints at the Medes' threat against Babylon under Cyrus in the 6th century."[39] But it does not necessarily refer to the same occasion. Isaiah 26:15, "but you have increased the nation, O Lord . . . you have enlarged all the borders of the land," surely requires a date after the restoration of Judah, and probably points to a date in the fifth century, as suggested by Lindblom.[40] In any case, there can be little doubt that the predictions arise from the desire to "take away the disgrace of my people" and see Babylon destroyed as it had destroyed Jerusalem.

The Reason for Destruction

The stated reason for destruction, however, is not revenge for the Babylonian conquest. The whole earth is to be destroyed, because "the earth lies polluted under its inhabitants; for they have transgressed laws, violated the statutes, broken the everlasting covenant." The everlasting covenant is usually recognized as the covenant with Noah. The objection is sometimes raised that this was not a conditional covenant, and that "the expression 'break the eternal covenant' . . . actually does not make sense."[41] Hans Wildberger seems to be right that the prophet construes the Noahic covenant on the analogy of the Sinaitic one[42] — hence the reference to laws and statutes. Later tradition knew of Noahide laws, which were binding on all humanity.[43] These include the shedding of blood. Already in Genesis, Noah is warned that God will require a reckoning for bloodshed: "Who-

38. As suggested by O. Kaiser, *Isaiah 13–39* (OTL; Philadelphia: Westminster, 1974) 177, 181; B. S. Childs, *Isaiah* (OTL; Louisville: Westminster, 2001) 178-81.

39. Sweeney, *Isaiah 1–39*, 319.

40. The suggestion of Wildberger, *Isaiah 13–27*, 565, cf. Blenkinsopp, *Isaiah 1–39*, 370, that this is an allusion to the time of David, seems to me quite implausible in the context.

41. Wildberger, *Isaiah 13–27*, 480. Cf. Johnson, *From Chaos to Restoration*, 28: "An everlasting covenant by definition cannot be broken."

42. Wildberger, *Isaiah 13–27*, 480.

43. David Novak, *Natural Law in Judaism* (Cambridge: Cambridge University Press, 1998) 149-73.

ever sheds the blood of a human, by a human shall that person's blood be shed" (Gen. 9:6). Moreover, blood defiles, and this would explain why the land is defiled; compare Numbers 35:33-34:

> you shall not pollute the land in which you live, for blood pollutes the land, and no expiation can be made for the land, for the blood that is shed in it, except by the blood of the one who shed it.[44]

Bloodshed is not necessarily the only way in which the earth has been polluted, but it is surely one of the ways. The priestly author in Genesis did not conceive of the covenant with Noah as one that could be broken. But the prophet of Isaiah 24 thought otherwise. In Genesis God had promised that he would never again curse the ground because of humankind (Gen. 8:21), but now we find that a curse devours the earth because of its inhabitants (Isa. 24:6).

The destruction of the earth, then, can be viewed as a punishment for breach of covenant, as if the whole earth were subject to a conditional agreement like the one between Yahweh and Israel. But the problem with the world is not just a matter of occasional acts of violence, like those perpetrated by Babylon against Israel. Defiling violence is endemic to human behavior, as it was in the generation of Noah. Perhaps at this point in the history of Israel and Judah it had become apparent that the threat to a small nation in the ancient Near East was not confined to any one empire. If Egypt did not dominate, then Assyria would, or Babylon, or Persia. Greece and Rome would later be added to the list. So, increasingly in postexilic prophecy, the call is for judgment not on any one nation but on all the nations. This tendency is found already in the oracle against Gog from the land of Magog in Ezekiel 38–39, and in Joel 3:2, where God gathers all the nations in the valley of Jehoshaphat.

Isaiah 24–27 actually goes farther than books such as Joel and calls for judgment, not just on all peoples, but on the world itself. Creation itself is awry. In the mythology of the ancient Near East, from Babylon to Jerusalem, creation was conceived in terms of combat, often dubbed the *Chaoskampf*.[45] The god of life and order had to defeat the forces of chaos.

---

44. Johnson (*From Chaos to Restoration*, 29) objects that the context makes clear that the prohibition against pollution is because of God's ownership of the land (of Israel), but this could be extended here to the whole world.

45. Hermann Gunkel, *Creation and Chaos in the Primeval Era and the Eschaton: A Religio-Historical Study of Genesis 1 and Revelation 12* (trans. W. Whitney; Grand Rapids:

From the perspective of Judeans in the Babylonian exile, or later under Gentile rule, the process needed to be repeated. In the following chapters, Isaiah 25 and 27, the prophet twice evokes explicitly the old cosmogonic myths. The first and more poignant passage is in 25:6-8, which promises that the Lord will make a feast for all peoples "on this mountain," presumably Mt. Zion:

> And he will destroy on this mountain
>> the shroud that is cast over all peoples,
>> the sheet that is spread over all nations;
>> he will swallow up death forever.
> Then the Lord GOD will wipe away the tears from all faces,
>> and the disgrace of his people he will take away from all the earth.

In the old Ugaritic myth, Mot, or Death, had swallowed Baal. In the prophetic future, Yahweh would swallow Death.[46] Death, of course, was not a problem that afflicted only the Israelites. The poignancy of this passage arises especially from its recognition that the basic problems that beset any people are universal problems that can only be addressed by addressing the whole created order.

The second mythological passage is briefer: "On that day the Lord with his cruel and great and strong sword will punish Leviathan the fleeing serpent, Leviathan the twisting serpent, and he will kill the dragon that is in the sea" (27:1). This is almost a direct quotation of an Ugaritic text in which Baal is said to have "smote Lotan the ancient dragon, destroyed the crooked serpent, Shilyat with the seven heads."[47] Slaying the dragon, in Near Eastern mythology, is the necessary prerequisite for building a new created order. While Isaiah 24–27 does not speak explicitly of a new creation, it clearly envisions the emergence of a new order.

Eerdmans, 2006; German original, 1895); Jon D. Levenson, *Creation and the Persistence of Evil* (San Francisco: Harper, 1985) 3-50; Richard J. Clifford, S.J., "The Roots of Apocalypticism in Near Eastern Myth," in J. J. Collins, ed., *The Encyclopedia of Apocalypticism*, vol. 1: *The Origins of Apocalypticism in Judaism and Christianity* (New York: Continuum, 1998) 3-38.

46. Johnson, *From Chaos to Restoration*, 65.

47. Cross, *Canaanite Myth*, 119; Bernhard W. Anderson, "The Slaying of the Fleeing, Twisting Serpent: Isaiah 27:1 in Context," in L. M. Hopfe, ed., *Uncovering Ancient Stones: Essays in Memory of H. Neil Richardson* (Winona Lake, IN: Eisenbrauns, 1994) 3-15.

Death and Resurrection

It has been argued that the literary structure of Isaiah 24–27 is determined by a mythic pattern of Threat-War-Victory-Feast, derived from Canaanite mythology and exemplified in the Baal Epic.[48] This, I think, is to force the evidence. But there is no doubt about the prominence of mythic motifs in these oracles, and these motifs imply a pattern, even if every element in these chapters does not necessarily fit into it. The pattern provides a context for the cosmic destruction of chapter 24. The myths are essentially circular rather than linear. The destruction is never the end of the story. Especially striking here is the language of death and resurrection. The swallowing of Death in chapter 25 does not promise the resurrection of those already dead, but it changes the conditions of human existence for the future. A more controversial reference to resurrection is found in chapter 26. The context is a contrast between the fate of other nations and that of Judah:

> O LORD our God,
>> other lords besides you have ruled over us,
>> but we acknowledge your name alone.
> The dead do not live;
>> Shades do not rise —
>> Because you have punished and destroyed them,
>> And wiped out all memory of them.
> But you have increased the nation, O LORD. . .
> Your dead shall live, their corpses shall rise.
>> O dwellers in the dust, awake and sing for joy!
> For your dew is a radiant dew,
>> and the earth will give birth to those long dead. (Isa. 26:13-15, 19)

Some scholars regard this passage as the earliest expression of a hope for the resurrection of the dead in the Hebrew Bible.[49] In my judgment, the reference is more likely to be to the restoration of Judah after the exile, as in Ezekiel's vision of the valley full of dry bones, which may be roughly

---

48. Millar, *Isaiah 24–27*, 65-81.

49. Emile Puech, *La Croyance des Esséniens en la Vie Future. Immortalité, Résurrection, Vie Éternelle?* (EBib 21; Paris: Gabalda, 1993) 66-73; G. W. E. Nickelsburg, *Resurrection, Immortality, and Eternal Life in Intertestamental Judaism and Early Christianity* (HTS 56; Cambridge, MA: Harvard University Press, 2006) 30-31.

contemporary.[50] The once-powerful Babylon will not rise again, but Judah will. The people of Judah had already suffered much destruction, but they are not the object of the Lord's wrath on this occasion. Rather, they are invited to hide in their chambers for a little while until the wrath is past. The Lord will pass them over, as the destroying angel had spared them at the time of the exodus. As in Zephaniah, the destruction of the whole earth does not include Mt. Zion, or the remnant of Judah.

Zion emerges in these oracles as the center of a restored world order. Though the moon be abashed and the sun ashamed, "the LORD of hosts will reign on Mt. Zion and in Jerusalem" (Isa. 24:23). This is the mountain on which the Lord makes a feast for all peoples (25:6). The universalism of this scenario is often noted, but it is a Zion-centric universalism. All peoples can be included, but in subordinate roles. Moreover, they are only included after they have suffered a destructive judgment. In chapter 26, Jerusalem is "a strong city" through whose gates "the righteous nation" may enter. This is ultimately a nationalistic vision, essentially in continuity with the ideology of the royal cult in pre-exilic Jerusalem, although, remarkably, there is no role here for a messianic king. The prophet was not entirely oblivious to the realities of Persian rule.

The mythic pattern that is reflected in Isaiah 24–27 is essentially the same one that informs Daniel 7[51] and Revelation.[52] Despite the continuity, however, there are some fundamental differences between Isaiah 24–27 and the later apocalypses. One concerns the nature of resurrection, and another concerns the constitution of the righteous people. According to Daniel, at the end of history the archangel Michael will arise:

> At that time your people shall be delivered, everyone who is found written in the book. Many of those who sleep in the land of dust shall awake, some to everlasting life, and some to shame and everlasting contempt. Those who are wise shall shine like the brightness of the sky, and those who lead many to righteousness like the stars forever and ever. (Dan 12:1-3)[53]

50. So also Blenkinsopp, *Isaiah 1–39*, 371.

51. John J. Collins, "Stirring Up the Great Sea: The Religio-Historical Background of Daniel 7," in J. J. Collins, ed., *Seers, Sibyls and Sages in Hellenistic-Roman Judaism* (JSJSup 54; Leiden: Brill, 1997) 139-55; idem, *Daniel* (Hermeneia; Minneapolis: Fortress, 1993) 280-94.

52. Adela Yarbro Collins, *The Combat Myth in the Book of Revelation* (HDR 9; Missoula: Scholars Press, 1976).

53. See Collins, *Daniel*, 390-94.

In this case there is no doubt that the resurrection of individuals who had died is in view. Not all will be raised, and those who are will be raised for different fates — eternal life for some and everlasting shame and contempt for others. The wise משכלים, some of whom suffered death in the persecution under Antiochus Epiphanes, will become like the stars, which is to say that they will be exalted to join the angelic host in heaven. One should not exaggerate the individualism of this scenario. It is still concerned with the deliverance of "your people," and it is quite compatible with the vision of Daniel 7, which is closer in idiom to Isaiah 24–27, and which envisions an ongoing earthly kingdom for "the people of the Holy Ones of the Most High" (Dan. 7:27).[54] But the novelty of Daniel's expectation over against the earlier biblical tradition should not be missed. It introduces a hope for salvation "out of this world," which would eventually have enormous implications for both Judaism and Christianity.

Marvin Sweeney has quite rightly protested that "Daniel does not abandon concern for this world in an attempt to achieve redemption in a heavenly realm beyond the bounds of human history."[55] Redemption in a heavenly realm is in no way incompatible with concern for this world, as the latter-day Islamic "martyrs" also know. But the hope for salvation outside the bounds of human history makes a difference nonetheless, as it changes the ultimate values for which one lives.

Jon Levenson has recently questioned the significance of the distinction between resurrection as a metaphor for national restoration, such as we find in Ezekiel 37 or Isaiah 26, and the hope for individual resurrection and vindication such as we find in Daniel 12:

> When personal identity is constructed in corporate terms — when, that is, the subject is profoundly embedded in familial, tribal, and national groupings — some questions natural to modern Westerners become unproductive, even dangerous. In the case at hand, the question of whether it is individuals or the nation, Israelites or Israel, that God revives has about it a certain artificiality. . . . The classical Jewish belief in the resurrection of the dead is not simply the notion that departed individuals will eventually receive their due. It is the confidence that

54. The corporate expectation is emphasized by J. D. Levenson, *Resurrection and the Restoration of Israel: The Ultimate Victory of the God of Life* (New Haven: Yale University Press, 2006) 197.

55. Marvin A. Sweeney, "The End of Eschatology in Daniel," *BibInt* 9 (2001): 121-40 (139).

God will in the end fulfill his outstanding promises to Israel, even to those worthy members of Israel who sleep in the dust.[56]

But whether or not "the classical Jewish belief in the resurrection of the dead" is necessarily what we find in Daniel, the hope for individual resurrection shows that personal identity is no longer constructed *only* in corporate terms. This is not to deny that corporate identity still has an important role in Daniel and other apocalyptic texts, but it is qualified by a new understanding of the self that admits of immortality and is concerned with other forms of salvation in addition to the fulfillment of God's promises to Israel.

The rise of the afterlife in the Hellenistic age was not peculiar to Judaism, and the Jewish phenomenon cannot be understood in isolation from its broader environment.[57] The conquests of Alexander and the subsequent cultural mingling led to changes in society quite apart from the influence of particular ideas. One of these changes was surely the weakening (not the obliteration!) of traditional bonds of tribe and family, especially in the context of growing urbanization. In the Jewish context, there was another factor that contributed to the hope for a judgment, and differentiated outcome, beyond the grave. This was the growth of divisions within the people of Judah, sometimes taking the form of full-blown sectarianism.[58] In the case of Daniel, those who rise to shame and everlasting contempt are not necessarily all Gentile. They presumably include "those who forsake the holy covenant" (Dan. 11:30), the Hellenizing faction that bore at least some of the responsibility for the persecution under Antiochus Epiphanes.[59] Division within the community was already a factor in the Persian period, and it is often associated with the late prophetic writings that are sometimes misleadingly dubbed "proto-apocalyptic."[60] Surprisingly enough,

---

56. Levenson, *Resurrection and the Restoration of Israel*, 200.

57. See Jan N. Bremmer, *The Rise and Fall of the Afterlife* (London: Routledge, 2002); Alan F. Segal, *Life after Death: A History of the Afterlife in the Religions of the West* (New York: Doubleday, 2004) 173-247.

58. Albert I. Baumgarten, *The Flourishing of Jewish Sects in the Maccabean Era: An Interpretation* (JSJSup 55; Leiden: Brill, 1997).

59. On the circumstances surrounding the persecution see John J. Collins, "Cult and Culture: The Limits of Hellenization in Judea," in J. J. Collins, ed., *Jewish Cult and Hellenistic Culture* (JSJSup 100; Leiden: Brill, 2005) 21-43.

60. See especially Paul D. Hanson, *The Dawn of Apocalyptic* (Philadelphia: Fortress Press, 1975).

such divisions play no part in Isaiah 24–27.[61] There "the nation" appears to be an unproblematic concept, one which does not seem to call for further distinctions, either in this world or in the next. It was possible, of course, to exclude some people from the commonwealth of Judah, as Ezra reportedly tried to do. A postmortem judgment, however, provided a neater and less problematic way of excluding the unworthy. In rabbinic idiom, they would have no share in the world to come. Even in the classical (rabbinic) Jewish theology of resurrection, the concept of Israel is more problematic than it was when identity was uniformly conceived in corporate terms.

Conclusion

"Universal destruction," writes Donald Polaski, "functions to present the reader with a hopeless nonsurvivable world. Having brought the audience down to a hyperbolically low point, the author/redactor is free to reconstruct the world. It is this project, not the exhilaration of survival, that will bond the community together."[62] In Isaiah 24–27, the world shown to be hopeless is the world with Babylon at its center, the city of chaos. We do not know whether Babylon had been physically destroyed when these oracles were uttered. Most probably, it had at least fallen from power. The hyperbole of cosmic destruction leaves the prophet free to imagine a new creation. Some later apocalypses would strive to make the destruction of the old order more emphatically complete, even punctuating it with a period of primeval silence (2 Esd. 7:30).[63] But the destruction is always a prelude to a new order. Polaski is right that it is the new order that defines the community. If the restoration is conceived in terms of national mythology, as in Isaiah 24–27, then the emphasis is on national solidarity. If provision is made for a judgment of the individual dead, then there is greater emphasis on individual character and decision, although national solidarity is not necessarily excluded. The apocalypses that conceive resurrection in otherworldly terms typically conceive of a community that does not necessarily coincide with ethnic Israel.

How one views the prospect of an end of this world naturally de-

61. Scholars, including Millar and Johnson, who identify the "city of chaos" as Jerusalem posit a deep division in the Jewish community, but the argument is not persuasive.

62. Polaski, "Destruction, Construction, Argumentation," 26.

63. Caird, *The Language and Imagery*, 256-57, misses this realist (though scarcely literal) depiction of the end in apocalyptic texts.

pends on one's vantage point. For Jeremiah, the return of the earth to waste and void was a disaster, as it served as an expressive metaphor for the destruction of Jerusalem. Isaiah 24, however, and indeed most apocalypses, are, in the words of Dan Johnson, "decidedly positive about Yahweh's activity within this world."[64] The destruction must be seen as an element in a mythic pattern, which ultimately leads to restoration or renewal.

I can think of only one Jewish text from antiquity where the destruction of the world appears to be final. This is a passage at the end of the fifth book of the *Sibylline Oracles* (*Sib. Or.* 5:512-31). It is a debatable example, as that book has its share of prophecies of eschatological renewal.[65] The placement of this particular oracle, however, at the end of the book, gives it a ring of finality. It describes a battle of the stars:

> I saw the threat of the burning sun among the stars
> and the terrible wrath of the moon among the lightning flashes.

In the end,

> Heaven itself was roused until it shook the fighters.
> In anger it cast them headlong to earth.
> Accordingly, stricken into the baths of ocean,
> they quickly kindled the whole earth.
> But the sky remained starless.

The book ends without any restoration. I submit that this is the bleakest use of end-of-the-world imagery that one finds anywhere in Jewish or Christian tradition. *Sibylline Oracles* 5 dates from some time in the late first or early second century CE. While we do not know the exact date of composition, it provides an apt metaphor for the desolation that befell Judaism in the Egyptian Diaspora after the revolt under Trajan. In this case, the end-of-the-world imagery is not part of a myth of cyclic renewal, but like the prophecy of Jeremiah is an anguished cry of someone whose world was coming to an end as if the sky were falling.

---

64. Johnson, *From Chaos to Restoration*, 99.
65. Collins, *The Sibylline Oracles of Egyptian Judaism*, 73-95.

CHAPTER 4

Apocalypticism and the Transformation of Prophecy in the Second Temple Period

A few years ago I was asked to give a talk on prophecy at a local church. I gave what I considered to be a standard talk, focusing on Amos and Jeremiah, emphasizing the demand for social justice, speaking truth to power, and so forth. After a while I noticed that a group of women were shaking their heads in disagreement. When I finished, one of them asked: Why didn't you speak about prophecy? I said that I had spoken about prophecy. No! she said. Prophecy is about the future. What does the Bible tell us about the end of the world? I quickly realized that no meeting of minds would ensue.

These women, of course, were not alone in their view of prophecy. Much of American popular religion is dominated by what Paul Boyer called "prophecy belief," a tradition rooted in the Dispensationalism of John Nelson Darby in the nineteenth century, and associated with Fundamentalism.[1] In this tradition, the entire Bible is read as prophecy, in the sense that it may be taken to contain coded information about the present, on the assumption that we are now living at the end of history. Hal Lindsey's best-selling book, *The Late Great Planet Earth,* updated through several editions, is a classic of the genre.[2] Needless to say, this way of reading the Bible is diametrically opposed to modern critical scholarship in any of its forms. It entails a radically different view of prophecy from the one that sees the prophets as social and religious critics of their own time. It collapses the distinction that has been standard in modern scholarship

---

1. Paul Boyer, *When Time Shall Be No More: Prophecy Belief in Modern American Culture* (Cambridge, MA: Harvard University Press, 1992).
2. Hal Lindsey with C. C. Carlson, *The Late Great Planet Earth* (Grand Rapids: Zondervan, 1970).

between prophecy and apocalypticism, but its view of apocalypticism is as alien to modern scholarship as its view of prophecy.

This view of prophecy, however, also had significant antecedents in the ancient world. The *pesharim,* or biblical commentaries in the Dead Sea Scrolls, exhibit a hermeneutic that is eerily similar to that of modern Fundamentalists.[3] The authors of these commentaries did not believe that the words of the prophets were primarily intended for their own time. We read in the pesher on Habakkuk:

> God told Habakkuk to write down that which would happen to the final generation, but He did not make known to him that time would come to an end. And as for that which He said, that he who reads may read it speedily; interpreted this concerns the Teacher of Righteousness, to whom God made known all the mysteries of His servants the Prophets.[4]

The underlying hermeneutic may reasonably be dubbed "apocalyptic." On the one hand, it assumes that truth is a mystery that is only revealed in coded form. Prophecy is as enigmatic as the visions of Daniel or Enoch, and requires further revelation for its interpretation. On the other hand, its content is concerned not, or not only, with the time of its composition, but with events that were far in the future from the perspective of the prophet, and especially with the end of history. Here again there is an analogy with the apocalypses, which are attributed pseudonymously to figures from the ancient past, who can then be credited with prophecies that span many centuries.

Moreover, the writings that are classified as apocalyptic in modern scholarship are often regarded as prophecy in the ancient texts. The Florilegium from Qumran (4Q174) cites the Book of Daniel the Prophet, and the Melchizedek Scroll cites Daniel's prediction about an anointed one just as it cites Isaiah. Daniel, of course, is classified among the Prophets

---

3. For a brief, lucid discussion, see F. F. Bruce, *Biblical Exegesis in the Qumran Texts* (Grand Rapids: Eerdmans, 1959). For a fuller analysis, see Maurya P. Horgan, *Pesharim: Qumran Interpretations of Biblical Books* (CBQMS 8; Washington, DC: Catholic Biblical Association, 1979). For a broader analysis of the understanding of revelation in the Dead Sea Scrolls and contemporary literature, see Alex P. Jassen, *Mediating the Divine: Prophecy and Revelation in the Dead Sea Scrolls and Second Temple Judaism* (STDJ 68; Leiden: Brill, 2007).

4. 1QpHab 7; trans. Geza Vermes, *The Complete Dead Sea Scrolls in English* (rev. ed.; London: Penguin, 2004) 512.

in the Greek Bible, and this classification may well be older than what we find in the Masoretic text.[5] Josephus and the New Testament also refer to Daniel as a prophet,[6] and Enoch is said to have prophesied in Jude, verse 14. The Book of Revelation refers to itself as "the book of this prophecy" (Rev. 22:19; cf. Rev. 1:3). In light of this, several scholars in recent years have questioned the distinction between prophecy and apocalypticism in the Second Temple period, and suggested, in the celebrated formulation of John Barton, that "the 'transition from prophecy to apocalyptic' is the title of a process that never occurred."[7]

Those who question the distinction between prophecy and apocalypticism do not all do so from the same perspective. We may distinguish three distinct positions:

1. One position holds that the texts commonly distinguished as prophecy and apocalypses are instances of the same broad phenomenon and that the differences between them are generically insignificant. This position has recently been defended by Lester Grabbe.

2. A second position, typified by Stephen Cook, acknowledges that prophecy changed significantly in the postexilic period, but sees considerable overlap between late prophecy and early apocalypticism. The distinction between the two is blurred by the phenomenon of "proto-apocalyptic" or "apocalyptic prophecy" in the Persian period.

3. A third position also acknowledges significant change but emphasizes that prophetic themes and language are integral to the apocalypses. In the words of Ron Hendel, "On many levels, the words of the prophets are the wellspring of apocalyptic mysteries."[8] Apocalypticism, on this reading, is a secondary transformation of prophecy, but "not a different genus."[9]

---

5. Klaus Koch, "Is Daniel Also among the Prophets?" *Interpretation* 39 (1985) 117-30.

6. *Antiquities* 10.246, 249, 266-68; Matthew 24:15.

7. John Barton, *Oracles of God: Perceptions of Ancient Prophecy in Israel after the Exile* (Oxford and New York: Oxford University Press, 1986) 200. Compare Ronald Hendel, "Isaiah and the Transition from Prophecy to Apocalyptic," in Chaim Cohen et al., eds., *Birkat Shalom: Studies in the Bible, Ancient Near Eastern Literature and Postbiblical Judaism Presented to Shalom M. Paul on the Occasion of His Seventieth Birthday* (Winona Lake, IN: Eisenbrauns, 2008) 261-79; Hindy Najman, "The Inheritance of Prophecy in Apocalypse," in John J. Collins, ed., *The Oxford Handbook of Apocalyptic Literature* (New York: Oxford University Press, 2014) chapter 3.

8. Hendel, "Isaiah and the Transition from Prophecy to Apocalyptic," 279.

9. Hendel, "Isaiah and the Transition from Prophecy to Apocalyptic," 276.

Each of these positions has some merit. I will argue, however, for a fourth view that sees prophecy and apocalypticism as distinct though related phenomena. On this view the issue is a matter of etic versus emic terminology. Granted that what we call apocalypses were often regarded as prophecy in antiquity, and were indebted to the prophetic writings in various ways, their difference from classical prophecy outweighs their continuity with it. All participants in this debate can agree that some transformation of prophecy occurred in the Second Temple period.[10] In dispute is whether the apocalyptic literature, beginning with the books of Daniel and Enoch, is adequately understood as a transformation of prophecy, and whether it is sufficiently distinctive to warrant classification as a new genre.

A Common Phenomenon

Lester Grabbe has argued that apocalypticism should be considered a subdivision of prophecy and that the differences between, say, Amos and Daniel are no greater than those between Amos and Nahum (or between Daniel and *1 Enoch*).[11] He argues that both prophecy and apocalypticism present themselves as delivering a divine message, presuppose a mythical worldview in which the heavenly world determines what will happen on earth, and look forward to an ideal age. He subsumes both, and also "mantic wisdom," under the label of divination. In part, the issue here is the level of abstraction one finds helpful. Both prophecy and apocalypticism are certainly forms of revelation.[12] (Divination has a narrower connotation and I do not find it helpful in this context. It usually refers to ways of seeking messages from the divine by technical means, as distinct from spontaneous prophecy.) The question is whether there are still significant differences between the apocalypses of the Hellenistic and early Roman periods and the canonical prophetic writings. I submit that there are.

---

10. On the transformation of prophecy, see especially Jassen, *Mediating the Divine.*

11. Lester L. Grabbe, "Introduction and Overview," in Lester L. Grabbe and Robert D. Haak, eds., *Knowing the End from the Beginning: The Prophetic, the Apocalyptic and Their Relationships* (London and New York: T&T Clark, 2003) 2-43, especially 22-24; and in the same volume Grabbe, "Prophetic and Apocalyptic: Time for New Definitions and New Thinking," 107-33.

12. Compare the definition of an apocalypse in *Semeia* 14: "A genre of revelatory literature. . . ." John J. Collins, "Introduction: Towards the Morphology of a Genre," in idem, ed., *Apocalypse: The Morphology of a Genre* (*Semeia* 14; Chico: Scholars Press, 1979) 9.

On the formal level, we seldom find direct inspired speech, which is typical of prophetic oracles, in the apocalypses. There is certainly continuity between the symbolic visions of the prophets and those of the apocalypses, although the latter are more elaborate, or, in Susan Niditch's terminology, "baroque."[13] But the heavenly journey, which provides the framework for a major subset of apocalypses,[14] has only faint precedents in the prophets. Isaiah describes his vision in the heavenly throne room, but he does not describe how he got there, or what he saw along the way. The greater interest in cosmology in the apocalypses reflects a shift in emphasis from the auditory reception of the message to a quest for broader understanding that is more akin to wisdom than to classical prophecy, as von Rad famously argued.[15] This is not to say that there is no formal continuity at all: there obviously is continuity in the case of symbolic visions. But the differences are considerable, and nothing is gained by overlooking them.

With regard to the content of the revelation, Grabbe has rightly argued that the prophets as well as the apocalypses have a mythical worldview. But not all mythical worldviews are alike. The prophecy of a lion eating straw like an ox in Isaiah 65 may be as "mythical" as Daniel 12, but its view of the world is very different. The difference lies in Daniel's expectation of judgment after death and the hope that the righteous *maskilim* will be exalted to the stars, or heavenly host. The belief in resurrection and judgment after death, which is fundamental to the apocalypses, entailed a fundamental shift in values from the worldview of ancient Israel. The goal of life was no longer to see one's children's children, but to live forever with the angels in heaven. This is why the *maskilim* in Daniel could let themselves be killed in a time of persecution. The hope for judgment after death is not an incidental motif among the many we find in any apocalypse. It is a key to the function and purpose of the work.[16]

13. Susan Niditch, *The Symbolic Vision in Biblical Tradition* (Harvard Semitic Monographs 30; Chico: Scholars Press, 1983); Klaus Koch, "Von profetischen zum apokalyptischen Visionsbericht," in David Hellholm, ed., *Apocalypticism in the Mediterranean World and the Near East* (Tübingen: Mohr Siebeck, 1983) 413-46.

14. Collins, "The Jewish Apocalypses," in *Semeia* 14, 36-44; *The Apocalyptic Imagination* (2nd ed.; Grand Rapids: Eerdmans, 1998) 6-7.

15. Gerhard von Rad, *Theologie des Alten Testaments* (2 vols.; 4th ed.; Munich: Kaiser, 1965) 2.315-30; see especially Michael E. Stone, "Lists of Revealed Things in the Apocalyptic Literature," in F. M. Cross et al., eds., *Magnalia Dei: The Mighty Acts of God* (Garden City, NY: Doubleday, 1976) 414-54.

16. See further my essay, "Apocalyptic Eschatology as the Transcendence of Death," in John J. Collins, *Seers, Sibyls and Sages in Hellenistic-Roman Judaism* (JSJSup 54; Leiden:

Late Prophecy and Early "Apocalyptic"

My argument so far is that *pace* John Barton, and despite the continued use of "prophecy" as a way of designating revelation in the postexilic period, some kind of transition, or transformation of prophecy if you will, occurred in those centuries. Several scholars have tried to trace that transformation and to provide a sociological explanation for it.[17] Otto Plöger found the origins of apocalypticism in eschatologically oriented post-exilic writings, such as Isaiah 24–27, Zechariah 12–14, and Joel.[18] He argued that these were products of prophetic conventicles that were marginalized by cultic establishment. He saw them as the forerunners of the Hasidim of the Maccabean period, whom he credited with the full-blown apocalyptic visions of Daniel. Paul Hanson looked to an earlier period, that of the restoration, but saw essentially the same dynamic at work.[19] For him, "the dawn of apocalyptic" was represented by Trito-Isaiah, which again reflected prophetic groups that were marginalized by the central cult. Stephen Cook continued the sociological line of explanation, but argued that apocalyptic expectations were not of concern only to marginalized groups. Instead he looked to such passages as Ezekiel 38–39 and Zechariah 1–8, which were priestly compositions, associated with the "cultic establishment" that Plöger and Hanson saw as the antithesis of the prophetic/apocalyptic conventicles.[20] All of these scholars, however, had similar views of what constituted apocalyptic characteristics. Hanson and Cook saw this primarily in the increased use of mythological imagery. For Hanson, apocalyptic eschatology differed from its prophetic counterpart insofar as it ceased to translate the divine revelation into "terms of plain history, real politics and human instrumentality," due to an increasingly pessimistic view of reality.[21]

Brill, 1997) 75-98. See also my response to Grabbe, "Prophecy, Apocalypse and Eschatology: Reflections on the Proposals of Lester Grabbe," in *Knowing the End from the Beginning*, 44-52, and the critique of Grabbe by Andrew Chester, *Future Hope and Present Reality*, vol. 1: *Eschatology and Transformation in the Hebrew Bible* (WUNT 293; Tübingen: Mohr Siebeck, 2012) 85-86.

17. See the overviews by Stephen L. Cook, *Prophecy and Apocalypticism: The Postexilic Social Setting* (Minneapolis: Fortress, 1995) 2-12; and Antonios Finitsis, *Visions and Eschatology: A Socio-Historical Analysis of Zechariah 1–6* (London and New York: T&T Clark, 2011) 5-36.

18. Otto Plöger, *Theocracy and Eschatology* (Richmond: John Knox, 1968).

19. Paul D. Hanson, *The Dawn of Apocalyptic: The Historical and Sociological Roots of Jewish Apocalyptic Eschatology* (Philadelphia: Fortress, 1975).

20. Cook, *Prophecy and Apocalypticism*.

21. Hanson, *Dawn of Apocalyptic*, 11.

For Cook, "apocalypticism relies *heavily* on the images and oppositions of mythology. One might justly call it 'mythopoeic,' since it insists on applying language of mythological proportions to a new work of God."[22] This mythological language is used to express eschatological expectation. "Eschatology in apocalyptic literature," writes Cook, "involves an imminent inbreaking by God inaugurating a future age qualitatively different from this age."[23] What makes certain postexilic prophetic writings "apocalyptic" is that they envision "a fundamental change in reality — a physical change. It is imminent, not far-flung. It ushers in a marvelous world beyond anything that humans have known."[24]

In his book *Prophecy and Apocalypticism,* Cook acknowledged that the prophetic texts of the Persian period "were not informed by many of the significant ideas and motifs found in the Hellenistic apocalypses," such as resurrection and the judgment of the dead.[25] Accordingly, he accepted the term "proto-apocalyptic," which had been proposed by Hanson, with the proviso that he was not "implying acceptance of any typology presupposing a trajectory from prophecy to apocalypticism."[26] In his more recent work he argues that "the roots of resurrection faith, at least in poetic potential, are arguably discoverable in proto-apocalyptic literature," and that "Israel was comfortable with the idea of resurrection by the time of the exile."[27] He finds the evidence for this in such passages as Ezekiel 37 and Isaiah 24–27. He recognizes that Ezekiel's use of resurrection language is symbolic, but argues that it "demonstrates how rising from death was not an anomalous idea in his era." Scholarly opinion is notoriously divided as to whether Isaiah 26:19 should also be taken metaphorically, or whether it expresses a literal hope for resurrection.[28] Nonetheless, there is

22. Stephen L. Cook, "Apocalyptic Prophecy," in Collins, ed., *The Oxford Handbook of Apocalyptic Literature,* chapter 2.

23. Cook, *Prophecy and Apocalypticism,* 24.

24. Cook, "Apocalyptic Prophecy," 20.

25. Cook, *Prophecy and Apocalypticism,* 34. He noted possible exceptions in Isaiah 26:19 and 24:21-22.

26. Cook, *Prophecy and Apocalypticism,* 34-35.

27. Cook, "Apocalyptic Prophecy," 28. In this he is influenced by the work of Jon D. Levenson, *Resurrection and the Restoration of Israel: The Ultimate Victory of the God of Life* (New Haven: Yale University Press, 2006) 156-65 (on Ezekiel), 198-200 (on Isa. 26:19).

28. For a recent review, see Chester, *Future Hope and Present Reality,* 287-90. Chester inclines to the view that literal resurrection is implied. Christopher B. Hays, *Death in the Iron Age II and in First Isaiah* (FAT 79; Tübingen: Mohr Siebeck, 2011) 328, is exceptional in dating Isaiah 24–27 to pre-exilic times.

a clear difference between Persian period prophecy and the apocalypses of the Hellenistic period in this regard. Resurrection is atypical of postexilic prophecy, whereas it is central to the later apocalypses.

Scholars such as Grabbe have disputed whether postexilic prophecy is any more mythical than its pre-exilic counterpart, which also expected divine inbreaking on "the Day of the Lord." Robert Alter has noted that the imagery of classical prophets like Isaiah often shifts the action to the cosmic scale, in a manner analogous to myth.[29] The so-called Isaianic apocalypse in Isaiah 24–27 presents an unusually dense cluster of mythological images,[30] but it is exceptional even within the post-exilic corpus. Only Jeremiah 4:23-28 provides a comparable vision of the undoing of creation.[31]

The sense that post-exilic prophets did not relate their message to "plain history" and "human instrumentality," to use Hanson's terms, is exacerbated by the fact that we often cannot discern the historical circumstances to which they refer. The poet/prophet of Isaiah 24–27 seems to have been reacting to the destruction of a particular city ("you have made the city a heap, the fortified city a ruin; the palace of aliens is a city no more, it will never be rebuilt"; Isa. 25:2), but we can only guess as to the actual occasion. (Most probably, the city in question was Babylon, but some scholars have argued that it was Jerusalem!)[32] Similarly, the setting of Zechariah 9–14 is notoriously obscure. It may be that these oracles were originally intended to address quite specific occasions, but we cannot now identify them with any confidence. The difficulty of identifying historical referents for these oracles undoubtedly contributed to the sense that they were intimating matters of cosmic and eschatological, rather than historical, import. Not all postexilic prophecy is so obscure. Zechariah 1–8, which is one of Cook's exemplars of "proto-apocalyptic,"

29. Alter, *The Art of Biblical Poetry* (New York: Basic Books, 1985) 152. Cf. Hendel, "Isaiah and the Transition," 267.

30. William R. Millar, *Isaiah 24–27 and the Origin of Apocalyptic* (Harvard Semitic Monographs 11; Missoula, MT: Scholars Press, 1976); Dan G. Johnson, *From Chaos to Restoration: An Integrative Reading of Isaiah 24–27* (JSOTSup 61; Sheffield: JSOT, 1988).

31. For a recent discussion of Jeremiah 4 in conjunction with Isaiah 24–27, see Chester, *Future Hope and Present Reality,* 53-81.

32. E.g., Johnson, *From Chaos to Restoration,* 29-35. Millar, *Isaiah 24–27,* even identifies the "city of aliens" in Isaiah 25 and 26 as Jerusalem. See my essay, "The Beginning of the End of the World in the Hebrew Bible," in John J. Ahn and Stephen L. Cook, eds., *Thus Says the Lord: Essays on the Former and Latter Prophets in Honor of Robert R. Wilson* (New York and London: T&T Clark, 2009) 137-55, especially 145-46, and Brian Doyle, *The Apocalypse of Isaiah: Metaphorically Speaking* (BETL 151; Leuven: Peeters, 2000) 31-37.

is highly specific in its historical references to the restoration period. Even Jeremiah 4:23-28 refers to the imminent destruction of Jerusalem, not to the end of the world as a whole. In the words of Dan Johnson, it is "an example of cosmic imagery applied to a specific geographical situation."[33] Nonetheless, while Grabbe makes a valid point about the mythic presuppositions of classical prophecy, there is surely a difference in degree in the use of mythological imagery in at least some postexilic texts, and this trend is continued in apocalypses such as Daniel and Revelation. (It should be noted, however, that both Daniel and Revelation have quite clear historical referents.)

In addition to the use of mythological imagery, there are some other developments in prophecy in the post-exilic period that are of relevance to later apocalyptic texts. The oracles of the classical prophets were usually directed to an immediate context, but when oracles were collected and edited for later generations the original context lost at least some of its relevance, if it was recognized at all. As Barton has remarked, "no one ever promoted predictive prophecies, old or new, whose import was that the crucial event in world history would happen after his hearers were all dead and buried."[34] Rather, the assumption was that the prophecies spoke to the readers' own time. Barton argues that this phenomenon, of collecting and preserving prophecies for future generations, lies at the root of the extended view of history that is typical of historically oriented apocalypses. He notes that a book like Isaiah contained material that obviously related to events long after the time of the prophet (e.g., the mention of Cyrus in Isa. 45:1). There may indeed be some relevance to the apocalyptic view of history here, but much better parallels to the apocalypses can be found in the Mesopotamian predictive texts (sometimes inaccurately dubbed "Akkadian apocalypses"), which contain *ex eventu* predictions of extended periods of history.[35] Neither do the edited prophetic books provide any good analogy for the division of history into periods that is typical of the later apocalypses. So while we may grant that the alienation of oracles from their original context was a necessary condition for the way they

33. Johnson, *From Chaos to Restoration*, 29.
34. Barton, *Oracles of God*, 200.
35. Matthew Neujahr, *Predicting the Past in the Ancient Near East: Mantic Historiography in Ancient Mesopotamia, Judah, and the Mediterranean World* (Brown Judaic Studies 354; Providence: Brown University Press, 2012). The relevance of these texts for the Jewish apocalypses was pointed out by W. G. Lambert, *The Background of Jewish Apocalyptic* (London: Athlone, 1978).

were interpreted in the Hellenistic period, it does not provide an adequate explanation of the extended view of history in the guise of prediction by ancient figures that we find in the apocalypses.

Another aspect of the transformation of prophecy in the postexilic period that is of some relevance for our topic is its textualization and scribalization.[36] As Hendel has remarked, "once it is a literary text, the prophetic oracle is to some degree unmoored from its historical context" and "becomes, at least potentially, a floating signifier."[37] Again, this was a necessary precondition for the reinterpretation of prophecy in an apocalyptic sense, but it did not in itself determine the form the reinterpretation would take. It is true, however, that many of the redactional additions to the prophetic books have eschatological overtones. Think for example of the numerous passages that begin "on that day." They give the impression that these books relate to the indefinite future, and so could be applied to new situations by an interpreter like the Teacher of Righteousness at Qumran. I would argue, however, that the kind of eschatology implied in the redaction of the prophetic books remains significantly different from the eschatology of the apocalypses.

It is not always clear whether passages added to a book like Isaiah were originally meant to be attributed pseudonymously to the eighth-century prophet. It is clear, however, that they were so understood from an early time. Whether this accumulative attribution of oracles to a well-known prophet is analogous to the phenomenon of pseudonymity in apocalyptic texts is debatable. Passages may have been added to the prophetic books because of some perceived affinity in style or content, but this is somewhat different from *de novo* pseudepigraphical composition. Moreover, it should be noted that the apocalyptic writers only rarely attributed their revelations to the classical prophets. Enoch is not cast as a prophet in the biblical text, although he may have been so regarded in the Hellenistic period. The name of Daniel may, perhaps, have been suggested by the mention of a Daniel in Ezekiel 14, but again he is not attested as a prophet before the second century BCE. Ezra and Baruch are scribes rather than prophets. In the Christian era we find apocalypses of Isaiah, Zephaniah, and Elijah, but also of Moses and Adam. Indeed the fact that so many apocalyptic visionaries were scribes or sages provided one of von Rad's

---

36. This has been emphasized by Ronald E. Clements, *Old Testament Prophecy: From Oracles to Canon* (Louisville: Westminster, 1996) 171-88.

37. Hendel, "Isaiah and the Transition," 265.

arguments for his thesis that apocalypticism was more closely related to wisdom than to prophecy.[38]

Barton argued that the fact that prophecy was already understood to refer to the distant future and/or the end of history showed that "the transition from prophecy to apocalyptic never occurred."[39] One might better argue, however, that it shows *how* it occurred, or rather that it shows how the transformation of prophecy may have been one factor that contributed to the rise of apocalypticism. Hendel's statement that "the two categories, as defined by modern scholarship, are already amalgamated in the biblical text"[40] is a considerable overstatement. We may perhaps agree that "prophecy is already interpreted in an apocalyptic direction in the editorial redaction and final form of the text," but the presence of some apocalyptic-like traits does not amount to generic amalgamation. The transformation of prophecy in the Persian period is important for any understanding of the relation between prophecy and apocalypticism, but it does not resolve all differences between prophecy and apocalypticism.

The Legacy of Prophecy in the Apocalypses

A third position on the relation between prophecy and apocalypticism provides a more subtle challenge to the distinction between the two categories. Hindy Najman speaks of the continuation of "the prophetic project in which humans served as the means whereby God spoke to the people."[41] What she has in mind, however, is not just the broader category of revelation to which Grabbe appealed. Rather: "it increasingly relied on *strategies of inheritance*."[42] In this, she appeals to the argument of Ron Hendel that apocalypticism arises from a close preoccupation with prophetic sources, perhaps including visionary experiences inspired by them.[43] "The shift in understanding," writes Hendel, "is precipitated not just by changed cir-

---

38. Von Rad, *Theologie*, 2.315-30.

39. Barton, *Oracles of God*, 200.

40. Hendel, "Isaiah and the Transition," 266.

41. Najman, "The Inheritance of Prophecy in Apocalypse," 40.

42. Najman, "The Inheritance of Prophecy in Apocalypse," 40.

43. Other scholars have made similar proposals, notably Christopher Rowland, *The Open Heaven: A Study of Apocalyptic in Judaism and Early Christianity* (London: SPCK, 1982) 214-17.

cumstances but also by an intensive, if selective, attention to the books of the classical prophets."[44]

Hendel illustrates his point by documenting the tissue of references to Isaiah in Daniel 12:1-4: he finds six references in four verses. It is well known that the exaltation of the *maskilim* to the stars echoes the poem on the suffering servant in Isaiah 53.[45] The statement in Daniel 12:2, that those who sleep in the land of dust will awake, echoes Isaiah 26:19 on the resurrection. Many other examples could be given, most obviously Daniel's reinterpretation of Jeremiah's prophecy that Jerusalem would be desolate for seventy years. Hendel sums up his discussion of Daniel 12 as follows:

> The eschatological prophecy of the angel is, to a considerable degree, an apocalyptic concatenation and recomposition of selected oracles from Isaiah. In other words, the angel gives an authoritative interpretation of what Isaiah has to say about the end time.[46]

I would rather say that what we have in Daniel is a reaction to the persecution under Antiochus Epiphanes, drawing on the linguistic resources of Isaiah, and that while Daniel draws heavily on Isaiah in this instance, he is by no means limited to the prophetic repertoire. It is possible that he understood this to be the true meaning of the passages in Isaiah, but allusion is not to be confused with interpretation. Daniel was composing a new text, not writing a pesher.

Hendel notes that "from our perspective, the angel may have got it wrong, because older prophecy had different things on its mind."[47] I had argued in my commentary on Daniel that here we see the difference between full-blown apocalyptic and older prophecy.[48] Hendel grants this, but counters:

> Yet, at the same time, this text shows that the older prophetic books were read as apocalyptic literature — that in this period there is no categorical difference between prophecy and apocalyptic. Isaiah is an

44. Hendel, "Isaiah and the Transition," 264.

45. See my commentary, *Daniel: A Commentary on the Book of Daniel* (Hermeneia; Minneapolis: Fortress, 1993) 385, and the classic essay of H. L. Ginsberg, "The Oldest Interpretation of the Suffering Servant," *VT* 3 (1953) 400-404.

46. Hendel, "Isaiah and the Transition," 270.

47. Hendel, "Isaiah and the Transition," 270.

48. Collins, *Daniel,* 402.

apocalyptic seer, even though it takes an angel (or a comparably inspired interpreter) to get his message right.[49]

This is an astute observation. To our knowledge, there was no school of literary or ideological criticism in ancient Jerusalem, concerned with distinguishing genres in the corpus of scripture. It is indeed likely that people viewed prophets and apocalyptic visionaries alike as mediators of divine revelation, and were not concerned with formal differentiation. But to say that people in Jerusalem in the second century BCE did not perceive a categorical distinction is not necessarily to say that there was none. Here we come back to the difference between emic and etic perceptions. At the very least, we must acknowledge with Barton that what we find in Daniel is a "second-mode" reading of prophecy.[50] Even if it seems presumptuous to say that the apocalyptic visionaries got the meaning of the older prophecies wrong, their reading was a reinterpretation, something different from what prophecy had meant in an earlier age. A transition, or transformation, had occurred.

Hendel insists, however, that the apocalyptic interpretation of Isaiah is not purely a matter of anachronistic misreading. Isaiah 26:19, "Your dead shall live, their bodies shall rise; awake and shout for joy, dwellers in the dust," is quite naturally read as a reference to the resurrection of individuals, whether it was originally so intended or not. Some passages in Isaiah also anticipate the theme of apocalyptic secrecy. Isaiah 29:11 says that the prophecy has become for you like the words of a sealed scroll, which if it is given to one who knows how to read, saying "Read this," he will say, "I cannot, because it is sealed."[51] That passage may well be redactional in Isaiah, inserted when the original context was forgotten and the prophecy had become mysterious. Moreover, Isaiah had been instructed in his call vision in Isaiah 6 to tell his listeners to hear but not understand, see but not comprehend. There was, then, an element of mystery in the prophetic book, although the book itself was never supposed to be kept secret. Isaiah's question, how long? (Isa. 6:11), is also taken up in a different context in Daniel.

---

49. Hendel, "Isaiah and the Transition," 270. On the apocalyptic reading of Isaiah see Joseph Blenkinsopp, *Opening the Sealed Book: Interpretations of the Book of Isaiah in Late Antiquity* (Grand Rapids: Eerdmans, 2006) especially 89-128, on the interpretation of Isaiah in the Dead Sea Scrolls.

50. Barton, *Oracles of God,* 197.

51. See Blenkinsopp, *Opening the Sealed Book,* 8-12. Blenkinsopp speaks of an "Isaianic-Danielic interpretive trajectory" (15).

It is apparent that the apocalyptic writers were deeply familiar with the prophetic heritage and drew from it a store of symbols of ancestral vitality that enriched their discourse by allusion to older tradition. It would be erroneous to suppose, however, that prophecy was the unique source on which the visionaries drew. Like Ben Sira's scribe, they sought out the wisdom of the ancients wherever it was to be found.[52] The imagery of Daniel 7, where a rider of the clouds is granted kingship by an Ancient of Days and the beasts from the unruly sea are subdued, reaches back to Canaanite mythology that we know only from second millennium sources, although it must have been transmitted somehow in Israel.[53] The Books of Enoch incorporate a wide range of cosmological lore of Babylonian origin, especially but not only in the Astronomical Book, or Book of the Heavenly Luminaries (*1 Enoch* 72–82).[54] The Mesopotamian background of the figure of Enoch is well established.[55] The apocalyptic writers, then, are not just "pastiche *prophets,*" in John Barton's phrase.[56] They are engaged in a wide-ranging bricolage that draws on many sources besides the prophets. Indeed, as Barton himself noted: "our witnesses do not turn to different kinds of books for different kinds of information. If one wants predictions, they are quite as likely to be found in the Psalms or the wisdom books as in the latter Prophets."[57]

A New Thing

But the apocalyptic writings are not just pastiches, prophetic or otherwise. They have their own *Gestalt,* structure, and coherence, which gives a more comprehensive view of cosmos and history than we ever find in the classical prophets, even in the redacted prophetic books. The extended view of

---

52. Sirach 39:1-3: He seeks out the wisdom of all the ancients, and is concerned with prophecies; he preserves the sayings of the famous and penetrates the subtleties of parables; he seeks out the hidden meaning of proverbs and is at home with the obscurities of parables.

53. Collins, *Daniel,* 280-94.

54. See, e.g., M. T. Wacker, *Weltordnung und Gericht. Studien zu 1 Henoch 22* (Würzburg: Echter, 1982). On the astronomical book and Babylonian astronomy see James C. VanderKam in George W. E. Nickelsburg and James C. VanderKam, *1 Enoch 2* (Hermeneia; Minneapolis: Fortress, 2012) 373-83.

55. James C. VanderKam, *Enoch and the Growth of an Apocalyptic Tradition* (CBQMS 16; Washington, DC: Catholic Biblical Association, 1984) 33-51.

56. Barton, *Oracles of God,* 148, emphasis added.

57. Barton, *Oracles of God,* 148.

history may be incidentally entailed in the attempt to relate the prophetic oracles to events long after their time of composition, but it is an integral feature of the apocalypses of the historical type, which regularly map out the periods of history either from the Exile or from Creation.[58] John Barton claimed that "the attempt to find any unifying theme among all the apocalypses that are extant is doomed to failure,"[59] but this contention cannot be sustained. The contents of the apocalypses are diverse, to be sure, but they are all bounded by the looming presence of supernatural agents and by the anticipation of a final judgment, which would determine the fate of individuals in the hereafter.[60] The coordinates of the worldview are set by the orientation to the supernatural world and the distinctive eschatological expectation. This literary and conceptual structure was a novelty in Judaism in the Hellenistic period.

Eschatology is also pervasive in the prophetic books in the Hebrew Bible,[61] and Hendel and Najman are right that the legacy of prophecy is taken up in the apocalyptic writings, but it was also transformed. Both the continuity and the transformation may be illustrated by the motif of a new creation, which is often taken to typify apocalyptic eschatology. Already in Isaiah 65:17, near the end of the redacted book of Isaiah, we read: "I am about to create new heavens and a new earth. The former things will not be remembered or come to mind." This verse is echoed in Revelation 21:1, where John of Patmos "saw a new heaven and a new earth; for the first heaven and the first earth had passed away, and the sea was no more." The new creation in Isaiah 65 is a mythical state, where the wolf and the lamb shall feed together, echoing the older Isaianic prophecy in Isaiah 11. But it is still an earthly utopia: "no more will there be in it an infant that lives but a few days or an old person who does not live out a lifetime; for one who dies at a hundred years will be considered a youth and one who falls short of a hundred will be considered accursed" (Isa. 65:20). In Revelation, however, the new creation follows the resurrection, and death has no longer any power over those who are raised. Even in its denial of

---

58. Collins, "The Jewish Apocalypses," 30-36.

59. Barton, *Oracles of God*, 201, relying on Rowland, *The Open Heaven*.

60. See my article "Genre, Ideology and Social Movements in Jewish Apocalypticism," in John J. Collins and James H. Charlesworth, eds., *Mysteries and Revelations: Apocalyptic Studies since the Uppsala Colloquium* (JSPSup 9; Sheffield: Sheffield Academic Press, 1991) 11-32, especially 16. Compare in the same volume George W. E. Nickelsburg, "The Apocalyptic Construction of Reality in 1 Enoch," 51-64.

61. See Chester, *Future Hope and Present Reality*.

death, Revelation uses prophetic language: "he will wipe every tear from their eyes. Death will be no more" (Rev. 21:4; compare Isa. 25:8: "he will swallow up death forever. Then the Lord will wipe away the tears from all faces"). The language is poetic in both cases, informed by the old Canaanite myth of Baal and Mot (or Death) and, in the case of Revelation, the myth of Baal and Yamm (the sea that will be no more in Rev. 21:1). But in the Isaianic passage the primary concern is that God take away "the disgrace of his people," and it is not clear whether the destruction of death is more than a metaphor for national deliverance. In Revelation, the destruction of death is meant quite literally and is the culmination of the hope for the future. The gulf between the present order and the future has grown wider, punctuated in Revelation by an intermediate reign of a thousand years (the original millennium) and in the contemporary apocalypse of *4 Ezra* by seven days of primeval silence (2 Esd. 7:30). Or, as most bluntly stated in *4 Ezra,* "the Most High has made not one world but two" (2 Esd. 7:50).

Hendel does not claim that reflection on older prophecy was the sole and sufficient cause of the rise of apocalypticism. "Apocalypticism," he concludes, "is the child of literacy and cultural disruption." In times of disruption, "one often looks to the past and its classic texts for stable and authoritative voices and strives to reconnect with their truer vision."[62] Older prophetic texts, which were themselves in many cases the products of earlier cultural disruption, figure prominently among the sources that nourished the apocalyptic imagination. Recent scholarship, as reviewed above, has shed much light on the various ways in which the legacy of prophecy lived on in the apocalyptic literature. There was indeed continuity between the two genres. Apocalypticism can arguably be viewed as prophecy transformed, but it can also be viewed as wisdom transformed, myth eschatologized, and various other things. Prophecy was not its only source, and the apocalypses are not simply a variant of older prophecy. It was a new phenomenon that entailed a novel view of the world that would have a transformative and long-lasting effect on western religion.

62. Hendel, "Isaiah and the Transition," 278.

PART II

Variations on a Genre

CHAPTER 5

Enochic Judaism: An Assessment

Introduction

The non-canonical literature from Qumran that has commanded most scholarly attention in the last decade or so is undoubtedly the literature associated with the name of Enoch. The Aramaic fragments of the Enoch literature had been published by J. T. Milik already in 1976.[1] They became a subject of intensive study, however, in the last decade, in part because of the monumental commentary by George Nickelsburg in the Hermeneia series,[2] and in part through the labors of Gabriele Boccaccini, not only in his own publications,[3] but also in his leadership of the international Enoch seminar, which devoted its first meeting to "the origins of Enochic Judaism,"[4] its second meeting to the subject of "Enoch and Qumran Origins,"[5]

1. Józef T. Milik, *The Books of Enoch: Aramaic Fragments of Qumrân Cave 4* (Oxford: Clarendon, 1976). For an up-to-date overview of the Enoch literature from Qumran see Loren T. Stuckenbruck, "The Early Traditions Related to 1 Enoch from the Dead Sea Scrolls: An Overview and Assessment," in Gabriele Boccaccini and John J. Collins, eds., *The Early Enoch Literature* (JSJSup 121; Leiden: Brill, 2007) 41-63.

2. George W. E. Nickelsburg, *1 Enoch 1. A Commentary on the Book of 1 Enoch, Chapters 1–36; 81–108* (Hermeneia; Minneapolis: Fortress, 2001).

3. Gabriele Boccaccini, *Beyond the Essene Hypothesis: The Parting of the Ways between Qumran and Enochic Judaism* (Grand Rapids: Eerdmans, 1998); *Roots of Rabbinic Judaism: An Intellectual History, from Ezekiel to Daniel* (Grand Rapids: Eerdmans, 2002).

4. Gabriele Boccaccini, ed., *The Origins of Enochic Judaism: Proceedings of the First Enoch Seminar, University of Michigan, Sesto Fiorentino, Italy, June 19-23, 2001 = Henoch* 24/1-2 (2002).

5. Boccaccini, *Enoch and Qumran Origins: New Light on a Forgotten Connection* (Grand Rapids: Eerdmans, 2005).

and also sponsored a comprehensive volume of essays on "The Early Enoch Literature."[6] It is on Boccaccini's theses that I wish to focus here, specifically his view of Enochic Judaism and the relationship he posits between this branch of Judaism and the sectarian movement known from the Dead Sea Scrolls.[7]

Enochic Judaism

According to Boccaccini, the books of Enoch attest to a tradition that extended over centuries, possibly beginning as early as the fourth century BCE and extending into the first century CE.[8] He recognized that this was "a complex and dynamic trend of thought . . . and therefore cannot be fit entirely into a unitary scheme or a universal definition." Yet "its generative idea . . . can be identified in a particular conception of evil, understood as an autonomous reality antecedent to humanity's ability to choose, the result of 'a contamination that has spoiled [human] nature,' an evil that 'was produced before the beginning of history.' "[9] He associates this tradition with a movement of dissent within the priesthood, reflected in the strong interest in the calendar and the negative reference to the temple in the *Animal Apocalypse*.[10] According to Boccaccini, writings preserved in *1 Enoch* were the constitutive documents of this tradition, but not the only ones. He finds the same conception of evil in some books in which the figure of Enoch was not central (*Jubilees, Testaments of the Twelve Patriarchs*) or

6. Boccaccini and Collins, eds., *The Early Enoch Literature*.

7. See already my essays " 'Enochic Judaism' and the Sect of the Dead Sea Scrolls," in Boccaccini and Collins, eds., *The Early Enoch Literature*, 283-99, and "How Distinctive Was Enochic Judaism?" in Moshe Bar-Asher and Emanuel Tov, eds., *A Festschrift for Devorah Dimant = Meghillot* 5-6 (2007) *17-*34. Also Matthias Albani, " 'Zadokite Judaism,' 'Enochic Judaism' und Qumran. Zur aktuellen Diskussion um G. Boccaccinis 'Beyond the Essene Hypothesis'," in Jörg Frey and Michael Becker, eds., *Apokalyptik und Qumran* (Einblicke 10; Paderborn: Bonifatius, 2007) 85-101.

8. Boccaccini, *Beyond the Essene Hypothesis*, 12. For the antiquity of the earliest Enoch literature see already M. E. Stone, "The Book of Enoch and Judaism in the Third Century B.C.E.," *CBQ* 40 (1978) 479-92; idem, *Scriptures, Sects and Visions: A Profile of Judaism from Ezra to the Jewish Revolts* (Philadelphia: Fortress, 1980).

9. Boccaccini, *Beyond the Essene Hypothesis*, 12. In this he builds on the work of his teacher, Paolo Sacchi, *Jewish Apocalyptic and Its History* (Sheffield: Sheffield Academic Press, 1997).

10. Boccaccini, *Roots of Rabbinic Judaism*, 89, 99-103.

was even missing (*4 Ezra*). He also argues that this Enoch tradition was in fact the early Essene movement.[11]

Some features of this construct are more widely accepted than others. The books that make up *1 Enoch* are indeed closely bound together by recurring motifs and allusions.[12] Moreover, several of the Enochic writings envision a distinct group of righteous within Israel. The *Book of the Watchers* refers to "the plant of righteousness and truth" (10:16). In the *Apocalypse of Weeks*, the elect are "the chosen righteous from the chosen plant of righteousness" (93:10). The *Animal Apocalypse* speaks of "lambs" whose eyes are opened (90:6). Even the *Similitudes of Enoch*, which are later in date than any other part of *1 Enoch* by at least a century, seem to envision the righteous as a community. It is not unreasonable, then, to suppose that these books of Enoch were composed within a movement of some sort, although continuity becomes problematic in the case of the *Similitudes*. The further "Enochic Judaism" is extended beyond the book of *1 Enoch*, however, the more problematic it becomes.

The notion that the story of the Watchers, understood as a paradigm for the origin of evil, was generative for the whole corpus, has been accepted, virtually without question, in Italian scholarship. But while this story is undoubtedly important, and reverberates in later Enochic books, it is only one motif among many.[13] A far more balanced account of the worldview of *1 Enoch* has been given by George Nickelsburg, who argues, quite rightly, that the focal point in all the Enochic books is the coming judgment.[14] The Enochic books share "an apocalyptic construction of re-

---

11. An independent formulation of "Enochic Judaism" as a paradigm of regularity and deviance can be found in David R. Jackson, *Enochic Judaism* (LSTS 49; London and New York: Continuum, 2004). Jackson distinguishes three "paradigm exemplars": the "Shemikhazah exemplar," focusing on the union of angels with human women; the " 'Aza'el exemplar," focusing on improper revelation; and the "cosmic exemplar," focusing on the rebellion of angels who were in charge of cosmic phenomena related to the calendar.

12. See my essay "Pseudepigraphy and Group Formation in Second Temple Judaism," in Esther G. Chazon and Michael E. Stone, eds., *Pseudepigraphic Perspectives: The Apocrypha and Pseudepigrapha in Light of the Dead Sea Scrolls* (STDJ 31; Leiden: Brill, 1999) 44-48.

13. Compare the criticism of Annette Yoshiko Reed, "Interrogating Enochic Judaism: 1 Enoch as a Source for Intellectual History, Social Realities, and Literary Tradition," in Boccaccini, ed., *Enoch and Qumran Origins*, 340.

14. Nickelsburg, *1 Enoch 1*, 37-56; idem, "The Apocalyptic Construction of Reality in 1 Enoch," in John J. Collins and James H. Charlesworth, eds., *Mysteries and Revelations: Apocalyptic Studies since the Uppsala Conference* (JSPSup 9; Sheffield: Sheffield Academic Press, 1991) 51–64.

ality" that became common in Judaism in the Hellenistic period, and that has both temporal and spatial dimensions. Revelation comes from above, mediated by angels and conveyed to earth by Enoch. Angelic and demonic forces influence human affairs. The entire sweep of history can be foreseen by the visionary. The judgment is a cosmic judgment not only of the earth, but of individuals, who attain everlasting reward or punishment. The interest in the temporal future is balanced by a corresponding interest in places beyond the range of ordinary human experience, including the throne of God and the resting places of the elect. While the different Enochic books vary in their emphasis and nuance, and sometimes even take issue with each other, Nickelsburg's sketch of a shared worldview is well founded. This apocalyptic worldview is also found, with variations, in the other apocalyptic writings of the era, including Daniel.[15]

There are also some distinctive features in the Enochic writings that distinguish them as a corpus within the apocalyptic writings. These include the specific story of the Watchers and the degree of interest in otherworldly geography, neither of which is attested in Daniel. Moreover, the negative reference to the temple in the *Animal Apocalypse (1 En.* 89:73) implies a rupture with what was arguably the most central symbol in Judaism at that time. The most obvious and basic distinguishing trait of this literature, however, is the fact that Enoch is the mediator of revelation, rather than Moses or any other figure drawn from Israelite tradition. This in turn raises the question of the status of the Mosaic, Sinaitic revelation in these books. Was this group Enochic, in the sense that it looked on the legendary patriarch as the primary mediator of revelation? Or was the invocation of the ante-diluvian hero merely a literary device in books that were solidly grounded in the Mosaic covenant?

Scholarship on this issue has in fact been rather evenly divided.[16] On the one hand, George Nickelsburg has argued that Enochic wisdom was an alternative to Mosaic Torah.[17] On the other, E. P. Sanders[18] and Mark

15. See my essay "Genre, Ideology and Social Movements in Jewish Apocalypticism," in Collins and Charlesworth, eds., *Mysteries and Revelations*, 11-32, and, more generally, *The Apocalyptic Imagination* (2nd ed.; Grand Rapids: Eerdmans, 1998) passim.

16. See the review of the debate by Kelley Coblentz Bautch, *A Study of the Geography of 1 Enoch 17–19: "No One Has Seen What I Have Seen"* (JSJSup 81; Leiden: Brill, 2003) 289-99.

17. Nickelsburg, "Enochic Wisdom: An Alternative to the Mosaic Torah?" in Jodi Magness and Seymour Gitin, eds., *Ḥesed ve-Emet: Studies in Honor of Ernest S. Frerichs* (BJS 320; Atlanta: Scholars Press, 1998) 123-32; *1 Enoch 1*, 50-56.

18. E. P. Sanders, *Paul and Palestinian Judaism* (Philadelphia: Fortress, 1977) 346-62.

Elliott[19] have viewed it as an example of covenantal nomism. The division of opinion is most acute in the case of the early Enochic *Book of the Watchers (1 Enoch* 1–36).

At the core of this book is the story of the fallen angels, in *1 Enoch* 6–11. This is usually regarded as a midrash on the story of the sons of God in Genesis 6,[20] although J. T. Milik famously argued that the Enochic story is older than the variant in Genesis.[21] The account of Enoch's ascent to heaven has various points of contact with prophetic traditions.[22] In his subsequent tour with an angelic guide he is shown a holy mountain in the center of the earth, which is evidently Mount Zion, and beside it a cursed valley, presumably Ge Hinnom or Gehenna.[23] He also sees the Garden of Righteousness and the tree of wisdom, from which "your father of old and your mother of old, who were before you, ate and learned wisdom. And their eyes were opened, and they knew that they were naked, and they were driven from the garden" (*1 En.* 32:6). Moreover, the opening chapters of the *Book of the Watchers* are a virtual tissue of biblical allusions, and Lars Hartman has argued that they find their referential background in covenant renewal ceremonies and that the entire passage must be understood in a covenantal context.[24]

Despite occasional arguments that the *Book of the Watchers* preserves old traditions independent of the Bible, it seems to me beyond reasonable doubt that, in all stages of its composition, it reflects knowledge of at least

19. Mark Elliott, *The Survivors of Israel: A Reconsideration of the Theology of Pre-Christian Judaism* (Grand Rapids: Eerdmans, 2000) 330-32, 529-33; "Covenant and Cosmology in the Book of the Watchers and the Astronomical Book," in Boccaccini, ed., *The Origins of Enochic Judaism*, 23-38.

20. See James C. VanderKam, "The Interpretation of Genesis in 1 Enoch," in Peter W. Flint, ed., *The Bible at Qumran: Text, Shape, and Interpretation* (Grand Rapids: Eerdmans, 2001) 129-48; idem, "Biblical Interpretation in 1 Enoch and Jubilees," in James H. Charlesworth and Craig A. Evans, eds., *The Pseudepigrapha and Early Biblical Interpretation* (JSPSup 14; Sheffield: Sheffield Academic Press, 1993) 96-125; Philip S. Alexander, "The Enochic Literature and the Bible: Intertextuality and Its Implications," in Edward D. Herbert and Emanuel Tov, eds., *The Bible as Book: The Hebrew Bible and the Judaean Desert Discoveries* (London: The British Library and Oak Knoll Press, in association with The Scriptorium: Center for Christian Antiquities, 2002) 57-69.

21. Milik, *The Books of Enoch*, 31. Nickelsburg, *1 Enoch 1*, 176-77, shows that the Enochic text follows Genesis 6 quite closely.

22. Nickelsburg, *1 Enoch 1*, 30.

23. *1 Enoch* 26–27; Nickelsburg, *1 Enoch 1*, 317-19.

24. Lars Hartman, *Asking for a Meaning: A Study of 1 Enoch 1–5* (ConBNT 12; Lund: Gleerup, 1979).

parts of the biblical tradition. This is not to say, however, that it is exegetical in intent or that it presupposes the authority of the Mosaic Torah. James Kugel, who more than any other scholar has made the case for the exegetical character of the Pseudepigrapha, grants that *1 Enoch* may well have passed on traditions originally unrelated to the biblical text.[25] There is, to be sure, an exegetical element in the story. In the *Book of the Watchers*, the flood is clearly the consequence of the sins initiated by the sons of God, while this connection is not explicit in Genesis. But there is no biblical basis at all for the stories of Asael and Shemihazah, the leaders of the fallen angels. The ascent of Enoch and his tour of the extremities of the earth are spun off from the biblical statement that he "walked with *elohim*" (Gen. 5:22) but many of the details of these chapters (e.g., the geography of chapters 17–19,[26] or the discussion of the chambers of the dead in chapter 22)[27] have little basis in biblical tradition.

A Distinct Form of Judaism?

There is no real doubt that the "chosen righteous from the chosen plant of righteousness," or the elect group envisioned in *1 Enoch*, constituted a Jewish sect. (I think the tendency to speak of Judaisms, in the plural, is unfortunate. Judaism is what all varieties of Judaism have in common.) They understood themselves as descendants of Abraham, the chosen plant of righteousness. In the *Animal Apocalypse* and in the *Apocalypse of Weeks*, it is quite clear that they are an offshoot of historic Israel. Yet, as George Nickelsburg has observed, the only *explicit* reference to the Sinai covenant appears in the *Apocalypse of Weeks* in *1 Enoch* 93:6, which says that "a covenant for all generations and a tabernacle" will be made in the fourth week. The *Animal Apocalypse,* in contrast, which clearly knows the story of the Exodus, refers to the ascent of Moses on Mount Sinai ("and that sheep

25. James L. Kugel, *Traditions of the Bible* (Cambridge, MA: Harvard University Press, 1998) 180; compare Andreas Bedenbender, *Der Gott der Welt tritt auf den Sinai. Entstehung, Entwicklung und Funktionsweise der frühjüdischen Apokalyptik* (Arbeiten zur neutestamentlichen Theologie und Zeitgeschichte 8; Berlin: Institut Kirche und Judentum, 2000) 157-63.

26. Coblentz Bautch, *A Study of the Geography*, 297, concludes that shared concerns about disobedience and illicit relationships do not necessarily demonstrate points of contact between these chapters and the Mosaic Torah.

27. See Marie-Theres Wacker, *Weltordnung und Gericht. Studien zu 1 Henoch 22* (Würzburg: Echter, 1982).

went up to the summit of a high rock") but conspicuously fails to mention either the making of a covenant or the giving of the law. At no point is there any polemic against the Mosaic Torah, but it is never the explicit frame of reference. In this respect, the Enochic literature stands in striking contrast to *Jubilees,* which retells the stories of Genesis from a distinctly Mosaic perspective, with explicit halachic interests.[28] The revelation to Enoch is anterior to that of Moses and in no way subordinated to it. As Nickelsburg has argued, "the general category of covenant was not important for these authors."[29] The word is rare. To quote Nickelsburg again:

> In short, the heart of the religion of *1 Enoch* juxtaposes election, revealed wisdom, the right and wrong ways to respond to this wisdom, and God's rewards and punishments for this conduct. Although all the components of "covenantal nomism" are present in this scheme, the word *covenant* rarely appears and Enoch takes the place of Moses as the mediator of revelation. In addition, the presentation of this religion is dominated by a notion of revelation — the claim that the books of Enoch are the embodiment of God's wisdom, which was received in primordial times and is being revealed in the eschaton to God's chosen ones.[30]

The understanding of the relationship between the elect and God may be covenantal, in the sense that it is based on laws which entail reward or punishment as their consequences, but it is not based on the Mosaic covenant, which was so widely accepted as the foundation of Jewish religion in the Hellenistic period.

It is often argued that the reason that *1 Enoch* is not specifically Mosaic is simply a reflection of its pseudepigraphic setting in the pre-diluvian period. But the choice of pseudonym and setting is not incidental. By choosing to attribute vital revelation to a figure who lived long before Moses, long before the emergence of Israel as a people, the authors of the Enoch literature chose to identify the core revelation, and the criteria for judgment, with creation, or the order of nature as they understood it, rather than with anything distinctively Israelite.

---

28. Compare the reflections of VanderKam, "The Interpretation of Genesis in 1 Enoch," 142-43.

29. Nickelsburg, "Enochic Wisdom," 125.

30. Nickelsburg, "Enochic Wisdom," 129.

The idea of a movement within Judaism that is not centered on the Mosaic Torah may seem anomalous in the context of the Hellenistic age, but it was not without precedent. The biblical wisdom literature is distinguished precisely by its lack of explicit reference to either the Mosaic Torah or the history of Israel, and it retains this character as late as the Book of Qoheleth, which may be roughly contemporary with the early Enoch literature. The Book of *Ben Sira,* which is close to the early Enoch literature in date, professes that all wisdom is the book of the covenant of the Most High. But *Ben Sira* remains a wisdom book rather than an exposition of the Torah. It pays no attention to the purity laws of Leviticus, and it sometimes adapts biblical narratives in surprising ways, most notably in its references to the creation stories.[31] 4QInstruction, a relatively early wisdom book found at Qumran, which has many points of contact with the Enoch literature, clearly reflects knowledge of the Torah at several points. Nonetheless, the Torah is not thematized there, as it is in *Ben Sira,* and the primary guides to wisdom appear to be the mysterious "vision of Hagi" and the teaching about "the mystery to come" that is transmitted by parents to their children.[32] Judaism in the early second century BCE was not uniformly Torah-centered, even among those who were familiar with the Torah and respected it as one source of wisdom among others.

I would agree then, with Boccaccini and others, that the Enoch literature reflects a distinctive form of Judaism (not "*a Judaism*") in the late third/early second centuries BCE.[33] (Whether this form of Judaism persisted into the first century BCE or later is another question, into which I do not wish to enter here.) The distinguishing marks of this form of Judaism were not only the explanation of the origin of evil by the myth of the Watchers, but also the invocation of the pre-diluvian Enoch rather than Moses as the revealer of essential wisdom and the view that angelic life was

31. See John J. Collins, *Jewish Wisdom in the Hellenistic Age* (OTL; Louisville: Westminster, 1997) 42-61.

32. See the essays in John J. Collins, Gregory E. Sterling, and Ruth A. Clements, eds., *Sapiential Perspectives: Wisdom Literature in Light of the Dead Sea Scrolls* (STDJ 51; Leiden: Brill, 2004). Note especially in the same volume the essay by Lawrence H. Schiffman, "Halakhic Elements in the Sapiential Texts from Qumran," 89-100, on the very limited use of legal material. See also Matthew J. Goff, *The Worldly and Heavenly Wisdom of 4QInstruction* (STDJ 50; Leiden: Brill, 2003) 225, with reference to 4QInstruction: "it uses the Torah without invoking it as a source of authority."

33. For a fuller treatment of this issue see Collins, "How Distinctive Was Enochic Judaism?" *17-34.

the ultimate ideal for humanity. Whether the authors of this literature were dissident priests is not so clear. Their interest in the calendar is congenial to such a hypothesis, the *Book of the Watchers* is certainly interested in the heavenly temple, and the *Animal Apocalypse* is explicitly critical of the Second Temple. Nonetheless, the failure to characterize Enoch explicitly as a priest would be remarkable if the movement were indeed priestly.

The Relation to the Sect Known from the Scrolls

The more controversial part of Boccaccini's thesis concerns the relation of this "Enochic Judaism" to the sectarian movement known from the Scrolls.[34] Boccaccini proposes the thesis that "Enochic Judaism is the modern name for the mainstream body of the Essene party, from which the Qumran community parted as a radical, dissident, and marginal off-spring."[35] This suggestion is not entirely without precedent. At one point in the history of research it was customary to associate all references to elect groups in the books of Enoch, Daniel, and *Jubilees* with the Hasidim, and regard them as the forerunners of the Essenes (and Pharisees).[36] In 1984 Devorah Dimant suggested that the *Animal Apocalypse* was an early sectarian work, and refers to the appearance of the Teacher of Righteousness.[37] In 1987 Philip Davies, who a decade earlier had debunked the all-embracing portrayal of the Hasidim,[38] threw caution to the winds and declared that it seemed "unnecessarily pedantic" not to call the authors of the Enochic texts and *Jubilees* "Essenes,"[39] and proceeded to equate the terms "pre-Qumran" and "Essene."[40] Davies also promoted the view that the *Damascus Document* reflected "the organization of the parent community, from which the Qumran group emerged," and that the latter group

34. Collins, "Enoch, the Dead Sea Scrolls, and the Essene Groups and Movements in Judaism in the Early Second Century B.C.E.," in Boccaccini, ed., *Enoch and Qumran Origins*, 345-50; " 'Enochic Judaism' and the Sect of the Dead Sea Scrolls," 283-99.

35. Boccaccini, *Beyond the Essene Hypothesis*, 16.

36. For a classic example, see Martin Hengel, *Judaism and Hellenism* (Philadelphia: Fortress, 1974) 1.175-80.

37. Devorah Dimant, "Qumran Sectarian Literature," in Michael E. Stone, ed., *Jewish Writings from the Second Temple Period* (CRINT 2/2; Philadelphia: Fortress, 1984) 544-45.

38. Philip R. Davies, "Hasidim in the Maccabean Period," *JJS* 28 (1977) 127-40.

39. Philip R. Davies, *Behind the Essenes: History and Ideology in the Dead Sea Scrolls* (BJS 94; Atlanta: Scholars Press, 1987) 109.

40. Davies, *Behind the Essenes*, 30.

originated in a schism not with Judaism as a whole but with the parent "Essene" group.[41] The "Groningen hypothesis" advanced by Florentino García Martínez in 1990 also tried "clearly to distinguish between the origins of the Qumran group and the origins of the parent group, the Essene movement, and to trace back to the Apocalyptic Tradition of the third century B.C. the ideological roots of the Essenes."[42] García Martínez also sought "the origins of the Qumran group in a split which occurred within the Essene movement in consequence of which the group loyal to the Teacher of Righteousness was finally to establish itself in Qumran."[43]

Boccaccini, then, is building on the results of earlier scholarship, although one cannot speak of a consensus on these issues. In my view, however, there are serious problems with this reconstruction of Essene origins, and the resulting identification of Enochic Judaism as Essene is at best an oversimplification. There are, to be sure, clear lines of continuity between the Enoch literature and the Dead Sea sect that are not in dispute. These include the common solar calendar, division of history into periods, and an interest in the angelic world that involves life after death, as well as the fact that the Enoch literature, like the *Damascus Document*, speaks of the emergence of an elect group late in the Second Temple period. But these affinities must be seen in perspective of what we know of the Essenes, of continuities with other literature, and of the range of interests that characterize the sectarian scrolls.

The Essenes

Let us begin with the issue of terminology. I still believe that the community (or communities) described in the *Community Rule* and *Damascus Rule* should be identified with the Essenes described in the Greek and Latin sources, despite some troubling discrepancies.[44] But it is important to remember the basis of the identification. This is primarily the similarity in community organization and process of admission. There are also some

41. Davies, *Behind the Essenes*, 18-19.

42. Florentino García Martínez, "A Groningen Hypothesis of Qumran Origins," *RevQ* 14 (1990) 537.

43. García Martínez, "A Groningen Hypothesis of Qumran Origins," 537.

44. See John J. Collins, *Beyond the Qumran Community: The Sectarian Movement of the Dead Sea Scrolls* (Grand Rapids: Eerdmans, 2010) 122-65. The most controversial point in the debate about the identification is the question of celibacy.

similarities in religious ideas, such as the Essene belief in determinism and the description of life after death, but I doubt that these would be sufficient to sustain the identification without the community structures. The closest parallels are found in the *Community Rule*. If, then, we are justified in speaking of Essenes in connection with the DSS at all, the *yaḥad* of the *Community Rule* should be our primary example of an Essene community. If we share the common assumption that the Qumran community was a settlement of this *yaḥad*, then that community is our touchstone of what it meant to be an Essene.[45] If we compare what is said about the "lambs" in the *Animal Apocalypse* or about the "chosen righteous" in the *Apocalypse of Weeks* with the accounts of the Essenes in Josephus, Philo, or Pliny, we find that they have almost nothing in common. The Enochic texts do not attest the kind of separatist community that is central to the classical accounts. It seems to me then that to speak of the tradents of the Enoch literature as Essenes is to sow confusion.

Now it may be objected that I am overlooking the evidence of the *Damascus Document,* which has been taken to reflect a middle ground between the Enoch literature on the one hand and the *yaḥad* (which is taken to reflect the Qumran community) on the other. CD col. 7 legislates for people who live in camps according to the order of the land and marry and have children. These people are often identified with "the marrying Essenes" who are mentioned by Josephus as another branch of the sect.[46] Josephus says that these were in agreement with the other Essenes on the way of life, usages, and customs, and differed only with respect to marriage. Presumably, people who married and had children cannot have lived the same kind of communal life as those who did not. But the mere absence of communal life is hardly sufficient grounds for identifying them with Enochic Judaism. In the end, the case for such an identification stands or falls on the degree of similarity that we find between the *Damascus Document* and the Enoch literature.

45. The *yaḥad* cannot be simply identified with "the Qumran community." 1QS 6:1-7 clearly presupposes multiple settlements of the *yaḥad*. See my article "The Yaḥad and 'The Qumran Community'," in Charlotte Hempel and Judith M. Lieu, eds., *Biblical Traditions in Transmission: Essays in Honour of Michael A. Knibb* (JSJSup 111; Leiden: Brill, 2006) 81-96. Torleif Elgvin also argues that "The Yaḥad Is More Than Qumran" in Boccaccini, ed., *Enoch and Qumran Origins*, 273-79, but his argument is based on the paleographic dating of some texts that refer to the *yaḥad* to a time before the establishment of the Qumran settlement. See the critical remarks of Florentino García Martínez, "Response: The Groningen Hypothesis Revisited," in Boccaccini, ed., *Enoch and Qumran Origins*, 314.

46. *Bellum Judaicum* 2.160.

The Alleged Schism

Before I turn to that question, however, I want to comment on the relation between the two orders of Essenes and between the *Damascus Document* and the *Community Rule*. Josephus gives no hint that the existence of the two orders of Essenes was due to a schism. Quite the contrary. He suggests that they differed only with respect to marriage. The best evidence for a distinction of two orders in the Scrolls is found in CD 7, which can be taken to distinguish between those who "walk in perfect holiness" and those who live in camps and marry.[47] The passage can be construed so that those who live in camps are a sub-group of those who walk in holiness, but there is still a distinction between two groups. But here again there is no suggestion of a schism. CD legislates for both. Whether the people of the *yaḥad* were celibate is much disputed, especially with reference to the evidence of the cemetery.[48] But in any case the people who are said to go into the desert to prepare the way of the Lord in 1QS 8 are not schismatics, but are people who are set aside within the community for a life of holiness.[49] There is no indication that the *Community Rule* and the *Damascus Document* represent different sides in a schism. Both texts are preserved at Qumran. The *Damascus Document,* it should be noted, pays explicit homage to the Teacher, who is not mentioned in the supposedly Qumranic *Community Rule* but is associated with the *yaḥad* in the *Pesharim*. It seems to me then that the two orders of Essenes represented different options within the sect, not dissenting factions. Equally, the *Damascus Document* represents both the "men of perfect holiness" and those who live in camps as loyal followers of the Teacher of Righteousness.[50]

The idea of schism within the parent movement is based above all on the references in the *Damascus Document* to the "Scoffer" (CD 1:14) and to

---

47. Joseph M. Baumgarten, "The Qumran-Essene Restraints on Marriage," in Lawrence H. Schiffman, ed., *Archaeology and History in the Dead Sea Scrolls* (Sheffield: Sheffield Academic Press, 1990) 13-24.

48. See Jürgen Zangenberg, "The 'Final Farewell': A Necessary Paradigm Shift in the Interpretation of the Qumran Cemetery," *Qumran Chronicle* 8 (1999) 273-78. For a recent assessment of the cemetery see Brian Schultz, "The Qumran Cemetery: 150 Years of Research," *DSD* 13.2 (2006) 194-228.

49. John J. Collins, "Forms of Community in the Dead Sea Scrolls," in Shalom M. Paul et al., eds., *Emanuel: Studies in Hebrew Bible, Septuagint, and Dead Sea Scrolls in Honor of Emanuel Tov* (Leiden: Brill, 2003) 105-7.

50. See further Collins, *Beyond the Qumran Community*, 12-87.

those who turned back with the Man of the Lie (CD 20:15).[51] It is clear that some people rejected the Teacher and broke with his community. One may well argue, then, that the whole Essene sect arose as the result of a schism within a wider movement (such as the Hasidim), and this was in fact the usual argument in the earlier phase of research on the Scrolls. But there is no reason to suppose that the people who settled at Qumran were the only ones loyal to the Teacher; CD 7 clearly regards those who lived in camps as members of the same movement. I see no justification for referring to those who left with the Man of the Lie as Essenes.[52]

As a first step towards reducing confusion, therefore, I suggest that the word "Essene" be restricted to the followers of the Teacher of Righteousness, whether celibate or married. Those who turned back with the Man of the Lie ceased to be Essenes (and may have become Pharisees),[53] but I see no evidence of any schism between two parties who remained Essene. I might add that I would not object to a complete moratorium on the word "Essene" in connection with the Dead Sea Scrolls. It is inevitable that we discuss the identification of the sect, but the information provided by the Greek and Latin sources is suspect anyway, and does not add anything reliable to what can be gleaned from the Scrolls themselves.

The *Damascus Document* and the Enoch Literature

But leaving aside the term "Essenes," can we say anything about the identification of the "plant root," the community that existed for some twenty years before the arrival of the Teacher? Was this community identical with the "chosen righteous" and "small lambs" of the Enoch literature?

The argument for the identification is clear enough: one should not multiply sectarian groups without cause. Since the Enoch literature was known and influential at Qumran, and it indicates the rise of an elect group late in the Second Temple period, why not identify this group with the "plant root" of the Dead Sea sect? Moreover, they have in common allegiance to the solar calendar, which set them at odds with the Jerusalem temple, and they shared ideas of reward and punishment after death. Even

51. See especially Hartmut Stegemann, *Die Entstehung der Qumrangemeinde* (Bonn: published privately, 1971) 48-52.

52. So also Mark Elliott, "Sealing Some Cracks in the Groningen Foundation," in Boccaccini, ed., *Enoch and Qumran Origins*, 263-72.

53. So Stegemann, *Die Entstehung*, 257.

the metaphor of planting figures prominently in *1 Enoch*.[54] These factors certainly show that there was some connection between the Enoch group and the plant root of CD. Are they enough to establish the identification?

I think not. The concept of covenant and the Torah of Moses are absolutely central to the *Damascus Document*.[55] As we have seen repeatedly, neither is at all prominent in the early Enoch literature. Conversely, while the *Damascus Document* knows the story of the Watchers, it never appeals to the authority of Enoch as a revealer, although it does appeal to Levi and cites *Jubilees*. It also attaches major importance to issues of purity, which are not especially prominent in the Enoch literature. There is, then, an ideological gulf between the Enoch literature and the Damascus covenant.

Boccaccini tries to bridge that gulf by appeal to the Book of *Jubilees*. Here we have a revelation that was allegedly given to Moses and that is greatly concerned with halachic issues.[56] It also draws on the Enoch tradition, notably on the myth of the Watchers, and attaches great importance to the solar calendar. Boccaccini concludes that "the Book of Jubilees gives us evidence that after the Maccabean crisis, the Enochians, or at least some Enochians, now considered the Mosaic revelation as no longer a competitive revelation to pass over in silence, as Dream Visions did, but as a common heritage that could neither be ignored nor dismissed."[57] But is the Book of *Jubilees* necessarily a product of Enochians? Might one not equally well suppose that some people who venerated Moses no longer regarded Enochian revelation as competitive? Or indeed that some people who were devoted to the Torah of Moses became aware of the Enoch literature and tried to incorporate it into "Mosaic religion"? There is a fusion of traditions in *Jubilees*, but can we be so confident that the people doing the fusing were the so-called Enochians? In his more recent work, Boccaccini grants that "it is unlikely that the authors of the Enoch apocalypses and the sectarian

54. Patrick A. Tiller, "The 'Eternal Planting' in the Dead Sea Scrolls," *DSD* 4 (1997) 312-35.

55. John J. Collins, "The Nature and Aims of the Sect Known from the Dead Sea Scrolls," in Anthony Hilhorst, Émile Puech, and Eibert Tigchelaar, eds., *Flores Florentino: Dead Sea Scrolls and Other Early Jewish Studies in Honour of Florentino García Martínez* (JSJSup 122; Leiden: Brill, 2007) 35-40; Stephen J. Hultgren, *From the Damascus Covenant to the Covenant of the Community: Literary, Historical and Theological Studies in the Dead Sea Scrolls* (STDJ 66; Leiden: Brill, 2007) 141-232.

56. See Gabriele Boccaccini and Giovanni Ibba, eds., *Enoch and the Mosaic Torah: The Evidence of Jubilees* (Grand Rapids: Eerdmans, 2009).

57. Boccaccini, *Beyond the Essene Hypothesis*, 88.

rule books once belonged to the same group or organization," although he still claims that they constituted one "intellectual movement."[58]

The impulse to apply Ockham's razor to the identification of groups in second-century Judaism is commendable up to a point, but it can be carried to excess.[59] The Enoch literature and the *Damascus Document* are not the only texts from this period that speak of the emergence of an elect group. We also have the *maskilim* in Daniel, and we have remnants in the pseudo-Daniel writings that do not seem to me to come from the same source as the canonical book.[60] Daniel was also known and influential at Qumran, and like *Enoch* had a great interest in the angelic world and hoped for an angelic afterlife. But as Boccaccini recognizes, Daniel cannot be subsumed into Enochic Judaism. Now we must also add 4QInstruction to the list.[61] This wisdom text is addressed to "people of the spirit" who are sharply distinguished from "the spirit of flesh." It has been suggested that this text, too, was influenced by the Enoch literature, especially by the *Epistle*,[62] but it never refers to Enoch, nor to distinctively Enochic themes like the fall of the Watchers. In each of these cases, *Enoch*, Daniel, and 4QInstruction, there are clear lines of continuity with central writings of the sectarian scrolls,[63] but they cannot be reduced to a single parent movement.

Conclusion

It seems to me that the safest conclusion from this evidence is that the Dead Sea sect drew its inspiration from various quarters. One of these was

---

58. Boccaccini, "Enochians, Urban Essenes, Qumranites: Three Social Groups, One Intellectual Movement," in Boccaccini and Collins, eds., *The Early Enoch Literature*, 315. In addition to the importance of the Torah of Moses in the *yaḥad*, he notes the clear sociological discontinuity entailed by the elaborate entry procedures in the *yaḥad*.

59. Compare James C. VanderKam, "Too Far Beyond the Essene Hypothesis?" in Boccaccini, ed., *Enoch and Qumran Origins*, 388-93.

60. See my article "Pseudepigraphy and Group Formation," 43-58.

61. John Strugnell and Daniel J. Harrington, *Qumran Cave 4. XXIV. Sapiential Texts, Part 2. 4QInstruction (Musar le Mevin)* (DJD XXIV; Oxford: Clarendon, 1999).

62. Torleif Elgvin, "Wisdom and Apocalypticism in the Early Second Century B.C.E. — The Evidence of 4QInstruction," in Lawrence H. Schiffman, Emanuel Tov, and James C. VanderKam, eds., *The Dead Sea Scrolls Fifty Years after Their Discovery* (Jerusalem: Israel Exploration Society, 2000) 226-47.

63. For the continuities with wisdom literature see especially Armin Lange, *Weisheit und Prädestination* (Leiden: Brill, 1995) 69-79.

certainly the Enoch literature. Another was the wisdom tradition attested in 4QInstruction. Daniel was another, and the Torah of Moses was yet another, arguably the most important of all. The reduction of all these to a single line of tradition is a temptation that should be avoided. Rather than being a splinter movement, an offshoot of a branch, it seems to me that the sectarian movement reflected in the Scrolls involved a synthesis of traditions, Enochic and Mosaic, sapiential and apocalyptic. It was still a sectarian movement, but it drew together traditions, and probably also people, from various sources. If the people who settled at Qumran were originally Enochians, I would expect *Enoch* to play a larger role in the sectarian writings. This is not at all to deny the important continuities between *Enoch* and Qumran, but these continuities must be seen in the broader context of elect communities in Judaism in the second century BCE.

CHAPTER 6

The Genre of the Book of Jubilees

Genre

Literary competence, writes John Barton, can be defined principally as *the ability to recognize genre*.[1] He defines genre as "any recognizable and distinguishable type of writing or speech — whether 'literary' in the complimentary sense of that word or merely utilitarian, like a business letter — which operates within certain conventions that are in principle (not necessarily in practice) statable."[2] The important thing is to know the *kind* of writing that is involved and the conventions that apply. As Carol Newsom puts it, "genres serve as proffered contracts between writers and readers, providing common expectations for what the text in question is intended to do and what means it is likely to use."[3] The expectations of readers are guided by association with other works that are perceived to be similar. Without some such associations, it is difficult, if not impossible, to understand a work at all. In the words of Jonathan Culler, "A work can only be read in connection with or against other texts, which provide a

1. John Barton, *Reading the Old Testament: Method in Biblical Study* (rev. ed.; Louisville: Westminster John Knox, 1996) 16. Barton's view of genre follows that of E. D. Hirsch, *Validity in Interpretation* (New Haven: Yale University Press, 1967) 68-126.
2. Barton, *Reading the Old Testament*, 16.
3. Carol A. Newsom, "Rhetorical Criticism and the Reading of the Qumran Scrolls," in Timothy H. Lim and John J. Collins, eds., *The Oxford Handbook of the Dead Sea Scrolls* (Oxford: Oxford University Press, 2010) 691.

It is a pleasure to dedicate this essay to Jim VanderKam, who has done more than any scholar since R. H. Charles to advance the study of the book of *Jubilees*.

grid through which it is read and structured by establishing expectations which enable one to pick out salient features and give them a structure."[4]

Recognition of genre is an art rather than a science, and there has been considerable debate about the appropriate criteria.[5] The phase of literary criticism known as "New Criticism" tended to favor formal criteria.[6] According to the influential introduction to literary theory of René Wellek and Austin Warren: "Genre should be conceived, we think, as a grouping of literary works based, theoretically, upon both outer form (specific metre or structure) and also upon inner form (attitude, tone, purpose — more crudely, subject and audience)."[7] More recent theorists have tended to deprecate classification. Alistair Fowler famously quipped that genres are more like pigeons than pigeonholes.[8] It is certainly true that generic classification has often been too rigid. Genres are not ontological entities. They are largely pragmatic configurations based on scholars' perceptions of affinities, and shaped in part by the perspective and interest of the analyst. There is no reason why a text might not have affinities with more than one genre, and genres inevitably change and are modified over time. Moreover, mere classification is only a prelude to many of the more interesting questions we can ask about texts, including that of function.[9] Yet it remains true that without classification there is no generic analysis at all.[10]

4. Jonathan Culler, *Structuralist Poetics: Structuralism, Linguistics, and the Study of Literature* (Ithaca, NY: Cornell University Press, 1975) 139.

5. See David Duff, *Modern Genre Theory* (Harlow, UK: Longman, 2000). For an excellent overview, with an eye to biblical studies, see Carol A. Newsom, "Spying Out the Land: A Report from Genology," in Roland Boer, ed., *Bakhtin and Genre Theory in Biblical Studies* (Semeia Studies 63; Atlanta: Society of Biblical Literature, 2007) 19-30 (originally published in Ronald L. Troxel et al., eds., *Seeking Out the Wisdom of the Ancients: Essays Offered to Honor Michael V. Fox on the Occasion of His Sixty-Fifth Birthday* [Winona Lake, Ind.: Eisenbrauns, 2005] 437-50).

6. R. S. Crane, *Critical and Historical Principles of Literary Criticism* (Chicago: University of Chicago Press, 1971) 38. See the comments of Amy J. Devitt, *Writing Genres* (Carbondale: Southern Illinois University Press, 2004) 6.

7. *Theory of Literature* (New York: Harcourt, Brace and World, 1956) 231.

8. Alastair Fowler, *Kinds of Literature: An Introduction to the Theory of Genres and Modes* (Cambridge, MA: Harvard University Press, 1982) 36.

9. Much recent genre theory seems to be concerned with the way genres work rather than with the more basic problem of identifying a genre in the first case. See, e.g., Devitt (*Writing Genres*) or, in the context of biblical studies, Christine Mitchell, "Power, *Eros*, and Biblical Genres," in Boer, ed., *Bakhtin and Genre Theory*, 31-43.

10. Devitt (*Writing Genres*, 7) says that "defining genre as a kind of text becomes circular, since what we call a kind of text depends on what we think a genre is," but quickly

Even if a text is judged to fall in the interstices between genres, and not to conform to any recognized category, this judgment is only possible on the basis of a classification of recognized genres.

That said, genres may be classified in various ways. The classic "new critical" approach to genres was based on the formal features of texts, and this mode of classification could be extended to take account of the thematic content of works.[11] The mere listing of features is not necessarily significant. It is necessary to identify the features that bear structural weight in a text.[12] In the wake of Fowler's work, a Wittgensteinian "family resemblance" approach gained popularity.[13] The appeal of this approach lay in its ability to recognize affinities without creating rigid classifications, but it has also been criticized for lack of precision. As another genre theorist, John Swales, remarked, "family resemblance theory can make anything resemble anything."[14] More recently, prototype theory has attracted attention. This theory is derived from cognitive psychology. As described by John Frow:

> [T]he postulate is that we understand categories (such as *bird*) through a very concrete logic of typicality. We take a robin or a sparrow to be more central to that category than an ostrich, and a kitchen chair to be more typical of the class of chairs than a throne or a piano stool. Rather than having clear boundaries, essential components, and shared and uniform properties, classes defined by prototypes have a common core and then fade into fuzziness at the edges. This is to say that we classify easily at the level of prototypes, and with more difficulty — extending features of the prototype by metaphor and analogy to take account of non-typical features — as we diverge from them.[15]

---

adds: "That conundrum does not mean that genres do not involve classification nor that devising a classification scheme is necessarily a waste of time." Indeed, if genre is not "a kind of text," one is left to wonder what the word means at all.

11. This was the approach followed in John J. Collins, ed., *Apocalypse: The Morphology of a Genre* (*Semeia* 14; Missoula, MT: Scholars Press, 1979).

12. Compare the comments of Newsom on the importance of *Gestalt* structures ("Spying Out the Land," 25).

13. Ludwig Wittgenstein, *Philosophical Investigations* (Oxford: Blackwell, 1958) 31-32; Fowler, *Kinds of Literature*, 41-42.

14. John M. Swales, *Genre Analysis: English in Academic and Research Settings* (Cambridge: Cambridge University Press, 1990) 51.

15. John Frow, *Genre* (London: Routledge, 2006) 54.

Membership in a category may be a matter of degree. It should be noted that prototypical exemplars of a genre are not necessarily historical archetypes, classic works that became models for later writers. Late exemplars may also be prototypical, if they exemplify especially well the typical features of the genre.

This approach to genre has considerable appeal. As Carol Newsom puts it:

> One of the advantages of prototype theory is that it provides a way for bringing together what seems so commonsensical in classificatory approaches, while avoiding their rigidity. At the same time it gives more discipline to the family-resemblance approach, because not every resemblance or deviation is of equal significance. As applied to genre categories, prototype theory would require an identification of exemplars that are prototypical and an analysis of the privileged properties that establish the sense of typicality.[16]

Both "family resemblance" and "prototype theory" are based on the identification of common distinctive features in a cluster of texts. Some other approaches are more intuitive. The thought of the Russian literary critic Mikhail Bakhtin has been widely influential. According to Michael Vines:

> For Bakhtin, genre is not about the presence or absence of particular literary forms (or linguistic devices). Genre is instead primarily about a work's meta-linguistic form: the formal structure of a work that transcends its linguistic devices . . . it is precisely the value-laden temporal and spatial quality of a work, or its chronotope, that is the primary indicator of its generic relationships.[17]

This would lead, if I understand Vines correctly, to a recognition of genre on the basis of worldview rather than of strictly literary features. Such an approach may have merit, but it seems to me to pursue a different question from that of literary genre, as traditionally understood. Again, many scholars would argue that genres should be identified on the basis of common

16. Newsom, "Spying Out the Land," 24.
17. Michael E. Vines, "The Apocalyptic Chronotope," in Boer, ed., *Bakhtin and Genre Theory*, 110-11.

function. So, for example, John Swales claims that "the principal criterial feature that turns a collection of communicative events into a genre is some shared set of communicative purposes."[18] There is an obvious objection to this approach, insofar as the purpose of a text is often implicit, and less overt and demonstrable than literary form. The deeper issue here, however, is whether there is a simple correlation between form and function. A form may be used ironically, and in any case literary forms can be adapted to new purposes in different settings. This is not to deny that function is an important issue in any literary analysis, but to question whether it provides a satisfactory basis for generic recognition.

In this chapter, my concern is with genre recognition, in the specific case of the Book of *Jubilees*. My concern is with literary form, not meta-linguistic chronotopes. I bracket for the present the question of function, although I believe that some light can be shed on it by generic analysis. Both "family resemblance" and "prototype theory" are somewhat helpful in this endeavor. The question can also be viewed in terms of the composition of the book. Were there literary models available to the author? Did he conform to them or bend them to his purpose, and is that purpose clarified by the literary presentation of the work?

Rewritten Scripture

While various suggestions have been made regarding the genre of *Jubilees*, by far the most common in recent scholarship has been "rewritten Bible."[19] This genre label was introduced by Geza Vermes to describe such works as *Jubilees*, the *Genesis Apocryphon*, the *Biblical Antiquities* of Pseudo-Philo, and the *Antiquities* of Josephus.[20] The *Temple Scroll* is often added to the list, though there is a vast corpus of Jewish writings from the Hellenistic period that is based on what we know as the biblical text. The designation

18. Swales, *Genre Analysis*, 46. See also Carolyn R. Miller, "Genre as Social Action," *Quarterly Journal of Speech* 70 (May 1984) 151-67; "Rhetorical Community: The Cultural Basis of Genre," in Aviva Freedman and Peter Medway, eds., *Genre and the New Rhetoric* (London: Taylor, 1994) 67-78.

19. James C. VanderKam, *The Book of Jubilees* (Guides to Apocrypha and Pseudepigrapha; Sheffield: Sheffield Academic Press, 2001) 135. Earlier, less successful, designations include "targum" and "haggadic midrash."

20. Geza Vermes, *Scripture and Tradition in Judaism: Haggadic Studies* (2nd ed.; Studia Post-Biblica 4; Leiden: Brill, 1973) 67-126.

"rewritten Bible" is problematic, since that which is rewritten was not yet "Bible," and so scholars increasingly refer to these texts as "rewritten scriptures."[21] There is certainly a "family resemblance" between these writings, insofar as they are all adaptations of older scriptures. Whether that resemblance is sufficient to designate a literary genre, however, is a matter of dispute.

In his article on "rewritten Bible" in the *Encyclopedia of the Dead Sea Scrolls*, George Brooke wrote: "Rewritten Bible texts come in almost as many genres as can be found in the biblical books themselves."[22] Vermes, of course, had only the narrative books of the Torah in mind. The supposed genre is complicated considerably if we include the *Temple Scroll*, which is a rewriting of biblical laws but not a narrative. There are also rewritten prophetic texts and a targum of Job. The fragments of Hellenistic Jewish literature in Greek include a tragedy on the subject of the Exodus by one Ezekiel, and epic poems based on Genesis by Theodotus and Philo (not the philosopher).[23] The Dead Sea Scrolls include examples of rewritten prophetic texts (e.g., Pseudo-Ezekiel). The question arises then whether the word "genre" is more appropriately used at the level of the umbrella term that embraces the different kinds of rewriting, or whether we should rather think of the relevant texts as narratives, legal texts, prophecies, etc. There is no doubt that the relation of these texts to the older scriptures is a significant generic feature, but it is not immediately apparent that all rewriting is alike. There is need for greater generic differentiation among the texts that rewrite the various older genres.

21. See, e.g., Anders Klostergaard Petersen, "Rewritten Bible as a Borderline Phenomenon — Genre, Textual Strategy or Canonical Anachronism?" in Anthony Hilhorst et al., eds., *Flores Florentino: Dead Sea Scrolls and Other Jewish Studies in Honour of Florentino García Martínez* (JSJSup 122; Leiden: Brill, 2007) 284-306; and Molly M. Zahn, "Rewritten Scripture," in Lim and Collins, eds., *The Oxford Handbook of the Dead Sea Scrolls*, 323-36. Jonathan G. Campbell, " 'Rewritten Bible' and 'Parabiblical Texts': A Terminological and Ideological Critique," in Jonathan G. Campbell, ed., *New Directions in Qumran Studies: Proceedings of the Bristol Colloquium on the Dead Sea Scrolls, 8–10 September 2003* (London: T&T Clark, 2005) 43-68, also objects to "rewritten scriptures." He suggests terminology along the lines of "scripture" and "parascripture."

22. George J. Brooke, "Rewritten Bible," in *EDSS* 2.777-81 (here 780). Compare already George W. E. Nickelsburg, "The Bible Rewritten and Expanded," in Michael E. Stone, ed., *Jewish Writings of the Second Temple Period* (CRINT 2.2; Assen: van Gorcum/Philadelphia: Fortress, 1984) 89: "It is clear that these writings employ a variety of genres."

23. For these texts see Carl R. Holladay, *Fragments from Hellenistic Jewish Authors*, vol. 2: *Poets* (Atlanta: Scholars Press, 1989).

Accordingly, several scholars have argued that rewriting scripture is a compositional technique, but does not in itself define a genre. As Daniel Harrington wrote in 1986: "it seems better to view rewriting the Bible as a kind of activity or process than to see it as a distinctive literary genre."[24] More recently, Daniel Falk argues: "Just as 'biblical text' is not a genre, 'rewritten Bible' cannot properly be a genre. It is a strategy of extending scriptural authority by imitation. It is possible to keep the same genre as the scriptural base, or to recast it into a new genre."[25]

In contrast to this trend in scholarship, Philip Alexander has sought to defend the view that a literary genre of "rewritten Bible" can be defined on the basis of the four texts adduced by Vermes: *Jubilees, Genesis Apocryphon*, the biblical *Antiquities* of Pseudo-Philo, and the *Antiquities* of Josephus.[26] He identifies nine characteristics of the proposed genre:

1. Rewritten Bible texts are narratives, which follow a sequential, chronological order.
2. They are free-standing compositions which replicate the form of the biblical books on which they are based.
3. Despite the superficial independence of form, these texts are not intended to replace, or to supersede the Bible.
4. Rewritten Bible texts cover a substantial portion of the Bible.
5. They follow the Bible serially, in proper order, but they are highly selective in what they represent.
6. Their intention is to produce an interpretative reading of Scripture that is fuller, smoother, and more doctrinally advanced.
7. The narrative form limits the text to a single interpretation of the original.
8. The narrative form also precludes explicit exegetical reading.

24. Daniel J. Harrington, S.J., "Palestinian Adaptations of Biblical Narratives and Prophecies," in Robert A. Kraft and George W. E. Nickelsburg, eds., *Early Judaism and Its Modern Interpreters* (Atlanta: Scholars Press, 1986) 243. The criticism of Harrington and Nickelsburg by Moshe Bernstein (" 'Rewritten Bible': A Generic Category Which Has Outlived Its Usefulness?" *Textus* 22 [2005] 176-80), that they do not satisfy "the need for more precise nomenclature for literary forms" (177), seems to miss the point they are making, that rewritten scripture is not a literary form at all.

25. Daniel K. Falk, *The Parabiblical Texts: Strategies for Extending the Scriptures in the Dead Sea Scrolls* (London: T & T Clark, 2007) 16.

26. Philip Alexander, "Retelling the Old Testament," in D. Carson and H. G. M. Williamson, eds., *It Is Written: Scripture Citing Scripture; Essays in Honour of Barnabas Lindars, SSF* (Cambridge: Cambridge University Press, 1987) 99-121.

9. Non-biblical tradition, oral or written, is integrated with the biblical narrative.[27]

There is no doubt that these common characteristics constitute a "family resemblance" and that they are significant characteristics of the Book of *Jubilees*. There were certainly precedents available to the author, whether they qualify as prototypes or not. The rewriting of Kings in Chronicles is often cited in this regard.[28] Nonetheless, the restriction to narrative form is significant and indicates that the "genre" in question is no more than one sub-genre of "rewritten scriptures," perhaps "rewritten narratives" or "rewritten scriptural narratives." Moreover, the common characteristics do not include the self-presentation of the books. In fact, the self-presentation of *Jubilees* is strikingly different from that of the other exemplars.

Yet the self-presentation of the texts is clearly crucial to the definition of "rewritten scriptures," and indeed of any genre. The case of "rewritten scriptures" has been complicated in recent years by the discovery of such texts as *4QReworked Pentateuch* (4Q158, 4Q364-67), a group of five fragmentary manuscripts, originally thought to make up a single composition, but now increasingly viewed as distinct but related compositions.[29] All five manuscripts reflect Pentateuchal texts, with variations, including rearrangements and additions (notably the "Song of Miriam"). In the words of Sidnie White Crawford, "these texts are the product of scribal interpretation, still marked mainly by harmonistic editing, but with one important addition: the insertion of outside material into the text, material not found in other parts of what we now recognize as the Pentateuch."[30] Many fragments correspond to the traditional text with minimal variation. The extant fragments do not suggest any changes of speaker or setting over against other forms of these texts. Consequently, they are increasingly viewed not

27. Alexander, "Retelling the Old Testament," 116-18.

28. See, e.g., VanderKam, *The Book of Jubilees*, 135, who also notes the difference in self-presentation between Chronicles and *Jubilees*.

29. On the fragmentary manuscripts considered a single composition, see Emanuel Tov and Sidnie White, "Reworked Pentateuch," *DJD* 13.187-351. On the manuscripts as distinct compositions, see Michael Segal, "4QReworked Pentateuch or 4QPentateuch?" in L. Schiffman et al., ed., *The Dead Sea Scrolls: Fifty Years After Their Discovery* (Jerusalem: Israel Exploration Society/Shrine of the Book, Israel Museum, 2000) 391-99; George Brooke, "4Q158: Reworked Pentateuch[a] or Reworked Pentateuch A?" *DSD* 8 (2001) 219-41. So now also Sidnie White Crawford, *Rewriting Scripture in Second Temple Times* (Grand Rapids: Eerdmans, 2008) 39.

30. White Crawford, *Rewriting Scripture*, 39-40.

as distinct compositions but as expansionistic variants of the text known from our Bible.[31]

As Michael Segal has pointed out, one of the distinctive features of "rewritten scriptures," as distinct from textual variants, is the self-presentation of these works: "In a number of rewritten compositions, the author has added a new narrative frame. This change places the composition as a whole into a new setting and thus offers a new ideological framework by which to understand the text."[32] Segal offers *Jubilees* and the *Temple Scroll* as paradigmatic examples of this phenomenon. The *Antiquities* of Josephus provides another clear example. But the nature of the narrative frame differs strikingly from one example to another, and this should cast some doubt on the adequacy of "rewritten scriptures," or even "rewritten narrative," as a designation of genre.

The Narrative Frame of *Jubilees*

In the case of *Jubilees*, we are fortunate that the beginning of the work has been preserved. Both the short prologue and the opening chapter are attested in the fragments of 4Q216 and preserved in full in Ethiopic. From allusions to Exodus 24:12-18, it appears that the setting is Moses' first forty-day sojourn on Mount Sinai.[33] Moses is told to write down "all these words which I will tell you on this mountain: what is first and what is last and what is to come during all the divisions of time which are in the law and which are in the testimony and in the weeks of their jubilees until eternity — until the time when I descend and live with them throughout all the ages of eternity" (*Jub.* 1:26).[34] The actual dictation is performed not by the Deity

31. For a list of scholars who hold this view, including now Emanuel Tov, see White Crawford, *Rewriting Scripture*, 56. See the discussion by Molly M. Zahn, "The Problem of Characterizing the 4QReworked Pentateuch Manuscripts: Bible, Rewritten Bible, or None of the Above?" *DSD* 15 (2008): 315-39; eadem, "Rewritten Scriptures"; and eadem, *Rethinking Rewritten Scripture: Composition and Exegesis in the 4QReworked Pentateuch Manuscripts* (STDJ 95; Leiden: Brill, 2011).

32. Michael Segal, "Between Bible and Rewritten Bible," in M. Henze, ed., *Biblical Interpretation at Qumran* (Grand Rapids: Eerdmans, 2005) 21.

33. See James C. VanderKam, "Moses Trumping Moses," in H. Najman et al., eds., *The Dead Sea Scrolls: Transmission of Traditions and Production of Texts* (Leiden: Brill, 2010) 25-44. Also VanderKam, *The Book of Jubilees*, 86-91.

34. Translations of *Jubilees* are from James C. VanderKam, *The Book of Jubilees* (2 vols.; CSCO 510-11; Scriptores Aethiopici 87–88; Leuven: Peeters, 1989).

but by the angel of the presence, who in turn derives the information from the heavenly tablets.[35]

It is apparent that this introductory frame is itself a rewriting of the story of the revelation at Mount Sinai. *Jubilees* presupposes that a basic story of that revelation is familiar to its readers. Hence, it does not recount the manner in which the Israelites arrived at Sinai. It also, unlike the *Temple Scroll*, explicitly acknowledges the existence and authority of "the first law" known from the Torah. The most explicit reference is in *Jubilees* 6:20-22, with regard to the laws of Shavuoth: "For I have written (this) in the book of the first law in which I wrote for you that you should celebrate it at each of its times. . . ." Again in *Jubilees* 30:12, à propos of Dinah and the Shechemites: "I have written for you in the words of the law everything that the Shechemites did to Dinah. . . ." But in addition to the Torah, there was also the "testimony" (תעודה), which, as VanderKam argues persuasively, should be identified with the contents of the Book of *Jubilees* itself, although they may not exhaust the testimony contained in the heavenly tablets.[36] As VanderKam has also pointed out, various passages in the Torah were taken as hints that God revealed more to Moses on Mount Sinai than is now contained in the biblical text.[37] According to Exodus 24:12, the Lord summoned Moses to give him "the law and the commandment." The expression would later be interpreted atomistically in the Talmud.[38] Further references to ordinances and laws given to Moses on Mount Sinai (Lev. 26:46) suggest that the revelation was more extensive than what is found in Exodus 20–31. VanderKam argues that *Jubilees* claims to present the initial revelation on Sinai, when the Lord gave the first pair of stone tablets to Moses:

> Those two tablets, however, were soon to suffer a violent end when Moses smashed them to pieces in Exod 32:19. Thus the field was left

35. Hindy Najman, "Interpretation as Primordial Writing: *Jubilees* and Its Authority Conferring Strategies," in *Past Renewals: Interpretive Authority, Renewed Revelation and the Quest for Perfection in Jewish Antiquity* (JSJSup 53; Leiden: Brill, 2010) 39-71. This article was originally published in *JSJ* 30 (1999) 379-410. On the heavenly tablets see Florentino García Martínez, "The Heavenly Tablets in the Book of Jubilees," in Matthias Albani et al., eds., *Studies in the Book of Jubilees* (Tübingen: Mohr Siebeck, 1997) 243-60.

36. VanderKam, "Moses Trumping Moses." Cana Werman, "'The תורה and the תעודה Engraved on the Tablets," *DSD* 9.1 (2002) 75-103, thinks that the "testimony" is "the preordained march of history."

37. VanderKam, "Moses Trumping Moses."

38. *b. Ber* 5a. See VanderKam, "Moses Trumping Moses."

clear for the revelation of *Jubilees* as the only product of Moses' first forty-day stay on Sinai — a revelation that survived his furious descent of the mountain. The second set of tablets (Exodus 34) repeated the limited contents of the first but came at least forty days later.[39]

The authority claimed for this "testimony," then, is at least as great as that of the Torah, arguably greater. As VanderKam puts it, "he (the author of *Jubilees*) was not seconding Sinai; he was initiating it."[40] The claim of priority is questionable, since *Jubilees* still acknowledges the traditional Torah as "the first law," but at the least it is claiming an equal authority.[41]

Mosaic Discourse?

Hindy Najman has argued that *Jubilees* is an example of "Mosaic discourse" and that it can be seen as an example of "discourse tied to a founder" by analogy with the way texts were attributed in philosophical schools.[42] In view of the setting at Sinai and the role of Moses as recipient of the revelation, this designation is reasonable. Yet it is worth noting that Moses is not the speaker in *Jubilees*. Rather, the revelation is dictated to him by the angel of the presence.[43] While much exegetical activity undoubtedly went into the composition of *Jubilees*, it is not presented as an exegetical text, and there is no admission that its authority is derivative from that of the first law. *Jubilees*, then, is angelic discourse, or even mediated divine discourse. Moses' authority here is not that of a founder, although he was

39. VanderKam, "Moses Trumping Moses."

40. VanderKam, "Moses Trumping Moses."

41. Martha Himmelfarb, *A Kingdom of Priests: Ancestry and Merit in Ancient Judaism* (Philadelphia: University of Pennsylvania Press, 2006) 54-55, writes: "Jubilees does not attempt to nudge the Torah out of its niche and replace it, but rather embraces the authority of the Torah even as it seeks to place itself alongside it." See also Martha Himmelfarb, "Torah, Testimony, and Heavenly Tablets: The Claim to Authority in the Book of Jubilees," in Benjamin G. Wright, ed., *A Multiform Heritage: Studies on Early Judaism and Christianity in Honor of Robert A. Kraft* (Atlanta: Scholars Press, 1999) 22-28.

42. Hindy Najman, *Seconding Sinai: The Development of Mosaic Discourse in Second Temple Judaism* (JSJSup 77; Leiden: Brill, 2003) 41-69.

43. See James C. VanderKam, "The Putative Author of the Book of *Jubilees*," *JSS* 26 (1981) 209-17; reprinted in James C. VanderKam, *From Revelation to Canon: Studies in the Hebrew Bible and Second Temple Literature* (JSJSup 62; Leiden: Brill, 2000) 439-47; also see his "The Angel of the Presence in the Book of *Jubilees*," *DSD* 7 (2000) 378-93.

often so viewed in the Hellenistic world. Ultimately, of course, all revelation comes from God, but *Jubilees* appeals to sources of authority that are higher than Moses in the chain of transmission: the angel and the heavenly tablets from which the revelation is derived.

Jubilees and Enoch

Precisely these sources of authority by which the Moses of *Jubilees* is able to "trump" the biblical Moses, per VanderKam's phrase, suggest a different "family resemblance" or a different generic prototype from that of rewritten scripture. The books of Enoch are also an important source for *Jubilees*. These books apparently have the status of "testimony," like *Jubilees* itself: Enoch also "wrote a testimony for himself and placed it upon the earth against all mankind and for their history" (*Jub.* 4:19). *Jubilees* draws extensively on Enochic lore, especially the story of the fallen Watchers in *1 Enoch* 6–11.[44] According to Genesis 5:22, Enoch walked with *elohim*, which was probably understood as "angels" in the Hellenistic period.[45] One of the revelations attributed to Enoch, the *Apocalypse of Weeks,* begins as follows: "The vision of heaven was shown to me, and from the words of the watchers and holy ones I have learned everything, and in the heavenly tablets I read everything and I understood" (*1 En.* 93:2).[46] Here, then, we have a prototype for *Jubilees* that is different from the Torah of Moses, from which so much of *Jubilees* is drawn.

Enoch supposedly lived long before Moses, and his revelations are prior to those of Moses. There has been extensive debate in recent years as to whether these traditions derive from a distinctively "Enochic Judaism" that was not based on the Torah.[47] At least it must be acknowledged that

44. Michael Segal, *The Book of Jubilees: Rewritten Bible, Redaction, Ideology and Theology* (JSJSup 117; Leiden: Brill, 2007) 103-43; John S. Bergsma, "The Relationship between *Jubilees* and the Early Enochic Books," in G. Boccaccini and G. Ibba, eds., *Enoch and the Mosaic Torah: The Evidence of Jubilees* (Grand Rapids: Eerdmans, 2009) 36-51; James C. VanderKam, "The Book of Enoch and the Qumran Scrolls," in Lim and Collins, eds., *The Oxford Handbook of the Dead Sea Scrolls*, 254-77.

45. James C. VanderKam, *Enoch and the Growth of an Apocalyptic Tradition* (CBQMS 16; Washington, DC: Catholic Biblical Association, 1984) 31.

46. George W. E. Nickelsburg and James C. VanderKam, trans., *1 Enoch: A New Translation* (Minneapolis: Fortress, 2004) 140.

47. See Gabriele Boccaccini and John J. Collins, eds., *The Early Enoch Literature* (JSJSup 121; Leiden: Brill, 2007).

Torah and covenant play no overt part in the earliest Enochic writings.[48] As George Nickelsburg has shown: "Although all the components of 'covenantal nomism' are present in this scheme, the word *covenant* rarely appears and Enoch takes the place of Moses as the mediator of revelation."[49] Gabriele Boccaccini has viewed the use of Enochic tradition in *Jubilees* as an attempt to merge two forms of Judaism.[50] Boccaccini's views on the alleged division between "Enochic" and "Zadokite" Judaism are not widely shared.[51] It is not necessary to view *Jubilees* as effecting reconciliation between two parties that were ideologically opposed. It is sufficient to view the use of Enoch in *Jubilees* in literary terms. The author of *Jubilees* adapted the Enochic writings for his purposes. The myth of the Watchers is transformed from a paradigm for the existence of evil in the world to a paradigm of sin and punishment.[52] More important for our present purpose is the fact that Enoch provided a model of revelation that could claim a form of divine authority distinct from the traditional Torah of Moses.

Jubilees as an Apocalypse

The early books of Enoch are prototypical apocalypses. Apocalypses are revelations of mysteries that go beyond the bounds of normal human knowledge.[53] The authority of the revelation is established in vari-

48. John J. Collins, "How Distinctive Was Enochic Judaism?" in Moses Bar-Asher and Emanuel Tov, eds., *Meghillot. Studies in the Dead Sea Scrolls V–VI: A Festschrift for Devorah Dimant* (Jerusalem: Bialik, 2007) 17-34.

49. George W. E. Nickelsburg, "Enochic Wisdom: An Alternative to the Mosaic Torah?" in J. Magness and S. Gitin, eds., *Hesed Ve-Emet: Studies in Honor of Ernest S. Frerichs* (BJS 320; Atlanta: Scholars Press, 1998) 129. See also Nickelsburg, "Enochic Wisdom and Its Relationship to the Mosaic Torah," in *The Early Enoch Literature*, 81–94; and Andreas Bedenbender, "The Place of the Torah in the Early Enoch Literature," in Boccaccini and Collins, eds., *The Early Enoch Literature*, 65-79.

50. Gabriele Boccaccini, "From a Movement of Dissent to a Distinct Form of Judaism: The Heavenly Tablets in Jubilees as the Foundation of a Competing Halakah," in Boccaccini and Ibba, eds., *Enoch and the Mosaic Torah*, 193-210. For Boccaccini's views on party divisions in Judaism in the second century BCE see his *Beyond the Essene Hypothesis: The Parting of the Ways between Qumran and Enochic Judaism* (Grand Rapids: Eerdmans, 1998).

51. See James C. VanderKam, "Mapping Second Temple Judaism," in Boccaccini and Collins, eds., *The Early Enoch Literature*, 1-20.

52. Segal, *The Book of Jubilees*, 143.

53. On the definition of an apocalypse see Collins, ed., *Apocalypse: The Morphology*

ous ways. The revelation is typically ascribed to a famous ancient figure, such as Enoch or Daniel, but the apocalypse does not rely only on human authority, however exalted. It pertains to the definition of the genre that the revelation is mediated by an otherworldly figure, typically an angel. It often takes the form of symbolic visions, interpreted by an angel. In other cases, the angel serves as tour guide. In yet others, the angel simply narrates the revelation. In the case of Enoch, there is also appeal to the heavenly tablets, which Enoch supposedly saw when he ascended to heaven. There is a certain redundancy, or overkill, in the ways in which revelation is authorized.[54]

Insofar as the manner of revelation is concerned, *Jubilees* is a classic apocalypse. Moses, rather than Enoch, is the pseudonymous recipient of the revelation, and he is associated with law rather than with astronomical mysteries. But formally the revelation is very similar. Should *Jubilees* then be classified as an apocalypse?

The problem is that the genre apocalypse, as commonly understood in the study of ancient Judaism and early Christianity, is defined not only by form but also by content. It discloses mysteries of the heavenly (or nether-) world and is concerned with eschatological reward and punishment. This content admits of a good deal of variation. Broadly speaking, we may distinguish two types of apocalypses, one that reviews the periods of history, often in the guise of prophecy, the other that describes otherworldly journeys. The eschatology may entail upheavals at the end of history and a public judgment, especially in the historical apocalypses, or it may focus on the judgment and abodes of the dead, especially in the otherworldly journeys. (The judgment of the dead is also important in the "public" eschatology of the historical apocalypses.) Apocalypses are not exclusively concerned with eschatology and may devote lengthy passages to historical reviews or cosmological descriptions, but they have an eschatological focus. Some scholars, to be sure, have argued that apocalypses should be defined on purely formal grounds, on the basis of the manner of revelation, and in that case the identification of *Jubilees* as an apocalypse would be

---

of a Genre; and John J. Collins, *The Apocalyptic Imagination* (2nd ed.; Grand Rapids: Eerdmans, 1998) 1-43.

54. It has been argued that the references to heavenly tablets in *Jubilees* are interpolations (so James L. Kugel, "On the Interpolations in the Book of Jubilees," *RevQ* 24 [2009] 215-72, building on the work of Segal, *The Book of Jubilees*), but it should be noted that angelic revelation and the heavenly tablets are juxtaposed in the Enochic *Apocalypse of Weeks*.

unproblematic.[55] But in prevailing scholarly usage, apocalypses are not only angelic revelations, but revelations with certain distinctive concerns.

An Ironic Apocalypse?

In a dissertation at the University of Notre Dame, directed by James VanderKam, Todd Hanneken has outlined well the anomalous character of *Jubilees* among the apocalypses.[56] With regard to the manner of revelation, he notes the absence of symbolic visions and consequently the lack of esotericism.[57] "Revelation," he concludes, "is not an angelic interpretation of cosmic mysteries to a bewildered recipient, followed by an esoteric chain of transmission."[58] The revelation is fully accessible to all Israel, not just to an elect group as in the Books of Enoch and Daniel.[59] While angels figure prominently in *Jubilees*, Hanneken denies that they do what they typically do in apocalypses: "particularly afflict, fight, judge, and restore in an eschatological context."[60] The role of demons, or evil spirits, is limited in *Jubilees* 10:7-14. Mastema is easily defeated. The dominant view of history in *Jubilees* is indebted to Deuteronomy more than to the apocalypses. Humans are the catalysts of evil. The hope for an ultimate change for the better in history is tied to human repentance, not to an apocalyptic timetable.[61] Hanneken concludes that *"Jubilees* imitates the apocalypses on the surface level of literary genre, but argues against the ideas typically conveyed thereby. . . . The basic tenets of the worldview are caricatured, inverted, and refuted."[62] In his view, the use of the genre apocalypse in *Jubilees* is ironic.

---

55. Jean Carmignac, "Qu'est-ce que l'Apocalyptique? Son emploi à Qumrân," *RevQ* 10 (1979) 3-33; Hartmut Stegemann, "Die Bedeutung der Qumranfunde für die Erforschung der Apokalyptik," in D. Hellholm, ed., *Apocalypticism in the Mediterranean World and the Near East* (Tübingen: Mohr Siebeck, 1983) 495-530.

56. Todd R. Hanneken, "*Jubilees* among the Apocalypses" (Ph.D. diss., University of Notre Dame, 2008).

57. This point is also noted by Armin Lange, "Divinatorische Träume und Apokalyptik im Jubiläenbuch," in Albani et al., eds., *Studies in the Book of Jubilees*, 25-38.

58. Hanneken, "*Jubilees* among the Apocalypses," 259.

59. Compare the argument of Himmelfarb (*A Kingdom of Priests*, 80-84) that *Jubilees* is not sectarian but addressed to all Israel.

60. Hanneken, "*Jubilees* among the Apocalypses," 309.

61. Hanneken, "*Jubilees* among the Apocalypses," 433.

62. Hanneken, "*Jubilees* among the Apocalypses," 461.

Hanneken does not engage in any theoretical study of irony, except to refer to the classical contrast between the gentle satire of Horace and the bitter caricatures of Juvenal.[63] Webster's dictionary defines irony as "a method of humorous or sarcastic expression in which the intended meaning of the words used is the direct opposite of their usual sense," or as "a combination of circumstances or a result that is the opposite of what might be expected or considered appropriate."[64] It would be difficult to think of a book more lacking in humor than *Jubilees*.[65] The content of *Jubilees* may be strikingly different from what we would expect in an apocalyptic revelation, but the difference hardly amounts to caricature. To say that *Jubilees* adapts and modifies elements of earlier apocalyptic writings does not necessarily mean that it argues against them or refutes them. After all, the writings of Enoch are acknowledged as "testimonies" in *Jubilees*. Hanneken's interpretation of *Jubilees* is in part a response to the thesis of Gabriele Boccaccini, cited above, that *Jubilees* attempts a reconciliation of the Enochic tradition with a covenantal based view of Judaism. He rightly notes that the reconciliation would be far too one-sided, since the covenantal theology that is conspicuously absent in Enoch predominates in *Jubilees*. Boccaccini's use of binary oppositions to characterize Judaism in this period is too simplistic, as VanderKam has shown;[66] Hanneken seems to fall into the same binary logic in positing an opposition between *Jubilees* and the apocalyptic tradition.

The use of apocalyptic tradition in *Jubilees* is especially evident in the opening chapter and again in chapter 23. At the beginning of *Jubilees*, the angel of the presence is told to "dictate to Moses (starting) from the beginning of the creation until the time when my temple is built among them throughout the ages of eternity. The Lord will appear in the sight of all, and all will know that I am the God of Israel, the father of all Jacob's children, and the king on Mt. Zion for the ages of eternity. Then Zion and Jerusalem will become holy" (1:27–28). Moreover, we are told that the tablets record the weeks of the *Jubilees*:

63. Hanneken, "*Jubilees* among the Apocalypses," 15. For a sampling of the theoretical discussion of irony see Carolyn J. Sharp, *Irony and Meaning in the Hebrew Bible* (Bloomington: Indiana University Press, 2009) 6-42.

64. *Webster's New World Dictionary of the American Language* (New York: World Publishing Company, 1962) 773.

65. *Pace* Hanneken, "*Jubilees* among the Apocalypses," 509, it is difficult to construe anything in the book as mischievous.

66. VanderKam, "Mapping Second Temple Judaism," 10-20.

from [the time of the creation until] the time of the new creation when the heavens, the earth, and all their creatures will be renewed like the powers of the sky and like all the creatures of the earth, until the time when the temple of the Lord will be created in Jerusalem on Mt. Zion. All the luminaries will be renewed for (the purposes of) healing, health, and blessing for all the elect ones of Israel and so that it may remain this way from that time throughout all the days of the earth. (1:29)

Hanneken argues that while "the description of the construction of the sanctuary and the indwelling of God sounds like an apocalyptic description of a future restoration, especially in the last verse," it "refers primarily to the sanctuary that was created in the very near future, relative to Moses, and the distant past, relative to the second century author."[67] But the temple in question cannot be identified with any temple that had been built before *Jubilees* was written, and must rather be seen in the context of speculation about a new Jerusalem, in the *Temple Scroll* and elsewhere in the Dead Sea Scrolls.[68] This passage establishes an eschatological horizon, which must be kept in mind in the remainder of the work. Eschatological transformation is not foregrounded in *Jubilees*, but it is affirmed.

The passage in *Jubilees* most often taken to be apocalyptic is 23:11-31, often called "the *Jubilees* apocalypse." It describes eschatological upheavals, marked by sinful behavior and general decline, including loss of longevity. The deeds of that generation will incur a mighty retribution. But then, "the children will begin to study the laws, to seek out the commands, and to return to the right way" (23:26), and life will be transformed and grow longer again. The righteous will drive out their enemies and will see all the punishments and curses that had been their lot falling on their enemies. In the end, "their bones will rest in the earth and their spirits will be very happy. They will know that the Lord is one who executes judgment" (23:31).

James Kugel has noted the affinities of this passage with Psalm 90, which also comments on the limited length of human life. The author's view of the decline in longevity in the biblical narratives, together with the sectarian politics of the second century BCE, shapes this passage "as

67. Hanneken, "*Jubilees* among the Apocalypses," 467.

68. Cf. 11Q19 (11QTemple) 29:9-10; 4Q174 (Florilegium) 1:3-7. See Michael O. Wise, "4QFlorilegium and the Temple of Adam," *RevQ* 15 (1991) 103-32. Also 11QNew Jerusalem, and Lorenzo DiTommaso, *The Dead Sea New Jerusalem Text: Contents and Contexts* (Tübingen: Mohr Siebeck, 2005).

much as any particular view of the future."[69] But most eschatological expectation is shaped by the past and present, so *Jubilees* 23 is not atypical of
apocalypses in that respect.

Hanneken notes, correctly, that there is no angelic agency in this passage and that no chronological framework is supplied for the eschatological sequence.[70] Sin and repentance are not predetermined. As throughout
Jubilees, the understanding of sin and punishment is Deuteronomistic. This
understanding of history contrasts with what we find in Daniel and *1 Enoch*
(with the exception of the prayer in Daniel 9).[71] Hanneken also argues that,
"whereas a historical apocalypse typically imagines a radical reversal and
graphic vindication and vengeance, *Jubilees* imagines a gradual fulfillment
of the original plan of creation."[72] But the contrast here may be overdrawn.
Jubilees 23:30, "then the Lord will heal his servants . . . they will see all their
punishments and curses on their enemies," may not be as graphic as the
Book of Revelation, but the net effect is much the same: radical reversal,
vindication, and vengeance. It is difficult to see here a "little spoof on a
historical apocalypse," as Hanneken would have it.[73]

It should also be said that Deuteronomistic theology is not inherently
incompatible with the apocalyptic genre, as can be seen from the (admittedly later) apocalypse of *2 Baruch*, which is just as focused on the Torah
as is *Jubilees*.[74] The essential elements of an apocalyptic worldview are the
way it frames human existence, by attention to the supernatural world on
the one hand and the expectation of eschatological judgment on the other.[75]
(Even the supernatural powers recede in the later apocalypses of *4 Ezra*
and *2 Baruch*.) These elements are present in *Jubilees*, but in an attenuated
form. *Jubilees* is not an anti-apocalyptic polemic, but apocalyptic beliefs
and expectations are not at the center of its concerns. In the perspective of
prototype theory, it may be regarded as a marginal member of the genre
apocalypse, on the "fuzzy edge" of the genre, without claiming that this is
its only generic affiliation.

69. James L. Kugel, "The *Jubilees* Apocalypse," *DSD* 1 (1994) 322-37 (here 337).

70. Hanneken, "*Jubilees* among the Apocalypses," 483.

71. See John J. Collins, *Daniel: A Commentary on the Book of Daniel* (Hermeneia;
Minneapolis: Fortress, 1993) 359-60.

72. Hanneken, "*Jubilees* among the Apocalypses," 497.

73. Hanneken, "*Jubilees* among the Apocalypses," 496.

74. See Collins, *The Apocalyptic Imagination*, 212-25.

75. John J. Collins, "Genre, Ideology and Social Movements in Jewish Apocalypticism,"
in *Seers, Sibyls and Sages in Hellenistic-Roman Judaism* (JSJSup 54; Leiden: Brill, 1997) 29.

Conclusion

In the end, *Jubilees* is a hybrid work. As most scholars have realized, it has a family resemblance to other rewritten scriptural narratives, from Chronicles to Pseudo-Philo's *Biblical Antiquities*. In this case, the narrative to be rewritten is the story of the revelation at Sinai. Unlike most rewritten scriptural narratives (Chronicles, *Biblical Antiquities*, the *Genesis Apocryphon*, or the *Antiquities* of Josephus), however, *Jubilees* claims the status of revelation. It does not dispute the authority of the "first Torah" that serves as the basis of its rewriting, but the authority it claims for itself is no less than that. There were not many ways in which such a claim could be formulated. The *Temple Scroll*, which has much in common with *Jubilees* but also differs from it in significant ways, presented itself as divine speech, the strongest possible claim an author could make.[76] *Jubilees* is only a little less audacious. It turned instead to the prototypical example of Enoch, who received his revelation from angels and the heavenly tablets. *Jubilees*, in effect, borrowed from the apocalypses key "authority conferring strategies," in Hindy Najman's phrase.

The influence of the apocalypses on *Jubilees* was not only formal. *Jubilees* also accepted key elements of the apocalyptic worldview: the agency of supernatural powers (the angel of the presence, Mastema, the demons, even if they are subject to control) and the expectation of eventual retribution and a new creation. These elements were modified and integrated with the Deuteronomistic view of history, which emphasized above all the observance of the Torah. This hardly amounted to a compromise, reconciling Enochic and covenantal Judaism; the end product is unambiguously covenantal. But neither was it an ironic subversion of the apocalyptic worldview. It was rather a strategic adaptation of it.

But if *Jubilees* does not fit neatly in a particular genre, this does not lessen the importance of generic analysis for understanding the book. One of the uses of genre analysis is to provide a foil against which the distinctive nature of an individual composition can be appreciated. There is, then, much to be gained from viewing *Jubilees* in the context both of rewritten narratives and of apocalypses, even it must be considered an exceptional and marginal member of both categories.

---

76. Lawrence H. Schiffman, "The Book of Jubilees and the Temple Scroll," in Boccaccini and Ibba, eds., *Enoch and the Mosaic Torah*, 99-115.

CHAPTER 7

The Sibyl and the Apocalypses:
Generic Relationships in Hellenistic Judaism and Early Christianity

The *Sibylline Oracles* constitute a distinct genre of literature in Hellenistic Judaism and early Christianity. They have been dubbed "the apocalyptic of Hellenistic Diaspora Judaism" by Philip Vielhauer, but it is now generally granted that they are not apocalypses.[1] The Sibyl's revelations are not presented as accounts of visions or of otherworldly journeys, but take the form of oracular speech. In this respect, they might be classified as prophecy rather than as apocalyptic. But it is certainly true that they differ from classical Hebrew prophecy in significant ways, and also that they have much in common with the apocalypses.[2]

Jane Lucy Lightfoot has recently argued that the *Sibylline Oracles*, especially book 3, can be illuminated by John Barton's study of the transformation of prophecy in the Second Temple period.[3] One feature of the age was the rise of pseudepigraphy, the attribution of revelatory (and other) writings to figures from the hoary past. This may have been a way of circumventing the belief that the age of prophecy had passed,

---

1. P. Vielhauer, "Apocalypses and Related Subjects," in E. Hennecke, ed., *New Testament Apocrypha* (rev. ed., ed. Wilhelm Schneemelcher; Louisville: Westminster John Knox, 1992) 2.560.

2. J. J. Collins, *The Apocalyptic Imagination* (rev. ed.; Grand Rapids: Eerdmans, 1998) 116-18. All references to Jewish and Christian Sibylline oracles in this essay are to J. J. Collins, "The Sibylline Oracles," in J. H. Charlesworth, ed., *The Old Testament Pseudepigrapha* (New York: Doubleday, 1983) 1.317-472.

3. J. L. Lightfoot, *The Sibylline Oracles, with Introduction, Translation, and Commentary on the First and Second Books* (Oxford: Oxford University Press, 2007) 60. Cf. J. Barton, *Oracles of God: Perceptions of Ancient Prophecy in Israel after the Exile* (Oxford: Oxford University Press, 1986).

but it also had implications for the nature of prophecy. It made possible long-range "predictions" that spanned the course of history from ancient times to the present of the real authors. Since these "predictions" were verifiably accurate, they enhanced the credibility of the things that remained to be fulfilled. Also notable were increased interest in the manner in which revelations were received, an expansion of the range of revealed things, and the inclusion of ethical instruction. In all of these matters, there are significant parallels between the *Sibylline Oracles* and the apocalypses.

The Pagan Sibyllina

While the oracles were indebted, quite decisively, to Jewish tradition, however, they were presented as the utterances of a figure from pagan antiquity, who had her own associations.[4] The earliest preserved reference, in Heraclitus, refers to her as "the Sibyl, with frenzied lips, uttering words mirthless, unembellished, yet reaches to a thousand years with her voice through the god."[5] Presumably, Heraclitus meant that the Sibyl's career endured for a thousand years. There is no evidence that she was ever credited with predicting the course of events over a thousand years. Only scattered examples of pagan Sibylline oracles have survived.[6] They are usually written in epic hexameters, like other Greek oracles. Most are brief predictions of war or natural disaster:

> As for the battle on Thermodon, may I be far away from it as an eagle in the clouds and the upper air, to behold it only. The vanquished weeps, but the victor is destroyed.

There was a famous collection of Sibylline oracles in Rome, which was consulted some fifty times between 496 and 100 BCE.[7] The accounts of

4. See the classic account of H. W. Parke, *Sibyls and Sibylline Prophecy in Classical Antiquity* (ed. B. McGing; London: Routledge, 1998).

5. Plutarch, *De Pythiae oraculis* 6 (397A).

6. I. Cervelli, "Questioni sibilline," *Studi Storici* 34.4 (1993) 895-1001, especially 895-934. See also Parke, *Sibyls and Sibylline Prophecy*, 1-22.

7. H. Cancik, "Libri Fatales. Römische Offenbarungliteratur und Geschichtstheologie," in D. Hellholm, ed., *Apocalypticism in the Mediterranean World and the Near East* (Tübingen: Mohr Siebeck, 1983) 549-76.

the consultations typically tell of some crisis or prodigy that provoked the consultation, and give some details of rituals prescribed by the oracles. Only one direct quotation from the Libri Sibyllini has been preserved, in the *Memorabilia* of Phlegon.[8] It tells of the birth of an androgyne, and prescribes a list of rituals and offerings to the gods. When the Roman collection was destroyed by fire in the first century BCE, replacement oracles were collected from Erythrae and elsewhere. The enduring impression of Sibylline oracles in the Roman world around the turn of the era can be inferred from Tibullus:

> [The Sibyls] told that a comet would be the evil sign of war, and how plenty of stones would rain down on the earth. They say that trumpets have been heard and weapons clashing in the sky, and that the groves have prophesied defeat.[9]

With the exception of the Roman Sibylline books, which appear to have prescribed rituals, the oracles seem to have been predictions of wars, political events, or natural disasters. While these predictions might be strung together, they do not appear to constitute developed literary units. In the words of Arnaldo Momigliano, "Pagan Sibylline oracles seldom went beyond individual events; they seldom pursued what we might call the great currents of world history."[10]

The pagan oracles, then, are quite different from the long oracles composed by Jews and Christians. Yet, as Momigliano also remarked, "even the most determined Jew, once he had accepted to play the part of a Sibyl, had also to accept some of the preoccupations and mental pre-suppositions of a pagan Sibylline text."[11] In fact, a long section in book 3 of the *Sibylline Oracles* (401-88) strings together a series of such predictions of destruction against various places, many of them in Asia Minor. This section of *Sibylline Oracles* 3 is often attributed to the Erythrean Sibyl. It would seem that these oracles were included precisely to lend an authentic Sibylline flavor to the Jewish oracles. Shorter strings of oracles of this type are also interspersed elsewhere in the Jewish Sib-

---

8. FGH 257F 37. L. Breglia Pulci Doria, *Oracoli Sibillini tra rituali e propaganda (Studi su Flegonte di Tralles)* (Naples: Liguori, 1983).

9. Tibullus 2.5.71-80. Parke, *Sibyls and Sibylline Prophecy*, 210.

10. A. Momigliano, "From the Pagan to the Christian Sibyl," *Nono contributo alla storia degli studi classici e del mondo antico* (Rome: Edizioni di Storia e Letteratura, 1992) 13.

11. Momigliano, "From the Pagan to the Christian Sibyl," 10.

yllines. It should be noted that these oracles were not entirely alien to the spirit of Hebrew prophecy. Jeremiah had famously said that a true prophet was one who prophesied "war, famine and pestilence," and the biblical prophetic books also include lengthy sections of oracles against nations other than Israel.

The Jewish Adaptation

The most conspicuous differences between the Jewish Sibylline oracles and their pagan counterparts are the lengthy exhortations put in the Sibyl's mouth and the framework of universal history.[12] The exhortations provide the vehicle for propaganda, which is arguably the *raison d'être* of the Jewish oracles. The framework of universal history, however, with the predictions of impending divine judgment, constitutes the main point of resemblance to the apocalypses, and it is on this aspect of the oracles that I wish to focus here.

Jane Lightfoot has argued that there is a special bond between the Sibyl and Enoch, and has even suggested that the earliest Jewish Sibyl-lists may have drawn on the books of Enoch, although she admits that the evidence is not conclusive.[13] Both Enoch and the Sibyl have more than mortal status. The Sibyl was granted as many years as the grains in a handful of sand, but without the gift of youth. Enoch, who had "walked with *elohim*" (God or angels) in his lifetime, was believed to have been taken up to heaven. Both are primordial figures, who are therefore in a position to "predict" events spanning the course of history. Both are associated, in different ways, with the Flood. It is therefore natural to ask whether the Sibyl's conception of universal history is not derived from the apocalypses of Enoch, and perhaps also that of Daniel. Lightfoot looks specifically to the *Apocalypse of Weeks* in *1 Enoch* 93:1-10 + 91:11-17, where the course of history is divided into ten "weeks," followed by "many weeks without number." Whether this Enochic text can be singled out as the source for the Sibylline conception of history, however, is open to question.

---

12. See my essay "The Jewish Transformation of Sibylline Oracles," in *Seers, Sibyls, and Sages in Hellenistic-Roman Judaism* (JSJSup 54; Leiden: Brill, 1997) 181-97; also published in I. Chirassi Colombo and T. Seppilli, eds., *Sibille e linguaggi oracolari* (Rome: Istituti Editoriali e Poligrafici Internazionali, for the University of Macerata, 1998) 369-87.

13. Lightfoot, *The Sibylline Oracles*, 70-77.

Universal History in the *Sibylline Oracles*

At this point it will be helpful to review the development of the Jewish Sibylline tradition, and specifically the development in the Sibylline treatment of history. Most scholars regard the core of *Sibylline Oracles* 3 as the oldest Jewish Sibylline oracles. By the core I mean *Sibylline Oracles* 3:97-349 and 489-829.[14] These oracles are dated to the mid-second century BCE by recurring references to the reign of the seventh king of Egypt of the line of the Greeks.[15] It is agreed that *Sibylline Oracles* 3:1-96 belong to the lost second book of the original collection, while verses 350-488 are a collection of oracles of diverse origin against various places. Some of this material dates to the Roman period.[16] It is the core oracles, in any case, that address the broader sweep of history in *Sibylline Oracles* 3.

The core material may be divided into five oracles: verses 93-161, 162-95, 196-294, 295-349, and 489-829.[17] The greatest sweep of universal history is found in verses 93-161, which begins with the tower of Babel and continues with a euhemeristic account of the Titans. It concludes with a list of kingdoms: "then as time pursued its cyclic course the kingdom of Egypt arose, then that of the Persians, Medes, and Ethiopians, and Assyrian Babylon, then that of the Macedonians, of Egypt again, then of Rome." The concluding reference to Rome might suggest a date after the battle of Actium in 31 BCE, but the passage dealing with the tower of Babel was paraphrased by Alexander Polyhistor in the mid-first century BCE. The sibyllist could have recognized Rome as a world power already in the sec-

14. The distinction of this core has been disputed in different ways by E. Gruen, *Heritage and Hellenism: The Reinvention of Jewish Tradition* (Berkeley: University of California Press, 1998) 271-83, and R. Buitenwerf, *Book III of the Sibylline Oracles and Its Social Setting* (SVTP 17; Leiden: Brill, 2003) 126-30. I have responded to their arguments in "The Third Sibyl Revisited," in my book *Jewish Cult and Hellenistic Culture* (JSJSup 100; Leiden: Brill, 2005) 82-98.

15. Collins, "The Third Sibyl Revisited," 87-94, against the argument of Gruen that the number seven is symbolic and "mystical," therefore without specific reference (Gruen, *Heritage and Hellenism*, 277). On the use of numerical symbolism in apocalyptic literature see A. Yarbro Collins, "Numerical Symbolism in Jewish and Early Christian Literature," in her *Cosmology and Eschatology in Jewish and Early Christian Apocalypticism* (JSJSup 50; Leiden: Brill, 1996) 57-89.

16. For full analysis see my book, *The Sibylline Oracles of Egyptian Judaism* (SBLDS 13; Missoula, MT: Society of Biblical Literature, 1974) 21-71.

17. I accept Buitenwerf's analysis of the units, except that I do not regard verses 350-488 as part of the original core. See Buitenwerf, *Book III of the Sibylline Oracles*, 137-300.

ond century BCE, but it is not certain that verses 93-161 constitute a literary unit. Either the passage on the tower or the list of kingdoms could have been composed separately. The passage on the tower is presumably based on Genesis. The account of the Titans is probably derived from Hesiod's *Theogony*, although it differs in details and in the euhemeristic interpretation. History between primeval times and the present is condensed into the list of kingdoms. This list is exceptional in several respects. The number of kingdoms, eight, does not fit any established schema, apocalyptic or other. While the concluding sequence (Macedonia, Egypt, Rome) is obviously historical, the sequence of Persians, Medes, Ethiopians, and "Assyrian Babylon" makes no historical sense and seems to be a rather random listing of the great powers known to the author. The only similarity to the apocalypses here lies in the idea that it was possible for the Sibyl to offer a synthetic view spanning all of history. The listing of world kingdoms is reminiscent of Daniel rather than of Enoch, but the idea that world kingship passed to various powers in succession was widely known in the Hellenistic world, beginning with Herodotus.

The oracle in *Sibylline Oracles* 3:162-95 also asks "how many kingdoms of men shall be raised up?" (v. 166). In this case "the house of Solomon" is listed first, followed by a random conglomeration of Phoenicians, Pamphylians, Persians, Phrygians, Carians, Mysians, and Lydians, of whom only the Persians could reasonably be said to have enjoyed world empire. Here again the picture clarifies in the Hellenistic period. First, a "great, diverse, race of Macedonia" will rule. Then (v. 175) "will be the beginning of another kingdom, white, and many-headed from the western sea." The reference is obviously to Rome, but not to the triumph of Octavian. Rather, Rome is said to "cut up everything . . . in many places, but especially in Macedonia" (v. 190). Macedonia was divided after the battle of Pydna in 168 BCE and was made a Roman province in 147 BCE. This is also the period suggested by the reference to "the seventh reign, when a king of Egypt, who will be of the Greeks by race, will rule" in verse 193. After that, "the people of the great God will again be strong" (v. 194).

Here again there is a general similarity to the apocalypses insofar as the Sibyl claims to predict the whole course of history. Again, the analogy is with Daniel rather than Enoch, in view of the focus on world kingdoms. But interest in world kingdoms was not peculiar to Daniel or Jewish apocalypticism. The Sibyl seems to be trying to integrate Judean history (beginning with Solomon, and ending with the restoration of the people of God) into a sequence of world kingdoms. The conclusion envisioned to this sequence is the restoration of "the people of God," perhaps to its Solomonic glory. There is no suggestion of an apocalyptic finale, with cosmic judgment or resurrection of the dead.

Sibylline Oracles 3:196-294 addresses the question, "what first, what next, what will be the final evil on all men?" (v. 197). The first evils, we are told, will befall the Titans. Then assorted evils will befall Greeks, Phrygians, Persians, Assyrians, Egyptians, Libyans, Ethiopians, Carians, and Pamphylians. The main concern of this oracle, however, is with "the pious men who live around the great temple of Solomon." The Sibyl digresses to eulogize this people and summarize the story of the Exodus. The oracle goes on to describe the Exodus, and the destruction of the temple. Eventually "the heavenly God will send a king" (v. 286). Most probably, Cyrus of Persia is meant. This oracle ends with the restoration of the temple "as it was before." Apart from the initial reference to the Titans, this oracle is a summary of biblical history down to the restoration after the Babylonian exile.

Sibylline Oracles 3:295-349 is part of a longer oracle that goes up to verse 488 and that consists of oracles against various places. Verses 350-80 are an oracle against Rome from the first century BCE. Verses 381-488 seem to be generic Sibylline oracles, and are sometimes attributed to the Erythrean Sibyl. Regardless of how we define the extent of this oracle, however, it contains no overview of universal history.

The last section of the book, on Buitenwerf's analysis, runs from verse 489 to verse 829. Buitenwerf distinguishes four admonitions within it, each of which begins with direct address: 545-623, 624-731, 732-61, and 762-808.[18] (Verses 809-29 constitute a conclusion by the Sibyl in which she identifies herself as the daughter-in-law of Noah.) None of these oracles provides an overview of universal history such as we found in the earlier sections of the book, but they include several passages that are eschatological in character.

Verses 545-623 begin with oracles of destruction against various places, followed by an appeal to the Greeks to worship the true God by sending offerings to his temple, and a eulogy of the Jews (vv. 573-600). They conclude with a prophecy of divine judgment on humanity as punishment for idolatry. This will happen "whenever the young seventh king of Egypt rules his own land, numbered from the dynasty of the Greeks" (vv. 608-9), and will involve an invasion of Egypt by a king from Asia. Then:

18. Buitenwerf, *Book III of the Sibylline Oracles,* 236-300.

God will give great joy to men
for earth and trees and countless flocks of sheep
will give to men the true fruit
of wine, sweet honey and white milk
and corn, which is best of all for mortals. (619-23)

Sibylline Oracles 3:624-731 begins with an appeal to the Greeks to sacrifice to the true God. Then it describes a period of great upheaval ("king will lay hold of king and take away territory"). Then "God will send a king from the sun, who will stop the entire earth from evil war" (vv. 652-53). The identity of this figure need not concern us here. I have argued elsewhere that the reference is to a Ptolemaic king rather than to a Judean messiah.[19] But the cessation of war is not final. Verses 657-68 describe an attack by the kings of the earth on Jerusalem and its temple. They will be destroyed by divine judgment. But then "the sons of the great God will all live peacefully around the temple, rejoicing in these things which the creator, just judge and sole ruler, will give" (vv. 702-4).

Verses 732-61 again begin with an appeal to the Greeks, and then proceed to the divine judgment, followed by the transformation of the earth and universal peace.

Finally, in verses 762-808 we are told that God will raise up a kingdom for all ages. The "maiden" Jerusalem is told to rejoice, for

... he will dwell in you. You will have immortal light.
Wolves and lambs will eat grass together in the mountains.
Leopards will feed together with kids.
Roving bears will spend the night with calves.
The flesh-eating lion will eat husks at the manger
like an ox, and mere infant children will lead them
with ropes. For he will make the beasts on earth harmless.
Serpents and asps will sleep with babies
and will not harm them, for the hand of God will be upon them.
  (*Sib. Or.* 3:785-95)

The oracle concludes with the signs of the end and an admonition to sacrifice to the true God.

19. See my essay, "The Sibyl and the Potter: Political Propaganda in Ptolemaic Egypt," in *Seers, Sibyls, and Sages*, 199-210.

There are parallels to the eschatological scenario found in these oracles in some apocalyptic texts, such as *4 Ezra*, from the late first century CE, which also has elaborate signs of the end and an assault by the nations on Mount Zion. The motif of the attack on Mount Zion has old biblical roots, however, as can be seen in Psalms 2 and 48. The final outcome of the eschatological conflict in *Sibylline Oracles* 3:785-95 is clearly modeled on Isaiah 11.

Conspicuously absent here is any role for angelic powers or any mention of resurrection or judgment after death, the distinctive trademarks of apocalyptic literature in the Books of Enoch and Daniel. In the Sibyl's retelling of primeval history, there is no place for the descent of the "sons of God" or Watchers before the Flood, although they could have been related to the Titans, and are in fact accommodated in the later Sibylline books 1 and 2 (*Sib. Or.* 1:87-104). So despite the common use of pseudepigraphy and long-term prophecy, *Sibylline Oracles* 3 does not exhibit an apocalyptic worldview. There is no reason to suppose that the Sibyl was influenced by the books of *Enoch*. There is one allusion to the Book of Daniel in *Sibylline Oracles* 3:396-400, which speaks of ten horns and a horn growing on the side (cf. Dan. 7:7-8). The reference is to the descendants of Alexander, most probably the Syrian kings in the second century BCE. The provenance of this oracle is uncertain. It at least raises the possibility that the Jewish sibyllist of the second century BCE knew the Book of Daniel. But the Sibyl did not adopt either Daniel's view of the sequence of world kingdoms or his view of the end of history and the resurrection of the dead.

World Kingdoms

It is true, however, that one of the major concerns of *Sibylline Oracles* 3 is paralleled in the Book of Daniel. This is the succession of world kingdoms. But this motif, too, had deeper roots. The earliest account of a succession of world empires is found in Herodotus: "the Assyrians had held the empire of upper Asia for the space of 520 years, when the Medes set the example of revolt from their authority." Later, "the Medes were brought under the rule of the Persians."[20] Herodotus claimed to be following "Persian authorities," and the inclusion of the Medes would seem to reflect a Persian perspective. Ctesias, who wrote in the early fourth century BCE and had

---

20. Herodotus, 1.95, 1.130.

been court physician to Artaxerxes II, has the same sequence.[21] According to Ctesias, Assyria had held a true world empire, from India to Egypt, and it was taken over first by Media and then by Persia. The sequence Assyria-Media is attested in the Jewish Book of Tobit (14:4) where there is no apparent Hellenistic influence.[22] The sequence of Assyrians, Medes, and Persians also appears in *T. Naphtali* 5:8, in a list where the last people mentioned are the Syrians. It has been suggested that the "three-kingdom" sequence of Assyria, Media, and Persia is the official Achaemenid view of history, intended to establish the legitimacy of Persia as the heir to the earlier empires of the Near East.[23] It must be admitted, however, that this motif is never attested in Persian inscriptions, and so its role as Persian ideology remains hypothetical.[24]

In the Hellenistic and Roman periods, the sequence of kingdoms is extended. Most probably, the inclusion of the Greek empire originated in the Seleucid kingdom.[25] Eventually, the sequence was extended to include Rome. A fragment of one Aemilius Sura, preserved in Velleius Paterculus, who wrote about the turn of the era, reads:

> The Assyrians were the first of all races to hold power, then the Medes, after them the Persians, and then the Macedonians. Then when the two kings, Philip and Antiochus, of Macedonian origin, had been completely conquered, soon after the overthrow of Carthage, the supreme command passed to the Roman people.[26]

---

21. According to Diodorus Siculus, 2.1-34.

22. J. C. H. Lebram, "Die Weltreiche in der jüdischen Apokalyptik: Bemerkungen zu Tob. 14:4–7," *ZAW* 76 (1964) 328-31.

23. R. G. Kratz, *Translatio Imperii: Untersuchungen zu den aramäischen Daniel-erzählungen und ihrem theologiegeschichtlichen Umfeld* (Göttingen: Vandenhoeck & Ruprecht, 1991) 198-212; K. Koch, *Europa, Rom und der Kaiser vor dem Hintergrund von zwei Jahrtausenden Rezeption des Buches Daniel* (Göttingen: Vandenhoeck & Ruprecht, 1997) 13.

24. J. Wiesehöfer, "Daniel, Herodot und 'Darius der Meder'. Auch ein Beitrag zur Idee der Abfolge von Weltreichen," in R. Rolliger, ed., *Von Sumer bis Homer. Festschrift für Manfred Schretter zum 60. Geburtstag* (AOAT 325; Münster: Ugarit-Verlag, 2005) 647-53.

25. J. Wiesehöfer, "Vom 'oberen Asien' zur gesamten bewohnten Welt.' Die hellenistische-römische Weltreiche-Theorie," in M. Delgado, K. Koch, and E. Marsch, eds., *Europa, Tausendjähriges Reich und Neue Welt. Zwei Jahrtausende Geschichte und Utopie in der Rezeption des Danielbuches* (Freiburg Schweiz: Universitätsverlag, 2003) 66-83.

26. J. W. Swain, "The Theory of the Four Monarchies: Opposition History under the Roman Empire," *CP* 35 (1940) 2.

The same sequence, with Rome as the fifth empire, is found in Polybius (38.22) from the late second century BCE; Dionysius of Halicarnassus (1.2.2-4), about 10 BCE; Tacitus (*Hist.* 5.8-9), about 100 CE; and Appian (Preface, 9) about 140 CE. The Book of Daniel evidently adapted the pre-Roman sequence by substituting Babylon for Assyria, in light of the impact of Babylon on Jewish history.[27] The fact that Daniel makes a place for the Medes, who had never conquered Israel or Judah, shows its indebtedness to the traditional schema. It should be noted that the sequence of Assyria, Babylonia, Persia, Macedonia is found in the Babylonian Dynastic Prophecy, which, like the Sibyl and the apocalypses, is a long-term prophecy of the course of history, and which has been construed as anti-Macedonian.[28] The Babylonian text, however, does not thematize the succession of kingdoms in the same way as the Greek and Roman texts.

Sibylline Oracles 3 does not attest the schema of four kingdoms, followed by a definitive fifth one, as we might have expected if it were influenced by the Book of Daniel. It does, however, speak of a succession of kingdoms, and it includes a Media kingdom in some lists. I would suggest that the Sibyl does not derive this interest in the succession of kingdoms from Jewish apocalyptic literature, but from Greek historiography. It should be noted that the oracles that address the succession of kingdoms in *Sibylline Oracles* 3 do not have eschatological conclusions. The succession of kingdoms is given a more apocalyptic cast in *Sibylline Oracles* 4 and *Sibylline Oracles* 1-2, but this does not seem to be the case in the earliest Jewish Sibylline oracles.

Sibylline Oracle 4

The *Fourth Sibylline Oracle* includes an extensive "prophecy" of the sequence of world kingdoms. First, the Assyrians will rule for six generations, beginning from the time of the Flood. Then the Medes will have two

27. It is disputed whether there was already an anti-Hellenistic use of the sequence, predicting the overthrow of the fourth kingdom, before Daniel. The anti-Hellenistic use was hypothesized by Swain, "The Theory of the Four Monarchies," and popularized by S. K. Eddy, *The King Is Dead: Studies in Near Eastern Resistance to Hellenism* (Lincoln: University of Nebraska, 1961) 19-20. Wiesehöfer, "Vom 'oberen Asien,'" 68-69, is dismissive of this idea, on the grounds that there is little evidence of anti-Hellenistic resistance outside of Judea.

28. A. K. Grayson, *Babylonian Historical-Literary Texts* (Toronto: University of Toronto Press, 1975) 24-37.

generations, the Persians one. When "the race of men comes to the tenth generation" the kingdom will pass to the Macedonians. But this again will be followed by Roman rule, and Rome too will be subject to the wrath of God, "because they will destroy the blameless tribe of the pious" (v. 136). Finally, the Sibyl warns that if humanity does not change its ways, and practice washing "in perennial rivers" as a sign of repentance, God will destroy the whole world by fire. The conflagration, however, will be followed by resurrection and judgment. The resurrection has a physical character, involving the bones of the dead. Sinners will be condemned to Tartarus, but the righteous "will live on earth again" (v. 188).

The *Fourth Sibylline Oracle*, as we have it, dates to the time after the destruction of Jerusalem. It mentions the eruption of Mount Vesuvius (vv. 130-32), which it takes to be a sign that the divine judgment is imminent. It has been argued, however, that the prophecy of the course of history, divided into four kingdoms and ten generations, is an older oracle from the early Hellenistic period.[29] In Daniel, the fourth numbered kingdom is followed by the kingdom of God. The tenth generation normally marks the end of history in Sibylline prophecy.[30] In *Sibylline Oracles* 4, the rule of Rome is not integrated into the numerical sequence, and neither is it a definitive, eschatological kingdom. The suspicion arises that it has been inserted here to update an older oracle. It is possible that the Jewish sibyllist was familiar with a form of the schema that had Rome as the definitive, fifth kingdom, but subverted that schema by prophesying that it, too, would be subject to divine judgment. It is unusual, however, to have history extended beyond the tenth generation, and so it is likely that the Sibyl is updating an older, pre-Roman oracle. Little can be said, however, about the provenance of that older oracle.

Even if we do not posit an older oracle from the Hellenistic period, however, *Sibylline Oracles* 4 is quite likely to be the oldest attestation of the ten-generation schema in the Jewish Sibylline tradition. The motif was certainly not original here. Jane Lightfoot looks to the Jewish apocalyptic tradition for a model.[31] It is clear that the Sibyl did not derive the four-kingdom schema from Daniel, since Assyria rather than Babylon is cast as the first kingdom. Lightfoot's concern, however, is primarily with the

29. D. Flusser, "The Four Empires in the Fourth Sibyl and in the *Book of Daniel*," *Israel Oriental Studies* 2 (1972) 148-75 (152); J. J. Collins, "The Place of the Fourth Sibyl in the Development of the Jewish Sibyllina," *JJS* 25 (1974) 365-80.

30. Compare *Sib. Or.* 2.15; 8.199.

31. Lightfoot, *The Sibylline Oracles*, 111-13.

schema of ten generations. She looks for a model to the Enochic *Apocalypse of Weeks* (*1 En.* 93:1-10 + 91:12-17), where history is divided into ten "weeks," followed by "many weeks without number." We may note that in the Hebrew *Melchizedek Scroll* from Qumran, the Day of Expiation is at the end of the tenth jubilee (11QMelch 2:7). The *Melchizedek Scroll* is certainly influenced by the jubilee theology of Leviticus 25-26, and also by the reinterpretation of Jeremiah's prophecy as 70 weeks of years in Daniel 9. None of these texts equates the ten generations with kingdoms. It should be noted that the eschatological scenario envisioned by the Sibyl (a conflagration, followed by resurrection) is quite different from what we find in the *Apocalypse of Weeks*.

Other possible backgrounds for the motif of ten generations have been proposed. Most intriguing here is the reference to the "*ultima aetas*" of the "Cumea" (presumably the Cumean Sibyl) in Virgil's *Fourth Eclogue*. A commentary on the *Fourth Eclogue* by Servius, a pagan grammarian, about 400 CE, claims that the Cumean Sibyl divided the *saecula* according to metals and said who would rule over each.[32] The last *saeculum* would be the tenth, and would be ruled by the Sun or Apollo. No such Sibylline oracle is known, although it is often supposed that Virgil must have known one.[33] It seems, at least, that speculation about an "*ultima aetas*" could be credibly associated with the Sibyl in Virgil's time, although this did not necessarily entail a tenfold division of history, as Servius assumed. It is possible, but not demonstrable, that this association was derived from Jewish Sibylline texts. The division of history into *saecula* had a native Italian background in Etruscan tradition.[34] Virgil may have cited the Sibyl as the authority on all things pertaining to the future.[35] Virgil says nothing

32. G. Thilo, ed., *Servii Grammatici qui feruntur in Vergilii Bucolica et Georgica Commentarii* (Leipzig: Teubner, 1887) 44-45; Flusser, "The Four Empires," 163.

33. G. Jachmann, "Die Vierte Ekloge Vergils," *Annali della Scuola Normale Superiore di Pisa* 21 (1953) 13-62; A. Kurfess, "Vergils Vierte Ekloge und die *Oracula Sibyllina*," *Historisches Jahrbuch der Görres Gesellschaft* 73 (1956) 121-22; R. G. M. Nisbet, "Virgil's Fourth Eclogue: Easterners and Westerners," *Bulletin of the Institute for Classical Studies* 25 (1978) 59-78; Parke, *Sibyls and Sibylline Oracles*, 146-47. Parke attributes the absence of such an oracle from our collection to "the fluidity of the Sibylline tradition."

34. H. Cancik, "Libri Fatales. Römische Offenbarungsliteratur," 557-58; B. Gladigow, "*Aetas, aevum und saeclorum ordo*: Zur Struktur zeitlicher Deutungssysteme," in D. Hellholm, ed., *Apocalypticism in the Mediterranean World and the Near East* (Tübingen: Mohr Siebeck, 1983) 262-65. A haruspex allegedly took the comets that appeared after Caesar's death as a sign of the end of the ninth saeculum and the beginning of the tenth.

35. See further Collins, "The Jewish Transformation of Sibylline Oracles," 195-96.

about a conflagration or resurrection. His *ultima aetas* is rather a return of the golden age.

David Flusser has argued that the tenfold division of history derives from the Persian millennium.[36] There is a noteworthy parallel in the *Bahman Yasht*, or *Zand-i Vohuman Yasn*. Zarathustra was shown a vision of a tree with four branches, one of gold, one of silver, one of steel, and one of mixed iron. The branches correspond to reigns. The fourth is "the evil sovereignty of the *divs* with disheveled hair . . . when thy tenth century will be at an end, O Zarathustra."[37] The *Bahman Yasht* is a Pahlavi text, and relatively late, and some of the reigns are assigned to Sassanian kings. The text as we have it is no earlier than the sixth century CE. Many scholars, however, have speculated that this view of history was found already in the lost *Yasht* of the *Avesta* on which this is a commentary.[38] The combination of four kingdoms and the tenth generation is arguably the closest parallel we have to the *Fourth Sibylline* view of universal history. The correspondence is not exact; the Sibyl does not divide the ages according to metals, although, as we have seen, Servius claimed that such a Sibylline oracle existed. We do not know exactly in what form these traditions were available in the first century of the Common Era. The Roman antiquarian Varro spoke of a Persian Sibyl, "of whom Nicanor spoke, who wrote of the deeds of Alexander of Macedon."[39] There is no other record, however, of Sibylline oracles of Persian provenance, and if we assume that Sibylline oracles were always written in Greek hexameters, it is unlikely that any existed.[40] The *Oracle of Hystaspes*, which is known primarily from Lactantius but also from other authors, including Justin and Clement of Alexandria, provides some evidence for the currency of Persian apocalyptic ideas in

---

36. Flusser, "The Four Empires," 162-74.

37. B. T. Anklesaria, *Zand-i Vohuman Yasn* (Bombay: Camay Oriental Institute, 1967) 101. The motif of four periods associated with metals is also found in *Denkard* IX, 8.

38. See especially A. Hultgård, "*Bahman Yasht:* A Persian Apocalypse," in J. J. Collins and J. H. Charlesworth, eds., *Mysteries and Revelations: Apocalyptic Studies since the Uppsala Colloquium* (JSPSup 9; Sheffield: Sheffield Academic Press, 1991) 114-34; "Myth et Histoire dans l'Iran Ancien. Etude de quelques thèmes dans le Bahman Yašt," in G. Widengren, A. Hultgård, and M. Philonenko, eds., *Apocalyptique iranienne et dualisme qoumrânien* (Paris: Maisonneuve, 1995) 63-162 (107).

39. Lactantius, *Divinae Institutiones* 1.6.8.

40. *Pace* the maximalist views of M. Boyce, "The Poems of the Persian Sibyl and the Zand I Vahman Yasht," in C. H. De Fouchécour and P. Gignoux, eds., *Études irano-aryennes offertes à Gilbert Lazard* (Cahiers de Studia Iranica 7; Paris: Association pour l'Avancement des Études Iraniennes, 1989) 59-77.

the Hellenistic-Roman world.[41] According to Aristocritus, Hystaspes said that "the fulfillment would take place after the completion of six thousand years," but this formulation seems to be indebted to biblical, sabbatical, ideas.[42] We cannot point to a specific Persian text that could have served as source for the Sibyl, but Persian traditions and motifs were certainly known in the Greco-Roman world. It is apparent that the *Apocalypse of Weeks* was neither the only nor the closest parallel to the formulation that we find in *Sibylline Oracles* 4. It is noteworthy that the motifs of conflagration and resurrection with which the oracle ends also have Persian parallels, although they are not integrated into Zarathustra's vision in the *Bahman Yasht*.[43]

Sibylline Oracles 4 also differs from the apocalypses in one notable respect. In the apocalypses, the coming judgment is inevitable. People may save themselves by repentance, but they cannot forestall the judgment. In *Sibylline Oracles* 4, however, the judgment is conditional and may yet be averted.

Sibylline Oracles 1–2

The most elaborate account of universal history, divided into ten generations, is found in *Sibylline Oracles* 1–2, which originally were one oracle. The Sibyl begins by looking back at creation. The Flood marks the end of the fifth generation. The Sibyl, as Noah's daughter-in-law, is located in the sixth. Noah is cast as a preacher of repentance. He is not as explicit as *Sibylline Oracles* 4 that the disaster can be avoided by repentance, but that seems to be implied. Unfortunately, the original sequence of generations has been interrupted after the seventh generation by an insertion dealing with the

41. J. R. Hinnells, "The Zoroastrian Doctrine of Salvation in the Roman World: A Study of the Oracle of Hystaspes," in E. J. Sharpe and J. R. Hinnells, eds., *Man and His Salvation: Studies in Memory of S. G. F. Brandon* (Manchester: Manchester University Press, 1973) 125-248.

42. Aristocritus, *Theosophy*, cited by Hinnells, "The Zoroastrian Doctrine," 128.

43. Belief in a coming conflagration is explicitly attributed to Hystaspes by Justin, *Apology* 1.20.1. The classic passage is in *Bundahishn* 30.19ff. For resurrection: *Bundahishn* 34. See A. Hultgård, "Persian Apocalypticism," in J. J. Collins, ed., *Encyclopedia of Apocalypticism: The Origins of Apocalypticism in Judaism and Christianity* (New York: Continuum, 1998) 1.56-60. Persian belief in the resurrection of the dead is attested already about 300 BCE by Theopompus in Diogenes Laertius, "Proem" 9.

incarnation and the career of Christ, in 1:324-400. The eighth and ninth generations are lost, but we are thrust into the tenth generation in 2:15.

The eschatology of *Sibylline Oracles* 2 goes through several phases. First, "the faithful chosen Hebrews will rule over exceedingly mighty men, having subjected them as of old, since power will never fail" (2:174-76). This passage is elaborated in decidedly Christian terms, by reference to the parable of the watchful servant. Then there is a passage dealing with the return of Elijah, which, again, is elaborated with allusions to the New Testament ("Alas for as many as are found bearing in the womb on that day . . ."). Then there is a passage (vv. 196-213) describing the destruction of the world by a river of fire. Then the archangels lead all the souls of men to judgment. The resurrection of the dead follows, described in physical terms (bones fastened with all kinds of joinings). The righteous pass safely through the river of fire, but the wicked are condemned to Gehenna. The righteous will live forever on a transformed earth, and will be able to save people from Hell by their intercession. It is well known that *Sibylline Oracles* 2 is closely related to the *Apocalypse of Peter*. There too the resurrection is described in very physical terms (v. 4), and "cataracts of fire are let loose" (v. 5) and the whole world is dissolved in conflagration. The archangels bring the sinners to judgment, and the fiery character of Hell is emphasized.

Lightfoot, following Dieterich, has observed that the account of the last judgment is disproportionately long and has a different source from the prophecy of history.[44] The interest in the punishment of the damned is typical of tour apocalypses rather than of historical ones.[45] Lightfoot has argued against the usual attempts to distinguish an underlying Jewish oracle in the eschatological section, and she contends that the entire oracle from 2:196 on is a consistent adaptation of the *Apocalypse of Peter*.[46] She entertains the possibility that all of books 1 and 2 may have been composed by a Christian, living in the second century CE or later: "He assembled it all in imitation of the structure of the Apocalypse of Weeks, but wad-

---

44. Lightfoot, *The Sibylline Oracles*, 129. Cf. A. Dieterich, *Nekyia: Beiträge zur Erklärung der neuentdeckten Petrusapokalypse* (Leipzig: Teubner, 1893) 189 n. 1.

45. See J. J. Collins, ed., *Apocalypse: The Morphology of a Genre* (*Semeia* 14; Chico, CA: Scholars Press, 1979); M. Himmelfarb, *Tours of Hell: An Apocalyptic Form in Jewish and Christian Literature* (Philadelphia: University of Pennsylvania Press, 1983).

46. The priority of the *Apocalypse of Peter* is widely but not universally granted. For a dissenting opinion see T. Adamik, "The Description of Paradise," in J. N. Bremmer and I. Czachesz, eds., *The Apocalypse of Peter* (Leuven: Peters, 2003) 78-90, especially 86.

ded with all sort of other material, Enochic, Petrine, Sibylline."[47] But the structure of *Sibylline Oracles* 1–2 does not in fact correspond to that of the *Apocalypse of Weeks*. It is true that the *Apocalypse* speaks of the Flood as "the first consummation," but it locates it in the second week, not the fifth. History is not divided symmetrically as it is in the Sibyl. Moreover, even Lightfoot recognizes that this hypothesis "does not explain the massive jolt to the structure at 1.323, between the Titans of the seventh generation and the coming of Christ,"[48] and admits that there is no evading the fact that the oracle is composite.[49] An older oracle that divided history into ten generations has been disrupted by an explicitly Christian passage, and the eschatology has been adapted to reflect the kind of interest in the afterlife that is more usually associated with the tour apocalypses.

There can be little doubt that the prophecy of universal history already had an eschatological ending. In light of the parallel in *Sibylline Oracles* 4, it is reasonable to assume that this ending included a conflagration, followed by resurrection and everlasting beatitude on earth. This scenario is made more elaborate in *Sibylline Oracles* 2, but the basic structure persists. There is reason to suspect that this structure was ultimately of Persian origin, or shaped by Persian influence, especially in view of the prominence of the river of fire, through which the righteous pass unharmed.[50] It is usually assumed that the older oracle was Jewish. Lightfoot has challenged this view, and in view of the thorough reworking of the end of the work, the origin of the older oracle remains uncertain. It should be noted, however, that the theme of universal history is much more prominent in Jewish than in Christian eschatological texts. The eschatological rule of the Hebrews in *Sibylline Oracles* 2:174-76 also suggests Jewish origins, although it has clearly been Christianized in the present form of the text. The older, presumably Jewish, redaction was dated to a time before 70 CE by Kurfess, on the grounds that it did not refer to the destruction of Jerusalem.[51] In view of the massive disruption of the second half of the oracle, no great confidence can be placed in this argument. But even the Christian redaction may be as early as the second century CE, in light of the parallels with the *Apocalypse of Peter;* so a date in the first century CE is not unreasonable for the Jewish stratum.

47. Lightfoot, *The Sibylline Oracles*, 149.
48. Lightfoot, *The Sibylline Oracles*, 149.
49. Lightfoot, *The Sibylline Oracles*, 150.
50. *Sibylline Oracles* 2:252; cf. *Bundahishn* 30:19.
51. A. Kurfess, "Oracula Sibylina I/II," *ZNW* 40 (1941) 151-65.

Conclusion

Despite their common features, the *Sibylline Oracles* were not modeled on the apocalypses. The oldest datable Jewish oracles, in *Sibylline Oracles* 3, do not embrace the distinctively apocalyptic eschatology that had already gained currency in the Books of Enoch and Daniel. They do not look for the destruction of this world or for the resurrection of the dead. Neither do they divide history into periods in a systematic way. All of these features appear somewhat later in *Sibylline Oracles* 4 and *Sibylline Oracles* 1–2, but even these oracles do not betray the influence of Enoch and Daniel on their formulation of the periods of history. The four kingdoms of *Sibylline Oracles* 4 differ from those of Daniel, by retaining Assyria as the first kingdom. The motif of succeeding generations is indebted to Hesiod more than to Enoch or Daniel. Neither Enoch nor Daniel envisioned a conflagration at the end of history, and neither emphasized the physical nature of the resurrection in the manner we find in the Sibyls.

This is not to deny that the later *Sibylline Oracles* were influenced by apocalyptic tradition, broadly speaking. In the second century BCE, belief in resurrection was a novelty in Jewish circles. By the first century CE, it was relatively commonplace. It is not necessary to suppose that the author of a given Sibylline oracle borrowed the idea from a specific source. The idea was broadly current, and individual authors were free to formulate it in different ways.

It is significant that the *Oracles* were written in Greek, while the earlier apocalypses were all in Hebrew or Aramaic. (Apocalypses written in Greek, such as 3 *Baruch* and the Revelation to John, begin to appear toward the end of the first century CE.) The authors of the *Oracles* were familiar with a wide range of Hellenistic sources, including Hesiod, and political theories about the succession of kingdoms. They were also familiar, of course, with the biblical tradition, and *Sibylline Oracles* 1:87-103 clearly reflects the Enochic *Book of the Watchers,* but their sources were eclectic. It seems likely that the authors of *Sibylline Oracles* 4 and *Sibylline Oracles* 1–2 were familiar with the Persian idea of a millennium, followed by a conflagration and resurrection, even though it is unlikely that they understood the Persian context of these motifs. Rather, it was a matter of finding ideas that bore some resemblance to native Jewish beliefs, but also had currency in the Hellenistic world, and so could be imputed with some credibility to the pagan prophetess.

Finally, we should not underestimate the creativity of either the apocalyptic or the Sibylline writers. To be sure, they cobbled together their compositions from all sorts of traditions, but their works had their own distinctive character and were not simply reproductions of sources. The prophecies of universal history that we find in books 4 and 1–2 of the *Sibylline Oracles* are more fully developed than anything we find in the Jewish apocalypses, or, indeed, in the putative Greco-Roman and Persian sources on which their authors may have drawn.

CHAPTER 8

Gabriel and David:
Some Reflections on an Enigmatic Text

Since its publication in 2007, the *Gabriel Revelation* has attracted a good deal of attention in the media.[1] "Ancient Tablet Ignites Debate on Messiah and Resurrection," announced the *New York Times* on July 6, 2008. On the following day, the *International Herald Tribune* asked, "Is 3-day resurrection an idea predating Jesus?" Similar articles appeared in Israeli newspapers, and a flurry of postings on the Internet followed.[2] Only a few scholars, however, have tried to engage the text on a scholarly level. We now have a new, although partial edition by Elisha Qimron and Alexey Yuditsky.[3] Moshe Bar-Asher and Gary Rendsburg have published studies of the language of the text.[4] Yuval Goren has published an analysis of the stone on which the in-

---

1. Ada Yardeni and Binyamin Elizur, "A Prophetic Text on Stone from the First Century BCE: First Publication" (in Hebrew), *Cathedra* 123 (2007) 155-66. See the English translation in Matthias Henze, ed., *Hazon Gabriel: New Readings of the Gabriel Revelation* (SBLEJL; Atlanta: SBL, 2011): "A Hebrew Prophetic Text on Stone from the Early Herodian Period: A Preliminary Report." See also Ada Yardeni, "A New Dead Sea Scroll on Stone? Bible-like Prophecy Was Mounted in a Wall 2,000 Years Ago," *BAR* 34.1 (2008) 60-61.

2. E.g., Victor Sasson, "The Vision of Gabriel and Messiah in Mainstream Judaism and in Christianity: Textual, Philological, and Theological Comments," http://victorsasson .blogspot.com/2009/09/vision-of-gabriel-and-messiah-in.html. Despite its pretensions, Sasson's blog is an ill-informed rant against any deviation from "mainstream Judaism" and against Christianity. It contributes nothing to the understanding of the text.

3. Alexey (Eliyahu) Yuditsky and Elisha Qimron, "Notes on the Inscription, 'The Vision of Gabriel'" (in Hebrew), *Cathedra* 133 (2009) 133-44. See the English translation in Henze, ed., *Hazon Gabriel*.

4. Moshe Bar-Asher, "On the Language of 'The Vision of Gabriel,'" *RevQ* 23 (2008) 491-524; Gary A. Rendsburg, "Linguistic and Stylistic Notes to the Hazon Gabriel Inscription," *DSD* 16 (2009) 107-16.

scription is written.[5] David Hamidović has published an independent reading of the text with some comments on genre and *Sitz im Leben*.[6] The most far-reaching attempt to make sense of the text and place it in a historical context, as of March 2010, is that of Israel Knohl, who has discussed it at length in a monograph and several articles.[7] Knohl deserves credit for his pioneering work on this text, and his interpretation is highly ingenious. It is also controversial and problematic, however, and calls for critical assessment.[8]

Since the circumstances of discovery remain unknown, there is inevitably some doubt about the authenticity of the inscription. Since the experts who have examined it are satisfied, however, we must proceed on the assumption that it is authentic until proven otherwise.[9] Ada Yardeni and Binyamin Elizur identified the script as "typical of the Herodian period" and dated it to the late first century BCE or early first century CE. While the text may, in principle, be somewhat older than the inscription, it is in this general context that we must try to locate it.

Genre and Structure

Since the beginning of the text is missing, and we are not sure of its extent, it is difficult to determine the genre with any confidence. It is clear that the text is a revelation of some sort. David Hamidović identifies the genre as an apocalyptic vision.[10] There is no report of a vision in the extant text,

---

5. Yuval Goren, "Micromorphologic Examination of the *Gabriel Revelation* Stone," *IEJ* 58 (2008) 220-29.

6. David Hamidović, "La *Vision de Gabriel*," *RHPR* 89 (2009) 147-68.

7. Israel Knohl, *Messiahs and Resurrection in 'The Gabriel Revelation'* (Kogod Library of Judaic Studies; London/New York: Continuum, 2009). See also idem, "'By Three Days, Live': Messiahs, Resurrection and Ascent to Heaven in *Hazon Gabriel*," *JR* 88 (2008) 147-58; and idem, "The Messiah Son of Joseph: 'Gabriel's Revelation' and the Birth of a New Messianic Model," *BAR* 34.5 (2008) 58-62.

8. I have already indicated the main lines of my critique in a short piece for nonspecialist readers, "The Vision of Gabriel," *Yale Alumni Magazine* (September/October 2008) 26-27.

9. Goren ("Micromorphological Examination," 228) finds "no indication of modern treatment of the surface of the stone," but he emphasizes that "by no means does this statement indicate that the entire inscription or parts of it were created in antiquity beyond any trace of doubt." Bar-Asher ("On the Language of 'The Vision of Gabriel,'" 517) accepts that the Hebrew dates from "the end of Second Temple times."

10. Hamidović, "La *Vision de Gabriel*," 159.

but there are questions in lines 31 and 77 that reflect a dialogue between the revealer and the recipient of the revelation. The question in line 31 asks about an object, variously identified as a frontlet or a tree, that may have been seen in a vision. It is apparent, in any case, that the revelation does not take the form of an extended symbolic vision, such as we find in Daniel 7 and 8, but is primarily a discourse, with elements of dialogue and perhaps visions of particular objects such as we find in Amos 7–8. Yardeni and Elizur suggest that it is "a collection of short prophecies dictated to a scribe, in a manner similar to prophecies appearing in the Hebrew Bible." Knohl interprets the text by unit. The main point of disjunction comes at line 77, where the speaker announces "I am Gabriel." Up to that point, the text appeared to be a speech of God, but a speech introduced by the formula "Thus says the Lord" can be spoken by a prophetic or angelic mediator, and so it is possible that Gabriel is the speaker throughout. Knohl is probably right, nonetheless, that the identification of the angel marks a new, concluding section of the composition. A partial analogy for the genre of the text can be found in the discourse of the angel Gabriel in Daniel 10–12, but that discourse describes a much clearer historical and eschatological sequence than is the case here. One might also compare the discourses of the angel Uriel in *4 Ezra,* which occur in the context of dialogues. There are hints of dialogue in the *Gabriel Revelation* insofar as the speaker occasionally addresses commands to the human recipient. The only passages that might be ascribed to the recipient are a response to a question in line 31 and the question about the revealer's identity in line 77. The *Gabriel Revelation* may well qualify as an apocalypse, insofar as it is a revelation mediated to a human recipient by an angel and is concerned with heavenly realities and eschatological events,[11] but this judgment must be qualified by the fragmentary nature of the available text.

Knohl further divides lines 1-76 into three subsections: lines 9-12, 13-42, and 56-76.[12] The first of these subsections is extremely fragmentary. It says something about someone asking questions of the Lord, and, as Knohl puts it, it "presumably served as an introduction to the revelation . . . that follows."[13] The other two sections are separated by text that is either barely intelligible or entirely unintelligible, but they are not marked off formally

---

11. On the definition of an apocalypse, see John J. Collins, ed., *Apocalypse: The Morphology of a Genre* (*Semeia* 14; Missoula, MT: Scholars Press, 1979) especially 9.

12. Knohl, *Messiahs and Resurrection,* 31.

13. Knohl, *Messiahs and Resurrection,* 32.

as distinct sections. There are several prophetic formulae ("thus says the Lord . . .") throughout the text (lines 13, 18, 20, 29, 57, 69), but these do not necessarily mark new units in the text.

An Eschatological Assault on Jerusalem

The revelation concerns an attack by the nations on Jerusalem (lines 13-14). This motif is familiar from the Psalms (2; 48), and from prophetic (Zechariah 14) and apocalyptic (*4 Ezra* 13) literature. Such a scenario could be inspired by an actual historical assault on Jerusalem, or it could be an eschatological fantasy, without historical basis.

According to Knohl, "lines 16-17 present the request from Ephraim to place the sign, probably portending the coming redemption, which is also announced by God's statement that His 'gardens' are ripe and ready for Israel (lines 18-19)."[14] In this, he is following the reading of Yardeni and Elizur in lines 16-17: "My servant, David, asked from before Ephraim(?) 17. [to?] put the sign(?)." They, however, leave blank the end of line 18, where Knohl finds the reference to gardens.[15]

Yuditsky and Qimron read these lines quite differently: "David, my servant, asked me: 'Answer me, I ask you for the sign.' Thus said YHWH, God of Hosts, the God of Israel: 'My son, I have a new testament for Israel.'"

Where Yardeni and Elizur read Ephraim, they read אמרים ("words," as in Prov. 22:21). Instead of "my gardens" (גני) they read בני ("my son"), a reading that Knohl now accepts. Insofar as one can judge from the photos published in Knohl's book,[16] and his article in *BAR*,[17] it seems possible to read the second letter of the last word on line 16 as a *pe*, as in Ephraim, but Yuditsky and Qimron, working from new, digital photographs, say that it "can hardly be a *pe*." The reading must be considered doubtful. Knohl makes much of the supposed reference to Ephraim here, and we will return to his interpretation at the end of this chapter. For the present, it must suffice to note that it is uncertain whether the text refers to Ephraim at all.

The person addressed by God as "my son" is presumably David, the

---

14. Knohl, *Messiahs and Resurrection*, 32.
15. Hamidović ("La *Vision de Gabriel*," 153) also reads the reference to "gardens."
16. Knohl, *Messiahs and Resurrection*, 104.
17. Knohl, "The Messiah Son of Joseph," 60.

person who asked for the sign. The idea that the Davidic king, or Messiah, can be addressed by God as "son" is familiar from Psalm 2 and 2 Samuel 7, and it is also reflected in a number of texts from the Hellenistic and Roman periods.[18] The request for a sign is answered by an assurance "in three days you will know," and by a further prophetic announcement that "evil is broken before righteousness." Knohl translates this in the perfect tense, but it is presumably a prophetic perfect, and so Yuditsky and Qimron rightly take it as future. The point is that the nations besieging Jerusalem will be defeated. The assurance is offered in place of a sign, since the deliverance itself will be seen shortly.

An Evil Branch

After this, the addressee is encouraged to ask about the identity of an "evil branch" (צמח רע). The word צמח is a designation for the Messiah, derived from Jeremiah 23:5 ("the days are coming, says the Lord, when I will raise up for David a righteous branch") and Jeremiah 33:15, and is used in eschatological contexts in the Dead Sea Scrolls, notably in 4Q285, 4Q252, and 4QpIsaª.[19] A צמח רע is presumably a false messiah. Several messianic pretenders appeared in the first century of the Common Era, especially in connection with the revolt against Rome.[20] In the Gospel of Mark, Jesus warns his disciples: "And if anyone says to you at that time, 'Look! Here is the Messiah!' or 'Look! There he is!' — do not believe it. False messiahs and false prophets will appear and produce signs and omens, to lead astray, if possible, the elect" (Mark 13:21-22). Knohl asserts that "this evil messianic figure must be distinguished from the more conventional type of false messiah, who wishes to redeem Israel but cannot achieve this goal. Here, emphasis is laid upon the sheer wickedness of the would-be redeemer."[21] Instead, Knohl associates the evil branch with the Antichrist, as that figure

---

18. See further Adela Yarbro Collins and John J. Collins, *King and Messiah as Son of God: Divine, Human, and Angelic Messianic Figures in Biblical and Related Literature* (Grand Rapids: Eerdmans, 2009) 48-74.

19. John J. Collins, *The Scepter and the Star: The Messiahs of the Dead Sea Scrolls and Other Ancient Literature* (New York: Doubleday, 1995) 57-63.

20. Richard A. Horsley and John S. Hanson, *Bandits, Prophets, and Messiahs: Popular Movements in the Time of Jesus* (New Voices in Biblical Studies; Minneapolis: Winston, 1985) 88-134; Collins, *Scepter and the Star*, 199-204.

21. Knohl, *Messiahs and Resurrection*, 12 n. 51.

appears in Christian literature, beginning with the Book of Revelation. The Antichrist is "characteristically duplicitous, presenting himself as the Messiah and Redeemer while actually being the Devil's spawn, seeking to corrupt and lead astray."[22] In support of this interpretation, Knohl reads the next word as לובנסד, an expression otherwise unattested, which he renders as "plastered white." Yuditsky and Qimron do not venture a reading here.[23] Again, Knohl's bold interpretation has a dubious textual basis. The idea of an Antichrist who apes the Christ is not reliably attested before the Book of Revelation and seems to be a distinctively Christian development.[24] The phrase צמח רע cannot bear the interpretive weight that Knohl lays on it.

Divine Deliverance

Shortly after this comes the promise of a theophany, formulated in the language of the prophet Haggai: "In a little while I shall shake heaven and earth" (lines 24-25). In line 26, Yardeni and Elizur, followed by Knohl and Hamidović, read: "these are the seven chariots." Yuditsky and Qimron, however, read "the God of chariots (parallel to 'the Lord God of hosts') will listen to (the cry of Jerusalem)," reading שמע as a prophetic perfect, instead of שבע ("seven"). Knohl, following Yardeni and Elizur, locates the supposed seven chariots at the gate (שער) of Jerusalem and the gates (שערי) of Judah,[25] but Yuditsky and Qimron read that (God will listen to

22. Knohl, *Messiahs and Resurrection*, 12. See further Knohl, "On 'the Son of God,' Armilus and Messiah Son of Joseph" (in Hebrew), *Tarbiz* 68 (1998) 13-38. Cf. David Flusser, *Judaism and the Origins of Christianity* (Jerusalem: Magnes, 1988) 207-13, 433-53. Knohl takes the figure who is called "Son of God" in 4Q246 to be an Antichrist figure and identifies him with the Roman emperor Augustus (*Messiahs and Resurrection*, 52-84). That figure is more plausibly interpreted as the Davidic Messiah. See Yarbro Collins and Collins, *King and Messiah as Son of God*, 65-73.

23. Yardeni and Elizur allowed Knohl's reading as one of several possibilities but offered no translation.

24. On the Antichrist, see Gregory C. Jenks, *The Origins and Early Development of the Antichrist Myth* (BZNW 59; Berlin: de Gruyter, 1991); L. J. Lietaert Peerbolte, *The Antecedents of Antichrist: A Traditio-Historical Study of the Earliest Christian Views on Eschatological Opponents* (JSJSup 49; Leiden: Brill, 1996); Bernard McGinn, *Antichrist: Two Thousand Years of the Human Fascination with Evil* (San Francisco: HarperSanFrancisco, 1994) especially 32-56 ("Christ's Alter Ego").

25. So also Hamidović, "La *Vision de Gabriel*."

the cry of) the devastation (שׁוֹד) of Jerusalem and the cities (עָרֵי) of Judah. Again, Knohl reads "three angels" in line 28,[26] where Yardeni and Elizur offer no reading and Yuditsky and Qimron read "the hosts" (צבאת). There is a reference to the angel Michael in line 28.

Readings diverge again in line 31, where Knohl followed the original reading of Yardeni and Elizur, הצץ "the frontlet,"[27] but they now accept the correction of Yuditsky and Qimron and read "the tree" (העץ). The two editions construe the tree in different ways. Yardeni and Elizur translate: "'What is it?' said the tree." Yuditsky and Qimron, more plausibly: "'What is it?' and I said, 'a tree.'" (Knohl has "he said, the frontlet.") In either case, there seems to be a vision implied. (Compare Amos's visions of a plumb line and a basket of summer fruit in Amos 7–8.) Unfortunately, very little of this passage is legible. If Knohl's reading were accepted, we might speculate that the "frontlet" was intended as a crown for the Davidic figure. It is difficult to imagine what the significance of the tree might be. Yuditsky and Qimron offer no reconstruction of lines 33 to 63, although they offer some new readings in these lines. Yardeni and Elizur read only scattered words between lines 32 and 44 (Jerusalem is mentioned twice, and there is possible mention of exile in line 37) and declare lines 45 to 50 to be unintelligible. Knohl and Hamidović read "a sign from Jerusalem" in line 36 and "a sign of exile" in line 37. In line 40, Knohl reconstructs "that his mist will fill most of the moon" and in line 41 "blood that the northerner would become maggoty." Even apart from the difficulty of reading anything in those lines, the meaning of the reconstructed text is not clear. Knohl's translation of line 40 is admittedly conjectural. He suggests an analogy to the signs of the Day of the Lord in Joel 2. Yuditsky and Qimron are probably wise to leave those lines almost entirely blank.

Blood and Chariots

When legible text resumes, there is mention of "three days" in line 54, marked with a question mark by Yardeni and Elizur but without context. We have an intriguing reference to "the blood of the slaughters (?)/sacrifices (טבחי) of Jerusalem" in line 57 (so Yardeni and Qimron, who think

26. So also Hamidović, "La *Vision de Gabriel.*"
27. So also Hamidović, "La *Vision de Gabriel.*"

it "more plausible to understand the word *ṭbḥy* as referring to the flesh of the sacrifices in the Jerusalem Temple" than to the slaughter on some occasion when Jerusalem was sacked). They also read the word סתום immediately before this phrase and comment: "the precise meaning of סתום in this context is obscure, either ending the preceding verse or perhaps referring to the interruption of the sacrifice-practice at the Jerusalem temple." Knohl construes the references as to "the blood of the slaughtered of Jerusalem," and reads סתום as "seal up." Compare Daniel 8:26, where Gabriel tells Daniel to "seal up the vision, for it refers to many days from now." "Sealing" can be applied more easily to a revelation than to "blood," but perhaps the blood is to be kept as evidence or testimony for a coming judgment. Knohl's reading at line 60, "He will have pity . . . his mercy are [sic] near," departs from Yardeni and Elizur, who read only a vague reference to "spirit" or "wind."[28]

The text becomes a little clearer beginning with line 65. There we find mention of שלושה קדשי העולם, "the three holy ones of the world." Knohl asserts that " 'holy ones' is used in the Hebrew Bible and early Jewish literature to designate both angels and human beings,"[29] but in fact the term is predominantly used to refer to angels.[30] He suggests that "holy ones of the world" must refer to "creatures of this world only" and suggests a reference to martyrs. This seems quite arbitrary. A reference to angels seems to me more likely, analogous, perhaps, to the angels who preside over the nations.[31] The Greek equivalent, *hagioi*, is used for martyred human beings in the Book of Revelation (11:18; 13:10; 14:12; 16:6; 17:6; etc.), but they are not called "holy ones of the world," and the usage derives from their association with the angels after death.

In lines 66-67, Knohl, following Yardeni and Elizur, reads: "in you we trust . . . Announce him of blood (בשר לו על דם), this is their chariot."[32] This is scarcely intelligible. Knohl offers a highly imaginative interpretation:

---

28. Hamidović reads differently: "Dieu n'est [pas] profane [הלל]. Ainsi il saisira c[es] biens . . ."

29. Knohl, *Messiahs and Resurrection*, 22.

30. See John J. Collins, *Daniel: A Commentary on the Book of Daniel* (Hermeneia; Minneapolis: Fortress, 1993) 313-17.

31. E.g., in Daniel 10. Compare also the seventy angelic shepherds in the Animal Apocalypse, in *1 Enoch* 89:59–90:19.

32. Hamidović reads the same words but construes slightly differently: "Informe-le au sujet du sang de ce char qui est à eux."

The good tidings are presumably connected to the fate of a group of people ("their chariot") killed by the enemies of Jerusalem. Through the recipient of the vision, God promises that the blood of the martyrs will serve as their chariot. The prophecy is probably based on the story in 2 Kings 2:11, in which Elijah goes up to heaven in a chariot of fire.[33]

Yuditsky and Qimron, however, take the word בשר not as a verb meaning "to preach good news" but as a noun meaning "flesh," which makes much better sense in conjunction with "blood." Their reconstruction also goes beyond their actual reading: "on you we rely [not on] flesh (and) not on blood. This is the chariot. . ." While this reconstruction is also speculative, it does not require nearly as great a flight of imagination as Knohl's transformation of the blood of the slain into the chariot of Elijah.

In line 70, Knohl and Yuditsky and Qimron agree against Yardeni and Elizur in reading "three shepherds." There is also mention of prophets at the beginning of the line, and Yuditsky and Qimron identify these with the shepherds. Knohl sees the "three shepherds" as an allusion to Zechariah 11:8.[34] In the biblical passage, however, the three shepherds are bad rulers whom the Lord has to replace: "In one month I disposed of the three shepherds, for I had become impatient with them, and they also detested me." In the *Gabriel Revelation*, the three shepherds are sent by the Lord. They are mentioned again in line 75. There is no indication in the extant text of divine disapproval. The term "shepherds" usually represents rulers rather than prophets, so the prophets here are probably distinct emissaries. Hamidović does not find any reference to shepherds here, reading ואני instead of רועי. There is, in any case, an undisputed reference to "three shepherds" who went out to (ל) Israel in line 75.[35]

Line 72: "the place for the sake of David, the servant of the Lord," may be part of a divine assurance, or it may be part of a prayer, since two lines later we read "showing kindness to thousands." In any case, the line confirms the importance of David in this composition.

In line 76, Yardeni and Elizur, Knohl, and Hamidović all read כהן, "priest," but Yuditsky and Qimron read בהן, "among them," a variant of בם in the preceding phrase. Again, where Yardeni and Elizur, followed by Knohl and Hamidović, read בני קדושים, literally "sons of holy ones,"

33. Knohl, *Messiahs and Resurrection*, 23.
34. Knohl, *Messiahs and Resurrection*, 24.
35. Knohl construes the preposition as "for" Israel.

Yuditsky and Qimron read בם קדושים. Even if בני קדושים should prove to be correct, however, it should be translated simply as "holy ones." Priests might be associated with angelic "holy ones," but it is uncertain whether there is any reference here to a priest at all.

The Concluding Section

Line 77 seems to mark a transition in the text, probably the beginning of the conclusion. The speaker is now identified as Gabriel, in a passage that implies a dialogue.[36] Someone is told, "you will rescue them" (line 78). Yuditsky and Qimron read the following statement as "A proph[et and a she]pherd will save you" and they reconstruct "three shepherds, three [pro]phets" in line 79. Yardeni and Elizur, Hamidović, and Knohl also recognize the word "three" in line 79, but they reconstruct the reference as "three signs." None of these readings, other than the word "three," is at all clear.

Knohl's reading of line 80 is the most controversial suggestion about this text to date. Yardeni and Elizur read only: "In three days . . . I, Gabriel . . ." Knohl read the word חאיה after "three days," and interpreted it as "live!" a command to rise from the dead.[37] Hence the headlines proclaiming "resurrection after three days before Jesus." The spelling, however, is anomalous. Knohl asserts that the use of *aleph* as a vowel is quite common,[38] but he provides no instance of its use in the verb "to live." Moreover, as Moshe Bar-Asher has pointed out, an *aleph* is never used to represent a *hatef patah;* it is always a whole vowel, usually a long one.[39] The parallel cited by Knohl from Ezekiel 16:6 ("in your blood, live") does not envision resurrection from the dead. Ronald Hendel resolved the problem by suggesting that the word should be read as האות, "the sign," and this reading is now accepted by Yuditsky and Qimron.[40] There are other references to signs in the text, and the *aleph* is not problematic. The main

---

36. Yardeni and Elizur, Hamidović, and Knohl read "who am I?" Yuditsky and Qimron read "who are you?"

37. Hamidović ("La *Vision de Gabriel*," 155) reads the same word, but translates as an injunctive future: "on vivra." In his note, however, he suggests that it may be an infinitive absolute and may be the equivalent of an imperative. He also notes, however, that the verb "to live" does not necessarily refer to resurrection (161).

38. Knohl, *Messiahs and Resurrection*, 26.

39. Bar-Asher, "On the Language," 501.

40. Ronald Hendel, "The Messiah Son of Joseph: Simply 'Sign,'" *BAR* 35 (2009) 8.

pillar on which Knohl's controversial interpretation of the text rests has disappeared on inspection.

In line 81, Knohl follows Yardeni and Elizur in reading "the Prince of Princes." This title, as he notes, is found in Daniel 8:25, where the "little horn," "a king of bold countenance," rises up against the Prince of Princes, who is also called "the prince of the host." Knohl argues that "if the 'host of heaven' represents the People of Israel, the 'prince of the host' represents their leader."[41] He then supposes that the author of the *Gabriel Revelation* read the prophecy of Daniel 8 to mean that the king of bold countenance will destroy Israel and attack, perhaps even kill, their leader — the "prince of princes." He concludes: "what our text adds to the original prophecy is that Gabriel will resurrect the executed leader."[42] But in Daniel, the host of heaven is clearly the angelic host, and the Prince of Princes is the Most High.[43] Daniel 8 is not describing an attack on a human leader at all. Moreover, even if the author of the *Gabriel Revelation* takes the title "Prince of Princes" from Daniel 8, it does not follow that he is offering an interpretation of the Danielic passage in which the phrase occurs. The *Gabriel Revelation* says nothing here of an attack on any human leader, much less his death or resurrection.

Line 83, "to me, from the three, the small one that I took," is too elliptic to make much sense. The "three" may well refer back to the three shepherds mentioned earlier. Knohl suggests that "it is possible that 'took' implies ascent to heaven," since the same verb is used for the taking of Enoch in Genesis 5:24. But of course the word need not have that meaning at all. The attraction of Knohl's interpretation depends on his reading of line 80 as a reference to resurrection, which we have already rejected.

Knohl finds a final reference to resurrection in line 85, "then you will stand." In this case, he has a plausible parallel in Daniel 12:13, where the visionary is told: "you shall rise for your lot at the end of days." While the legible text in the *Gabriel Revelation* is far too elliptic to warrant confidence, it is not implausible that the revelation would end as Daniel's had. In that case, however, the reference is to the future resurrection of the visionary, whose death is not a subject of the revelation.

From this perusal of the reconstructions of the text that have been

41. Knohl, *Messiahs and Resurrection*, 28.
42. Knohl, *Messiahs and Resurrection*, 28.
43. See Collins, *Daniel*, 333. Cf. Daniel 11:36, where the upstart king offends "the God of gods." The archangel Michael has also been proposed as a possible identification for the prince of princes.

offered to date, it is clear that many of the readings are uncertain, and that only a very elliptic text is available to us. The text contains a revelation about an attack of the nations on Jerusalem. God, apparently speaking through the angel Gabriel, promises deliverance very soon. ("In three days" should not be taken literally.) It is apparent that the Davidic Messiah has a role to play in this eschatological drama, and it would seem from line 72 that God delivers Jerusalem "for the sake of David, the servant of YHWH." Some other figures (prophets, shepherds) also have a role, but the text is too elliptic to allow us to fill in the details. There is also mention of a false messiah, "an evil branch," but there is nothing to indicate that this figure is an eschatological adversary of the Messiah like the Antichrist in Christian tradition, or the much later figure of Armilus in *Sefer Zerubbabel*.[44]

A Messiah of Ephraim?

Knohl has argued that the Davidic Messiah is not the only, or even the most important, messianic figure in this text. He also finds reference to the "Messiah son of Joseph," known from the Babylonian Talmud, or "Messiah of Ephraim," who is mentioned in the medieval *Pesiqta Rabbati*, and he claims that the *Gabriel Revelation* provides evidence that this figure was known already around the turn of the era. This claim is highly problematic.

As noted above, Yardeni and Elizur read the word "Ephraim" at the end of line 16 (with a question mark to indicate that the reading was uncertain). They translate: "my servant, David, asked from before Ephraim [to?] put the sign (?). I ask from you . . ." Knohl, reading the same text, translates the verb "ask" as an imperative: "My servant David, ask of Ephraim [that he] place the sign; (this) I ask of you." Yuditsky and Qimron reject the reading Ephraim and read: "David, my servant, asked me: Answer me, I ask you for the sign." Where Yardeni and Knohl read שׂים[ ] at the beginning of line 17, Yuditsky and Qimron read [הש]יבני, "answer me." It is not possible to decide between the readings on the basis of the published photos. If we accept the reading "Ephraim," however, it would be very odd to ask a human figure, even a messiah, to "place the sign." In the entire biblical and Jewish tradition, one asks God for a sign (e.g., Isaiah 7) or asks what

---

44. On Armilus, see Joseph Dan, "Armilus: The Jewish Antichrist and the Origins and Dating of the *Sefer Zerubbavel*," in Peter Schäfer and Mark Cohen, eds., *Toward the Millennium: Messianic Expectations from the Bible to Waco* (SHR 77; Leiden: Brill, 1998) 73-104.

the signs will be (e.g., *4 Ezra* 5–6). The construal of the text proposed by Yuditsky and Qimron is much more plausible than the alternatives in this respect.

Knohl infers from his reading of this passage that the Messiah of Ephraim is superior in status to the Davidic Messiah: "the fact that David is sent by God to request Ephraim to place the sign may attest that Ephraim has superior rank. He, and not David, is the key person who is asked to place the sign; David is only the messenger!"[45] When the Messiah son of Joseph appears in the Talmud, however, the relationship is quite different. There, the Messiah son of Joseph precedes the Davidic Messiah and is killed:

> Our Rabbis taught: The Holy One, blessed be He, will say to the Messiah, the son of David (May he reveal himself speedily in our days!), "Ask of me anything, and I will give it to thee," as it is said, "I *will tell of the decree*" etc. "*this day have I begotten thee, ask of me and I will give the nations for thy inheritance*." But when he will see that the Messiah the son of Joseph is slain, he will say to Him, "Lord of the Universe, I ask of Thee only the gift of life." "As to life," He would answer him, "Your father David has already prophesied this concerning you," as it is said, *He asked of thee life, thou gavest him [even length of days for ever and ever].* (*b. Sukkah* 52a)[46]

Nowhere in Jewish tradition does the Messiah son of Joseph take precedence over the Davidic Messiah.[47] The Messiah son of Joseph is introduced in this talmudic passage (*Sukkah* 52a) in the context of a discussion of the referent of Zechariah 12:10 ("they will look on him whom they have pierced").[48] It is apparent that this figure was well known by talmudic times, but his origin is uncertain. The most plausible explanation remains that the idea of a dying messiah took hold after the defeat of Bar

---

45. Knohl, "Messiah Son of Joseph," 60.

46. Trans. I. W. Slotki, the Traditional Press edition. The italicized passages are citations from Psalm 2:7-8 and Psalm 21:4.

47. On the Messiah son of Joseph, see Joseph Heinemann, "The Messiah of Ephraim and the Premature Exodus of the Tribe of Ephraim," *HTR* 68 (1975) 1-15, and the older literature cited there, especially in n. 1. In addition to the talmudic passages, the Messiah son of Joseph is mentioned in the Palestinian Targumim and in late medieval midrashim.

48. See George Foot Moore, *Judaism in the First Centuries of the Christian Era, the Age of the Tannaim* (2 vols.; 1927-30; repr., New York: Schocken, 1971) 370.

Kokhba, in the second century CE. In the words of Joseph Heinemann, "we must look for a dramatic, even traumatic event to account for this transfiguration of the legend [i.e., of messianic expectation]; and no other would supply as likely a cause for the creation of the new version as the defeat and death of Bar Kokhba."[49] There is certainly no hint of the expectation of such a figure in the surviving Jewish literature from the period before Bar Kokhba.

Moreover, while Ephraim was certainly a son of Joseph, it is not certain that the Messiah who is called Ephraim in the medieval *Pesiqta Rabbati* should be identified with the Messiah son of Joseph known from the Talmud. At least some parts of the relevant passage, *Pesiqta Rabbati* 36, suggest rather that "Ephraim" is a name for the Davidic Messiah.[50]

The *Pisqa* begins with a consideration of Isaiah 60:1-2: "Arise, shine, for thy light is come." These words, we are told, are to be considered in the light of what David, king of Israel, was inspired to say: "For with thee is the fountain of life; in Thy light we see light" (Ps. 36:9). The light is identified as "the light of the Messiah," and the verse is cited as proof that "the Holy One, blessed be he, contemplated the Messiah and his works before the world was created, and then under his throne of glory put away his messiah until the time of the generation in which he will appear." Satan then asks to see the Messiah. When he sees him, he is shaken, and he asks, "Who is this through whose power we are to be swallowed up? What is his name? What kind of being is he?" The Holy One replies: "He is the Messiah, and his name is Ephraim, my true Messiah, who will pull himself straight and will pull up straight his generation, and who will give light to the eyes of Israel and deliver his people; and no nation or people will be able to withstand him." The passage goes on to say that God tells the Messiah that he will have to suffer for a period of seven years for the sins of those who are put away with him under the throne. The Messiah responds: "Master of the universe, with joy in my soul and gladness in my heart I take this suffering upon myself, provided that not one person in Israel perish; that not only those who are alive be saved in my days, but also those who are dead, who died from the days of Adam up to the time of redemption."[51]

The *Pisqa* continues: "During the seven-year period preceding the

---

49. Heinemann, "Messiah of Ephraim," 8-9.
50. This was suggested to me orally by Martha Himmelfarb.
51. *Pesikta Rabbati: Discourses for Feasts, Fasts, and Special Sabbaths,* trans. William G. Braude (2 vols.; Yale Judaica Series 18; New Haven: Yale University Press, 1968) 2.678-79.

coming of the son of David, iron beams will be brought and loaded upon his neck until the Messiah's body is bent low. . . . It was because of the ordeal of the son of David that David wept, saying My strength is dried up like a potsherd (Ps. 22:16). During the ordeal of the son of David, the Holy One, blessed be He, will say to him: Ephraim, my true Messiah, long ago, ever since the six days of creation, thou didst take this ordeal upon thyself."[52] In this passage, it is difficult to distinguish the Messiah named Ephraim from the son of David.

The following *Pisqa*, 37, also refers many times to the Messiah as Ephraim and cites Jeremiah 31:20: "Is Ephraim my dear son?" It may be that the fact that Ephraim is said to be the son of God in Jeremiah (compare Hos. 11:1, 8) gave rise to the assumption that Ephraim and the Messiah son of David were one and the same.[53]

If the reading proposed by Yuditsky and Qimron is correct, there is no reference here to Ephraim at all, and so the consideration of the Messiah of Ephraim loses its relevance to the discussion. But even if Knohl's reading is correct, it does not follow that Ephraim is a name for a messiah in this text. Ephraim is often used in the Bible as a metonym for Israel, and it could be so used here.[54] In short, Knohl's attempt to find the Messiah son of Joseph in the *Gabriel Revelation* is problematic on many counts.

In contrast to the supposed references to the Messiah son of Joseph, "my servant David" appears unambiguously in this text. In line 16, he is either said to ask God for a sign or is commanded to ask for one. He is most probably the person addressed by God as "my son" in line 18.[55] The question arises, then, whether "my servant David" is the addressee throughout or at least from line 18 forward. This is perhaps unlikely, since David is referred to in the third person again in line 72, where something happens "for the sake of David, the servant of YHWH." It is true that other figures,

---

52. *Pesiqta Rabbati*, 2:680.

53. Michael Fishbane notes correctly that there is only one messianic figure in this text and that he is the sufferer called Ephraim, but he argues that this is a polemical position and that "any other messianic figure, like David, is excluded" ("Midrash and Messianism: Some Theologies of Suffering and Salvation," in Schäfer and Cohen, *Toward the Millennium*, 57-71 [here 65]). But then we must wonder why the *Pisqa* also refers to "the ordeal of the son of David."

54. See further Hamidović, "La *Vision de Gabriel*," 156 n. 16. He concludes: "En contexte il demeure difficile de reconnaître la désignation d'un messie, fils de Joseph, à la lecture du nom Éphraim" (161).

55. As noted above, Ephraim is said to be the son of God also in Jeremiah 31 and Hosea 11.

prophets, and shepherds play a role in this revelation, but it is clear that the primary agent of God is the Davidic Messiah.

The Setting

One of the many uncertainties about this text is whether it was inspired by a historical siege of Jerusalem or should rather be understood as an eschatological fantasy of the final attack of the Gentiles on Jerusalem. The urgency of the request for a sign probably argues for a historical crisis. If Yardeni's dating of the paleography is correct, then the siege of Jerusalem during the first Jewish revolt may be too late. The siege under Pompey in 63 BCE provides one possible occasion. The *Psalms of Solomon*, which reflect on that event, are also notable for their expectation of a Davidic Messiah.[56] Knohl's suggestion of the suppression of a revolt in Judea by Varus in 4 BCE is also possible, but his attempt to fill out the events by using the passage in Revelation 11 about the death of two witnesses[57] is highly fanciful.[58]

Much remains unclear about this text, even in the elementary matter of the actual readings. In either setting, however, the chief significance of this text is as a witness to the importance of the *Davidic* Messiah around the turn of the era. It is unfortunate that this simple fact has been obscured by speculation about a suffering and dying messiah who is simply not attested in the inscription, insofar as it can be deciphered.

56. See especially Psalms of Solomon 17; and Kenneth Atkinson, *I Cried to the Lord: A Study of the Psalms of Solomon's Historical Background and Social Setting* (JSJSup 84; Leiden: Brill, 2004).

57. Knohl, *Messiahs and Resurrection*, 66-71.

58. See John J. Collins, "An Essene Messiah? Comments on Israel Knohl, *The Messiah before Jesus*," in John J. Collins and Craig Evans, eds., *Christian Beginnings and the Dead Sea Scrolls* (Acadia Studies in Bible and Theology; Grand Rapids: Baker Academic, 2006) 37-44.

CHAPTER 9

The Idea of Election in 4 Ezra

The book of *4 Ezra,* composed near the end of the first century CE,[1] is rightly classified as an apocalypse,[2] but it is a distinctive work that is in many ways *sui generis.* The first three (of seven) sections are taken up with dialogues between Ezra and an angel,[3] in which Ezra presses the question of theodicy with a degree of persistence surpassed only by Job. Ezra was supposedly in Babylon "in the thirtieth year after the destruction of our city."[4] The historical Ezra lived more than a century later.[5] The setting is quite transparently typological: Babylon stands for Rome, and Ezra's questions are prompted by the destruction of 70 CE. Of course, Ezra did not live in the Roman era either. He is evoked here as an authoritative spokesperson, to serve as the mouthpiece for the agonized reflections of the author. It would be too simple to regard Ezra as the author's *alter ego.* There is, after all, another authoritative voice in these dialogues, that of the archangel Uriel. The tension between these two voices is one of the most intriguing features of this book and has to be reckoned with in any study that attempts to address the meaning of *4 Ezra.*

1. Michael E. Stone, *Fourth Ezra: A Commentary on the Book of Fourth Ezra* (Hermeneia; Minneapolis: Fortress, 1990) 9-10, dates it to the latter part of the reign of Domitian (81-96 CE).

2. On *4 Ezra* as an apocalypse see John J. Collins, *The Apocalyptic Imagination* (rev. ed.; Grand Rapids: Eerdmans, 1998) 195-212; Stone, *Fourth Ezra,* 36-37.

3. On the structure of the book see Stone, *Fourth Ezra,* 50-51. The sections are (1) 3:1–5:19; (2) 5:20–6:34; (3) 6:35–9:25; (4) 9:26–10:59; (5) 10:60–12:51; (6) 13:1-58; (7) 14:1-48.

4. The "thirtieth year" may be an allusion to Ezekiel 1:1, or may betray the actual date of composition.

5. The identification of Ezra with Salathiel (Shealtiel, father of Zerubbabel) in 4:1 may be an attempt to solve this problem.

What Benefit Is Election?

One of the issues where the tension between Ezra and Uriel becomes explicit concerns the election of Israel, which seemed paradoxical in the wake of the destruction of Jerusalem. Ezra appears to accept the election of Israel as a datum of tradition. In the first dialogue, in chapter 3, he reminds God that, when most of humanity was sinning after the Flood, "you chose for yourself one of them, whose name was Abraham, and you loved him. . . . You made with him an everlasting covenant, and promised him that you would never forsake his descendants" (3:13-15). The divine freedom (or arbitrariness?) in choosing Abraham is underlined by the rejection of Esau. Integral to the idea of election are the covenant and the Mosaic law, which Ezra sees as standing in continuity with the covenant with the patriarchs. He readily admits that Israel did not keep the law very well, because of "the evil heart" (3:20),[6] but then he asks poignantly: "Are the deeds of Babylon better than those of Zion? Or has another nation known you besides Israel? . . . Or what nation has kept your commandments so well? . . . You may indeed find individual men who have kept your commandments, but nations you will not find" (3:31-36).

The angel Uriel responds to Ezra much as God did to Job, by asking him impossible questions ("Go, weigh for me the weight of fire, or measure for me a measure of wind, or call back for me the day that is passed," 4:5). When Ezra presses the question: "why has Israel been given over to the Gentiles as a reproach?" the angel answers indirectly that a great judgment is coming. Presumably then, the reproach of Israel will be taken away, but Uriel does not refer to Israel at all in his response. It is somewhat ironic that the angel draws analogies from the sphere of nature (e.g., the sea and the forest in 4:13-18), as he concludes that "those who dwell upon earth can understand only what is on earth" (4:21): the world to come is discontinuous with this one.[7] When Ezra insists that he only wants to understand what is on earth, the fate of Israel, the angel again refers to the coming judgment and distracts Ezra by describing the signs of the end.

Ezra takes up the question again, however, in the second dialogue (5:20–6:34). Here he formulates the issue in terms of a contrast between "the one and the many."

---

6. See Stone's excursus, *Fourth Ezra*, 63-65.
7. Stone, *Fourth Ezra*, 102.

From all the multitude of peoples you have gotten for yourself one people; and to this people whom you have loved, you have given the law, which is approved by all. And now, O Lord, why have you given over the one to the many . . . and scattered your only one among the many? And those who opposed your promises have trodden down those who believed your covenants. If you really hate your people, they should be punished by your own hand. (5:28-30)

The suggestion here that Yahweh "hates" Israel should be taken in the sense of "repudiates," in the way that God repudiates Israel in Hosea chapter 2. Nonetheless, it is clear that Ezra does not question the doctrine of election as such. He is merely suffering cognitive dissonance because of the gulf between the belief in divine election and the historical fate of Israel. Uriel responds by asking whether Ezra thinks he loves Israel more than God does, and he insists that it is not possible to discover the goal of the promises to Israel. He again proceeds to distract Ezra with the prospect of an eschatological judgment.

The most extreme formulation of Ezra's theology of election comes at the beginning of the third dialogue (6:35–9:25). Ezra reviews the works of creation and says of Adam, "from him we have all come, the people whom you have chosen." He then concludes:

All of this I have spoken before thee, O Lord, because you have said that it was for us that you created this world. As for the other nations which have descended from Adam, you have said that they are nothing, and that they are like spittle, and you have compared their abundance to a drop from a bucket. And now, O Lord, behold, these nations, which are reputed as nothing, domineer over us and devour us. But we your people whom thou hast called your first-born, only begotten, zealous for you and most dear, have been given into their hands. If the world has indeed been created for us, why do we not possess our world as an inheritance? How long will this be so? (6:55-59)[8]

The suggestion that Adam is the progenitor of the chosen people is somewhat startling. Jacob Jervell comments: "Adam was therefore an Isra-

---

8. The idea that the nations are like spittle or as nothing is based on Septuagint of Isaiah 15:17. The idea that the world was created for the sake of Israel is found frequently in rabbinic literature, e.g., Sifre Deuteronomy 11:21; *b. Berakhot* 32b; *Genesis Rabbah* 12:2. See Stone, *Fourth Ezra*, 188-89.

elite."[9] But Ezra does not deny that other peoples are descended from Adam too. Herein lies one of the central problems of the book: Jews and Gentiles alike suffer because of the sin of Adam (7:118), or rather because of the evil heart that afflicted Adam from the start. The chosen people are children of Adam too, and, despite the disparaging references to other peoples, they cannot be entirely indifferent to the fate of humanity at large.

Uriel responds on behalf of the Lord by affirming that he did indeed make the world for Israel's sake. But this does not appear to put Israel at much of an advantage, for "when Adam transgressed my statutes, what had been made was judged. And so the entrances of this world were made narrow and sorrowful and toilsome; . . . but the entrances of the greater world are broad and safe, and really yield the fruit of immortality. Therefore unless the living pass through the difficult and vain experiences, they can never receive those things that have been reserved for them" (7:10-16).

In short, admission to eternal life would seem to be on an individual basis. The rules for those who belong to the covenant people are no different than for those who do not. As Paul would say, "All who have sinned apart from the law will also perish apart from the law, and all who have sinned under the law will be judged by the law. For it is not the hearers of the law who are righteous in God's sight, but the doers of the law who will be justified. When Gentiles, who do not possess the law, do instinctively what the law requires," they too are justified. Ezra might well ask with Paul, "Then what advantage has the Jew?"[10]

Uriel's response shifts the focus of his discussion with Ezra, who promptly notes that this may be satisfactory for the righteous but gives cold comfort to anyone else. The angel's reply is brutal: "Let many perish who are now living, rather than that the law of God which is set before them be disregarded" (7:20). Uriel assumes here that "God strictly commanded those who came into the world, when they came, what they should do to live, and what they should do to avoid punishment" (7:21). This would seem to require, in effect, some kind of natural law, as the law of Moses is not known to all who come into the world.[11] But the fact that

9. Jacob Jervell, *Imago Dei* (Göttingen: Vandenhoeck & Ruprecht, 1960) 34.

10. Romans 2:12-14; 3:1. On the numerous points of analogy between Romans and *4 Ezra* see further B. W. Longenecker, *Eschatology and the Covenant: A Comparison of 4 Ezra and Romans 1–11* (JSNTSup 57; Sheffield: Journal for the Study of the Old Testament Press, 1991).

11. Compare Romans 2:14: "when Gentiles, who do not possess the law, do instinc-

the law is known to everyone only makes people guilty. As Uriel puts it in 8:1, "The Most High made this world for the sake of many, but the world to come for the sake of only a few."

Uriel's harsh dismissal of "the many" who are not righteous evokes some of the most poignant sentences in *4 Ezra:* "O earth, what have you brought forth, if the mind is made out of the dust like the other created things! For it would have been better if the dust itself had not been born, so that the mind might not have been made from it" (7:62), or again, "O Adam, what have you done? For though it was you who sinned, the fall was not yours alone, but ours also who are your descendants" (7:118). In light of these statements, and of the third dialogue as a whole, Alden Thompson argued that Ezra was more concerned for general humanity than for Israel.[12] This inference is hardly warranted. Rather, Ezra recognizes, under pressure from the angel's formulation of the issue, that the fate of Israel cannot be separated from that of all humanity. In 8:15-16 he tries to draw the dialogue back to his original concern: "And now I will speak out. About all human-kind you know best; but I will speak about your people, for whom I am grieved, and about your inheritance, for whom I lament, and about Israel, for whom I am sad, and about the seed of Jacob, for whom I am troubled." By the end of this prayer, he has switched back to speaking about all who are born.[13] The fact that there are no human beings who have not acted wickedly strengthens the case for mercy towards Israel, but it does not change the fact that Ezra's primary concern is for his own people.

---

tively what the law requires . . ." On the question of natural law in *4 Ezra,* see Stefan Beyerle, " 'Du bist kein Richter über dem Herrn'. Zur Konzeption von Gesetz und Gericht im 4. Esrabuch," in S. Beyerle, G. Mayer, and H. Strauss, eds., *Recht und Ethos im Alten Testament* (Festschrift für Horst Seebass; Neukirchen: Neukirchener Verlag, 1999) 315-37, and the comments of Karina M. Hogan, "Theologies in Conflict in 4 Ezra: Wisdom Debate and Apocalyptic Solution" (Ph.D. dissertation, University of Chicago, 2002) 165-66, who notes that while *4 Ezra* shows no awareness of Greek philosophy, Uriel's way of instructing Ezra implies that God is the source of the laws governing the natural order. (Hogan's dissertation was published in JSJ Supplements, Leiden: Brill, 2008.) On the relation between natural law and Mosaic law in Second Temple Judaism see Hindy Najman, *Seconding Sinai: The Development of Mosaic Discourse in Second Temple Judaism* (Jewish Studies Journal Supplement Series 77; Leiden: Brill, 2003), and D. T. Runia, G. E. Sterling, and H. Najman, eds., *Laws Stamped with the Seals of Nature: Law and Nature in Hellenistic Philosophy and Philo of Alexandria* (*The Studia Philonica Annual* 15; Brown Judaic Studies Supplement Series 337; Providence: Brown University Press, 2003).

12. Alden Lloyd Thompson, *Responsibility for Evil in the Theodicy of 4 Ezra* (Society of Biblical Literature Dissertation Series 29; Missoula: Scholars Press, 1977) 269.

13. See Hogan, "Theologies in Conflict," 154-55.

Bruce Longenecker is closer to the mark when he categorizes Ezra's theology as "ethnocentric covenantalism,"[14] a phrase he proposes as a replacement for E. P. Sanders's "covenantal nomism." Sanders regarded *4 Ezra* as an exception to the standard Palestinian Jewish pattern of covenantal nomism, because it allows little if any place for atonement and divine mercy.[15] This, however, is only true of Uriel, insofar as Ezra at least argues that there should be a place for mercy, even if it is not apparent that there is. But while the angel's voice is certainly important, it cannot simply be equated with that of the author. Rather, as Karina Martin Hogan has shown in her 2002 Chicago dissertation, the form of the dialogue must be taken seriously.[16] The voices of Ezra and the angel must be held in tension. Both contribute to the discussion of a complex issue. Ezra bears an authoritative name and speaks with passion. He is not merely the voice of heresy, as Harnisch and Brandenburger have suggested.[17]

A Debate within the Wisdom Tradition

As Hogan has shown, the dialogue between Ezra and Uriel reflects the tensions that had arisen in the Jewish wisdom tradition from the second century BCE on. By wisdom tradition here I mean a style of writing that is indebted to ancient Near Eastern wisdom teaching, and especially to the biblical wisdom books of Proverbs, Qoheleth, and Job. These biblical wisdom books were distinguished in the biblical corpus by their lack of attention to the specific people of Israel and its history or covenant. Rather, they were concerned with all creation, and with humanity as such.[18] Their theology might be understood as a kind of natural theology that arrived at the knowledge of God through observation of nature and of the pattern of act and consequence in human relations.[19] In the Hellenistic period, however, this tradition underwent some significant changes.

14. Longenecker, *Eschatology and the Covenant*, 34.

15. E. P. Sanders, *Paul and Palestinian Judaism* (Philadelphia: Fortress, 1977) 409-18.

16. Hogan, "Theologies in Conflict" (see n. 11).

17. W. Harnisch, *Verhängnis und Verheissung der Geschichte* (Göttingen: Vandenhoeck & Ruprecht, 1969) 60-67; E. Brandenburger, *Die Verborgenheit Gottes im Weltgeschehen* (Zürich: Theologischer Verlag, 1981) 42-51.

18. Leo G. Perdue, *Wisdom and Creation: The Theology of Wisdom Literature* (Nashville: Abingdon, 1994).

19. John J. Collins, "The Biblical Precedent for Natural Theology," *Journal of the*

First of these was the attempt to integrate the specific history of Israel and the covenant into a sapiential theology. Ben Sira famously declared that all wisdom was "the book of the covenant of the Most High God, the law that Moses commanded us" (Sir. 24:23), and praised the heroes of Israelite history, with the implication that they were exemplars of wisdom. Yet Ben Sira remains a wisdom teacher rather than an exegete, and the relation between wisdom and the Torah is never clarified: Does it mean that the Torah is self-sufficient, so that those who have it have no need of further wisdom? Or does it mean that the wisdom found in the Torah is an example of universal wisdom, which can also be found in other sources?[20] The Wisdom of Solomon does not repeat Ben Sira's identification of wisdom and the Torah, and it speaks in good sapiential fashion of the righteous and the wicked. Yet the second half of the book is a paraphrase of Israelite history. There is still no specific mention of Israel, but the "holy people and blameless race" that is brought through the Red Sea is evidently Israel.[21] Implicit here is the assumption that Israel can be identified with the righteous, and that the story of Israel can be used typologically to illustrate the workings of God with all people. But the assumption that Israel is holy and righteous is sometimes problematic. There is a real tension between the sapiential dualism of justice and wickedness, and any doctrine of election by which one side of that dualism is identified with a specific people.

Ezra's indebtedness to the wisdom tradition can be seen in the recurring references to creation in his laments.[22] It can also be seen in his concern with the limits of human understanding and his expectation that at least the things of earth should be within his grasp. The fact that at least occasionally he is concerned for non-Israelite humanity and frames his questions in universal terms also testifies to the influence of this tradition. But, as Hogan has noted, "Ezra's preoccupation with God's election of and covenant with Israel is a more obvious feature of his theology than its sapiential basis."[23] Ezra stands, then, in the tradition of the covenantalized

---

American Academy of Religion 15.1 Supplement Series B 35-67 (1977), reprinted in idem, *Encounters with Biblical Theology* (Minneapolis: Fortress, 2005) 91-104.

20. See Hogan, "Theologies in Conflict," chapter 2.

21. Wisdom of Solomon 10:15-21. See further my essay, "Natural Theology and Biblical Tradition: The Case of Hellenistic Judaism," *Catholic Biblical Quarterly* 60 (1998) 1-15, reprinted in *Encounters with Biblical Theology*, 117-26.

22. See Michael A. Knibb, "Apocalyptic and Wisdom in 4 Ezra," *Journal of Jewish Studies* 13 (1983) 56-74; Hogan, "Theologies in Conflict," 117-29.

23. Hogan, "Theologies in Conflict," 121.

wisdom of Ben Sira. His preoccupation with election is troubled, however, by empirical reality, in the manner of Job and Qoheleth, for there is little in Ezra's situation to support the view that Israel is especially chosen or loved by God.

A second development in the Jewish wisdom tradition in the Hellenistic age is the acceptance of belief in reward and punishment after death.[24] Such a belief was viewed with extreme skepticism by Qoheleth and was categorically rejected by Ben Sira. The earliest Jewish wisdom text to embrace such a belief was 4QInstruction, a text preserved among the Dead Sea Scrolls, but not necessarily sectarian.[25] A kindred text, in many ways, is found in the *Epistle of Enoch* (*1 Enoch* 91–104), the only part of *1 Enoch* that is not in the form of a revelation and that relies to a considerable degree on sapiential forms of address.[26] Neither the Epistle nor 4QInstruction accords any special role to Israel, although both are evidently familiar with the Torah.

Hogan argues that Uriel's theology stands in this tradition. Uriel presents himself as a teacher and makes frequent use of analogies from nature, but in his view there is a sharp disjunction between this world and the world to come. Unlike 4QInstruction, he attaches great importance to the Torah, but he divorces it from its covenantal context. This Law is apparently available to all human beings. Like 4QInstruction, however, Uriel emphasizes individual salvation. He reinterprets Deuteronomy 30:19, "I have set before you life and death," so that the choice is presented to individuals rather than to Israel. Of course individual reward and punishment could be combined with a concern for the covenant people. The

---

24. See now Samuel Adams, *Wisdom in Transition: Act and Consequence in Second Temple Instructions* (JSJSup 125; Leiden: Brill, 2008).

25. See my essay "The Eschatologizing of Wisdom in the Dead Sea Scrolls," in John J. Collins, Gregory E. Sterling, and Ruth A. Clements, eds., *Sapiential Perspectives: Wisdom Literature in Light of the Dead Sea Scrolls* (Studies of the Texts of the Desert of Judah 51; Leiden: Brill, 2004) 49-65; Matthew J. Goff, *The Worldly and Heavenly Wisdom of 4QInstruction* (Studies of the Texts of the Desert of Judah 50; Leiden: Brill, 2003) 168-215.

26. See George W. E. Nickelsburg, *1 Enoch 1: A Commentary on the Book of Enoch, Chapters 1–36; 81–108* (Hermeneia; Minneapolis: Fortress, 2001) 34. On the relation between the Epistle and 4QInstruction see Torleif Elgvin, "An Analysis of 4QInstruction" (Ph. D. dissertation, Hebrew University, 1998) 168-72; Loren T. Stuckenbruck, "4QInstruction and the Possible Influence of Early Enochic Traditions: An Evaluation," in C. Hempel, A. Lange, and H. Lichtenberger, eds., *The Wisdom Texts from Qumran and the Development of Sapiential Thought* (Bibliotheca Ephemeridum Theologicarum Lovaniensium 159; Leuven: Peeters, 2002) 245-61; Goff, *The Worldly and Heavenly Wisdom*, 186-89.

Wisdom of Solomon adapts the Platonic theory of the immortality of the soul, which was notoriously individualistic. Yet it also continues to speak of God's people and to invest the story of the Exodus with typological significance. Uriel, too, acknowledges the election of Israel, but, to a far greater degree than the Wisdom of Solomon, his focus is on the judgment of individuals. This belief in individual judgment after death was introduced into the Jewish tradition in the apocalyptic Book of Daniel, where it coexisted with the hope for a kingdom (on earth) for the people of God. But the apocalyptic hope for reward and punishment after death also lent itself to an individualistic eschatology, as can be seen especially in later apocalypses such as *3 Baruch* and *2 Enoch*.

An Apocalyptic Solution

4 Ezra, however, does not remain an inconclusive dialogue between Uriel and Ezra. In the end, both of the sapiential theologies of the dialogues are superseded by apocalyptic revelations. Practically all students of *4 Ezra* have recognized that Ezra's vision of a woman in 9:26–10:26 is the turning point of the book.[27] Ezra undergoes something like a conversion experience. In the process, he moves beyond the covenantalized wisdom of the dialogues, which is seen to be inadequate. Many scholars have assumed that he succumbs to Uriel's eschatologized wisdom and accepts it. Wolfgang Harnisch realized that this assumption is problematic, as the theology of the visions is actually quite different from that of Uriel in the dialogues. Consequently, he proposed to excise these chapters as secondary additions.[28] Hogan also recognizes the difference in perspectives, but rejects the textual surgery. It is not the case that the angel of the dialogues simply prevails. While Ezra lets himself be persuaded and consoled by the visions,

27. M. E. Stone, "On Reading an Apocalypse," in John J. Collins and James H. Charlesworth, eds., *Mysteries and Revelations: Apocalyptic Studies since the Uppsala Colloquium* (Journal for the Study of Pseudepigrapha Supplement Series 9; Sheffield: Sheffield Academic Press, 1991) 65-78.

28. W. Harnisch, "Der Prophet als Widerpart und Zeuge der Offenbarung. Erwägungen zur Interdependenz von Form und Sache im 4. Buch Esra," in D. E. Hellholm, ed., *Apocalypticism in the Mediterranean World and the Near East* (Tübingen: Mohr, 1983) 461-93. Sanders, *Paul and Palestinian Judaism*, 409-18, takes a similar position, arguing that the last vision plus chapter 14 constitute "a 'saving' appendix" and that the author's view is the same as the angel's.

the angel also concedes something. In his concluding speech in 9:20-22 he says:

> So I considered my world, and behold, it was lost, and my earth, and behold it was in peril because of the devices of those who had come into it. And I saw and spared some with great difficulty, and saved for myself one grape out of a cluster, and one plant out of a great forest. So let the multitude perish which has been born in vain, but let my grape and my plant be saved, because with much labor I have perfected them.

Here, for the first time in Uriel's speech, is the suggestion that the righteous few are saved by an initiative of divine mercy.[29] They are also, in effect, a chosen people. Uriel is not explicit as to whether the reference is to Israel. The imagery of grape and plant certainly lends itself to such an interpretation, although one grape can hardly represent all Israel. The image of a vine is already used for the election of Israel in *4 Ezra* 5:23.[30] Hogan argues, however, that "the remnant symbolism is undeniably present, but in light of Uriel's willingness to extend biblical motifs to humanity in general (cf. 7:127-31) the whole from which the part is spared need not be Israel."[31] The reference is certainly to "the eschatological survivors," in Michael E. Stone's phrase.[32] This passage at least admits of interpretation in terms of the election, not of all Israel, but of a remnant thereof. Up to this point, Uriel had allowed no place for election at all.

Uriel appears again at the end of chapter 10, after Ezra's vision of the woman, but thereafter he is not named again. He may be identified as the *angelus interpres* who interprets the last two visions to Ezra, but here he acts only as the mouthpiece of the Lord. The theology that he propounded in the dialogues also fades from view.

In any case, the last two visions use the language of national resto-

---

29. M. Knibb, "2 Esdras," in R. J. Coggins and M. Knibb, *The First and Second Books of Esdras* (The Cambridge Bible Commentary; Cambridge: Cambridge University Press, 1979) 217.

30. Stone, *Fourth Ezra*, 300. For the plant imagery, compare Isaiah 60:21 and 61:3. This imagery is widely used in the Dead Sea Scrolls. Cf. Patrick A. Tiller, "The 'Eternal Planting' in the Dead Sea Scrolls," *Dead Sea Discoveries* 4 (1997) 312-35.

31. See Hogan, "Theologies in Conflict," 174. In contrast, Thompson assumes that "the few" in *4 Ezra* who are saved are Israel, and that "the many" who are not are the Gentiles. *Responsibility for Evil*, 212.

32. Stone, *Fourth Ezra*, 300.

ration. The interpretation of the vision of the lion and the eagle (chaps. 11–12) concludes by promising that the messiah, "from the posterity of David," will first rebuke and then destroy the Roman rulers. Then "he will deliver in mercy the remnant of my people, those who have been saved throughout my borders." In this case there is no doubt as to the ethnic origin of the remnant. In chapter 13, the man from the sea, who is also called "my son," acts in a manner reminiscent of Psalm 2.[33] He reproves the assembled nations, tells them how they are to be tortured, and destroys them without effort. Then he gathers a peaceful multitude: "These are the ten tribes which were led away from their own land into captivity in the days of King Hoshea, whom Shalmaneser the king of the Assyrians led captive" (13:40). Only a remnant of the people left in the land of Israel will be saved, but that remnant is not determined by its righteousness. They are saved because they are the remnant of the chosen people. In the end, an ethnic criterion for salvation prevails.

This apocalyptic theology is distinct both from the covenantal theology of Ezra and from the eschatologized wisdom of Uriel. The covenantal theology is abandoned, because it is not the case that Israel is saved if it keeps the law. The apocalyptic salvation will come at its own proper time, whether Israel keeps the law or not. A remnant is saved because it belongs to the chosen people, not because of its moral superiority. But Uriel's individualistic theology is also tacitly rejected. The visions in chapters 11–12 and 13 conjure up messianic figures who act on behalf of the nation, even if only a remnant of it is spared. It is understandable, then, that some critics have thought these chapters extraneous to the book. A more satisfactory explanation sees progress in the argument, so that neither Uriel nor Ezra prevails, but both are superseded by apocalyptic revelation.

Hogan rightly notes that the apocalyptic solution is not any more satisfying intellectually than the views of Ezra and Uriel.[34] It satisfies Ezra, in part because it addresses the destiny of Israel, which Uriel failed to address. But Hogan also realizes, following Stone, that its impact lies largely in its symbolism. If Ezra was distracted from his questions by Uriel's descriptions of the coming judgment, he is overwhelmed by these visions, much as Job was by the voice from the whirlwind. Unlike the sapiential tradi-

---

33. The Greek *pais*, which was presumably the underlying term here, can mean either servant or son. See Stone, *Fourth Ezra*, 207-14, who argues that the original reference was to "my servant," and Collins, *The Apocalyptic Imagination*, 207-8, for the allusion to Psalm 2, which would favor reading "son."

34. Hogan, "Theologies in Conflict," 272.

tions, apocalyptic revelation did not appeal to the intellect. It appealed to the imagination, and to basic emotions of hope and fear. As Plato also knew, a myth is sometimes more persuasive than an argument.

The belief that Israel is God's chosen people, then, survives in *4 Ezra*, despite Uriel's insistence on individual judgment, on the one hand, and the crushing weight of disconfirming evidence in the destruction of Jerusalem, on the other. The peculiarly difficult circumstances in which this book was written offer an exceptionally good opportunity to reflect on the function of belief in election and on its advantages and disadvantages.

The Function of Belief in Election

"The biblical idea of election," writes Jeremy Cott, "is the ultimate anti-humanistic idea."[35] This assessment of the idea of election rests largely on the story of the conquest of Canaan, and the genocide implied in the biblical account, whether that account is deemed historical or not. Joel Kaminsky has objected to "the assumption that election theology inherently leads to destructive violence directed against those not elected."[36] Election did not normally imply the mistreatment of non-Israelites. In the case of *4 Ezra,* mistreatment of Gentiles is hardly an issue. The book speaks from a situation in which Israel has been defeated and humiliated, and has no power to mistreat anyone. Nonetheless, Gentiles can scarcely fail to find Ezra's language of election offensive. Consider the corollary: "As for the other nations which have descended from Adam, thou hast said that they are nothing, and that they are like spittle, and thou hast compared their abundance to a drop from a bucket." And even if Ezra's theology is not affirmed, the concluding apocalyptic visions are not much better: in the eschatological finale, the nations will be assembled, rebuked, and destroyed, to make way for the remnant of Judah and the lost tribes of Israel. No doubt, Christian claims to have "the one true faith" and predictions of what will happen to infidels at the final judgment are just as offensive to Jews and other non-Christians, and Muslims ring their own variation on the theme. But the fact that other religions have analogous problems does not really mitigate the offence.

35. Cott, "The Biblical Problem of Election," *Journal of Ecumenical Studies* 21 (1984) 199-228 (204).

36. Joel Kaminsky, "Did Election Imply the Mistreatment of Non-Israelites?" *Harvard Theological Review* 96 (2003) 397-425 (398). See also his book, *Yet I Loved Jacob: Reclaiming the Biblical Concept of Election* (Nashville: Abingdon, 2007) 107-36.

Kaminsky points out, again quite properly, that election may serve various purposes.[37] It can, for example, be election for service, or it can serve a teleological purpose in relation to the world as a whole. In the case of *4 Ezra,* the question of election is not raised for the benefit of Gentile humanity. What is at stake is the salvation of Israel, in some form. In fairness to Ezra, he is not looking for the destruction of the Gentiles in his complaints. He is only asking for the consolation of Israel. The response of Uriel, which says in effect that the important thing is what happens after death, provides only cold comfort: people are judged on their merits, and there is no special consideration for Israel. The apocalyptic visions, however, promise not only the restoration of the lost tribes, but also the destruction of the Gentiles.

That *4 Ezra* is ethnocentric can hardly be denied. Ethnocentrism is not always regarded as a vice in the postmodern age. It is an essential means of maintaining minority identity. It is only malignant when it is combined with the exercise of political power, and it can be justifiable in contextual terms. Ethnocentrism, in short, can be redeemed, to a degree, by a postmodern "ethic of difference."[38]

Such redemption is easy enough in the case of *4 Ezra.* The idea that God loves you more than anyone else is not only forgivable but perhaps admirable in the wake of a disaster like the destruction of Jerusalem or the Holocaust. It is arguable that the belief in divine election always functioned to reassure a relatively small and powerless people and bolster their self-esteem and confidence. This argument is not entirely compelling. The tensions in the wisdom tradition, which Hogan has shown to underlie *4 Ezra,* are not peculiar to situations of crisis, and ethnocentrism survives and flourishes in times of prosperity. But a belief in divine election is certainly more palatable when it is held as a consolation in times of despair than when it is held by the rich and powerful.

If the idea of election is redeemed in the case of *4 Ezra,* this is mainly because of the flashes of deeply felt human solidarity exhibited by Ezra, especially in the third dialogue: "O earth, what have you brought forth? . . . O Adam, what have you done?" Ironically, such sympathy for the common lot of humanity is not intrinsic to any of the theological perspectives found

37. "Did Election Imply the Mistreatment of Non-Israelites?" 423.

38. Mark Brett, "The Ethics of Postcolonial Criticism," *Semeia* 75 (1996) 219-28 (222), paraphrasing Daniel Boyarin, *A Radical Jew: Paul and the Politics of Identity* (Berkeley: University of California Press, 1994) 247-50.

in the book. The "ethnocentric covenantalism" of Ezra regards the nations as spittle; the eschatological wisdom of Uriel seems to care only whether they keep the law; the apocalyptic visions consign them to destruction. But, to paraphrase George Bernard Shaw, no one can be theological all the time.[39] Every now and then one forgets, and something comes out quite naturally. Ezra, in effect, puts a human face on the stern eschatological wisdom of Uriel when he momentarily forgets the special plight of his particular people and mourns the common fate of the children of Adam. He can still find warrants and precedents in the biblical tradition for doing so. Uriel says that salvation is like agriculture: not all seeds planted by a farmer grow, and not all who are "sown" in the world are saved (8:41). Ezra retorts effectively: if seed does not come up, it perishes. "But man, who has been formed by your hands and is called your own image because he is made like you, and for whose sake you formed all things — have you made him like the farmer's seed? No, O Lord, who are over us! But spare your people and have mercy on your inheritance, for you have mercy on your own creation." Here Ezra does not claim that creation was for the sake of one people, Israel, but that it was for humanity at large, made in the image of God, according to the opening chapter of Genesis, and that Israel is an instance of it. The election of one people must be seen in the broader perspective of creation, even in a time of crisis.

39. In *Androcles and the Lion:* "I don't think anyone can be Christian all the time."

PART III

Themes in Jewish Apocalyptic Literature

CHAPTER 10

Jerusalem and the Temple in Jewish Apocalyptic Literature of the Second Temple Period

The category of apocalyptic literature takes its name from the New Testament Book of Revelation, or Apocalypse of John, which is often called simply The Apocalypse. Although that book is one of the foundational writings of Christianity, its author was a Jew and regarded himself as a true Israelite. His book is replete with imagery drawn from the Hebrew scriptures, and he was heir to a long tradition of Jewish apocalyptic literature. At the heart of the book is a bitter polemic against Rome, which is called Babylon, a name it is also given in several Jewish apocalypses from the end of the first century of the Common Era. Rome was the new Babylon, because it had destroyed Jerusalem and its temple, just as Babylon had done in the era of Nebuchadnezzar. At the end of the book, however, in chapter 21, the visionary turns his eyes to the future:

> Then I saw a new heaven and a new earth; for the first heaven and the first earth had passed away, and the sea was no more. And I saw the holy city, the new Jerusalem, coming down out of heaven from God, prepared as a bride adorned for her husband. And I heard a loud voice from the throne saying: See, the home of God is among mortals. He will dwell with them as their God. (Rev. 21:1-3)

Later in the same chapter, the visionary is taken by an angel to a great and high mountain, and shown the holy city Jerusalem coming down out of heaven from God. He is shown its wall and its gates, adorned with pearls and precious stones. He breaks with Jewish tradition, however, at one point: "I saw no temple in the city, for its temple is the Lord God the Almighty" (v. 22). Jerusalem, of course, was always associated with the presence of God, but that presence was normally located in the temple. We shall see, however, that even in this matter Jewish tradition was complex and that the temple was often problematic, especially in apocalyptic literature.

Much of Jewish apocalyptic literature was inspired by three major crises that befell Jerusalem and its temple. The first was the destruction of city and temple in the Babylonian era. While the literature of this period is prophetic rather than apocalyptic, it develops already many of the themes and motifs that appear again in the apocalyptic literature of the Hellenistic and Roman periods. The second was the crisis of the Maccabean era, when the temple was defiled, first by the Hellenizing High Priests and then by the Syrian soldiers of Antiochus Epiphanes. This upheaval was the occasion for the first great outpouring of apocalyptic literature in the Books of Daniel and Enoch, and also initiated the course of events that led to the formation of the sect that we know from the Dead Sea Scrolls. The third was the destruction of Jerusalem by the Romans in 70 CE. This too was the occasion of several apocalyptic visions, including the New Testament Book of Revelation. The Jewish apocalypses of *4 Ezra, 2 Baruch,* and *3 Baruch* were all written near the end of the first century CE, and expressed reactions to the great disaster that had befallen the Jewish people.

Exile and Restoration

The prophet Ezekiel had two great visions concerning the Jerusalem temple, one concerning its destruction and one envisioning its restoration. The first of these is found in chapters 8–10. Here Ezekiel has a fantastic vision of abominations that are said to take place in the temple. These involve the veneration of an image that provokes jealousy, creeping things of various sorts, and women weeping for Tammuz. The consequence, we are told, is "to drive me far from my sanctuary" (Ezek. 8:6). There follows a vision of slaughter, in which all who do not bear a mark on their foreheads are put to the sword. Before this, however, the glory of the Lord goes up from the cherub on which it had rested. Eventually, it lifts up from the city and rests on the mountain east of the city. Ezekiel here acknowledges an ancient belief that a city could not be captured so long as its patron deity was in it, a belief that is already attested in connection with the destruction of the Mesopotamian city of Ur at the beginning of the second millennium. The second great vision in the Book of Ezekiel concerning the temple is the vision of the restored land of Israel that concludes the book, in chapters 40–48. In this new and utopian dispensation, Jerusalem is not mentioned by name but is referred to as "the city." It is subsumed into the consecrated area or תרומה, which is a strip of land from the Jordan to the sea, separating the territories of Judah to the north and Benjamin to the south. Within this area, strips of land are set aside for the priests, the levites, the city, and the prince. The temple is located in the middle of the territory of the priests. The area of the city proper is declared profane (48:15: חל הוא), and the territory of the city is only half the area of that of the priests. Ezekiel's vision, then, entails a radical re-evaluation of Jerusalem, which becomes virtually an appendage of the temple precinct under the control of the Zadokite priests.[1]

The purpose of this re-evaluation is clear enough. In Ezekiel's view, the disaster that befell Israel was caused by the failure to protect the sanctity of the temple. In future, "no foreigner, uncircumcised in heart and flesh" is to enter the sanctuary (44:9). Levites and ordinary Israelites were restricted to the outer court. Pride of place in the new cultic order is given to the descendants of Zadok, who are credited with preserving the sanctuary when the rest of the people sinned, and who alone may enter the inner court. It is their concern to teach the people the difference between the sacred and the profane. If impurity was the cause of disaster, purity must henceforth be of paramount importance. The emphasis has shifted from Jerusalem, the ancient seat of the monarchy, to the sanctuary and its regulation. The Davidic prince retains a role and is given his own allotment of land in the תרומה, but he is, in the words of Jon Levenson, an apolitical messiah,[2] charged with providing the offerings for the sacrificial cult (46:17, 22-25).

Ezekiel's vision was eschatological; it was not a pragmatic program for renewal, and it was never realized in the Second Temple period.[3] Its

---

1. On Ezekiel's vision see W. Zimmerli, *Ezekiel 2: A Commentary on the Book of the Prophet Ezekiel, Chapters 25–48* (Hermeneia; Philadelphia: Fortress, 1983) 325-553; also J. D. Levenson, *The Theology of the Program of Restoration of Ezekiel 40–48* (Missoula, MT: Scholars Press, 1976). I am indebted to the essay of Adela Yarbro Collins, "The Dream of the New Jerusalem at Qumran," presented at the Princeton Conference on the Dead Sea Scrolls in November 1997, and published in James H. Charlesworth, ed., *The Bible and the Dead Sea Scrolls,* vol. 3: *The Scrolls and Christian Origins* (Princeton Symposium on Judaism and Christian Origins; Waco, TX: Baylor University Press, 2006) 231-54.

2. Levenson, *The Theology of the Program of Restoration,* 75.

3. S. S. Tuell, "Ezekiel 40–42 as Verbal Icon," *Catholic Biblical Quarterly* 58 (1996)

importance for our theme is that it inaugurated a tradition of speculation about an ideal temple and city. Other prophets of the exilic period also spoke of Jerusalem in utopian terms. The prophet we know as Second Isaiah promised that God would "set your stones in antimony, lay your foundations with sapphires, make your pinnacles of agate, your gates of carbuncles, and all your wall of precious stones" (Isa. 54:11-12). Another prophecy in the Book of Isaiah predicted that the glory of Lebanon, the cypress, the plane, and the pine, would be brought to Jerusalem to glorify the place of the sanctuary (Isa. 60:13). Measured against such expectations, the actual temple that was built in the Persian period was a considerable disappointment. The Book of Ezra reports that the old men who remembered Solomon's temple wept at the sight of its replacement (Ezra 3:12). The prophet Haggai asked those who remembered the first temple, "How do you see it now? Is it not in your sight as nothing?" But Haggai went on to prophesy that the Lord would, "in a little while, shake the heavens and the earth and the sea and the dry land, and shake all nations so that the treasures of all nations would come in and fill this house with splendor" (Hag. 2:6-7). The final glory would be greater than the former. But this prophecy, too, was not fulfilled. It is no wonder, then, that another prophet expressed skepticism and disillusionment about this promised temple:

> Heaven is my throne and earth is my footstool;
> What is the house that you would build for me? (Isa. 66:1)

This question had been raised before by the Deuteronomistic historians, in Solomon's prayer at the consecration of the first temple in 1 Kings 8, and less directly in Nathan's oracle to David in 2 Samuel 7. In those passages the objection was overcome. The prophet whose oracles are preserved in the last chapters of Isaiah was more radical: "For I am about to create new heavens and a new earth" (Isa. 65:17). In this new creation, Jerusalem would be a delight, but there is no mention of a temple. Perhaps the Isaianic prophet thought, like the much later prophet of Revelation, that the immediate presence of God would render the temple unnecessary.

The hope for a new heaven and a new earth is typical of apocalyptic literature, and may fairly be taken as one of the motifs that distinguishes

---

649-64, goes farther and proposes that Ezekiel's vision concerns the heavenly temple, but this is difficult to maintain in view of the location of the temple within the land of Israel. Full bibliography of the debate about the meaning of Ezekiel's vision may be found in Tuell's article.

the hope of the apocalyptists from that of the prophets. Accordingly, Paul Hanson has argued that Isaiah 56–66, usually called Trito-Isaiah, should be regarded as "the dawn of apocalyptic."[4] This argument has some merit. These oracles, like later apocalypses, hold out little hope for fulfillment in this world without the aid of some miraculous divine intervention. Isaiah 66 is atypical of Jewish apocalyptic literature, however, in questioning the need for a temple. Much more typical is the tradition emanating from Ezekiel, which dreamed of a new Jerusalem, or a new temple, in terms that surpassed any historical reality.

The Maccabean Crisis

The high standards of purity set by Ezekiel were not maintained throughout the Second Temple period. This is clear from the narrative of Nehemiah and from the prophetic denunciations of Malachi. One early apocalypse of the Hellenistic period, the *Animal Apocalypse* in *1 Enoch,* went so far as to claim that all the offerings in the second temple were impure (*1 En.* 89:73). In this apocalypse, the Jews are represented by sheep, and the other nations by various wild animals.[5] The temple is symbolized by a tower, and the period after the exile is described as follows: "And they began again to place a table before the tower, but all the bread that was upon it was polluted, and it was not pure" (*1 En.* 89:73). This apocalypse goes on to envision a new "house," which God will set up in the last times: "And I saw until the owner of the sheep brought a house, new and larger and loftier than the former, and he erected it in the place of the former one which had been rolled up. And all of its pillars were new and the ornaments were new and larger than those of the former old one which he had taken out. And all the sheep were in the midst of it" (*1 En.* 90:28-29). Since the temple is called a tower in the earlier passage, the "house" here should probably be identified as Jerusalem. Surprisingly, there is no tower in the new house, and so one might infer that the new Jerusalem will have no temple. If this is correct, the *Animal Apocalypse* is an important witness to a minority tradition, in which there is no temple in the eschatological age. The *Animal Apocalypse* was written in the Maccabean period, when

---

4. P. D. Hanson, *The Dawn of Apocalyptic* (Philadelphia: Fortress, 1975).
5. See the commentary of P. A. Tiller, *A Commentary on the Animal Apocalypse of 1 Enoch* (Atlanta: Scholars Press, 1993).

the Jerusalem temple was not destroyed but underwent severe disruption. The problems were initiated by the Hellenizing High Priests, Jason and Menelaus, but became acute when Antiochus Epiphanes gave over the temple area to his Syrian soldiers. The traditional cult was suspended and replaced with pagan observances. A Syrian-style altar was superimposed on the sacrificial altar in the temple, and this was dubbed "the abomination that makes desolate" in the Book of Daniel,[6] a phrase that reverberates in later apocalyptic literature, especially in the New Testament. It is possible that the *Animal Apocalypse* is reacting in a hyperbolic way to these events, and dismissing the entire second temple because of its recent pollution. It is also possible that it represents a tradition of dissent that had been critical of the Jerusalem priesthood even before these developments.

The main apocalyptic reaction to the crisis of the Maccabean era is found in the Book of Daniel. The profanation of the temple looms large in this apocalypse. One of the burning questions in the book concerns the length of the period of trial: "For how long is this vision concerning the regular burnt offering, the transgression that makes desolate and the giving over of the sanctuary and host to be trampled?" (8:13). The book famously gives more than one answer to this question. The most general formulation is "a time, times, and half a time," or three and a half years. In chapter 8 we are given a more specific number: "For two thousand three hundred evenings and mornings [= 1,150 days]; then the sanctuary shall be restored to its rightful state" (8:14). At the end of the book, however, we are given two further calculations: "From the time that the regular burnt offering is taken away and the abomination that desolates is set up, there shall be one thousand two hundred ninety days. Happy are those who persevere and attain the thousand three hundred thirty-five days" (12:11-12). All of these figures can be regarded as approximations of three and a half years. It would seem that when the 1,150 days had passed, the author revised his calculation, and did so again after the 1,290 days had passed. This kind of re-calculation is well known in other millennial groups, such as the Millerites in nineteenth-century America. What is remarkable in the case of Daniel is that, according to the books of Maccabees, Judas Maccabee had actually restored the temple three years to the day after it had been profaned (1 Macc. 4:52-54; 2 Macc. 10:5). All the predictions in the Book of Daniel anticipate a longer period of profanation. If we are right that the later calculations were added after the first predicted dates had passed, it follows that the author

6. See J. J. Collins, *Daniel* (Hermeneia; Minneapolis: Fortress, 1993) 357-58.

of the Book of Daniel did not recognize the restoration by Judas Maccabee as satisfactory. He was looking for a more spectacular restoration, which would include the resurrection of the dead.[7] But he did not think that the pollution of the temple had been really removed. Daniel does not offer a vision of a restored Jerusalem or temple, although he clearly expected that the sanctuary would be set right at the end of days.

The Dead Sea Scrolls

The author of Daniel was not the only devout Jew of the second century BCE who was dissatisfied with the Maccabean restoration of Jerusalem. The Dead Sea Scrolls contain the literature of a movement that disapproved so strongly of the Hasmonean priesthood that it broke away from the temple cult. This movement is most plausibly to be identified with the Essenes, who are known to us from the writings of Philo and Josephus. Philo tells us that the Essenes worshiped God "not by offering sacrifices but by resolving to sanctify their minds" (*Quod Omnis* 75). Josephus, in contrast, says that they "send votive offerings to the temple, but perform their sacrifices employing a different ritual of purification. For this reason they are barred from those precincts of the temple that are frequented by all the people and perform their sacrifices by themselves" (*Ant.* 18.19). In the Dead Sea Scrolls, in the Damascus Document, we are told that "none of those who have entered the covenant shall enter the sanctuary to kindle his altar in vain" (CD 6:11-13). This statement is ambiguous, depending on how we take the phrase "in vain." It may mean that the Essenes should refrain from all temple sacrifice, but it can more plausibly be taken to mean that they should not follow rituals that the sect regarded as improper. In any case, it seems clear that the Essenes were unhappy with the way the sacrificial cult was being carried out in the Jerusalem temple. From the evidence of the Scrolls, both in the Damascus Document and in 4QMMT, it would seem that a major factor was that they followed a different cultic calendar from the one followed in the temple. This disagreement made participation in the temple cult practically impossible. Since the High Priest is often characterized as the Wicked Priest in the pesharim from Qumran, many scholars have supposed that the sect broke with the temple because the

---

7. J. J. Collins, "The Meaning of the End in the Book of Daniel," in idem, *Seers, Sibyls and Sages in Hellenistic-Roman Judaism* (Leiden: Brill, 1997) 157-65.

Hasmoneans were not from the legitimate priestly line, but this objection is not voiced explicitly in the Dead Sea Scrolls.[8]

But if the Essenes were unhappy with current temple practice, this did not mean that they did not value temple cult in principle.[9] They had a strong priestly ideology, and consequently their exile from the temple presented them with a considerable problem. We can distinguish at least two kinds of response that they developed to cope with this problem.[10]

First, the sect regarded itself, or an elite community within it, as a spiritual temple. The Rule of the Community stipulates:

> When these are in Israel, the Council of the Community shall be established in truth. It shall be an everlasting Plantation, a House of Holiness (בית קדש) for Israel, an Assembly of Supreme Holiness for Aaron, with everlasting knowledge of the covenant of justice, and shall offer up sweet fragrance. . . . And they shall be an agreeable offering, atoning for the Land and determining the judgment of wickedness, and there shall be no more iniquity. (1QS 8:4-10)

The Pesher on Isaiah interprets the prophecy of a new Jerusalem in Isaiah 54 with reference to this "Council of the Community":

> And I will lay your foundations with sapphires: Interpreted, this concerns the priests and the people who laid the foundations of the Council of the Community . . . the congregation of His elect . . . like a sapphire among stones. [And I will make] all your pinnacles [of agate]: Interpreted, this concerns the twelve . . . who shall enlighten by judgment of the Urim and Thummim. (4Q164: 1-7)

Second, the community turned its mind to the heavenly temple and its cult. Already in the Hebrew Bible, Isaiah chapter 6 had reported a scene from a heavenly liturgy, where the cherubim called to one another, "holy, holy, holy is the Lord of hosts." This scene is developed in the apocalyptic

---

8. See further Collins, "The Origin of the Qumran Community: A Review of the Evidence," in *Seers, Sibyls and Sages*, 239-60.

9. On the paradoxical relationship of the Qumran sect to the temple, see especially F. Schmidt, *La Pensée du Temple. De Jérusalem à Qoumrân* (Paris: Seuil, 1994).

10. See Yarbro Collins, "The Dream of a New Jerusalem." Also L. H. Schiffman, "Jerusalem in the Dead Sea Scrolls," in M. Poorthuis and C. Safrai, eds., *The Centrality of Jerusalem: Historical Perspectives* (Kampen: Kok/Pharos, 1996) 73-88.

literature.[11] Daniel chapter 7 envisions God as a white-headed Ancient of Days seated on his throne. "A thousand thousands served him, and ten thousand times ten thousand stood before him." In *1 Enoch* 14, Enoch is taken up to heaven. There he enters "a large house which was built of hail stones, and the wall of that house was like a mosaic made of hail stones, and its floor was snow. Its roof was like the path of the stars and flashes of lightning, and among them were fiery Cherubim, and their heaven was like water. . . it was hot as fire and cold as snow, and there was neither pleasure nor life in it." From there he enters another house, which was larger than the former and was built of a tongue of fire. This house surpassed description. Its floor and roof were burning fire. In this house he saw the divine throne. Again, "ten thousand times ten thousand stood before him, but he needed no holy counsel. And the Holy Ones who were near to him did not leave by night or day and did not depart from him."[12]

In the Dead Sea Scrolls, the most elaborate account of the heavenly temple and its liturgy is found in the *Songs of the Sabbath Sacrifice,* which provide songs for each of thirteen sabbaths.[13] The first five are concerned with the establishment and responsibilities of the angelic priesthood. God "has established for himself priests of the inner sanctum, the holiest of the holy ones." They are "ministers of the Presence in his glorious *debir* (or inner sanctuary)." The sixth to eighth songs are dominated by repetitive structures in which the number seven appears prominently. The seventh song calls on the angels, and also various parts of the heavenly temple, to praise God. The ninth to thirteenth songs contain a systematic description of the heavenly temple that is based in part on Ezekiel 40–48. The twelfth song opens with a lengthy description of the throne-chariot, similar to Ezekiel chapter 1. The final song refers to the sacrifices of the holy ones and describes the glory of the angelic high priests.

While there is debate about the function of the *Songs,* the most persuasive view, in my opinion, is that they constitute "a quasi-mystical liturgy, designed to evoke a sense of being present in the heavenly temple."[14]

---

11. I. Gruenwald, *Apocalyptic and Merkavah Mysticism* (Leiden: Brill, 1979); M. Himmelfarb, *Ascent to Heaven in Jewish and Christian Apocalypses* (New York: Oxford University Press, 1993).

12. On the temple connotations of Enoch's vision see especially Himmelfarb, *Ascent to Heaven,* 14-16.

13. C. Newsom, *Songs of the Sabbath Sacrifices* (Atlanta: Scholars Press, 1985).

14. Newsom, *Songs of the Sabbath Sacrifices,* 59, 72. See further J. J. Collins, *Apocalypticism in the Dead Sea Scrolls* (London: Routledge, 1997) 140-43.

As we know from the prophet Isaiah, the idea of a heavenly temple and cult is very ancient. Normally, the cult in the earthly temple was thought to harmonize with the heavenly liturgy, and so the two were complementary. In the case of Qumran, however, the cult of the earthly temple in Jerusalem was judged invalid, and so the heavenly liturgy functioned in effect as a replacement for it. The sectarians could not participate in the sacrifices in the temple. Instead they recited their songs about the heavenly temple, where they participated in their imagination. This procedure is in fact typically apocalyptic. When the actual empirical world is out of joint, the apocalypses imagine an alternative universe where everything is in order.

But while the Qumran community disapproved of, and was barred from, the Jerusalem temple, it had not given up on it entirely. Two compositions found at Qumran provide elaborate descriptions of a new temple and a new Jerusalem. These are the *Temple Scroll* and the *New Jerusalem* text. It is not certain that either was strictly a composition of the Dead Sea sect. It is possible that both come from related priestly circles and were composed before the sect broke away from the Jerusalem temple. If this is the case, then these texts provide evidence of an ongoing tradition of utopian thinking with regard to the temple. Even if they were not composed at Qumran, it is clear that they held important places in the sectarian library.

The *Temple Scroll* is a synthetic edition of laws from Leviticus and Deuteronomy. It is presented as the revelation of God to Moses, but it is very unlikely that it was intended to replace the traditional Torah. Rather it was a guide to the Torah, which emphasized some things, omitted others, and advanced a particular line of interpretation. About two-thirds of the sixty-six chapters of the scroll are taken up with matters relating to the temple (columns 3:1–13:7), the cult (13:8–29:10), and the city (columns 30:1–47:18). The temple envisioned is about three times the size of the Herodian enclosure,[15] and is distinguished by the strictness of its purity laws and ritual observances. The attention to the architectural design of the temple and courtyards is reminiscent of Ezekiel 40–48, but the *Temple Scroll* differs from the biblical model in important respects.[16] It refers to numerous cities in the land of Israel, whereas Ezekiel refers to only one.

15. M. Broshi, "The Gigantic Dimensions of the Visionary Temple in the Temple Scroll," *Biblical Archaeology Review* 13 (1987) 36-37.

16. L. H. Schiffman, "Sacred Space: The Land of Israel in the Temple Scroll," *Biblical Archaeology Today, 1990. Proceedings of the Second International Congress on Biblical Archaeology* (Jerusalem: Israel Exploration Society, 1993) 398-410; Yarbro Collins, "The Dream of a New Jerusalem."

More important is the relation of the city to the temple. In Ezekiel's vision they were separated, and the city was declared profane, although it too was located in the תרומה or strip of land set aside for the Lord. In the *Temple Scroll,* however, the city is identified as "the city of the sanctuary" and shares in its sanctity:

> The city which I will sanctify, causing my name and [my] sanctuar[y] to abide [in it], shall be holy and pure of all impurity with which they can become impure. Whatever is in it shall be pure. Whatever enters it shall be pure: wine, oil, all food and all moistened (food) shall be clean. No skin of clean animals slaughtered in their cities shall be brought there (to the city of the sanctuary). . . . You shall not profane the city where I cause my name and my sanctuary to abide. (47:3-11)

The concern for the purity of the city is such that the latrine (one for the entire city!) must be located at least three thousand cubits outside it (46:13-16) and a man who has intercourse with his wife may not enter any part of the city of the sanctuary for three days (45:11-12). While this concern for the purity of the city was extreme, it was in accordance with a trend in the Hellenistic period. Josephus tells us that when Antiochus III of Syria captured Jerusalem he passed an edict, presumably at the request of the High Priest, that "It is unlawful for any foreigner to enter the enclosure of the temple which is forbidden to the Jews, except to those of them who are accustomed to enter after purifying themselves in accordance with the law of the country. Nor shall anyone bring into the city the flesh of horses or of mules or of wild or tame asses, or of leopards, foxes or hares or, in general, of any animals forbidden to the Jews. Nor is it lawful to bring in their skins or even to breed any of these animals in the city. But only the sacrificial animals known to their ancestors and necessary for the propitiation of God shall they be permitted to use" (*Ant.* 12.145-46). If such a concern for the purity of the city was at one time enacted as the law of the land, we should not be surprised to find the concern intensified in a utopian text like the *Temple Scroll.*

For the *Temple Scroll,* the Temple City was at the center of the land and the temple was at the center of the city. Ezekiel had distinguished an outer court and an inner court. The *Temple Scroll* provides for three concentric courtyards surrounding the temple, one reserved for the priests, the second for the men of Israel over the age of twenty, and the third for the women of Israel and for foreigners who were born in the land of Israel

169

(40:6).[17] Ezekiel makes no allowance for foreigners. In the *Temple Scroll*, both the temple and the city are constructed as squares. This idea also had some wider currency in Second Temple Judaism. In the *Jewish War* 6.310-11, Josephus says that when the rebels seized the temple area during the revolt against Rome, they "reduced the temple to a square, although they had it recorded in their oracles that the city and the sanctuary would be taken when the temple should become four-square." Josephus does not explain these statements. The holy area off-limits to foreigners in Herod's temple already was a square. It has been suggested that what the rebels did was eliminate the court of the Gentiles, and leave only the area from which foreigners were excluded.[18] We do not, however, know of any oracle containing the prediction mentioned by Josephus.

The plan of the temple in the *Temple Scroll* does not conform either to any biblical model or to the reality of Herod's temple. Larry Schiffman has suggested that it represents the layout of the Tabernacle and the desert camp combined.[19] The territories of the tribes are arranged around the holy city so that each has equal access to it. Most fundamentally, it seems to be an attempt to take the commandment "have them make me a sanctuary so that I may dwell in the midst of them" (Exod. 25:8) quite literally, by giving geographical expression to the centrality of the dwelling of God.

We have noted already that the size of the temple was unrealistic. It would have required major alterations of the terrain of Jerusalem to allow for its construction. Nonetheless, it is not strictly an eschatological temple. At the end of the discussion of the festivals in column 29 we are told: "I will dwell with them forever and ever and will sanctify my [sa]nctuary by my glory. I will cause my glory to rest on it until the day of creation on which I shall create my sanctuary establishing it for myself for all time according to the covenant which I have made with Jacob at Bethel." From this it appears that this temple is an interim one, and that it will be replaced by a divinely constructed temple in the new creation.[20] This would be

---

17. See the edition of E. Qimron, *The Temple Scroll: A Critical Edition with Extensive Reconstructions* (Jerusalem: Israel Exploration Society, 1996) 57. J. Maier, *The Temple Scroll: An Introduction, Translation and Commentary* (Sheffield: JSOT, 1985) 37, translates "proselytes born in . . ." but the reference is clearly to non-Jews.

18. J. Maier, "The Temple Scroll and Tendencies in the Cultic Architecture of the Second Commonwealth," in L. H. Schiffman, ed., *Archaeology and History in the Dead Sea Scrolls* (Sheffield: JSOT, 1990) 71.

19. Schiffman, "Sacred Space," 402.

20. The idea that God would build an eschatological temple in the new creation is

the "gate of heaven," like Bethel in the story of Jacob. Contrary to what is often asserted, the *Temple Scroll* is not designed for the messianic age.[21] The king in the *Scroll* is not said to fulfill messianic prophecy and his rule is conditional. The *Scroll* is certainly utopian in character, but it stops short of the definitive claims characteristic of apocalyptic visions.

The idea of a temple made directly by God at the end of days is also found in 4QFlorilegium, which is certainly a product of the Dead Sea sect. The passage in question begins by citing 2 Samuel 7:10-11: "I will appoint a place for my people Israel and will plant them so that they may dwell there and be troubled no more by their enemies. No evildoer shall afflict them again as formerly, from the day that I set judges over my people Israel." This text is explained as follows: "This is the House which [He will build for them in the] last days, as it is written in the book of Moses, in the sanctuary which Thy hands have established, O Lord, the Lord shall reign for ever and ever (Exod. 15:17-18). This is the House into which [the unclean shall] never [enter, nor the uncircumcised,] nor the Ammonite, nor the Moabite, nor the half-breed, nor the foreigner, nor the stranger, ever; for there shall my Holy Ones be. [Its glory shall endure] forever; it shall appear above it perpetually. And strangers shall lay it waste no more, as they formerly laid waste the Sanctuary of Israel because of its sin. And he said to build for him a temple of men (מקדש אדם), that there they may send up to him proper sacrifices" (1:1-13).

The phrase מקדש אדם has been the subject of intense controversy. The text clearly distinguishes between "the temple of Israel," which must be taken to refer to both the first and the second temples, and the eschatological temple made by the hands of the Lord. Some scholars argue that the מקדש אדם should be translated "temple of Adam," and identified with the eschatological "temple of the Lord."[22] Other texts among the Scrolls say that the elect will inherit "the glory of Adam" (CD 3:20) or "the inheritance of Adam" (4QpPss), and the latter text also says that they will inherit "the high mountain of Israel," a phrase that denotes the temple mount in Ezekiel. It is also true that the Book of *Jubilees,* a text closely related to the Dead Sea Scrolls, regards the garden of Eden as analogous to the temple in

---

also found in *Jubilees* 1:17, 27, 29. See J. C. VanderKam, "The Temple Scroll and the Book of Jubilees," in G. Brooke, ed., *Temple Scroll Studies* (Sheffield: JSOT, 1989) 232, 236.

21. J. J. Collins, *The Scepter and the Star: The Messiahs of the Dead Sea Scrolls and Other Ancient Literature* (New York: Doubleday, 1995) 109-11.

22. M. O. Wise, "4QFlorilegium and the Temple of Adam," *RevQ* 15 (1991) 103-32. So also Yarbro Collins, "The Dream of a New Jerusalem."

sanctity (*Jub.* 2:13) and as one of four holy places of the Lord, with Mount Sinai, "the mount of the east," and Mount Zion (*Jub.* 4:26). Further, we read in 2 *Baruch* that God made the future temple that is yet to be revealed when he made Paradise, and that he showed it to Adam, Abraham, and Moses (2 *Baruch* 4). Nonetheless, the concept of "the temple of Adam" is problematic. It is not apparent why the eschatological temple should be called "the temple of Adam" rather than "the temple of Moses," to whom it was also supposedly shown. Moreover, the מקדש אדם, which God said to build for him, can scarcely be identified with "the sanctuary which thy hands have established," and indeed the phrase would seem to stand in deliberate contrast to it.

If we assume that the מקדש אדם is a human temple, there are still two possible interpretations. It could mean "a temple consisting of men," as the Council of the Community is described in the *Community Rule*.[23] Alternatively, we could understand it by analogy with the *Temple Scroll*. In this case, the מקדש אדם is an ideal temple built by men, like the temple of the *Temple Scroll*, but not the temple built by God in the new creation.[24] Either interpretation is possible. The use of the verb "to build" and the focus on the proper sacrifices can be understood most directly if the reference is to an actual temple, but it is also possible that this language should be taken metaphorically.

The other major work from Qumran that describes an eschatological temple is the *Vision of the New Jerusalem,* which is preserved in several manuscripts but in very fragmentary condition.[25] This text, written in Aramaic, is more directly modeled on Ezekiel than is the *Temple Scroll.* The text is narrated in the first person by a visionary who is given a guided tour by an angel. It resembles the *Temple Scroll* insofar as the measurements are unrealistically large, the temple is located within the city, and the outer

---

23. So M. Knibb, *The Qumran Community* (Cambridge: Cambridge University Press, 1987) 258-62; D. Dimant, "4QFlorilegium and the Idea of the Community as Temple," in A. Caquot et al., eds., *Hellenica et Judaica. Hommage à Valentin Nikiprowetzky* (Paris/Leuven: Peeters, 1986) 165-89.

24. So Y. Yadin, "Le Rouleau du Temple," in M. Delcor, ed., *Qoumrân. Sa piété, sa théologie et son milieu* (Leuven: Leuven University Press, 1978) 115-19.

25. F. García Martínez, "The 'New Jerusalem' and the Future Temple of the Manuscripts from Qumran," in idem, *Qumran and Apocalyptic* (Leiden: Brill, 1992) 180-213; M. Chyutin, "The New Jerusalem: Ideal City," *Dead Sea Discoveries* 1 (1994) 71-97; E. Puech, "À propos de la Jérusalem nouvelle d'après les manuscrits de la Mer Morte," *Semitica* 43-44 (1995) 64-73.

wall has gates for each of the twelve tribes. The *New Jerusalem,* however, envisages the city as an immense rectangle. It is divided by six large avenues linking the twelve gates and forming sixteen big blocks of houses.[26] One of these avenues runs through the center of the city, and so the temple is slightly off-center. While the relation of this text to the *Temple Scroll* is not clear, the Hebrew text is the more symmetrical. It is likely that the *New Jerusalem* text was influenced by Hellenistic city planning, and while it shared many of the same values as the *Temple Scroll* its design was less perfectly symmetrical.

The buildings in the *New Jerusalem* are built with precious stones: "And all the buildings in it are of sapphire and rubies, and the windows (?) of gold . . ." (4Q554 frag. 2, col. 2:14-16). This description suggests that the city is the fulfillment of the prophecy of Isaiah 54:11-12, which was applied to the community in the Pesher on Isaiah. Mention of "living waters" and "water from . . ." in another fragment (11Q18 frag. 24:1, 3) evokes Ezekiel 47, which describes waters flowing from below the threshold of the temple and making the Dead Sea fresh. These parallels suggest that the temple of the *New Jerusalem* text is an eschatological temple, created miraculously by God.[27] It is not difficult to see the attraction of such a vision for the Qumran community when it was shut out from the actual temple cult in Jerusalem. It remains possible that this vision of a new Jerusalem and that of the *Temple Scroll* are both older compositions, which appealed to the Dead Sea sect but were not composed within it. It should be noted, however, that the *War Rule* makes provision for the cult during the eschatological war, and so clearly presupposes that there will be a functioning, acceptable temple in the end of days.[28] The Dead Sea sect evidently expected some kind of restoration of the temple before the new creation.

The Roman Period

The long and controversial history of the Jerusalem temple was brought to an end by the Roman soldiers when they captured the city in 70 CE. No event in Jewish history, down to the Holocaust in the last generation, was so traumatic as the destruction of the temple. The trauma was felt wherever

---

26. García Martínez, "The 'New Jerusalem' and the Future Temple," 188.
27. See Yarbro Collins, "The Dream of a New Jerusalem."
28. Schiffman, "Jerusalem in the Dead Sea Scrolls," 83-84.

Jews were scattered in the eastern Mediterranean world. The fifth Sibylline Oracle, written in Egypt early in the second century CE, laments that "I saw the second Temple cast headlong, soaked in fire by an impious hand, the ever-flourishing, watchful Temple of God, made by holy people and hoped by their soul and body to be always imperishable . . . But now a certain insignificant and impious king has gone up, cast it down and left it in ruins" (*Sib. Or.* 5:397-410). The Sibyl finds consolation in a vision of future restoration: "then on that day it will come to pass that the divine and heavenly race of the blessed Jews, who live around the city of God in the middle of the earth, are raised up even to the dark clouds, having built a great wall round about, as far as Joppa" (5:248-52). The extension of the city limits recalls the *Temple Scroll.* Its purpose is similar, to protect the purity of the city: "No longer will the unclean foot of Greeks revel around your land" (5:264-65). The Sibyl predicts a day when a man will come from heaven, holding a scepter given to him by God (5:414-28). The capstone of his work will be the restoration of Jerusalem: "And the city which God desired, this he made more brilliant than stars and sun and moon, and he provided ornament and made a holy temple . . . and he fashioned a great and immense tower over many stadia touching even the clouds and visible to all, so that all faithful and righteous people could see the glory of eternal God, a form desired."

Here again we see the persistent dream for an enlarged Jerusalem and temple that would dominate the land of Israel, and even the inhabited world.

Another, archetypically apocalyptic reaction to the destruction of Jerusalem is found in the book of *4 Ezra.* There Ezra is depicted as grieving over "the desolation of Jerusalem and the wealth of those who live in Babylon" (3:2). The angel Uriel tries to console him by telling him of the coming messianic age, and how "the city that now is not seen will appear" (7:26). Ezra remains disconsolate until he has a vision of a woman grieving over the death of her son. Ezra reacts impatiently: "You most foolish of women, do you not see our mourning and what has happened to us? For Zion the mother of us all is in deep grief and great affliction. It is most appropriate to mourn now, because we are all mourning, and to be sorrowful, because we are all sorrowing; you are sorrowing for one son, but we, the whole world for our mother" (10:7-8). As he speaks to her, however, the woman is transformed before his eyes. The angel explains to him that "This woman whom you saw, whom you now see as an established city, is Zion" (10:44), and that "no work of man's building could endure in a place where the city of the Most High was to be revealed" (10:54). The pain of the loss of Zion is eased by the assurance that a far more splendid city will be revealed by God in due time.

The apocalypse that speaks most directly to the crisis of the destruction of Jerusalem is the *Syriac Apocalypse of Baruch* or *2 Baruch*.[29] In the opening chapter of this work, the word of the Lord comes to Baruch to warn him that God is about to destroy Jerusalem because of the sins of its inhabitants. Baruch is dismayed: "If you destroy your city and deliver up your land to those that hate us, how will the name of Israel again be remembered? How will anyone proclaim your praises? Is the human race to be destroyed and humankind to be blotted out?" The Lord assures him that the city and people are to be given up only for a time, and that the world will not be consigned to oblivion. Then follows one of the more remarkable statements about the temple in the entire literature of the Second Temple period:

> Do you think that this is the city about which I said, On the palms of my hands have I engraved you? This building which now stands in your midst is not the one that is to be revealed, that is with me now, that was prepared beforehand here at the time when I determined to make Paradise, and showed it to Adam before he sinned (though when he disobeyed my commandment it was taken away from him, as was also Paradise). And after this I showed it to my servant Abraham by night among the divided pieces of the victims. And again I showed it also to Moses on Mount Sinai when I showed him the pattern of the tabernacle and all its vessels. And now it is preserved with me, as is also Paradise. (4:3-7)

Nonetheless, God does not allow this temple to be destroyed by the enemy. Instead he sends his angels. First they take the temple vessels and the ornamental vestments of the priests and hide them in the earth:

> Earth, earth, earth, hear the word of the mighty God,
> And receive what I commit to you
> And guard them until the last times,
> So that when you are ordered you may restore them
> And strangers may not get possession of them.

29. F. J. Murphy, "The Temple in the Syriac Apocalypse of Baruch," *JBL* 106 (1987) 671-83.

For the time has come when Jerusalem also will be delivered for a
time,
Until it is said that it shall be restored again forever. (5:8-9)

Then the angels proceed to destroy the city "so that the enemy cannot
boast and say, We have thrown down the wall of Zion and we have burnt
the place of the mighty God."

This opening scene would seem to imply that Zion would again be restored. Yet there is no clear reference to restoration in the remainder of the
book's eighty-seven chapters. The temple is not mentioned in connection
with the messianic age. Chapter 68 refers to the restoration after the first
destruction, noting that it did not measure up to the original temple. Some
scholars see a reference to a future restoration in chapter 32, which states
that "After a little time the temple of Zion will be shaken that it may be
built again. But that building will not remain, but will again after a time be
rooted out, and will remain desolate until the time. And afterwards it must
be renewed in glory and perfected for ever more." The shaking here refers
to the destruction of the first temple. The second temple, too, will not last.
The restoration envisaged, however, is not a human construction, but the
glorious temple that will be revealed from heaven in the new creation. This
is in accordance with *4 Ezra,* which also anticipates the revelation of the
new Jerusalem. If we compare this schema with that of the *Temple Scroll*
and *Florilegium,* there is no place for the interim temple, the מקדש אדם.
After the demise of the second temple there is only desolation until the
new creation when a new temple will be revealed in glory. In the wake of
the destruction, these apocalypses were not composed to give encourage-
ment to further rebellions or to attempts to restore Jerusalem and rebuild
its temple. Rather, they counseled resignation and patient waiting until
God would intervene in due time. For *2 Baruch,* the heavenly temple was
more important than the temple made by hands. For the present, Baruch
tells the people to pay attention to the Torah and to wait in patient hope.

The last apocalyptic reaction to the fall of Jerusalem that I will discuss
here, the *Greek Apocalypse of Baruch* or *3 Baruch,* takes this tendency a
step further.[30] This work, too, begins with Baruch grieving over the fall of
Jerusalem. In this case, however, the angel who appears to him offers no
extended explanation. Instead he tells him, "do not be so distressed about

---

30. See now D. C. Harlow, *The Greek Apocalypse of Baruch (3 Baruch) in Hellenistic
Judaism and Early Christianity* (Leiden: Brill, 1996).

the condition of Jerusalem. . . . Come and I will show you the mysteries of God." He then takes Baruch on a guided tour of the heavens. In the course of this Baruch learns that "the builders of the tower" (the Babylonians) are punished in the hereafter, and that the decisive question for all mortals is whether they have merits to present on the day of judgment. Nothing is said of the restoration of Jerusalem. This apocalypse was written in the diaspora, probably in Egypt, and, like most of the Jewish literature between the Bible and the Mishnah, was preserved by Christians. It might be regarded, then, as atypical of Judaism, and indeed the advice that Baruch should not be so distressed about Jerusalem is extreme. But in another sense it represents the culmination of a trend in apocalyptic literature, to look away from the painful realities of the present to another world, whether in the heavens or in the new creation. Baruch is not admitted beyond the fifth heaven, and so he does not get to witness the heavenly liturgy, but the effect of his vision is not unlike that of the *Songs of Sabbath Sacrifice* from Qumran, insofar as it turns attention away from this world and focuses on the mysteries of God.

Conclusion

The apocalyptic literature is only one strand in the thought of Second Temple Judaism. Other Jews found the second temple quite satisfactory. The apocalyptic visionaries, by definition, wanted something more. This literature was called into being first of all by the great crises of the two destructions and the profanation of the temple by Antiochus Epiphanes. When it was not related to these crises, as in the case of the texts from Qumran, it still reflects a deep dissatisfaction with the actual Jerusalem temple. The solutions it proposes are basically of two kinds, the expectation of an ideal temple in the future or the transfer of attention to the temple not made by human hands that already exists in the heavens. Ultimately no perishable temple was satisfactory. In the words of the Deuteronomist, "will God indeed dwell on earth? when even the heavens and the highest heaven cannot contain him." Precious though the temple was as a symbol of the divine presence, it was ultimately dispensable, something the people had to learn to live without. Perhaps that is why the prophet of Patmos, in the Book of Revelation, would have no temple in the new Jerusalem. The only adequate fulfillment of apocalyptic hopes would be a city where the role of the temple was filled by the actual presence of God. Such a city, of course, could only be part of a new creation, not of the world as we know it.

CHAPTER 11

Journeys to the World Beyond in Ancient Judaism

"Who has ascended to heaven and come down?" asks the weary sage Agur in Proverbs 30:4. Much of the biblical tradition, as edited by priestly writers and Deuteronomists, would answer "no one." Nonetheless, the motif of ascent to heaven became relatively popular in post-biblical Judaism, and a subgenre of apocalypses was devoted to describing such alleged experiences. In part, this development reflects a widespread interest in the world beyond in late antiquity, throughout the Hellenistic world. In part, it responded to concerns and experiences that were specifically Jewish. In this chapter I will focus on the earliest Jewish ascent apocalypses.[1] I will examine the ostensible purposes of the heavenly travels, and reflect on the functions that may be attributed to the texts describing them.

---

1. For reviews of this material see I. Gruenwald, *Apocalyptic and Merkavah Mysticism* (Leiden: Brill, 1980) 29-72; A. F. Segal, "Heavenly Ascent in Hellenistic Judaism, Early Christianity and Their Environment," in H. Temporini and W. Haase, eds., *Aufstieg und Niedergang der römischen Welt*, II.23.2 (Berlin: De Gruyter, 1980) 1352-68; M. Dean-Otting, *Heavenly Journeys: A Study of the Motif in Hellenistic Jewish Literature* (Frankfurt: Lang, 1984); J. D. Tabor, *Things Unutterable: Paul's Ascent to Paradise in Its Greco-Roman, Judaic, and Early Christian Contexts* (Lanham, MD: University Press of America, 1986); idem, "Heaven, Ascent to," in D. N. Freedman et al., eds., *The Anchor Bible Dictionary* (New York: Doubleday, 1992) 3.91-94; M. Himmelfarb, *Ascent to Heaven in Jewish and Christian Apocalypses* (New York: Oxford University Press, 1993); J. J. Collins, *The Apocalyptic Imagination* (2nd ed.; Grand Rapids: Eerdmans, 1998) 43-84, 177-93, 241-55; J. E. Wright, *The Early History of Heaven* (New York: Oxford University Press, 2000).

Ancient Near Eastern Precedents

The idea that a human being could journey to the world beyond and return was no innovation of ancient Judaism. The oldest Near Eastern stories of such journeys are found already in the Sumerian literature from the third millennium BCE, and they are developed in the Akkadian literature of the subsequent millennia.[2] Best known and most influential of these is the epic journey of Gilgamesh to the land of the living, in search of an antidote to death.[3] Gilgamesh travels through the mountain where the sun sets in the west and comes eventually to the shore of the sea that encircles the earth. He is ferried by a boatman to the land of the living to meet with Utnapishtim, the flood hero, who had been taken away to live with the gods. Utnapishtim gives him a twig from the tree of life. Despite the apparent success of his mission, Gilgamesh ultimately fails when he loses the precious twig. Access to the land of the living may not be utterly impossible, but it is clearly beyond the reach of most mortals, and even Gilgamesh, who is two-thirds divine, cannot secure it in a lasting way. Other Mesopotamian stories about journeys to the beyond are also somewhat pessimistic. Etana, the first king after the Flood according to the Sumerian King List, is called "the shepherd who ascended to heaven."[4] Etana's quest is for "the plant of birth" so that he might have an heir. He is carried aloft by an eagle, which he had saved from certain death. After they have ascended three leagues, Etana apparently loses his nerve and asks to be brought back to earth. One fragment of the myth, however, reports that they pass through the gate of the gods, and it is unclear whether the ascent ultimately succeeds.[5] In either case, access to the realm of the gods is deemed to be not entirely impossible but virtually so for most humans. The story of Adapa, who ascends to heaven and is offered the bread and water of life only to refuse them, on the advice of the god Ea, confirms this impression.[6]

2. G. Widengren, *The Ascension of the Apostle and the Heavenly Book* (Uppsala: Lundequist, 1950); Wright, *The Early History*, 26-51.

3. E. A. Speiser, "The Epic of Gilgamesh," in J. B. Pritchard, ed., *Ancient Near Eastern Texts Relating to the Old Testament* (3rd ed.; Princeton: Princeton University Press, 1969) 72-99; A. K. Grayson, "The Epic of Gilgamesh — Notes and Additions," in Pritchard, ed., *Ancient Near Eastern Texts*, 503-7; S. Dalley, *Myths from Mesopotamia* (New York: Oxford University Press, 1989) 39-153.

4. J. V. Kinnier-Wilson, *The Legend of Etana* (Warminster, UK: Aris & Phillips, 1985); Dalley, *Myths*, 189-202.

5. Dalley, *Myths*, 200, concludes her translation with this passage.

6. E. A. Speiser, "Adapa," in Pritchard, ed., *Ancient Near Eastern Texts*, 101-3; Dalley, *Myths*, 182-88.

Descent to the Netherworld is even more hazardous, as can be seen from the story of the Sumerian goddess Inanna and her Akkadian counterpart Ishtar, who descend to the Netherworld and are trapped there, and are rescued only with great difficulty by the gods.[7] Enkidu, the companion of Gilgamesh, is also trapped in the Netherworld in the fragmentary Sumerian myth "Gilgamesh, Enkidu and the Netherworld."[8] Gilgamesh pleads for him, but all the gods can do is open a vent to allow Enkidu's ghost to come up to speak to him. Nonetheless we have some cases where people are said to negotiate the round trip successfully. Enmeduranki, the ante-diluvian king of Sippar and ancestor of the *bārû* guild of diviners, was taken up to the divine assembly and shown the arts of divination and the heavenly tablets.[9] (Geo Widengren argued that "this divine wisdom, imparted to the ruler at the occasion of his enthronement, is not any exclusive right only belonging to mythical Enmeduranki. On the contrary! It is a distinctive trait of the Mesopotamian royal ideology that the ruler is endowed by the gods with surpassing knowledge and heavenly wisdom."[10] Whether the endowment with wisdom always entailed a heavenly ascent, however, is not so clear.) We also find a case of a human being who descends to the Netherworld and returns, if only in a dream. An Assyrian prince, Kumma, is said to have had this experience at his own request, in a tablet from Asshur, from the seventh century BCE. He awakes in terror, a chastened man.[11] There is also some evidence of Akkadian rituals for ascent to heaven and descent to the Netherworld.[12]

This rather scattered evidence from ancient Mesopotamia gives some

7. S. N. Kramer, "Inanna's Descent to the Nether World," in Pritchard, ed., *Ancient Near Eastern Texts*, 52-57; E. A. Speiser, "The Descent of Ishtar to the Nether World," in Pritchard, ed., 106-9; Dalley, Myths, 154-62.

8. See T. Jacobsen, *The Treasures of Darkness: A History of Mesopotamian Religion* (New Haven: Yale University Press, 1976) 212.

9. W. G. Lambert, "Enmeduranki and Related Matters," *Journal of Cuneiform Studies* 21 (1967) 126-38. Another ante-diluvian sage, Utuabzu, was also believed to have ascended to heaven. See R. Borger, "Die Beschwörungsserie *bīt mēseri* und die Himmelfahrt *Henochs*," *Journal of Near Eastern Studies* 33 (1974) 183-96.

10. Widengren, *The Ascent of the Apostle*, 12.

11. E. A. Speiser, "A Vision of the Nether World," in Pritchard, ed., *Ancient Near Eastern Texts,* 109-10. See H. S. Kvanvig, *Roots of Apocalyptic: The Mesopotamian Background of the Enoch Figure and of the Son of Man* (Wissenschaftliche Monographien zum Alten und Neuen Testament 61; Neukirchen-Vluyn: Neukirchener Verlag, 1988) 389-441.

12. T. Abusch, "Ascent to the Stars in a Mesopotamian Ritual: Social Metaphor and Religious Experience," in J. J. Collins and M. Fishbane, eds., *Death, Ecstasy and Otherworldly Journeys* (Albany: State University of New York Press, 1995) 15-39.

impression of the reasons why some people in antiquity wanted to transcend the limitations of earthly existence. I would suggest that there are three fundamental themes in these stories. Ascent to heaven, or the claim to have ascended to heaven, is a way to establish authority of a revealer or of a king, such as Enmeduranki. Related to this is the desire for knowledge and revelation, curiosity about things beyond the range of human knowledge. A distinct theme, no less fundamental, is the desire for eternal life, which figures prominently in the stories of Gilgamesh and Adapa, and indirectly in that of Etana, who sought immortality in his progeny. In these stories, however, that desire is frustrated.

Ancient Israel

The culture of ancient Israel was part of the wider culture of the Semitic world. Here too the basic understanding was that heaven was the Lord's while the earth was the proper domain of human beings. After death, people would descend to Sheol, where the dead could not even praise the Lord. Again, some exceptions were possible, but their exceptional nature was emphasized. In the cryptic phrase of Genesis, Enoch walked with the elohim, and was not, for the elohim took him.[13] Presumably he was taken to live with the elohim (angels or divine beings) either in heaven or at the ends of the earth, like Utnapishtim. Elijah, more spectacularly, was taken up to heaven in a whirlwind.[14] While Moses was explicitly said to have died, the fact that no one knew his burial place allowed for later speculation about his "disappearance" and possible apotheosis.[15] While Enoch and Elijah had gone up to heaven, however, they were not said to have come down, even if Elijah was expected to make a cameo appearance before the eschaton.

The idea of a round trip to heaven for purposes of revelation was

---

13. Genesis 5:21-24. See J. C. VanderKam, *Enoch and the Growth of an Apocalyptic Tradition* (Catholic Biblical Quarterly Monograph Series 16; Washington, DC: Catholic University of America, 1984) 30-31.

14. 2 Kings 2:11.

15. Deuteronomy 34:5-6. On the later speculation see J. D. Tabor, "'Returning to the Divinity': Josephus's Portrayal of the Disappearances of Enoch, Elijah and Moses," *Journal of Biblical Literature* 108 (1989) 225-38; C. Begg, "Josephus's Portrayal of the Disappearances of Enoch, Elijah and Moses: Some Observations," *Journal of Biblical Literature* 109 (1990) 691-93.

probably implied in the claim of prophets to have stood in the council of the Lord. According to Jeremiah, the lack of such an experience disqualified a prophet as inauthentic: "For who has stood in the council of the Lord so as to see and to hear his word?" (Jer. 23:18). We have several descriptions of such experiences, in the case of Micaiah ben Imlah in 1 Kings 22, in Isaiah, and in Ezekiel, although it is sometimes unclear whether the prophet is in heaven or in the temple on earth. What is remarkable about these scenes, however, is their focus on the divine audience. The description of the surroundings is minimal and there is no description at all of an ascent.[16] Nonetheless, the prophets are given temporary admission to the divine council, and this would seem to imply that they have ascended to heaven. This alleged experience established their authority and reliability.

It is possible that similar access was granted to the king, in the pre-exilic period. In Psalm 110 he is invited to sit at the Lord's right hand, although here again it is possible that the reference is to a temple ritual.[17] The line between temple and heaven is often blurred in any case. Similar access to the divine council is promised to the High Priest Joshua in Zechariah 3, after his trial, which also took place in heaven: "If you will walk in my ways and keep my requirements . . . I will give you the right of access among those standing here."[18]

Ancient Israel, like ancient Mesopotamia, then, held a rather restrictive view of access to the world beyond. Ascent to heaven was not altogether impossible, but it was severely limited, and little curiosity is expressed about it. Of course this restraint may be due in part to the editors of the biblical corpus. Deuteronomy famously asserted that the word of the Lord was not in heaven that one should ask, who will ascend to heaven and bring it down.[19] Even where ascent seems to be implied, as in the case of the prophets, it is not described. Moreover, ascent to heaven is invoked more than once in taunt songs, to deride the hybris of Gentile kings. So the king of Babylon is compared to Helal ben Shachar, Day Star son of Dawn:

16. Ezekiel's great vision of the new Jerusalem is a journey in the spirit (as also his vision of the abominations of the old Jerusalem), but it is not a journey to heaven.

17. H.-J. Kraus, *Psalms 60–150* (Augsburg: Minneapolis, 1989) 346-47. On the later interpretation of this passage see M. Hengel, "'Setze dich zu meiner Rechten!' Die Inthronisation Christi zur Rechten Gottes und Psalm 110,1," in M. Philonenko, ed., *Le Trône de Dieu* (Tübingen: Mohr, 1993) 108-94.

18. Zechariah 3:7. See C. L. Meyers and E. M. Meyers, *Haggai, Zechariah 1–8* (Anchor Bible 25B; New York: Doubleday, 1987) 195.

19. Deuteronomy 30:12.

"You said in your heart, 'I will ascend to heaven; I will raise my throne above the stars of God. I will sit on the mount of assembly on the heights of Zaphon; I will ascend to the tops of the clouds, I will make myself like the Most High.'"[20] Ezekiel taunts the king of Tyre: "Because your heart is proud and you have said, 'I am a god; I sit in the seat of the gods in the heart of the seas'; yet you are but a mortal, and no god."[21] A similar taunt is directed against Nabonidus by the clergy of Babylon: "(It was) he (who) stood up in the assembly to praise hi[mself]: 'I am wise, I know, I have seen (what is) hid[den]. (Even) if I do not know how to write (with the stylus), yet I have seen se[cret things].'"[22] These taunts lend some support to the view of Widengren that the claim of ascent to heaven was part of Near Eastern royal ideology, although they fall well short of establishing it as a constant element.[23] They also show that such claims sometimes met with considerable skepticism in the ancient world. Such skepticism was more prominent in the Greek world, where it found expression in the satires of Menippus of Gadara in the third century BCE and those of Lucian of Samosata, who wrote his *Nekyiamanteia and Icaromenippus* in the second century CE. In the older biblical and Near Eastern sources, the skepticism was not philosophical but arose from political dissent.

The *Book of the Watchers*

The earliest Jewish account of an otherworldly journey, in which the journey itself is a focus of interest, is found in the *Book of the Watchers* in *1 Enoch* 1–36. While this book can be classified as an apocalypse in terms of its macro-genre,[24] it is clearly a composite work and experimental in its literary genre. George Nickelsburg distinguishes five main sections:

(1) an introduction, in chapters 1–5;
(2) the rebellion of the angels, in chapters 6–11;
(3) Enoch's vision of heaven, chapters 12–16;
(4) Enoch's journey to the west, chapters 17–19;

20. Isaiah 14:13-14.
21. Ezekiel 28:2.
22. The Verse Account of Nabonidus: A. L. Oppenheim, "Nabonidus and the Clergy of Babylon," in Pritchard, ed., *Ancient Near Eastern Texts*, 314.
23. Widengren, *The Ascension of the Apostle*, 7-21.
24. J. J. Collins, "The Jewish Apocalypses," *Semeia* 14 (1979) 21-49.

(5) Additional journey traditions:
a list of accompanying angels, in chapter 20;
journey back from the west in 21–27;
journey to the east, in 28–33, and
journeys to the four corners of the earth, in 34–36.[25]

It seems likely that this text grew incrementally, but the actual history of composition is obscure.

The ascent proper is found in the third of these sections, chapters 12–16. Since Enoch is not mentioned at all in chapters 1–11, it is reasonable to assume that this is an addition to the story of the Watchers, but that story provides the occasion for Enoch's ascent. He is given a message to deliver to the fallen Watchers, informing them that they will have neither mercy nor peace. But they then prevail on him "to write out for them the record of a petition that they might receive forgiveness, and to take the record of their petition up to the Lord in heaven" (*1 Enoch* 13:4).[26] The purpose of his ascent, then, is intercession. This is usually taken to be a task of priests.[27] He takes the petition up to the heavenly temple. There are manifold connections between priests and angels, as can be seen explicitly in the *Songs of the Sabbath Sacrifice* from Qumran.[28] The depiction of the fallen Watchers, who are told that "you ought to intercede for men, not men for you," has been taken as a critique of the Jerusalem priesthood in the Hellenistic period.[29] Moreover, in the Book of *Jubilees* Enoch is said to have burned the incense of the sanctuary (*Jub.* 4:25), certainly a priestly function. Yet he is not called a priest in the *Book of the Watchers*, but a scribe. No doubt many priests were scribes, and scribes priests. The two roles are certainly not incompatible. But it is Enoch's scribal role that is emphasized here — specifically, his ability to write out a petition. Nickelsburg claims that "Enoch's call to preach to the rebel angels has been shaped according to

---

25. G. W. E. Nickelsburg, *Jewish Literature between the Bible and the Mishnah* (Philadelphia: Fortress, 1981) 48.

26. Translations of *1 Enoch* are taken from that of M. A. Knibb, "1 Enoch," in H. F. D. Sparks, ed., *The Apocryphal Old Testament* (Oxford: Clarendon, 1984) 169-319.

27. So, e.g., Himmelfarb, *Ascent to Heaven*, 20.

28. C. A. Newsom, "'He Has Established for Himself Priests': Human and Angelic Priesthood in the Qumran Sabbath Shirot," in L. H. Schiffman, ed., *Archaeology and History in the Dead Sea Scrolls* (Sheffield: Journal for the Study of the Old Testament, 1990) 101-20.

29. D. W. Suter, "Fallen Angel, Fallen Priest: The Problem of Family Purity in *1 Enoch* 6–16," *Hebrew Union College Annual* 50 (1979) 115-35.

the form of biblical prophetic commissioning," especially Ezekiel 1–2.[30] Again, there are clear analogies in the message of judgment that he is told to convey. But no prophet was asked to write out a petition for the accused. The role of the intercessor here has been modified in light of the legal practice of the literate Hellenistic age. In view of the implicit critique of the priesthood that many scholars have detected in the story of the fallen angels, we may wonder whether there is not a contrast here between the angel-priests, who have failed in their role of intercession, and the human scribe who assumes that role in their place; in short, whether Enoch is not substituting a new kind of intercession for that of the priesthood. The efficacy of this kind of intercession requires ecstatic experience on the part of the visionary scribe. In this respect there is indeed an analogy with the commissioning of a prophet.

Enoch's experience, however, is more complicated than that of the typical prophet. The late Ioan Culianu distinguished three main types of apocalypses according to the manner of the revelation: those whose hero is called from above, those whose hero is a victim of accident or illness (such as Er, in the myth of Er), and those whose hero strives to obtain a revelation. The last category he dubbed "Quest Apocalypses."[31] Enoch, however, combines the call and the quest. The quest aspect appears in his incubation by the waters of Dan, where he reads out the petition until he falls asleep. Dan, of course, was an old sacred site in Israelite tradition, and was also close to the Hellenistic shrine of Pan.[32] It is possible that some form of incubation ritual was associated with the site. Other apocalyptic visionaries of the Hellenistic and Roman periods also take measures to initiate their experiences. (Daniel fasts in Daniel 10, and Ezra eats the flower that is in the field, in 2 *Esdras* 9:26.) These measures distinguish the apocalyptic visionaries from the classical biblical prophets. Unlike some other visionaries (such as Isaiah), Enoch is not formally invested or commissioned in heaven, but the authorization of his message and role must be reckoned nonetheless among the functions of his ascent.

The actual account of the ascent describes in some detail the progression of Enoch through the heavenly temple until he comes to the throne of God. The description of the throne, again, is indebted to Ezekiel, and

---

30. Nickelsburg, *Jewish Literature*, 53.

31. I. P. Culianu, *Psychanodia* I (Leiden: Brill, 1983) 6.

32. G. W. Nickelsburg, "Enoch, Levi, and Peter: Recipients of Revelation in Upper Galilee," *Journal of Biblical Literature* 100 (1981) 575-600.

is rightly recognized as an important document in the development of Jewish mysticism.[33] Herewith we come to another function of the ascent texts, which would come to the fore in later Jewish mysticism: the contemplation of the divine throne. The experience here is not one of union, but of heightened presence, as is often the case in Jewish and Christian mysticism.[34] The written account of Enoch's experience enables the reader to share in it. This contemplation of the heavenly world also seems to be a major function of the *Songs of the Sabbath Sacrifice* from Qumran.[35]

Like the visions of Isaiah or Ezekiel, that of Enoch does not dwell on the throne vision as its final purpose. Enoch is again given a message of judgment to convey to the Watchers. Central to this message is the diagnosis of their error: "Why have you left the high, holy, and eternal heaven, and lain with the women and become unclean with the daughters of men, and taken wives for yourselves? . . . And you were spiritual, holy, living an eternal life, but you became unclean upon the women" (15:3). More is at issue in the ascent of Enoch than the reporting of judgment. There is also a contrast between two levels of existence, the immortal life of the angels and the corruptible life of human beings on earth. The *Book of the Watchers* claims that one can pass from one kind of existence to the other: the fallen angels presumably lose their immortality while the human Enoch ascends to the level of the immortal, although he does not immediately remain there. This issue of access to eternal life figures more directly in several other Jewish ascent apocalypses.

The ascent of Enoch in *1 Enoch* 12–16, then, touches on all three of our fundamental themes: it establishes the authority of Enoch, provides information about the heavenly temple and divine throne, and touches on the question of eternal life. The remainder of the *Book of the Watchers* expands the revelation, and provides more specific information about life after death. After Enoch has received his message for the Watchers, he is taken on a tour to the ends of the earth, which is extended in several units through chapters 17–36. This material is different in kind and in interest from the ascent to the divine throne for the purpose of intercession. It is

---

33. Gruenwald, *Apocalyptic and Merkavah Mysticism*, 32-37.

34. B. McGinn, "Love, Knowledge and Mystical Union in Western Christianity: Twelfth to Sixteenth Centuries," *Church History* 56 (1987) 7; *The Foundations of Mysticism* (New York: Crossroad, 1991) xvii.

35. C. A. Newsom, *Songs of the Sabbath Sacrifice: A Critical Edition* (Atlanta: Scholars Press, 1985) 59, describes the Songs as "a quasi-mystical liturgy designed to evoke a sense of being present in the heavenly temple."

not an ascent to heaven, but a tour of places that are not normally accessible. Much of what Enoch sees can only be attributed to cosmological curiosity — the storehouses of the wind, the foundations of the earth, and so forth.[36] It has been noted that the model of the earth implied in these journeys was already antiquated in the Hellenistic age: it is "conceived as a flat surface upon which one can travel to a certain point where it ends and drops off into a vast chasm — the classic ancient Near Eastern model of the earth."[37] At the end of heaven and earth is the fiery prison for the stars of heaven and the host of heaven (18:14-15). This provides a link with the story of the Watchers, who are said in 10:13 to be shut up in a prison of fire for all eternity, after they have been confined for seventy generations under the hills of the earth. The theme of judgment runs through much of Enoch's travel, and a major purpose of the account is to lend an aura of realism to the judgment by associating it with specific places, even if these are places that no one but Enoch has seen.

The eschatological focus of Enoch's tour can be seen most clearly in chapter 22 and in chapters 24–27. In chapter 22, Enoch sees "in the west a large and high mountain, and a hard rock and four beautiful places, and inside it was deep and wide and very smooth" (22:1-2). He is told that these places are intended for "the spirits of the souls of the dead," until the day of judgment. The spirits are divided into various categories: righteous, sinners, victims of murder, and a second category of sinners.[38] The location, inside a mountain in the west, recalls the journey of Gilgamesh through the mountain where the sun sets, but there is no Mesopotamian precedent for the separation of souls on the basis of their conduct in life.[39] Orphic influence has been detected in the chamber of the righteous, which has a spring of water and light.[40] This passage is unique among the Jewish apocalypses in failing to locate the abode of the righteous in heaven, and it probably reflects an early tradition. What is typical of the

---

36. See M. E. Stone, "Lists of Revealed Things in Apocalyptic Literature," in F. M. Cross et al., eds., *Magnalia Dei: The Mighty Acts of God* (Garden City, NY: Doubleday, 1976) 414-52.

37. Wright, *The Early History*, 121.

38. The text is corrupt. In 22:9 we are told that there are three divisions rather than four.

39. See M.-T. Wacker, *Weltordnung und Gericht. Studien zu 1 Henoch 22* (Würzburg: Echter, 1982) 173-77; G. W. E. Nickelsburg, *Resurrection, Immortality and Eternal Life in Intertestamental Judaism* (Cambridge, MA: Harvard University Press, 1972) 134-37.

40. T. F. Glasson, *Greek Influence on Jewish Eschatology* (London: SPCK, 1961) 19.

apocalypses, however, is the curiosity about the fate of the souls or spirits of people after death.

Equally typical is the interest in the final judgment. Enoch sees "a high mountain, whose summit is like the throne of the Lord," where God will sit "when he comes down to visit the earth for good" (25:3). Near it is a beautiful fragrant tree, the tree of life, from whose fruit life will be given to the righteous. It is planted "in a holy place, by the house of the Lord" (25:5). Later (chap. 32) he encounters another tree, over the mountains to the east, which is identified as the tree of wisdom from which Adam and Eve ate. Two distinct trees are implied in Genesis, but the way they are separated here probably reflects different stages of composition. Adam and Eve appear only in chapter 32. The earlier story of the fall of the Watchers ignores the myth of Adam and seems to imply a quite different explanation of the origin of sin. The tree of life here is not found in the Garden of Righteousness, but near the mountain of the Lord. This recalls Ezekiel 28, where the king of Tyre is taunted that he was "in Eden, the garden of God" (v. 13) and on "the holy mountain of God" (v. 14), with the implication that the two locations are one. Both Ezekiel and Enoch are probably reflecting a different tradition from what we find in Genesis 2–3. The judgment of the damned is located in an "accursed valley," presumably Gehenna. Some of Enoch's vision, then, concerns not the ends of the earth but the center of it, in the environs of Jerusalem. Nonetheless, as J. E. Wright has observed, they concern the mythical places of the earth.[41] The places of punishment are located at the ends of the earth, on the edge of the abyss. The waiting places of the dead are inside the mountain in the west, but the place of reward of the righteous is in the center of the earth, around the throne of God. The *Book of the Watchers,* then, provides an exceptional and rather archaic view of the mythical world where the afterlife of humanity is located. One function of the narrative is surely to affirm that view of the world, which must have been put in question by the spread of Hellenistic cosmology. The narrative, however, is not a disinterested account of cosmology. Much of it has to do with the theme of judgment, of the stars as well as of humanity. This interest is by no means exceptional in the Hellenistic era. All the Jewish apocalypses have a major interest in the fate of the dead.[42]

41. Wright, *The Early History*, 123.
42. See J. J. Collins, "Apocalyptic Eschatology as the Transcendence of Death," *Catholic Biblical Quarterly* 36 (1974) 21-43 (= idem, *Seers, Sibyls and Sages in Hellenistic-Roman Judaism* [Leiden: Brill, 1997] 75-98).

Other Early Enoch Traditions

The validation of Enoch's authority is only implicit in the *Book of the Watchers*. Elsewhere in the corpus it is addressed explicitly: Enoch imparts instruction to his children "according to that which appeared to me in the heavenly vision, and which I know from the words of the holy angels and understand from the tablets of heaven" (93:2). None of the narratives of Enoch's ascent describe his consultation of the tablets. It has been suggested plausibly that he is given this privilege by analogy with the ancient Sumerian king, Enmeduranki.[43] In accordance with the associations of the tablets of destiny, the range of Enoch's revelation is extended to include history as well as cosmology. The cosmology undergoes gradual development. We hear no more of chambers for the souls of the dead, or of a cosmic mountain in the middle of the earth. Rather, the abode of the righteous is transferred to heaven. We find this already in the *Epistle of Enoch,* which may be older than the Book of Daniel.[44] There the righteous are promised that the gate of heaven will be opened to them and that they will be companions to the stars of heaven (*1 Enoch* 104:2-6). The wicked, in contrast, will be wretched in Sheol.

This is also the case in the latest component of *1 Enoch,* the *Similitudes,* which were probably written around the time of Christ.[45] There, as in the *Book of the Watchers,* Enoch ascends to heaven on a storm-cloud (39:3). In this case, however, he has no mission of intercession for the Watchers. He is there simply to discover the mysteries of heaven. Immediately, we are told, "I saw another vision, the dwelling of the righteous and the resting-places of the holy. There my eyes saw their dwelling with the angels and their resting-places with the holy ones, and they were petitioning and supplicating and praying on behalf of the sons of men" (39:4-5). Later we are told that the wicked go down "into the flames of torment of Sheol" (63:10). Enoch is given no tour in the *Similitudes,* but he does learn various astronomical and cosmological secrets. The primary emphasis of the book, however, is on the judgment, and the role therein of the figure called "that Son of Man" who is subject to God but nonetheless sits on a throne of glory.[46]

43. VanderKam, *Enoch and the Growth of an Apocalyptic Tradition,* 43-45; idem, *Enoch: A Man for All Generations* (Columbia: University of South Carolina Press, 1995) 6-8.
44. VanderKam, *Enoch: A Man for All Generations,* 89-101.
45. See Collins, *The Apocalyptic Imagination,* 177-78.
46. J. J. Collins, *The Scepter and the Star* (New York: Doubleday, 1995) 177-82.

The most controversial part of the *Similitudes* is undoubtedly the epilogue to the visions found in *1 Enoch* 70–71. There are really two epilogues here, and it is unlikely that they come from the same author. First, we are told that

> it came to pass after this that, while he was living, his name was lifted from those who dwell upon the dry ground to the presence of that Son of Man and to the presence of the Lord of Spirits. And he was lifted on the chariots of the spirit and his name vanished among them. And from that day I was not counted among them [i.e. human beings], and he placed me between two winds between the north and the west, where the angels took the cords to measure for me the place for the chosen and the righteous. And there I saw the first fathers and the righteous who from the beginning of the world dwelt in that place. (70:1-4)

This passage provides a fitting conclusion to the *Similitudes*. The ascent on the chariots of the spirit recalls that of Elijah and also parallels Enoch's ascent at the beginning of the *Similitudes* in chapter 39. There is a clear homology between his ascent as a visionary and his final ascent to the abode of the righteous. This passage also makes a clear distinction between Enoch and "that Son of Man," a distinction that seemed to be presumed throughout his visions.[47]

This epilogue, however, is complemented by another one in chapter 71. In this case we are told that "my spirit was carried off, and it went up into the heavens" (*1 Enoch* 71:1). There he is met by the archangel Michael, who shows him all the secrets of the end of heaven and all the storehouses of the stars and the lights. Then he is again transported "to the highest heaven" (71:5). From this it appears that there are at least two heavens, more probably three.[48] This detail is significant, as the rest of 1 *Enoch* envisions only one heaven. The multiple heavens in chapter 71 are a strong

---

47. J. J. Collins, "The Son of Man in First Century Judaism," *New Testament Studies* 38 (1992) 448-66 (see 453-54), contra M. Casey, "The Use of the Term 'Son of Man' in the Similitudes of Enoch," *Journal for the Study of Judaism* 7 (1976) 25-26; idem, *Son of Man: The Interpretation and Influence of Daniel* 7 (London: SPCK, 1979) 105. Casey's argument is based on one manuscript, Abbadianus 55, which has a different reading in 70:1, but the difference is due to the omission of one word and is most probably accidental.

48. H. Bietenhard, *Die himmlische Welt im Urchristentum und Spätjudentum* (Wissenschaftliche Untersuchungen zum Neuen Testament 2; Tübingen: Mohr, 1951) 11; Wright, *The Early History*, 141.

indication that this chapter is a secondary addition. In the highest heaven, Enoch sees the heavenly temple. Most remarkably, Enoch is greeted, "You are the Son of Man who was born to righteousness" (71:14). I am not sure that Enoch is necessarily identified with "that Son of Man" whom he had seen in his visions. Throughout the *Similitudes*, there is a close parallelism between the righteous on earth and their counterparts in heaven. The heavenly Son of Man is the Righteous One *par excellence*. It may be that Enoch is being greeted in language that emphasizes his similarity to the heavenly figure.[49] Other righteous people will likewise be assimilated to Enoch and will walk in his way. It is true, however, that the later Enoch tradition emphasizes his heavenly transformation.[50] In 2 *Enoch* he is stripped of his earthly garments, anointed with oil, and clothed in glorious garments (2 *Enoch* 9:17-18) so that he becomes "like one of the glorious ones, and there was no apparent difference."[51] In the much later 3 *Enoch*, or Sepher Hekalot, he becomes Metatron, enlarged to the size of the world and enthroned on a throne of glory.[52] His assimilation to the Son of Man in *1 Enoch* 71 is certainly a step in this development. It may well have been intended to counter the Christian identification of Jesus as the Danielic Son of Man. Enoch, too, becomes a paradigm of divinization, or angelification. He is presented as a man taken up and transformed in heaven, with a clear implication that those who walk in his ways may hope for a similar fate.

Moses and Levi

Thus far we have focused on the Enoch tradition, which is the main locus of heavenly ascent in pre-Christian Judaism. Leaving aside a problematic text in the Dead Sea Scrolls,[53] we have only two non-Enochic Jewish stories of

49. Collins, "The Son of Man in First Century Judaism," 456-57.

50. This point is made by J. R. Davila, "Of Methodology, Monotheism and Metatron," in C. C. Newman, J. R. Davila, and G. S. Lewis, eds., *The Jewish Roots of Christological Monotheism* (Leiden: Brill, 1999) 11-12.

51. See Himmelfarb, *Ascent to Heaven*, 40, who argues for the priestly character of Enoch's investiture.

52. 3 *Enoch* 4:1. P. Alexander, "3 (Hebrew Apocalypse of) Enoch," in J. H. Charlesworth, ed., *The Old Testament Pseudepigrapha* (London: Darton, Longman & Todd, 1983) 1.258.

53. See M. Smith, "Ascent to the Heavens and Deification in 4QM," in Schiffman, ed., *Archaeology and History in the Dead Sea Scrolls*, 181-88; J. J. Collins, "A Throne in the Heavens: Apotheosis in Pre-Christian Judaism," in Collins and Fishbane, eds., *Death, Ecstasy,*

ascent that can be dated to the pre-Christian period. One is the dream of Moses in Ezekiel the Tragedian, and the other is the dream of Levi in the Aramaic *Apocryphon of Levi*.

In Moses' dream, he sees a man enthroned on the summit of Mount Sinai.[54] This "man," presumably God, vacates the throne and bids Moses sit on it, wearing a crown and holding a scepter. The dream is interpreted as a symbolic expression of Moses' leadership and knowledge, but it surely implies a tradition of the apotheosis of Moses. (The ultimate inspiration of this tradition is found in Exod. 7:1: "I have made you a god to Pharaoh." The divinity of Moses was linked with the ascent of Mount Sinai by Philo, who was probably drawing on older tradition.)[55] The enthronement of Moses clearly establishes his authority. It is not clear whether his exaltation was assumed to be permanent.

The other pre-Christian Jewish ascent is that of Levi in the *Levi Apocryphon* from Qumran, which is later adapted in the Greek *Testament of Levi*. The Apocryphon is very fragmentary. The relevant passage is found in 4Q213a:

Then I was shown visions [
in the vision of visions and I saw the heaven[s
beneath me, high until it reached to the heaven[s
to me the gates of heaven, and an angel[[56]

Fragmentary though it is, it is of interest, as it shows that Levi ascended through more than one heaven, but not yet through the numbered series that we find in later apocalypses. The corresponding passage in the Greek

---

and Otherworldly Journeys, 43-58; idem, *Apocalypticism in the Dead Sea Scrolls* (London: Routledge, 1997) 143-47. A new, controversial interpretation of this text has been proposed by I. Knohl, *The Messiah before Jesus* (Berkeley: University of California Press, 2000).

54. For the text, see Eusebius, *Praeparatio Evangelica* 9.29.4-5; C. R. Holladay, *Fragments from Hellenistic Jewish Authors*, vol. 2: *Poets* (Atlanta: Scholars Press, 1989) 363-65. See also P. W. van der Horst, "Moses' Throne Vision in Ezekiel the Dramatist," *Journal of Jewish Studies* 34 (1983) 21-29.

55. Philo, *De Vita Mosis* 1.155-58. See W. Meeks, "Moses as God and King," in J. Neusner, ed., *Religions in Antiquity: Essays in Memory of Erwin Ramsdell Goodenough* (Leiden: Brill, 1968) 354-71.

56. M. E. Stone and J. C. Greenfield, "Aramaic Levi Document," in G. Brooke et al., eds., *Qumran Cave 4. XVII. Parabiblical Texts, Part 3* (Discoveries in the Judaean Desert XXII; Oxford: Clarendon, 1996) 31. In the text cited, open square brackets mean that this is the edge of the fragment and that some words are missing at the end of the line.

Testament of Levi is preserved in two recensions.[57] In one of these, Levi ascends through three heavens. In the third, "you will stand near the Lord, and you will be a minister to him, and you will announce his mysteries to men" (*T. Levi* 2:6-10). In the other recension, there are seven heavens, but Levi is said to ascend only through the first three. Then he is told: "Do not marvel at these; for you will see four other heavens more brilliant and incomparable."[58] The description of the seven heavens in the following chapter proceeds at first from the bottom, through the first three, and then changes direction and proceeds downward from the highest heaven. There can be little doubt, then, that the vision of three heavens is original, and is expanded secondarily.[59]

Levi's vision in the Testament reaches its climax in *Testament of Levi* 5: "And the angel opened to me the gates of heaven, and I saw the holy temple and the Most High upon a throne of glory. And he said to me: Levi, I have given to you the blessings of the priesthood until I come and sojourn in the midst of Israel. Then the angel brought me down to the earth and he gave me a shield and a sword and said: Execute vengeance on Shechem because of Dinah." The goal of the ascent, then, is the authorization of Levi's priesthood and the legitimation of his violent action against Shechem. The vision is unusual among the apocalyptic ascent narratives insofar as it is not at all concerned with the theme of eternal life. It is closer to the older ascents of the prophets or to a figure like Enmeduranki than to the later apocalypses.

The Plurality of Heavens

The idea of three heavens had old precedents in Mesopotamia, as indeed did the seven heavens.[60] It may have been implied in the biblical phrase

57. See R. H. Charles, "The Testaments of the Twelve Patriarchs," in R. H. Charles, ed., *The Apocrypha and Pseudepigrapha of the Old Testament* (Oxford: Clarendon, 1913 [reprint 1963]) 2.304-6.

58. *Testament of Levi* 2:9. Trans. M. de Jonge and H. Hollander, *The Testaments of the Twelve Patriarchs: A Commentary* (Leiden: Brill, 1985) 132.

59. Contra Wright, *The Early History*, 147-48, who relies on the text-critical judgment of H. J. de Jonge, "Die Textüberlieferung der Testamente der zwölf Patriarchen," in M. de Jonge, ed., *Studies on the Testaments of the Twelve Patriarchs: Text and Interpretation* (Leiden: Brill, 1975) 45-62.

60. See A. Yarbro Collins, "The Seven Heavens in Jewish and Christian Apocalypses,"

שמי שמים, but that phrase has also been taken as a hyperbolic reference to the height and expanse of heaven.[61] The three heavens had some currency in Judaism around the turn of the era, as we can see from the *Levi Apocryphon, 1 Enoch* 71, and St. Paul's famous reference to a man who was caught up to the third heaven, whether in the body or out of the body, in 2 Corinthians 12:2.[62] It is unlikely that all references to three heavens can be attributed to Christian scribes taking the ascent of Paul as normative.[63]

In the late first and early second century CE, however, we see the emergence of a new form of heavenly journey, where the visionary ascends through a numbered sequence of heavens, usually seven — the number found in the second recension of the *Testament of Levi*, the Greek *Apocalypse of Moses*, *2 Enoch*, the *Apocalypse of Abraham,* and the (Christian) *Ascension of Isaiah.*[64] *3 Baruch* deviates from this number and describes only five heavens. Some scholars have argued that the climactic chapters of the book have been lost, but this does not appear to be the case. It may well be, however, that *3 Baruch* presupposes a schema of seven heavens and changes it for its purpose, to make the point that the visionary does not ascend all the way to the presence of God.[65] The seven heavens are associated with the seven planets in Hermetic texts, Mithraic monuments, and Celsus's discussion of the Mithraic mysteries, but not in Jewish or early Christian texts.[66] Nonetheless, it is difficult to avoid the impression that the late emergence of the seven-heaven cosmology in Jewish and Christian texts was prompted by the Hellenistic cosmology of seven spheres and planets surrounding the earth.[67] Admittedly, the apocalypses do not reproduce this cosmology accurately. They typically put the planets, sun,

---

in Collins and Fishbane, eds., *Death, Ecstasy, and Otherworldly Journeys*, 64-65 (= eadem, *Cosmology and Eschatology in Jewish and Christian Apocalypticism* [Leiden: Brill, 1996] 27-28), following F. Rochberg-Halton, "Mesopotamian Cosmology," in N. S. Hetherington, ed., *Encyclopedia of Cosmology: Historical, Philosophical, and Scientific Foundations of Modern Cosmology* (New York: Garland, 1993) 398-407, especially 401.

61. Wright, *The Early History*, 55.

62. On 2 Corinthians 12, see Tabor, *Things Unutterable.*

63. *Pace* Wright, *The Early History*, 148.

64. Yarbro Collins, "The Seven Heavens."

65. D. C. Harlow, *The Greek Apocalypse of Baruch (3 Baruch) in Hellenistic Judaism and Early Christianity* (Leiden: Brill, 1996) 34-76.

66. Yarbro Collins, "The Seven Heavens," 86.

67. On Hellenistic cosmology see M. R. Wright, *Cosmology in Antiquity* (London: Routledge, 1995).

moon, and stars in one or two heavens.[68] But the rather sudden popularity of the seven-storey heavens may nonetheless reflect the influence of Hellenistic cosmology, however garbled. The triumph of the seven-heaven cosmology, however, was by no means complete. Other, simpler cosmologies persist into the Christian period, as can be seen from such works as the Latin *Life of Adam and Eve* and the *Testament of Abraham*. Conversely, some apocalypses count a larger number of heavens. The J recension of 2 *Enoch* has ten.[69]

The apocalypses, of course, are mythological rather than scientific documents. They typically include a variety of cosmological mysteries, but all pay considerable attention to the punishment of the damned, which is located in a heaven rather than in Sheol in the later apocalypses,[70] and to the abode of the blessed. This attention is related to their predominant interest in moral formation, by impressing on their readers the ultimate consequences of righteous or impious actions.

Conclusion

In his classic study of the ascent of the soul, Wilhelm Bousset argued that the ecstatic ascent of the visionary was nothing other than an anticipation of the heavenly journey of the soul after death.[71] From the texts we have reviewed, it is clear that this is an over-generalization. There were old, if limited, traditions of ascent to heaven in the ancient Near East, which had as their focus the authority of the visionary rather than immortality, and some of the early Jewish ascents, such as those of Levi and Moses, are still of this type. In the Books of Enoch, however, and in the ascent apocalypses of the first century CE and later, there is a pervasive interest in life after death. The increased availability of this hope marks the main difference between the ascent literature of the Hellenistic and Roman periods and the older traditions of the ancient Near East.

68. Wright, *The Early History*, 183.

69. Wright, *The Early History*, 179.

70. In 3 *Baruch*, there are punishments in the first three heavens. In 2 *Enoch* there are places of punishment in the second and third heavens. The idea that spirits are tortured in a place above the earth but close to it is found already in Cicero's *Somnium Scipionis* (*Republic* 6.29). Cf. Plutarch, *De facie in orbe lunae* 27–29; *De genio Socratis* 590B.

71. W. Bousset, "Die Himmelsreise der Seele," *Archiv für Religionswissenschaft* 4 (1901) 136.

Various factors contributed to the hope for a heavenly afterlife in Hellenistic Judaism, including questions of theodicy and the desire for retribution in times of persecution. But this hope was too widespread in the Hellenistic world to be explained by inner-Jewish factors alone.[72] All the major cultures with which the Jews came in contact in the Second Temple period, Persian, Greek, and Roman, had stories of ascending visionaries and of heavenly immortality. Scholars such as Bousset and Richard Reitzenstein looked to Persia as the source of the phenomenon. More recent scholarship has been skeptical of this theory because of the difficulty of dating Persian traditions that are preserved in sources from the Byzantine period or the Middle Ages.[73] The relevance of the Greek and Roman material cannot be denied. From the sixth century BCE on, the belief in the immortality of the soul was spread by Pythagoreans and Orphics, and it was given great prominence in the philosophy of Plato. Increasingly the abode of the blessed was transferred to the heavens. A memorial commemorating the Athenians who died in the battle of Potidaia in 432 BCE states, "the ether has received their souls, the earth their bodies."[74] Around the same time, Aristophanes joked about "what people say, that when we die we straightaway turn to stars."[75] The popularity of astral immortality in the Hellenistic period is attested in epitaphs.[76] It can be no coincidence that the first clear reference to individual resurrection in the Hebrew Bible, in Daniel 12, says that "the wise will shine like the splendor of the firmament, and those who lead the common people to righteousness like the stars forever and ever."[77] This hope is essentially similar to the belief of Cicero

72. Major surveys of the belief in immortality and resurrection in ancient Judaism have been written by Nickelsburg, *Resurrection, Immortality and Eternal Life*, and E. Puech, *La Croyance des Esséniens en la Vie Future. Immortalité, Résurrection, Vie Eternelle?* (Paris: Gabalda, 1993). Neither pays much attention to the broader international context in which this belief developed.

73. See especially Culianu, *Psychanodia*. Also Segal, "Heavenly Ascent," 1342-43. For a discussion of Persian apocalypticism and the problems of dating see A. Hultgård, "Persian Apocalypticism," in J. J. Collins, ed., *The Encyclopedia of Apocalypticism*, vol. 1: *The Origins of Apocalypticism in Judaism and Christianity* (New York: Continuum, 1998) 39-83. The main Persian account of an otherworldly journey is the late Pahlavi Book of Arda Viraf, but there are indications that the motif is much older in Iranian tradition.

74. G. Kaibel, ed., *Epigrammata graeca ex lapidibus conlecta* (Berlin: Reimer, 1878) 2; cited by Wright, *The Early History*, 115.

75. *Peace* 832-34.

76. F. Cumont, *Lux Perpetua* (Paris: Geuthner, 1949) 142-288.

77. J. J. Collins, *Daniel* (Hermeneia; Minneapolis: Fortress, 1993) 393-94.

in the *Somnium Scipionis* that "all those who have preserved, aided, or enlarged their fatherland have a special place prepared for them in the heavens, where they may enjoy an eternal life of happiness."[78]

This is not to suggest that belief in immortality can be viewed as a cultural borrowing. In fact, Hellenistic influence is more pronounced in the later apocalypses; the cosmology of the *Book of the Watchers* is largely informed by older Near Eastern traditions.

The accounts of ascents in such authors as Cicero (primarily in the *Somnium Scipionis*) and Plutarch[79] are colored by Platonic philosophy, which regarded the spirit or soul as the true seat of the personality and the upper heavens as the realm of purest spirit. Among Jewish authors, only Philo of Alexandria fully appropriated this philosophy.[80] But even in such an unphilosophical work as the *Book of the Watchers*, there is a contrast between the high and holy heaven, which is the proper home of holy immortal beings, and the corruptible earth. The novelty of the Hellenistic age was the spread of the belief that mortals could pass from one realm to the other. An adequate explanation of this phenomenon would have to explore the *Zeitgeist* of the Hellenistic age and its expression in diverse local traditions, a task that goes well beyond the limits of this chapter.[81] But however this development is to be explained, it transformed the traditional worldview of Israel and the ancient Near East and had enormous consequences for the development of Christianity.

---

78. Cicero, *Republic* 6.13.

79. *De genio Socratis* 589F-592E; *De sera numinis vindicta* (563B-568A).

80. For the motif of heavenly ascent in Philo, see Segal, "Heavenly Ascent," 1354-58.

81. See J. Z. Smith, "Native Cults in the Hellenistic Period," *History of Religions* 11 (1971) 236-49; J. J. Collins, "Jewish Apocalyptic against Its Hellenistic Near Eastern Environment," *Bulletin of the American Schools of Oriental Research* 220 (1975) 27-36 (= *Seers, Sibyls and Sages*, 59-74); "*Cosmos* and Salvation: Jewish Wisdom and Apocalyptic in the Hellenistic Age," *History of Religions* 17 (1977) 121-42 (= *Seers, Sibyls and Sages*, 317-38).

CHAPTER 12

The Afterlife in Apocalyptic Literature

The apocalyptic literature was a new phenomenon in Judaism in the Hellenistic period.[1] Some of its distinctive characteristics can be found already in the late prophetic literature of the Second Temple period, which is sometimes called "proto-apocalyptic" literature.[2] But the apocalypses of the third and second centuries BCE, written in the names of Enoch and Daniel, have a significantly different worldview from the Book of Zechariah or the incorrectly labeled "Apocalypse of Isaiah" (Isaiah 24–27). The difference appears precisely in the understanding of life after death. Hope for a differentiated afterlife, where the good are rewarded and the wicked are punished, first appears in Jewish tradition in the apocalypses of Enoch and Daniel, and it is in this area that the apocalyptic literature makes its most significant contribution to Jewish tradition.[3]

---

1. J. J. Collins, *The Apocalyptic Imagination* (2nd ed.; Grand Rapids: Eerdmans, 1998); "The Place of Apocalypticism in the Religion of Israel," in idem, ed., *Seers, Sibyls and Sages in Hellenistic-Roman Judaism* (JSJSup 54; Leiden: Brill, 1997) 39-58.

2. P. D. Hanson, *The Dawn of Apocalyptic* (Philadelphia: Fortress, 1975).

3. J. J. Collins, "Apocalyptic Eschatology as the Transcendence of Death," in *Seers, Sibyls and Sages*, 75-98. For surveys of apocalyptic texts dealing with resurrection or eternal life, see G. W. Nickelsburg, *Resurrection, Immortality and Eternal Life in Inter-testamental Judaism* (HTS 56; exp. ed.; Cambridge, MA: Harvard University Press, 2006); G. Stemberger, *Der Leib der Auferstehung. Studien zur Anthropologie und Eschatologie des palästinischen Judentums im neutestamentlichen Zeitalter* (Rome: Pontifical Biblical Institute, 1972); H. C. Cavallin, *Life after Death: Paul's Argument for the Resurrection of the Dead in 1 Cor 15* (Lund: Gleerup, 1974); E. Puech, *La Croyance des Esséniens en la Vie Future. Immortalité, Résurrection, Vie Éternelle?* (EB 21; Paris: Gabalda, 1993) 99-154.

Resurrection in Late Prophetic Texts

The language of resurrection can be found already in prophetic texts of the exilic and early post-exilic periods. The most famous example is found in Ezekiel's vision of a valley full of dry bones (Ezekiel 37). The interpretation of the vision is quite explicit, however: "these bones are the whole house of Israel" (37:11). The resurrection, then, is metaphorical, although the passage would be interpreted literally in the Dead Sea Scrolls (4Q385) and later tradition. What is at issue is the restoration of the people of Israel. This is most probably also the case in the so-called "Apocalypse of Isaiah." Isaiah 26:19 declares: "your dead shall live, their corpses shall rise. O dwellers in the dust, awake and sing for joy! For your dew is a radiant dew and the earth will give birth to those long dead." Some scholars think that this passage reflects a belief in actual resurrection.[4] Those who will rise, however, are contrasted with another group, of whom it is said: "The dead do not live; shades do not rise — because you have punished and destroyed them and wiped out all memory of them. But you have increased the nation, O Lord . . . you have enlarged all the borders of the land" (26:14-15). In view of the contrast between the dead who do not rise and the nation that is enlarged, it is likely that the resurrection is the resurrection of the people, as in Ezekiel.[5] Isaiah 25:8 promises that God "will swallow up Death forever," an allusion to an old Canaanite myth that said that Death *(Mot)* swallowed the god Baal. That passage would seem to imply that at some future time there will be no more death, but not necessarily that those who have died will rise again.

The fact that the language of resurrection is introduced in these texts may be due to the acquaintance of Jews with Persian thought, where resurrection had an integral place in future expectation.[6] But belief in actual resurrection of individuals was not accepted widely if at all in Judaism in the Persian period. One of the passages that is most frequently dubbed "proto-apocalyptic" is Isaiah 65:17-25, which begins: "For I am about to create new heavens and a new earth." In this new creation, one who dies at

---

4. Nickelsburg, *Resurrection*, p. 18; Puech, *La Croyance des Esséniens*, pp. 66-73; G. F. Hasel, "Resurrection in the Theology of Old Testament Apocalyptic," *ZAW* 92 (1980) 267-84.

5. J. Day, "Resurrection Imagery from Baal to the Book of Daniel," in J. A. Emerton, ed., *Congress Volume 1995* (VTSup 66; Leiden: Brill, 1997) 125-34.

6. B. Lang, "Street Theater, Raising the Dead, and the Zoroastrian Connection in Ezekiel's Preaching," in J. Lust, ed., *Ezekiel and His Book* (Leuven: Leuven University Press, 1986) 297-316.

a hundred will be considered a youth, and one who falls short of a hundred will be considered accursed. Life will be longer and better, but it will still be mortal. This remained the standard Jewish eschatological expectation down to the Hellenistic period.

The *Book of the Watchers*

This expectation is changed radically in the Enochic literature. The *Book of the Watchers* (*1 Enoch* 1–36) is a composite text, which took shape in the third or early second centuries BCE. These chapters show no awareness of the Maccabean revolt and were probably written prior to it. Enoch ascends to heaven to present the petition of the Watchers, or fallen angels. The petition is rejected, because angels should intercede for men, not men for angels (15:2). The Watchers had abandoned a spiritual, eternal life to have intercourse with human women and produce children of flesh and blood, "as those do who die and are destroyed" (15:4). One of the essential contrasts throughout the Enoch literature is between the spiritual, eternal life, on the one hand, and the fleshly, mortal life, on the other. The fall of the angels is a fall into mortality, while conversely the ascent of Enoch is an ascent to eternal life.

After Enoch is given the reply to the Watchers, he is taken on a guided tour to the ends of the earth, in which he sees the mysteries of the cosmos. In the course of this tour he sees "in the west a large and high mountain, and a hard rock and four beautiful[7] places" (*1 En.* 22:1). The angel Raphael explains that these places were created that "the spirits, the souls of the dead might be gathered into them." There they would be kept until the day of judgment. The different compartments are meant to separate the souls of the dead:

> And thus the souls of the righteous have been separated; this is the spring of water, and on it is the light. Likewise a place has been created for sinners when they die and are buried in the earth and judgment has not come upon them during their life . . . and thus a place has been separated for the souls of those who complain and give information about their destruction, when they were killed in the days of the sinners. Thus a place has been created for the souls of men who are not

7. The Ethiopic here appears to be a misreading of the Greek word for "hollow."

righteous but sinners, accomplished in wrongdoing, and with the wrongdoers will be their lot. But their souls will not be killed on the day of judgement, nor will they rise from here. (22:9-14)

There is no close parallel to this passage in other Jewish apocalyptic writings, not even in the other Enochic books.[8] Various traditions about the afterlife are reflected in it.[9] The location of the chambers of the dead inside a mountain recalls the *Epic of Gilgamesh,* where Gilgamesh has to enter the base of a mountain to reach the Netherworld. The motif of water and light is associated with the afterlife of the blessed in Orphic tradition. The main significance of the passage is that it shows distinctions between the fate of the righteous and of sinners, in a manner not attested in earlier Jewish tradition.[10]

These chambers, however, are only the waiting places. Enoch goes on to see a mountain "whose summit is like the throne of the Lord" (*1 En.* 25:3). This, he is told, is the throne where the Lord will sit when he comes down to visit the earth for good. It is surrounded by fragrant trees, one of which is the tree of life that will be given to the righteous. "It will be planted in a holy place, by the house of the Lord, the Eternal King. Then they will rejoice with joy and be glad in the holy place; they will each draw the fragrance of it into their bones, and they will live a long life on earth as your fathers lived" (25:5-6). It is not clear that they will enjoy strictly eternal life; the language suggests extremely long lives like the first patriarchs. Elsewhere in the *Book of the Watchers* we are told that the Watchers hoped "for eternal life, and that each of them would live five hundred years" (10:10). The location of the tree of life is separate from that of the tree of wisdom from which Adam ate, which is in the Garden of Righteousness, far away to the east (chapter 33).

Enoch further sees "an accursed valley" (Gehenna?), which is for "those who are cursed for ever; here will be gathered together all who speak with their mouths against the Lord words that are not fitting and say hard things about his glory" (27:2). The Watchers, in chapter 10, are

---

8. The closest parallel is found in the fragmentary *Apocalypse of Zephaniah.* See further below.

9. M. T. Wacker, *Weltordnung und Gericht. Studien zu 1 Henoch 22* (Würzburg: Echter, 1982).

10. T. F. Glasson, *Greek Influence in Jewish Eschatology* (London: SPCK, 1961) 8-19, argues for Greek influence in this respect. On the detail of the distinctions see Nickelsburg, *Resurrection,* 134-37.

imprisoned under the hills of the earth for seventy generations and then condemned to the abyss of fire for all eternity (10:13). In chapter 21, Enoch sees the fiery prison of the angels, where they are held forever (cf. 18:14-16). We have here the beginnings of the idea of Hell, even though the valley of the accursed is not explicitly said to be fiery.[11] There is a precedent for the prison of the host of heaven in Isaiah 24:22 ("they will be shut up in a prison, and after many days they will be punished"), but the prison there is not fiery. The idea of Hell as a place of fiery punishment, which became standard in Christianity, seems to have been first developed in Judaism. The idea of a place of punishment in the Netherworld is found in Plato (*Republic* 10.614-21; *Gorgias* 523) and is thought to derive from Orphic teachings. In Persian eschatology, the wicked were destroyed by a stream of molten metal (*Bundahishn* 34). The idea of eternal punishment by fire, however, first appears here in *1 Enoch*. There was a precedent in Isaiah 66:24, where we are told that dead bodies of people who rebel against God will be on permanent display: "their worm shall not die and their flame shall not be quenched." It is not suggested, however, that they are alive to experience everlasting torment.

Other Enochic Apocalypses

The *Book of the Watchers* has the most elaborate mythical geography of the early Enoch apocalypses. Some of the other booklets that make up *1 Enoch* also have important ideas about life after death. The *Animal Apocalypse* in *1 Enoch* 85-90 presents an allegorical account of the history of Israel, in which the Israelites are represented as sheep and the nations as predatory animals.[12] Adam and the prediluvian patriarchs are bulls. The fallen angels of Genesis 6 are stars that fall from heaven. Noah is born a bull but becomes a man. Moses is a sheep at first but becomes a man. Otherwise, men in this apocalypse symbolize angels. The seventy shepherds that rule over the sheep in the post-exilic period are most plausibly interpreted as the patron angels of the nations. The "man" who records all their deeds (90:14) is a recording angel. The history culminates in a judgment, when

11. For a general treatment, see A. E. Bernstein, *The Formation of Hell: Death and Retribution in the Ancient and Early Christian Worlds* (Ithaca, NY: Cornell University Press, 1993).

12. P. A. Tiller, *A Commentary on the Animal Apocalypse of 1 Enoch* (Atlanta: Scholars Press, 1993).

"the Lord of the sheep" is enthroned in "the pleasant land" (Israel), and the sealed books are opened. The fallen angels and the seventy shepherds are condemned and thrown into "a deep place full of fire, burning and full of pillars of fire" (90:25). The "blind sheep" (Jewish apostates) are likewise thrown into an abyss of fire. All that had been destroyed and scattered are reassembled (90:33: probably a reference to the resurrection of the dead). Finally the sheep are all transformed into white bulls, the pristine Adamic form of existence. The emphasis here seems to be on the transformation of the elect rather than restoration to a previous form of existence.

The *Epistle of Enoch* (*1 Enoch* 91–105) also predicts resurrection at the end of history. The Lord will execute judgment and the idols of the nations will be destroyed in a judgment of fire. Then "the righteous will rise from sleep, and wisdom will rise and will be given to them" (*1 Enoch* 90:9-10). Elsewhere, however, the Epistle asserts the future vindication of the righteous in terms that do not suggest bodily resurrection but the transformation of the spirit after death:[13]

> Do not be afraid, you souls of the righteous, and be hopeful, you who have died in righteousness. And do not be sad that your souls have gone down into Sheol in sadness, and that your bodies did not obtain during your life a reward (102:4-5) . . . much good will be given to you in recompense for your toil, and your lot will be more excellent than that of the living. And the spirits of you who have died in righteousness will live, and their spirits will rejoice and be glad, and the memory of them will remain. (103:3-4)

Sinners will be committed to "darkness and chains and burning flames" (103:8), but the righteous "will shine like the lights of heaven and will be seen, and the gate of heaven will be opened to you . . . for you will have great joy like the angels of heaven . . . for you shall be associates of the host of heaven" (104:2-6).

The reward of the righteous is to share the eternal, spiritual life of the angels in heaven. This is not the Greek idea of immortality of the soul, but neither is it the resurrection of the body. Rather it is the resurrection, or exaltation, of the spirit from Sheol to heaven. The bodies of the righteous will presumably continue to rest in the earth. A similar understanding of the resurrection is found explicitly in the Book of *Jubilees*, another writing

13. Nickelsburg, *Resurrection*, 112-29.

from the second century BCE that may be some decades later than the *Epistle of Enoch.* There we are told that at a future time when people return to the path of righteousness their lives will grow longer until the number of their years becomes greater than once was the number of their days. After that "their bones shall rest in the earth, and their spirits shall have much joy" (*Jub.* 23:26-31).

The theme of angelic transformation is continued in the latest section of *1 Enoch,* the *Similitudes* (*1 Enoch* 37–71), which probably dates from the first century CE. The focus of this text is on the day of judgment, when the appearances of the present will be reversed.[14] Sinners will be confounded by the apparition of the heavenly Righteous One, who is identified as "that Son of Man" by allusion to the vision of "one like a son of man" in Daniel 7. The sinners have denied the existence of this heavenly vindicator and also of the resting places of the righteous after death. Enoch claims to have seen these resting places in a vision: "there my eyes saw their dwelling with the angels and their resting-places with the holy ones. . . . And I saw their dwelling under the wings of the Lord of Spirits, and all the righteous and chosen shone before him like the light of fire, and their mouth was full of blessing" (*1 Enoch* 39:5-7). When "that Son of Man" appears, "he will cast down the faces of the strong, and shame will fill them, and darkness will be their dwelling, and worms will be their resting-place; and they will have no hope of rising from their resting-places" (45:5).

Another section of the *Similitudes* looks forward to a general resurrection: "And in those days the earth will return that which has been entrusted to it, and Sheol will return that which has been entrusted to it, that which it has received" (51:1). In his visions, Enoch sees "the angel of punishment going and preparing all the instruments of Satan" (53:3) and a deep valley of burning fire that is prepared for the hosts of Azazel (chapter 54). The sinners also expect a fiery punishment. When they are confronted by the Son of Man, they confess: "Our souls are sated with possessions gained through iniquity, but they do not prevent our going down into the flames of the torment of Sheol" (53:10). Here it appears that Sheol has become identified as a place of punishment. The sinners cannot hope to rise from there. The righteous, in contrast, may expect eternal life in the company of the Son of Man: "with you will be their dwelling, and with you their lot, and they will not be separated from you, for ever and ever and ever" (71:16).

14. See Collins, *The Apocalyptic Imagination,* 177-93.

The Resurrection in Daniel

The exaltation of the righteous after death to join the host of heaven is also fundamental to the understanding of the resurrection in the Book of Daniel.[15] The prediction of resurrection in Daniel 12:1-3 comes at the end of a long revelation to Daniel by the angel Gabriel, which outlines the course of Hellenistic history in the form of a prophecy after the fact. This history reaches its climax in the career of Antiochus Epiphanes and his persecution of the Jews. Daniel incorrectly predicts that the king will meet his death in the land of Israel, but the real climax of history comes after that (Dan. 12:1-3):

> At that time Michael will arise, the great prince who stands over your people. There will be a time of distress such as had not been from the beginning of the nation to that time. At that time your people will be delivered, everyone who is found written in the book. Many of those who sleep in the dusty earth will awake, some to everlasting life and some to reproach and everlasting disgrace. The wise will shine like the splendor of the firmament, and those who lead the common people to righteousness like the stars forever and ever.

This is the only passage in the Hebrew Bible that clearly predicts the resurrection of individuals. It does not predict universal resurrection: many of those who sleep will arise, but not all. Those who are raised are the very good, for their reward, and the very bad, for punishment. The phrase "dusty earth" *('admat 'apar)* may refer either to the grave or Sheol or both. It does not necessarily imply that the resurrection must be physical; it may be a resurrection of the spirit from Sheol. The fate of the sinners is expressed briefly by means of an allusion to Isaiah 66:24. Daniel does not refer to the fiery abyss that is the standard place of punishment in the Enoch literature. The description of the eternal life of the righteous is equally terse. We are told only that the wise *(maskilim)* will shine like the stars. The *maskilim* were the heroes who stood fast in the time of persecution (11:33-35) and instructed the people, even though some of them lost their lives. The elevation to the stars has overtones of astral immortality, the belief that the dead become stars, which was widespread in the Greco-Roman world.[16] In the context of

---

15. J. J. Collins, *Daniel* (Hermeneia; Minneapolis: Fortress, 1993) 390-98.

16. F. Cumont, *Lux Perpetua* (Paris: Geuthner, 1949) 142-288; M. P. Nilsson, *Geschichte der griechischen Religion* (3rd ed.; Munich: Beck, 1967) 2.470-71.

Jewish apocalyptic literature, however, the stars are the host of heaven, or the angelic host. The destiny of the wise in Daniel, then, is exactly the same as that of the righteous in the *Epistle of Enoch:* to become companions of the host of heaven. The angelic host looms large in the visions of Daniel, which often involve angelic activity and always require an angelic interpreter. The resurrection is ushered in by the victory of the archangel Michael in his battle against the patron angels of Persia and Greece (Daniel 10). In chapter 7, Israel is called "the people of the holy ones," or the people who are the earthly counterpart to the heavenly host.

Sources of the Belief

The Books of Enoch and Daniel may be regarded as the formative documents of Jewish apocalyptic tradition. The belief in a blessed afterlife for the righteous and eternal punishment for the damned is an integral part of that tradition and is one of the factors that distinguishes apocalypticism from earlier Jewish tradition. In the case of Daniel, the hope for resurrection resolves a problem arising from religious persecution. In traditional Israelite belief, the righteous were rewarded in this life, by prosperity and longevity. During the persecution of the Maccabean era, however, it was precisely the righteous who lost their lives. Faith in the justice of God could be maintained if the righteous could hope for a reward after death.

It would be too simple, however, to view the apocalyptic hope for the afterlife entirely as a response to the problem of persecution. The *Book of the Watchers* is certainly older than the Maccabean era. The *Epistle of Enoch* may be older too. Neither of these books is set in a time of persecution, but both depict a world out of joint. The *Book of the Watchers* describes a world turned upside down by the Watchers, who taught humanity charms and spells and also the making of weapons and the arts of ornamentation: "and the world was changed. And there was great impiety and much fornication, and they went astray, and all their ways became corrupt" (*1 En.* 8:2). The account of the Watchers can be read plausibly as an allegory for the Hellenistic age, and the impact of western culture on a traditional Near Eastern society.[17] If this is correct, the apocalypse was written as a response to cultural trauma and offered an alternative reality in its visions of hidden

---

17. G. W. Nickelsburg, "Apocalyptic and Myth in 1 Enoch 1–11," *Journal of Biblical Literature* 96 (1977) 383-405.

places and life beyond death. The *Epistle of Enoch* and the later *Similitudes* place the emphasis rather on social tensions:

> Woe to those who build their houses with sin, for from their whole foundation they will be thrown down, and by the sword they will fall, and those who acquire gold and silver will quickly be destroyed in the judgment. Woe to you, you rich, for you have trusted in your riches but from your riches you will depart, for you did not remember the Most High in the days of your riches. (*1 En.* 104:7-8)

In the *Similitudes,* the wicked who are discomfited on judgment day are "the kings and the mighty." Here again the hope for life beyond death can be correlated with dissatisfaction with life in the present.

Other nations in the ancient Mediterranean world had well-developed notions of life after death. These notions were perhaps best developed in Egypt, where portrayals of the judgment of the dead date back to the dawn of history.[18] Greek ideas of reward and punishment after death are associated with Orphic religion and are documented in the dialogues of Plato and now in the gold tablets from burial sites in Italy.[19] Neither the Egyptians nor the Greeks conceived of an end of history that might be the occasion of a general resurrection. Such an idea was, however, an integral part of Persian eschatology and can be documented already in Hellenistic times.[20] There is surely some influence from these sources on the early Jewish apocalypses. (The overtones of astral immortality in Daniel 12 provide a case in point.) But the ideas of immortality that we find in these texts cannot be categorized as simple borrowings. They adapt motifs from the surrounding cultures, but they reconfigure them in a distinctive way. Immortality in these apocalypses is primarily life with the heavenly host, the holy ones known from Near Eastern mythology since the second

---

18. J. G. Griffiths, *The Divine Verdict: A Study of Divine Judgement in the Ancient Religions* (Leiden: Brill, 1991) 160-242.

19. E. Rohde, *Psyche: The Cult of Souls and Belief in Immortality among the Greeks* (New York, 1925); F. Graf, "Dionysian and Orphic Eschatology: New Texts and Old Questions," in T. H. Carpenter and C. A. Faraone, eds., *Masks of Dionysus* (Ithaca, NY: Cornell University Press, 1993) 239-58.

20. On Persian eschatology, see A. Hultgård, "Persian Apocalypticism," in J. J. Collins, B. McGinn, and S. Stein, eds., *The Encyclopedia of Apocalypticism* (New York: Continuum, 1998) 1.39-83. The Persian belief in resurrection is corroborated by Theopompus in the third century BCE (Diogenes Laertius, *Proem* 6-9).

millennium BCE. The notion of a fiery hell is more novel, but here again the novelty is achieved by *bricolage*. The Orphics did not conceive of fire as the main means of punishment in the afterlife. Persian eschatology knew the idea of a fiery destruction of the world, and the Stoics had their own conception of a final conflagration or *ekpyrosis*. The notion of a fiery Hell, however, appears to be a Jewish invention, which was later elaborated by Christianity.

It is often claimed that Jews believed in resurrection of the body, while Greeks believed in immortality of the soul.[21] Such a claim fails to do justice to the Books of Enoch and Daniel. What we find in these apocalypses is the resurrection of the spirit. It is not the Greek idea of the soul, but neither is it a physical body. In the terminology of St. Paul, it might be described as a spiritual body (cf. 1 Cor. 15:44). Ideas of physical resurrection also gained currency in Judaism in the second century BCE, as can be seen from the account of the martyrdoms in 2 Maccabees 7. But restoration of the body was only one of a number of ways in which the resurrection could be imagined. It was never the sole, nor even the dominant, concept of afterlife in ancient Judaism.

The Spread of Beliefs in Afterlife

The ideas of afterlife that we find in the early apocalypses were adapted in other bodies of literature. In the Dead Sea Scrolls, the fellowship with the angels, which was reserved for life after death in Enoch and Daniel, is conceived as a present possibility.[22] In Alexandrian Judaism, the resurrection of the spirit is reconceived as the immortality of the soul.[23] Ideas of resurrection spread to different segments of Jewish society around the turn of the era. The Pharisees accepted them; the Sadducees did not.[24] Belief in a judgment of the dead ceased to be a distinctive characteristic of apocalyptic movements. We do, however, have two clusters of apocalyptic

---

21. E.g., O. Cullmann, "Immortality of the Soul or Resurrection of the Dead," in K. Stendahl, ed., *Immortality and Resurrection* (New York: Macmillan, 1971) 9-35. See the comments of Nickelsburg, *Resurrection*, 177-80.

22. J. J. Collins, *Apocalypticism in the Dead Sea Scrolls* (London: Routledge, 1997) 110-29.

23. J. J. Collins, *Jewish Wisdom in the Hellenistic Age* (OTL; Louisville: Westminster, 1997) 185-87.

24. Puech, *La Croyance*, 201-42.

texts from the late first or early second centuries CE that show significant developments in Jewish conceptions of afterlife.

4 Ezra *and* 2 Baruch

The first cluster is found in the apocalypses of *4 Ezra* and *2 Baruch,* written after the destruction of Jerusalem in 70 CE, toward the end of the first century. In *4 Ezra,* an angel assures Ezra that the time will come when the messiah will be revealed and will rule for four hundred years. After the messianic age, the world will be turned back to primeval silence for seven days. Then it will be roused again, and "that which is corruptible shall perish. And the earth shall give up those who are asleep in it, and the dust those who dwell silently in it; and the chambers shall give up the souls which have been committed to them" (*4 Ezra* 7:30-33). Then follow judgment and recompense. "Then the pit of torment shall appear, and opposite it shall be the place of rest; and the furnace of hell shall be disclosed, and opposite it the paradise of delight" (7:36). Ezra asks about the interval, "whether after death, as soon as everyone of us yields up his soul, we shall be kept in rest until those times come when thou wilt renew the creation, or whether we shall be tormented at once" (7:75). He is told that the souls of the unrighteous do not immediately enter into habitations but wander grieving in torments, because they realize the error of their ways. The righteous immediately see the glory of God and rejoice. Their faces are to shine like the sun, and they are to be made like the light of the stars. There will no longer be any intercession on the day of judgment, but everyone will be judged on his or her own merits. Ezra objects that "there are more who perish than those who will be saved as a wave is greater than a drop of water" (9:15-16). But Ezra's angelic dialogue partner offers little consolation on this issue: "The Most High made this world for the sake of many, but the world to come for the sake of few. But I will tell you a parable, Ezra. Just as, when you ask the earth, it will tell you that it provides very much clay from which earthenware is made, but only a little dust from which gold comes; so is the course of the present world. Many have been created, but few shall be saved" (8:1-3).

The roughly contemporary apocalypse of *2 Baruch* also predicts a messianic age, when the earth shall yield its fruit ten thousandfold (29:3). Then, when this age has run its course, the messiah will return in glory (to heaven), and then all who have died and set their hopes on him will rise again. Then the treasuries where the souls are preserved will be opened, the righteous will rejoice, and the wicked will be discomfited (2 *Baruch* 30). Later, Baruch asks the Lord, "in what form will those live who live in thy day, and what will they look like afterwards?" (2 *Bar.* 49:2). He is told:

> the earth will certainly then restore the dead it now receives so as to preserve them: it will make no change in their form, but as it has received them, so it will restore them, and as I delivered them to it, so also will it raise them. For those who are still alive must be shown that the dead have come to life again, and that those who had departed have returned. (2 *Bar.* 50:2-3)

After the judgment, however, appearances will be changed. "The appearance of the evil-doers will go from bad to worse, as they suffer torment" (51:2), but the righteous "will assume a luminous beauty so that they may be able to attain and enter the world which does not die, which has been promised to them" (51:3). "Time will no longer age them, for in the heights of the world shall they dwell, and they shall be made like the angels and be made equal to the stars" (51:10). The extent of paradise will be spread before them, and in fact they will exceed even the splendor of the angels (51:12).

These apocalypses stand in the tradition of Daniel, insofar as there is a general resurrection at the end of history, and the righteous are eventually transformed to shine like the stars. Unlike the Enoch tradition, they pay little attention to the torment of the damned and the fires of Hell. But they have given thought to some of the problems involved in resurrection. At this point, what is envisioned is a bodily resurrection, to facilitate recognition of the dead. Ultimately, however, the emphasis is on transformation, as the body is then made luminous in an angelic state.

Apocalyptic Writings from the Diaspora

A different view of the afterlife can be found in the sub-genre of apocalypses that takes the form of ascent of the visionary through the heavens.[25] This

---

25. M. Himmelfarb, *Ascent to Heaven in Jewish and Christian Apocalypses* (New York: Oxford University Press, 1993); A. Yarbro Collins, "The Seven Heavens in Jewish and Christian Apocalypses," in eadem, *Cosmology and Eschatology in Jewish and Christian Apocalypticism* (Leiden: Brill, 1996) 21-54.

kind of apocalypse was pioneered in the *Book of the Watchers,* but there Enoch did not ascend through multiple heavens but rather traveled outward to the ends of the earth. The first case of an ascent through multiple heavens is found in the Aramaic Levi document from Qumran (4Q213a).[26] In the later, Greek, *Testament of Levi,* in the *Testaments of the Twelve Patriarchs,* this ascent is stylized. In one recension, Levi ascends through three heavens, in another through seven. Even the longer Greek recension, however, makes no mention of the abodes of the dead in any of the heavens.

In contrast, we find considerable attention to the dead in the ascent apocalypses of *2 Enoch* and *3 Baruch. 2 Enoch* is preserved only in Slavonic and is notoriously difficult to date.[27] Most scholars opt for a date no later than the first century CE because of the importance attached to animal sacrifice. It is located in Egypt, on the basis of allusions to Egyptian mythology and some affinities with Philo and other diaspora writings.[28] Nonetheless, the provenance of this apocalypse is far from certain. The situation is further complicated by the existence of two recensions, one of which is much longer than the other.

Two kinds of material, cosmological and eschatological, are emphasized in the account of Enoch's ascent. The descriptions of the first, fourth, and sixth heavens are concerned with the regulation of the heavenly bodies and the order of the universe. The second, third, and fifth heavens are the scenes of eschatological rewards and punishments. The second heaven contains the prison of the rebellious angels, who are tormented unceasingly. The third is the location of Paradise. The tree of life is there, and the Lord takes a rest under it whenever he walks in Paradise. Enoch is told by his angelic guide, Uriel, that this place has been prepared for the righteous. In the north of the third heaven, however, is "a very frightful place, and all kinds of torture and torment are in that place, cruel darkness and lightless gloom. And there is no light there, and a black fire blazes up perpetually, with a river of fire that comes out over the whole place . . . and very cruel places of detention and dark and merciless angels, carrying instruments of atrocities, torturing without pity" (*2 En.* 10:2-3). This place has been prepared for the punishment of sinners. In the sixth heaven, Enoch encounters

---

26. M. E. Stone and J. C. Greenfield, "Aramaic Levi Document," in G. Brooke et al., eds., *Qumran Cave IV-XVII* (DJD 22; Oxford: Clarendon, 1996) 30-31.

27. F. Andersen, "2 Enoch," in J. H. Charlesworth, ed., *The Old Testament Pseudepigrapha* (Garden City, NY: Doubleday, 1983) 1.91-221.

28. C. Böttrich, *Weltweisheit, Menscheitsethik, Urkult. Studien zum slavischen Henochbuch* (Tübingen: Mohr Siebeck, 1992) 192.

the Grigori, or Watchers, who are distinguished from the rebel angels of the second heaven. They are dejected, but not in torment, and at Enoch's exhortation they perform a liturgy of praise to God.

Two features of this heavenly eschatology are noteworthy. First, Paradise is not located in the highest heaven, in the presence of the Lord. We have noted that one recension of Aramaic Levi has only three heavens, and this was the most conventional number of heavens in traditional Babylonian cosmology.[29] The Hebrew Bible often refers to the "heaven, and the heaven of heavens," which could also be interpreted as three heavens. It would seem that the third heaven was at one time the highest, and this would account for the location there of Paradise. When Paul claims to "know a person in Christ who . . . was caught up to the third heaven — whether in the body or out of the body I do not know; God knows" and that he was also "caught up into Paradise" (2 Cor. 12:2-4), he is not referring to two different raptures; Paradise was located in the third heaven.

More surprising than the location of Paradise is the location of Hell. Three of the seven heavens contain places of punishment, and the place of human sinners is located like Paradise in the third heaven. In earlier Jewish and general Near Eastern tradition, the abode of the dead who were not beatified was always in the Netherworld. Hellenistic cosmology, however, had no place for a Netherworld, and so philosophical authors increasingly located Hades in the heavens.[30] 2 Enoch represents a Jewish adaptation of the new cosmology, in which all the dead ascend to the heavens, regardless of their destiny.

One other feature of 2 Enoch is significant for the understanding of the afterlife. When Enoch reaches the seventh heaven, he is transformed at the command of God: "Michael extracted me from my clothes. He anointed me with the delightful oil, and the appearance of that oil is greater than the greatest light, its ointment is like sweet dew, and its fragrance like myrrh; and its shining is like the sun. And I gazed at all of myself, and I had become like one of the glorious ones, and there was no observable difference" (2 En. 22:9-10). It is not apparent in 2 Enoch that all the righteous are so transformed, but the episode recalls the account of the resurrection in Daniel 12, where the wise are said to shine like the stars.[31]

29. Yarbro Collins, "The Seven Heavens," 27-28. Seven heavens are also attested as early as the second millennium BCE.
30. M. P. Nilsson, *Geschichte der griechischen Religion* (3rd ed.; Munich: Beck, 1974) 240-41. The earliest authority for the new location was Heracleides Ponticus, a pupil of Plato.
31. See further Himmelfarb, *Ascent to Heaven*, 47-71.

Like *2 Enoch, 3 Baruch* is generally believed to come from Egyptian Judaism, because of affinities with other Egyptian Jewish writings. The apocalypse begins with Baruch's lamenting the fall of Jerusalem, a setting that suggests the book was written in the years after 70 CE. Unlike *2 Enoch, 3 Baruch* has undergone a clear Christian redaction, but the core of the book is recognized as Jewish. It is preserved in Greek and also in Slavonic.[32]

The extant text of *3 Baruch* mentions only five heavens. Whether this number is original, or is an abbreviation of a seven-heaven schema, is disputed. It has been argued that the author was familiar with the seven-heaven cosmology, but that Baruch's ascent is aborted to make the point that humans cannot attain full unmediated access to the divine.[33] Unlike Enoch, Baruch is not transformed to angelic status.

The first two heavens are occupied respectively by those who built the tower of Babel and those who gave counsel to build the tower. They now have hybrid animal forms (faces of oxen, horns of stags, etc.) but are not otherwise in torment. The third heaven contains complex cosmological mysteries. The abode of righteous souls is apparently in the fourth heaven,[34] where they appear as a multitude of birds, singing the praises of the Lord. The gate to the fifth heaven is closed until Michael opens it to receive the prayers of humanity. He takes human merits up to God in a higher heaven and returns with rewards for the righteous and a stern insistence that those without merits have only themselves to blame. There is no vision of Hell, but in 4:16 the angel warns that sinners "will secure for themselves eternal fire." This passage, however, may be part of the Christian redaction of the book.

The transfer of Hell to the heavens was not universally followed. The *Apocalypse of Zephaniah,* which is preserved in a single Akhmimic manuscript from the fourth or fifth century CE, seems to be a Jewish Egyptian work of much earlier date.[35] It describes a tour of the abodes of the dead

---

32. D. C. Harlow, *The Greek Apocalypse of Baruch (3 Baruch) in Hellenistic Judaism and Early Christianity* (Leiden: Brill, 1996).

33. Harlow, *The Greek Apocalypse of Baruch,* 34-76.

34. *3 Baruch* 10. The Greek text reads "third heaven," but this is evidently a mistake or scribal alteration, since Baruch proceeds from there to the fifth heaven.

35. M. Himmelfarb, *Tours of Hell: An Apocalyptic Form in Jewish and Christian Literature* (Philadelphia: University of Pennsylvania Press, 1983) 13-14. There are two fragments, of which only the shorter mentions Zephaniah. The identification of the longer fragment, which is cited here, seems probable but is not certain. See K. H. Kuhn, "The Apocalypse of Zephaniah and an Anonymous Apocalypse," in H. F. D. Sparks, *The Apocryphal Old Testament* (Oxford: Clarendon, 1984) 915-25.

by Zephaniah. First he is taken to the abode of the righteous, which is full of light: "for where the righteous and saints are there is no darkness, but they are always in the light" (1:5). He also sees the punishment of the wicked and a host of punishing angels. Then he follows his guide through metal gates into a beautiful city. But the gates begin to breathe out fire, and he sees a sea of fire coming against him. Then he encounters a great angel, whom he mistakes for the Lord Almighty. He is told: "I am the great angel Eremiel, whose place is in the world below, and I have been appointed over the abyss and hell, in which all souls have been imprisoned from the end of the flood, which was upon the earth, until to-day" (2:12).[36] He informs Zephaniah that he is now in Hell and identifies the accuser, who has a catalogue of everyone's sins. Because of his righteousness, however, Zephaniah is allowed to come up from Hell and to cross at the ferry place to the land of the living. In some respects, the picture of the Netherworld given here is quite primitive. It parallels the *Book of the Watchers,* insofar as the spirits of the dead are held in waiting for the judgment day, and the righteous are in a place of light.[37] But the fiery picture of Hell is developed beyond what we find in *1 Enoch.* The uncertainty about the provenance of this apocalypse unfortunately undercuts its value for tracing the development of beliefs about the afterlife.

The apocalypses we have reviewed from the diaspora, originally written in Greek, show no interest in a general resurrection at the end of history but focus on the fate of the spirit or soul after death. There was a tradition of historical eschatology in the diaspora, which finds expression in the *Sibylline Oracles.* These typically review the rise and fall of kingdoms and culminate either with a glorious kingdom or with cosmic destruction. The main Sibylline books that can be ascribed to Egyptian Judaism, books 3 and 5, are remarkably void of interest in resurrection or afterlife. The fourth book has a different character, and probably comes from a different location (perhaps Syria) in the late first century CE. Here history ends with a conflagration, but after God extinguishes the fire he "will again fashion the bones and ashes of men, and he will raise up mortals again as they were before" (*Sib. Or.* 4:179-82). Sinners are banished to Gehenna, but the righteous will live on earth again and enjoy the light of the sun. The physical, earthly character of the resurrection here is remarkable in a text from the

---

36. An angel named Jeremiel converses with Ezra about the chambers of the dead in *4 Ezra* 4:36.

37. Himmelfarb, *Tours of Hell,* 151-53.

diaspora written in Greek but goes to show that Hellenistic culture did not always give rise to a belief in immortality of the soul, any more than Semitic culture necessarily gave rise to belief in resurrection of the body.

One final text from the diaspora requires mention here although its apocalyptic character is questionable. The *Testament of Abraham,* written in Egypt in the late first or early second century CE, is primarily a narrative about the death of Abraham.[38] (He conspicuously fails to make a testament.) When it is time for Abraham to die, God dispatches the angel Michael to fetch him. But Michael cannot bring himself to break the news, and when Abraham finally learns it he is reluctant to go. So Abraham is given a tour of the heavens and allowed to witness the judgment of the dead. There is then an apocalyptic judgment scene of considerable interest embedded in the narrative.[39] Abel, son of Adam, presides over the judgment, like a son of God. He is attended by recording angels and by an angel who holds a balance. A fiery angel, Purouel, tests the work of mortals through fire. Those whose works are burnt up are condemned to torment, while those whose works withstand the fire are saved. Unlike the judgment in *4 Ezra,* intercession is possible here. The judgment scene in the *Testament of Abraham* is exceptional insofar as it emphasizes the mercy of God and qualifies the strict dichotomy of righteous and wicked that is characteristic of most apocalypses.

Conclusion

The earliest Jewish apocalypses, in the Books of Enoch and Daniel, conceive of a resurrection of the dead at the end of history. While there is some variation among the different texts, the righteous are typically exalted to share the life of the angels, while the wicked are condemned to a fiery Hell. (Daniel is less explicit than Enoch about the punishment of the damned.) These apocalypses envision a resurrection of the spirit or spiritual body, and its relation to the physical body that died is not clarified.

The apocalyptic writings of the first and early second centuries CE adapt this tradition in two quite different ways. *4 Ezra* and *2 Baruch* look

---

38. For the text, see E. P. Sanders, "The Testament of Abraham," in Charlesworth, ed., *The Old Testament Pseudepigrapha,* 1.882-902.

39. See G. W. Nickelsburg, "Eschatology in the Testament of Abraham: A Study of the Judgement Scenes in the Two Recensions," in idem, ed., *Studies on the Testament of Abraham* (Missoula, MT: Scholars Press, 1976) 23-64.

for a general resurrection at the end of history. *2 Baruch* is especially clear on the form of the resurrection. Those who rise must be recognizable as those who have died, but they are subsequently transformed by the glory or the torment that they attain. The discussion in these apocalypses helps illuminate the background of Paul's discussion of the resurrection in 1 Corinthians 15. Paul sees the resurrection of Christ as harbinger of the general resurrection, but he insists that the body that is raised is not that which was buried but rather a spiritual body. We also find a general resurrection, in explicitly physical terms, in *Sibylline Oracles* 4, which was written in Greek in the diaspora (probably in Syria).

The more typical form of apocalypse from the diaspora, however, is the heavenly ascent. Here considerable attention is paid to the reward and punishment of the dead, but there is no expectation of a general resurrection. The focus on individual afterlife in these apocalypses was compatible with the Greek belief in the immortality of the soul, but it is expressed in mythological rather than philosophical idiom.

In most of the texts we have discussed, the belief in judgment after death serves the purpose of theodicy by upholding the ultimate justice of God. It thereby provides hope to the oppressed and relieves the resentment caused by injustice in this life. The judgment scene could, however, also be used for other purposes, as we see in the *Testament of Abraham,* which encourages compassion for human sinners and insists on the mercy as well as the justice of God.

PART IV

Pseudepigraphy

CHAPTER 13

Pseudepigraphy and Group Formation
in Second Temple Judaism

The device of pseudepigraphy offered many advantages to writers of the Hellenistic period, most obviously the prestige of antiquity.[1] In the pseudepigraphic writings found at Qumran, another factor is prominent. Several of them utilize the antiquity of the pseudonymous author to present a pseudo-prophecy that outlines a long expanse of history after the fact. Examples are found in the *Apocalypse of Weeks* and the *Animal Apocalypse* of *1 Enoch;* in Daniel 10–12; in *Jubilees* 23; in 4Q390 (Pseudo-Moses); and in the Pseudo-Daniel fragments. This device of prophecy after the fact, authorized by a venerable pseudonym, is well known throughout the Hellenistic world from Persia to Rome. On the one hand, it conveys a sense that history is predetermined, since it could be predicted centuries in advance. On the other, it inspires confidence in the real prediction with which these prophecies typically conclude. There is another feature of these prophecies, on which I wish to focus here, which comes at or near the point of transition between prophecy after the fact and real prediction. This concerns the rise of an elect group that is foretold from ancient times and thereby legitimated. It is reasonable to suppose that the real authors of the works in question belonged to these elect groups.

Since the best-known elect group to emerge in the second century BCE was the Dead Sea sect, the question of the relationship between these

---

1. See the overviews by B. M. Metzger, "Literary Forgeries and Canonical Pseudepigrapha," *JBL* 91 (1972) 3-24; W. Speyer, "Religiöse Pseudepigraphie und literarische Fälschung im Altertum," in *Frühes Christentum im antiken Strahlungsfeld* (Tübingen: Mohr, 1989) 21-58; W. Speyer, "Fälschung, pseudepigraphische freie Erfindung und 'echte religiöse Pseudepigraphie,'" in *Frühes Christentum im antiken Strahlungsfeld,* 100-139.

pseudepigraphic writings and that sect inevitably arises. Many scholars have argued that the Books of Enoch and *Jubilees* derive from a parent movement of the Dead Sea sect, and Daniel is sometimes also included in the same broad movement.[2] In her contribution to the Madrid Qumran Congress, Devorah Dimant claimed that the Pseudo-Moses text, 4Q390, "now provides for the first time solid textual data for reconstructing different strands within the growing corpus of works related to the Qumran community."[3] While this claim, in my opinion, exaggerates the significance of the Pseudo-Moses text, we do indeed have a complex body of data relevant to this issue. In this chapter I wish to take up Dimant's challenge by outlining some of the different strands in this literature and reflecting on the significance of the pseudepigraphic attributions.

The Enoch Apocalypses

The figure of Enoch is the subject of a few enigmatic verses in Genesis: he lived 365 years; then he walked with אלהים and was no more, for God took him.[4] It would seem that he was already associated with the solar calendar in Genesis. His primary qualification as a pseudepigraphic author, however, lies in the claim that he walked with אלהים, whether that word is understood to refer to God or to angels. Enoch's journeys to the ends of the earth in the *Book of the Watchers* may be understood as an attempt to spell out how he walked with אלהים. Consequently, he was uniquely qualified to impart wisdom about the mysteries of cosmos and history. The earliest Enochic writings, the *Book of the Watchers* and the *Astronomical Book,* contain compendia of cosmic revelations, including such matters

2. E.g., M. Hengel, *Judaism and Hellenism* (Philadelphia: Fortress, 1974) 1.175-80; D. Dimant, "Qumran Sectarian Literature," in M. E. Stone, ed., *Jewish Writings of the Second Temple Period* (Compendia Rerum Iudaicarum ad Novum Testamentam 2.2; Philadelphia: Fortress, 1984) 542-47; F. García Martínez, "Qumran Origins and Early History: A Groningen Hypothesis," *Folia Orientalia* 25 (1989) 119; P. R. Davies, *Behind the Essenes* (Atlanta: Scholars Press, 1987) 107-34. See also G. Boccaccini, *Beyond the Essene Hypothesis: The Parting of the Ways between Qumran and Enochic Judaism* (Grand Rapids: Eerdmans, 1998).

3. D. Dimant, "New Light from Qumran on the Jewish Pseudepigrapha — 4Q390," in J. Trebolle Barrera and L. Vegas Montaner, eds., *The Madrid Qumran Congress: Proceedings of the International Congress on the Dead Sea Scrolls* (Studies on the Texts of the Desert of Judah 2; Leiden: Brill, 1992) 2.447.

4. On the figure of Enoch see J. C. VanderKam, *Enoch: A Man for All Generations* (Columbia: University of South Carolina Press, 1995).

as the movements of the stars, the storehouses of the elements, and the abodes of the dead.

The extant Enoch literature contains several hints that there was a community in the Hellenistic period that claimed to possess a wisdom derived from Enoch. The clearest allusions to this community are provided by the *Apocalypse of Weeks* in *1 Enoch* 93:1-10; 91:11-17. This apocalypse pays much less attention to cosmic revelations than was the case in the *Book of the Watchers* and the *Astronomical Book.* Instead, it presents a schematic outline of patriarchal and Israelite history that highlights a pattern of sin and salvation. In the second week, culminating in the Flood, great wickedness arises, but a man (Noah) is saved. After the Flood, iniquity grows again, but at the end of the third week "a man will be chosen as the plant of righteous judgment and after him will come the plant of righteousness for ever." The pattern continues until the seventh week, which is dominated by an apostate generation, but "at its end the chosen righteous from the eternal plant of righteousness will be chosen, to whom will be given sevenfold teaching concerning his whole creation." At this point the course of history changes and sinners are destroyed by the sword. The sword continues to rage in the eighth generation, and at the end the elect acquire houses because of their righteousness and "a house will be built for the great king in glory for ever." In the ninth "week" the world is written down for destruction, and in the tenth the judgment of the Watchers takes place and the old heaven is replaced with a new one.

It is clear that the rise of the "chosen righteous" is a pivotal moment in this process and that one of the purposes of the apocalypse is to accredit this group as the elect of God. The author of the *Apocalypse of Weeks* most probably belonged to the number of the chosen righteous. We are not told much about this group, except that it is given "sevenfold teaching concerning the whole creation." Since the entire apocalypse is attributed to Enoch, it is reasonable to assume that this teaching is related to other books in the Enochic corpus, such as the *Book of the Watchers* and the *Astronomical Book,* both of which purport to describe "the whole creation." The *Book of the Watchers* uses the phrase "the plant of righteousness" to refer to the emergence of righteousness on earth after the Watchers are destroyed (*1 En.* 11:16). Books are important for this group. Enoch reads from books. But the righteous are not necessarily reclusive scholars. They are evidently willing to wield the sword by which the wicked are destroyed. It is arguable that the mention of the sword in the eighth week is a reference to the Maccabean revolt, but the apocalypse is clearly written before the building of the "great house" at the end of that week. Even if the sword is part of the real prophecy, however, and is still in the future from the perspective of the real author, it is clear that the Apocalypse endorses the use of violence. We have, then, a group that is both learned, in its way, and militant, playing an active role in implementing the divine judgment.

If there is doubt as to whether the *Apocalypse of Weeks* is referring to the Maccabean revolt, there is no such doubt about the *Animal Apocalypse.* Here too there is an elect group, identified allegorically as "small lambs." The character of this group is even more difficult to discern than was the case in the *Apocalypse of Weeks* because of the allegorical language. They are said to open their eyes and to see, in contrast to the blindness of their contemporaries. Whether their vision entailed "a sevenfold teaching about all creation," like the *Apocalypse of Weeks,* is not stated. When we are told that "horns came upon those lambs," however, the symbolism is clear, and when "a big horn grew on one of those sheep" the reference is unmistakably to Judas Maccabee.[5] Many scholars have identified the "lambs" with the Hasidim of the Maccabean books who are described as "mighty warriors" (1 Macc. 2:42)[6] and whose leader is said to be Judas Maccabee (2 Macc. 14:6). The Hasidim may also have been, or at least included, scribes.[7] In 1 Maccabees 7:12-13 the statement that a group of scribes appeared before the High Priest Alcimus is followed by a statement that the Hasidim were the first among the Israelites to seek peace.

There is no apparent reason why a vision predicting the rise of a militant group should be attributed to Enoch. If militancy were the defining characteristic of the group, more suitable pseudonyms could be found, such as Joshua or Elijah. Presumably the pseudonym was chosen for other reasons and the author of this apocalypse comes from the same circles that produced the other early Enochic writings, such as the *Book of the Watchers* and the *Apocalypse of Weeks.* The *Animal Apocalypse* at least shows familiarity with the myth of the Watchers. It seems reasonable to associate the lambs of the *Animal Apocalypse* with the chosen righteous of the *Apocalypse*

---

5. See P. A. Tiller, *A Commentary on the Animal Apocalypse of 1 Enoch* (Atlanta: Scholars Press, 1993) 355.

6. Note, however, J. Kampen, *The Hasideans and the Origin of Pharisaism* (Atlanta: Scholars Press, 1988) 95-107, who argues that the phrase could equally well be translated as "leading citizens."

7. V. A. Tcherikover, *Hellenistic Civilization and the Jews* (New York: Atheneum, 1970) 197-98; Tiller, *A Commentary,* 109; J. Sievers, *The Hasmoneans and Their Supporters* (Atlanta: Scholars Press, 1990) 39-40.

of Weeks. If the lambs are the circle from which the author of this Enochic apocalypse came, however, we should attribute to them a range of interests in cosmic speculation that are otherwise unattested for the Hasidim. Conversely, the Hasidim are represented in 1 Maccabees 2:42 as devoted to the law rather than to esoteric wisdom.[8] There may have been more than one group of militant scribes that supported the Maccabean revolt.[9]

If we include the *Epistle of Enoch* in the profile of the Enoch movement, then this group would seem to come from a socially underprivileged class, despite its literacy, since much of the criticism of the Epistle is directed against the rich. ("Woe to those who build their houses with sin, for from their whole foundation they will be thrown down, and by the sword they will fall; and those who acquire gold and silver will quickly be destroyed in the judgment. Woe to you, you rich, for you have trusted in your riches, but from your riches you will depart, for you did not remember the Most High in the days of your riches," 94:7-8). The *Apocalypse of Weeks,* also, hopes for "houses" for the righteous in the eschatological time. Again, there is no apparent reason why Enoch should be chosen as the mouthpiece of social criticism. Presumably he was the pseudonym of choice because of the wisdom revealed to him and because of the literate character of the group. The social criticism of the Epistle was incidental to the pseudonymity.

In her *Compendia* article of 1984 Devorah Dimant suggested that the "lambs" of the *Animal Apocalypse* correspond to the Dead Sea sect, which is described as a "plant root" in CD (the *Damascus Document*).[10] Her main argument is that the time of emergence appears to be the same in both documents. In CD column 1, as the passage is usually read, God causes a "plant root" to spring from Aaron and Israel 390 years after the destruction of Jerusalem by Nebuchadnezzar.[11] Dimant takes as her starting point 605 BCE, the date of the accession of Nebuchadnezzar, so that the plant root would emerge in 215 BCE and the Teacher of Righteousness in 195. She also calculates the chronology of the postexilic period in the *Animal Apocalypse* from 605 BCE and arrives at a date of 199 BCE for the emergence of the lambs. It is doubtful, however, whether the chronological data can

8. Kampen, *The Hasideans,* 107-14.

9. Cf. Tiller, *A Commentary,* 114-15, who argues that the *Animal Apocalypse* should not be ascribed to the Hasidim.

10. Dimant, "Qumran Sectarian Literature," 544.

11. On the difficulties of reading CD 1, see P. R. Davies, *The Damascus Covenant* (Sheffield: JSOT, 1982) 61-72.

be pressed in this way.[12] The 390 years of CD is a symbolic number and should not be taken precisely, and even if it were, the calculation should more reasonably begin from 586 BCE.

It is true that both the Enochic apocalypses and the Dead Sea sect regard the second temple as polluted. (This does not appear to be the case with the Hasidim.)[13] According to the *Apocalypse of Weeks,* the second temple generation is apostate. According to the *Animal Apocalypse,* the bread offered in the second temple was unclean and impure (*1 En.* 90:73). Calendrical disputes, and specifically the solar calendar, figure prominently in both corpora, as does the metaphor of planting.[14] Nonetheless, the character of the "plant root" of CD appears to be quite different from that of the "lambs." The movement in CD is said to grope in blindness at first and then to recognize that they were guilty men. It is, in short, a penitential movement concerned with the observance of the Torah, as CD proceeds to make clear.[15] There is no hint of militancy, and the movement does not arise in reaction against foreign rule. Conversely, the Torah of Moses receives scant attention in the Enochic apocalypses and there is no admission of guilt on the part of the "lambs," although they appear to have been in blindness before they began to see. The Torah is acknowledged in the *Apocalypse of Weeks* (93:6: "a law for all generations"), and the *Animal Apocalypse* singles out Moses as a sheep that became a man (89:38), but the revelations of Enoch are not derived from or based on the Torah of Moses. Enoch came first, and his revelations concern matters on which the Torah had little to say. Although the Enochic writings were preserved at Qumran and CD makes reference to the Watchers of heaven, it seems quite unlikely that these two groups should be identified with each other.

Daniel as a Pseudonym

The name of Daniel is also used to lend authority to a group or movement in the second century BCE. The biblical Book of Daniel develops the

---

12. J. J. Collins, "The Origin of the Qumran Community: A Review of the Evidence," in M. P. Horgan and P. J. Kobelski, eds., *To Touch the Text* (New York: Crossroad, 1989) 169-70 (= Collins, *Seers, Sibyls and Sages in Hellenistic-Roman Judaism* [Leiden: Brill, 1997] 250).

13. Tiller, *A Commentary,* 104-5.

14. Davies, *Behind the Essenes,* 130-32.

15. Compare 4Q306, "Men of the People Who Err," the subject of a presentation by T. H. Lim at the annual SBL meeting in New Orleans, November 24, 1996.

identity of the protagonist in a collection of Aramaic stories about Jewish courtiers in Babylon. The second half of the book purports to report the visions of one of these sages, which point to climactic events in the Hellenistic period. Daniel 11 builds up to a crisis when "the people who know their God stand firm and take action." The heroes of the story, however, are the משכילים, the wise among the people who give instruction to the common people. These are the ones who are singled out to shine like the stars at the resurrection. It is reasonable to suppose that the authors of the Book of Daniel belonged to the circles of these משכילים.[16] Like the elect in the *Apocalypse of Weeks,* these people are distinguished by their wisdom; as Philip Davies has noted, books play a prominent role in Daniel, even more than in *1 Enoch.*[17] Like the "lambs" of the *Animal Apocalypse,* the משכילים emerge in response to a political crisis. Unlike the lambs, however, they do not appear to take up arms. At most, they regard the Maccabees as "a little help" (11:34), and it is not clear that they regarded them as any help at all. While these משכילים bear some similarity to the group or groups described in the Enoch literature, they cannot be simply identified with them. Neither can they be identified with the Torah-oriented tradents of *Jubilees* or CD, since Daniel barely refers to the Law of Moses.

The specific associations evoked by the choice of Daniel as a pseudonym would seem to be twofold. First, there is the claim to revealed wisdom, grounded in Daniel's reputation as an interpreter of dreams and mysterious signs. Second, there is the political context. Daniel functions as adviser and critic to kings and predicts the rise and fall of kingdoms. The apocalyptic predictions of Daniel 7–12 are similarly political in character. If we take the court tales in Daniel 1–6 as in some sense indicative of the social roles to which the משכילים aspired, we might cast them in the role of religious advisers in political affairs, not unlike some of the ancient prophets, but such a correlation of narrative and social roles is admittedly risky.[18]

The name Daniel occurs in three manuscripts found at Qumran that are not part of the Book of Daniel: 4Q243, 244, and 245, known respectively as Pseudo-Daniel a, b, and c.[19] 4Q243 and 244 overlap, and clearly belong

---

16. See further J. J. Collins, *Daniel* (Hermeneia; Minneapolis: Fortress, 1993) 385-86.

17. P. R. Davies, "Reading Daniel Sociologically," in A. S. van der Woude, ed., *The Book of Daniel* (Leuven: Leuven University Press, 1993) 352-55.

18. Davies, "Reading Daniel Sociologically," 355, attributes to the משכילים a more direct political ambition.

19. See the edition of these texts by J. J. Collins and P. W. Flint, "Pseudo-Daniel," in G. Brooke et al., eds., *Qumran Cave 4. XVII. Parabiblical Texts, Part 3* (DJD 23; Oxford:

to the same manuscript. Milik tentatively proposed that 4Q245 belonged to the same work,[20] but this now seems doubtful.[21] 4Q243-44 present a speech by Daniel in a royal court. His speech is an overview of history, beginning with Noah and the Flood and continuing down to the Hellenistic period. The document contained several personal names. Only one, Balakros, is preserved. This name was borne by several figures in the early Hellenistic period. 4Q245 contains a long list of names. In part, this list gives the names of high priests from the patriarchal period (Qahat) down to the Hellenistic age (Onias, Simon). It then continues with a list of kings, including David, Solomon, and Ahaziah. It is difficult to see how these lists could be integrated into the document preserved in 4Q243 and 244. The latter document views Israel in the context of universal history and is concerned with the problem of foreign domination. 4Q245 is focused on the internal history of Israel. The two documents may come from the same or related circles, but their relationship seems to be one of complementarity rather than identity. The so-called "Son of God" text, 4Q246, is also often called "Pseudo-Daniel" and uses phrases that are also found in, and probably derived from, the biblical book. Since the name Daniel is not found in the extant fragments, however, we shall not consider it in the present discussion.

The text preserved in 4Q243 and 4Q244 is in a very fragmentary state. We have forty fragments of 4Q243 and fourteen fragments of 4Q244. Both manuscripts are written in Herodian script (late first century BCE). Milik found affinities between this text and the Book of Daniel in allusions to seventy years and a four-kingdom schema, while he found a reference to resurrection in 4Q245. Neither the seventy years nor the four-kingdom schema is actually found in the fragments. The reconstruction of "seventy years" seems more plausible than any alternative in 4Q243 fragment 16. The reference, however, is not necessarily to the Exile, as it is in Daniel 9. (4Q390, the Pseudo-Moses text, has two references to seventy years, neither of them in an exilic context.) The four-kingdom schema is inferred from the fourth line of the same fragment, which reads .[היא מלכותא קד. Milik restored קדמיתא "first." This reconstruction is problematic on two counts. First, two lines earlier in the same fragment we read that "he will

---

Clarendon, 1996) 95-164. See also J. J. Collins, "Pseudo-Daniel Revisited," *RevQ* 17 (1996) 111-35, and P. W. Flint, "4Qpseudo-Daniel arc and the Restoration of the Priesthood," *RevQ* 17 (1996) 137-50.

20. J. T. Milik, "'Prière de Nabonide' et autres écrits d'un cycle de Daniel," *RB* 63 (1956) 411-15.

21. Collins, "Pseudo-Daniel Revisited," 112.

save them." It seems unlikely that an act of salvation would be followed immediately by the inauguration of the first of a series of Gentile kingdoms. Second, if Milik's interpretation were correct this would be the only case where the four-kingdom sequence (familiar from the Book of Daniel and the fourth Sibylline Oracle) is inaugurated after deliverance from the Exile.[22] The first kingdom is always either Babylon or Assyria. Alternative reconstructions are possible. The phrase can be read as מלכותא קדישתא "holy kingdom," and the passage may be located in the eschatological phase of the prophecy.

4Q245 survives in four fragments, one of which contains the list of names already noted. The second fragment contains a passage reminiscent of CD 1, where some people are said to wander in blindness. There follows a statement that "these then will rise" (יקומון). Milik saw here a reference to resurrection and a parallel to Daniel 12, but the verb קום is not used in Daniel 12 and does not necessarily refer to resurrection. The following line says that some people "will return" (יתובון). There is, then, little evidence for direct literary dependence of these texts on the Book of Daniel. There is no mention of dreams or visions in either text. Each refers to a writing, and this may have been expounded by Daniel. Both texts presuppose that Daniel is an authoritative source of historical revelations, and, while this presupposition may derive from the biblical book, it could arguably be derived from part of the Daniel tradition, such as the stories preserved in Daniel 1–6, which circulated independently before the Maccabean era. The pseudo-Daniel texts do not necessarily derive from the same משכילים to whom we ascribed the Book of Daniel.

Both 4Q243-44 and 4Q245 appear to have had eschatological conclusions and to have spoken of elect groups in the eschatological time. 4Q243 frg. 24 speaks of the gathering of the elect and frg. 25 seems to imply an eschatological battle ("the land will be filled . . . with decayed carcasses"). Pseudo-Daniel a-b shares several motifs with other quasi-prophetic pseudepigrapha of the time. Israel at large lives in error, due to the influence of demonic spirits. Eschatological restoration is the destiny of an elect group that walks in the way of truth, in contrast to the "error" of others. The eventual emergence of this elect group is surely one of the major themes of this work. In this respect it resembles such works as the *Animal Apocalypse* and the *Apocalypse of Weeks*, which we have discussed above. Unfortunately little can be said about this group, however, because

---

22. On the four-kingdom sequence see Collins, *Daniel,* 166-70.

of the fragmentary state of the text. It seems clear enough that the elect are only a segment of Israel and that their emergence is set in the context of foreign oppression. It is not clear whether they constitute an organized community or are scattered individuals who adhere to the way of truth. There are distinct parallels between the Pseudo-Daniel text and CD in the account of the Exile as the giving of Israel into Nebuchadnezzar's hands, for the desolation of the land (cf. CD 1:12; 5:20; cf. also 4Q390 1:7-8). Yet there is no mention of a יחד and no unambiguously sectarian language. Pseudo-Daniel's relation to the Dead Sea sect may be analogous to that of *Jubilees* or the Enoch literature, which were evidently treasured at Qumran but which derived from separate, older movements.

4Q245 also envisages a group that wanders in blindness and another group that "returns." The key to the provenance of this document, however, lies in the list of names. The priestly names include חוניה (Onias) and, in the following line, שמעון (Simeon). The name preceding Simeon ends in ן- and the trace of the preceding letter seems more like ת than נ. It is possible (though not certain) that the text refers to Jonathan and Simon Maccabee (especially since Onias is represented as חוניה, rather than יוחנן).[23] The final fragment of this text speaks of people wandering "in blindness and error" and envisages some eschatological reversal. It is not clear whether the "error" is due to the priests at the end of the list or to some other cause. Whether the list included the early Maccabees or not, I would suggest that the separate lists of kings and priests were meant to show that the two offices, the kingship and the high priesthood, had always been distinct (even Jonathan and Simon had not laid claim to kingship). In this case, the lists of priests and kings in 4Q245 may be setting up a critique of the combination of priesthood and kingship under the Hasmoneans. Such a critique would be highly compatible with the expectation of two messiahs, of Aaron and Israel, at Qumran.[24] While much of this cannot be proven, due to the fragmentary state of the text, it is certainly the case that the Danielic writings focus on political events and institutions, in contrast to the halachic focus of works like *Jubilees* and the *Damascus Document.* While they were evidently congenial to the Dead Sea sect, their focus and sphere of interest are somewhat different and we should hesitate to ascribe them to one and the same movement.

23. See Collins and Flint, "Pseudo-Daniel," 160.
24. See further J. J. Collins, *The Scepter and the Star* (New York: Doubleday, 1995) 74-101.

Moses as Pseudonym

The use of pseudonymity in connection with Moses is somewhat different from the cases of Enoch and Daniel. With the exception of the *Testament* or *Assumption of Moses,* which is presented as the farewell speech of Moses to Joshua, Moses is not usually the speaker. In contrast, such works as 4Q390 and the *Temple Scroll* are presented as divine speech addressed to Moses. In *Jubilees,* the principal speaker is the angel of the presence, but again Moses is the addressee. As we might expect, the Torah is of central importance in all these Mosaic writings and there is extensive influence of the Book of Deuteronomy. We will confine our attention here to the use of *ex eventu* prophecy, especially as it relates to group formation.

The Book of *Jubilees* shares several areas of interest with the Enoch literature, notably the calendar and the origins of demonology. It differs from the Enoch literature, however, in one important respect: it has a pervasive interest in halachic rulings. The evils that later generations do are specifically related to transgression of the Sinai covenant (1:5), even though the halacha of *Jubilees* often differs from that of the Pentateuch.

The fate of future generations is most explicitly addressed in an *ex eventu* prophecy in *Jubilees* 23, although the historical allusions are not as transparent as in the Enochic books.[25] The passage refers to "an evil generation that transgresses on the earth and practices un-cleanness and fornication and pollution and abominations" (23:14).[26] This generation is characterized by a decline in the human lifespan. It is marked by strife between the generations, and also by calendrical error (23:19). Moreover, some in that generation "will take their stand with bows and swords and other weapons of war to restore their kinsmen to the accustomed path, but they will not return until much blood has been shed on either side" (23:20). The deeds of that generation will bring retribution from God, who will "abandon them to the sword and to judgment and captivity" and "stir up against them the sinners of the Gentiles" (23:23). Most scholars have taken these verses as allusions to events of the Maccabean period.[27] The

25. See the cautionary comments of R. Doran, "The Non-dating of Jubilees: Jub 34-38; 23:14-32 in Narrative Context," *JSJ* 20 (1989) 1-11.

26. *Jubilees* 23:10-13 is found at Qumran in 4Q221 (DJD 12.70-71), but the following passage is not.

27. G. W. E. Nickelsburg, *Jewish Literature between the Bible and the Mishnah* (Philadelphia: Fortress, 1981) 77.

allusions, however, take on a mythical quality: "the heads of the children will be white with grey hair" (23:25).

In this context, as in the Enoch apocalypses, we find a decisive turning point toward final salvation. In this case the turning point comes when "the children will begin to study the laws, and to seek the commandments, and return to the paths of righteousness." It is not clear that the reference here is to a specific group. The point may be simply that the turning point will come when people begin to study the law. The "children" are not said to take up arms like the "lambs" of the *Animal Apocalypse.* The earlier reference to those who do take up arms is ambivalent at best, and may be read as disapproving. The "children" of *Jubilees* are closer to the "plant root" of CD than to the Enoch movement. While the calendar remains a common concern in all these books, the interest in the law indicates a closer link between *Jubilees* and CD.

The law is also of central importance in 4Q390. The problems that befall the people of Israel come about because "they will not walk [in] my w[ays], which I command you so that you may warn them" (4Q390 1:3). Like other pseudepigrapha that we have discussed, this one is critical of the second temple establishment: "the sons of Aaron will rule over them, and they will not walk [in] my w[ays]." A notable, and unique, exception is made for "the first to come up from the land of their captivity in order to build the temple" (4Q390 1:5), but this variation hardly alters the document's ideological stance. As Dimant has shown, the text is not only indebted to Deuteronomy but shows great affinity with *Jubilees* and CD.[28] The affinities with *Jubilees* include a division of history into jubilees and various stylistic and terminological parallels. Especially noteworthy is the reference to the Angels of Mastemoth, to whom the Israelites are given over in punishment. In *Jubilees,* the Satan figure is called Mastema, and he is called "Angel of Mastema" in CD 16:5 and 1QM 13:11.[29] The Pseudo-Moses text also refers, however, to "the rule of Belial." The name Belial, which occurs frequently in the Scrolls, is not found in *Jubilees* and may indicate that this text is closer than *Jubilees* to the cultural milieu of Qumran. This impression is strengthened by the numerous terminological parallels between 4Q390 and CD that have been pointed out by Dimant.[30]

Dimant has also suggested a correlation between the Angels of Mas-

---

28. Dimant, "New Light on the Jewish Pseudepigrapha," 437-39, 444-45.
29. 1QS 3:23 refers to the domain of the Angel of Darkness as ממשלת משטמתו.
30. Dimant, "New Light on the Jewish Pseudepigrapha," 444-45.

temoth and the angelic shepherds to whom Israel is handed over in the
Animal Apocalypse:

> As a matter of fact, the Angels of Mastemoth play precisely the role
> assigned by the *Animal Apocalypse* to the shepherds. In both texts they
> serve as instruments for the punishment of Israel, in both the Israelites
> are unaware of the source of their distress. In addition, both works
> place the evil rule of these angels in a chronology of sabbatical years
> and jubilees.[31]

While all this is true, there is also an important difference between
the angels and the shepherds. The shepherds are most satisfactorily explained as the patron angels of the nations, who also appear as the adversaries of Israel in Daniel 10.[32] In 4Q390, there is no such national correlation. The Angels of Mastemoth are functionally indistinguishable from
Belial, and should be regarded as the agents of his reign. Here again, the
Pseudo-Moses text is closer to the cultural milieu of Qumran than are the
other pseudepigraphic apocalypses. The division that it envisages is not
between Israel and the nations but between God and Belial, righteous and
unrighteous. This division is not far removed from the dualism of light and
darkness that we find in the *Community Rule* and the *War Rule* at Qumran.

By analogy with other examples of *ex eventu* prophecy, it is reasonable to suppose that 4Q390 predicts a decisive turn for the better in the
eschatological time. Unfortunately, that part of the document is not extant. Consequently we do not know whether it speaks of an elect group
or what language it might use to describe it. It should be noted that the
Testament of Moses, which has a fully preserved *ex eventu* prophecy in the
name of Moses and has many parallels with 4Q390, does not refer to an
elect community within Israel, although it singles out the mysterious Taxo
and his family for a special role. But neither does the *Testament of Moses*
have significant parallels with the sectarian rule books from Qumran. What
it shares with 4Q390 and CD is simply the heritage of Deuteronomy, which
was available to all strands of ancient Judaism. 4Q390 is much more likely
to have envisaged an elect community. One thing that we may safely infer is
that if such a community was envisaged, it would be defined by its fidelity
to the Torah of Moses, whatever halachic interpretations it might have.

---

31. Dimant, "New light on the Jewish Pseudepigrapha," 442.
32. Tiller, *A Commentary,* 51-54.

The Absence of Pseudepigraphy in the Sectarian Scrolls

We have seen several texts that speak of the elect groups which will emerge in the eschatological time and establish the legitimacy of these groups by the authority of a famous ancient figure. I have argued that the groups in question should not be conflated. Rather, we should postulate a multiplicity of groups in the early second century BCE, groups that were probably quite small and loosely structured. In a recent essay on the social location of Ben Sira, Benjamin Wright suggested that the Enoch books, Aramaic Levi, and Ben Sira represent "competing groups/communities (and with Ben Sira and 1 Enoch competing notions of wisdom), who know about each other, who don't really like each other and who actively polemicize against each other, although not necessarily directly."[33] In the case of Ben Sira, the group or community consisted simply of a teacher and his pupils, and the Enoch group may not have been much more complex. The various groups I have discussed in this chapter, however, did not necessarily dislike each other, although they had different emphases. It may well be that they all came together eventually in the community of the new covenant that we know from the Scrolls, but we should probably imagine them as distinct communities or schools, nonetheless.

None of the texts we have considered gives any indication of the social organization of the group in question, and it remains unclear how far they were organized at all. The use of pseudepigraphy seems to coincide with low group definition. It may be that the pseudo-prophetic texts are intended to encourage the formation of the groups in question rather than reflect well-established entities.

CD 1 has served as a point of comparison for each of these texts mentioning the rise of an elect group. The Qumran text, however, is not pseudepigraphic, and it does not use the device of *ex eventu* prophecy to provide legitimization for the group. The same can be said of all the major sectarian scrolls, such as the *Community Rule, War Rule,* or the pesharim. Those who were like blind men groping their way (CD 1:9) may well have found comfort in ostensibly ancient prophecies that spoke of blindness and error while predicting that the elect would prevail. Once "God raised up for them a Teacher of Righteousness," however, the revelations of Enoch and Daniel faded to

---

33. B. G. Wright, "Putting the Puzzle Together: Some Suggestions concerning the Social Location of the Wisdom of Ben Sira," *SBL Seminar Papers* (Atlanta: Scholars Press, 1996) 146.

secondary importance. The prophets of old were superseded. According to the pesher on Habakkuk, God made known to the Teacher all the mysteries of the words of his servants the prophets (1QpHab 7). New prophecies, in the names of ancient prophets, would still be in need of interpretation and would in turn be subordinated to the authority of the Teacher. While the sectarians evidently took an interest in the pseudepigraphic Enoch and Daniel writings, perhaps because they seemed to predict the rise of the sect, there is no clear case of a new pseudepigraphic prophecy composed to legitimate the rise of the Dead Sea sect itself, although the provenance of the pseudo-Daniel and pseudo-Moses texts remains uncertain.

Two reasons suggest themselves for the lack of pseudonymity in the sectarian scrolls. One is the new authority of the Teacher of Righteousness and the other is a new method of self-legitimization, through the exegesis of biblical prophecy. We might have expected that the Teacher himself would be depicted as the fulfillment of prophecy, as Jesus is in the New Testament, and to some degree this is so. The title "Teacher of Righteousness" implies that he is the fulfillment of Hosea 10:12. 1QpHab identifies the Teacher as "the one who runs" in Habakkuk 1:2. On the whole, however, there is remarkably little concern (or need) to justify the authority of the Teacher. Presumably he established his own authority by the charisma of his personality.

Yet, unlike Jesus in the Gospels, the Teacher does not teach in his own name. Rather, he appears as the expositor of the traditional scriptures. He is the interpreter of prophecy, rather than its fulfillment. Primary authority is vested in the Torah and the prophetic books.

Interpretation of older scripture is not incompatible with pseudepigraphy, as can be seen from the case of Daniel 9. Yet exegesis plays only a minor role in the pseudepigrapha of Enoch and Daniel. One would scarcely infer the existence of a canonical or quasi-canonical scripture from the Enoch writings or pseudo-Daniel. The books that they expound are fictive writings, unavailable to the actual readers of the Hellenistic period. The Mosaic pseudepigrapha are more similar to the sectarian scrolls, but even *Jubilees* and the *Temple Scroll* are reformulations of the Torah rather than interpretations of it, thus demonstrating a different understanding of revelation than what we find in CD or the pesharim.[34]

---

34. Cf. the argument of L. H. Schiffman, *Sectarian Law in the Dead Sea Scrolls* (Chico, CA: Scholars Press, 1983) 17, that the grounding of legal rulings in the *Temple Scroll* is fundamentally different from what we find in CD, since the rulings of the latter are derived by interpretation.

The interpretation of scripture, no less than *ex eventu* prophecy, could also be used to establish the place of the sectarian community in the divine plan. CD expounds the "priests, Levites and sons of Zadok" of Ezekiel 44:15 so that "the Priests are the converts of Israel who departed from the land of Judah, and (the Levites are) those who joined them. The sons of Zadok are the elect of Israel, the men called by name who shall stand at the end of days" (CD 4:2-4). Those who go out into the wilderness, according to 1QS 8:12-14, do so in order to fulfill the prophecy of Isaiah 40:3. It seems to me, then, that the sectarian scrolls evidence a view of prophecy and legitimization that is quite different from what we find in the pseudepigraphic apocalypses.

In recent years we have had a growing appreciation of the diversity of traditions, and probably also of social groups, that went into the composition of the Dead Sea sect. What emerges from the evidence reviewed here, sketchy as it is, is a picture of several small parties or conventicles in the Maccabean era, with interests that overlapped in some respects and differed in others. It is a commonplace in the study of ancient Judaism that divergent biblical interpretation was a major factor in the rise of sectarianism.[35] The material we have reviewed here suggests that this is only half the picture. The incipient movements described in the pseudepigraphic apocalypses do not find their *raison d'être* in biblical interpretation but in the quest for esoteric wisdom. These movements surely played a part in the emergence of the Dead Sea sect.[36] But biblical interpretation was also a flourishing enterprise in the early second century, as we see from the veneration of the Torah in Ben Sira and from the new sapiential texts from Qumran.[37] The Teacher, whose authority prevailed at Qumran, was evidently more sage and interpreter than apocalyptic visionary. Under his tutelage, the Dead Sea sect dispensed with pseudepigraphy, but the pseudepigraphic prophecies retained an important place in the sectarian library.[38]

---

35. See, e.g., J. Blenkinsopp, "Interpretation and the Tendency to Sectarianism: An Aspect of Second Temple History," in E. P. Sanders, ed., *Jewish and Christian Self-definition: Aspects of Judaism in the Graeco-Roman Period* (Philadelphia: Fortress, 1981) 1-26.

36. I have explored the continuities between the apocalypses and the scrolls in my book, *Apocalypticism in the Dead Sea Scrolls* (London: Routledge, 1997).

37. The wisdom texts from Qumran are lucidly presented by D. J. Harrington, *Wisdom at Qumran* (London: Routledge, 1996).

38. The first generation of the Christian movement also dispensed with pseudonymity, under the charismatic influence of Jesus and Paul, but pseudonymous writing flourished in the following century. See D. G. Meade, *Pseudonymity and Canon* (Tübingen: Mohr, 1986).

CHAPTER 14

Enoch and Ezra

Pseudepigraphy is a common feature of ancient apocalypses, and a constant feature in extant Jewish exemplars of the genre. The pool of names from which the pseudonyms is drawn is quite limited: Enoch, Daniel, Ezra, Baruch, Abraham, Levi. If one loosens the definition of apocalyptic literature from criteria of literary form, Moses might be added, and some of the Hebrew prophets are credited with apocalyptic revelations in Christian tradition (Isaiah, Zephaniah, Elijah). But even within the limited range of the formal apocalypses, the variation in the pseudonyms is significant. Enoch and Ezra may reasonably be taken as the ends of the spectrum, figures who seem *prima facie* to have little in common in the biblical tradition, except that both have high standing with God.

Pseudepigraphy was widely practiced in antiquity.[1] Undoubtedly it served various purposes. Presumably, the name of a venerable ancient figure lent authority to a new revelation. Hindy Najman writes that, "by extending a discourse attached to a founder of an earlier period, writers in the late Second Temple period and even after the destruction of the Second Temple are able to authorize and link their new texts to old established traditions and founders."[2] In this way they could recover "an idealized past,

---

1. See the wide-ranging collection of essays in Jörg Frey, Jens Herzer, Martina Janssen, and Clare K. Rothschild, with Michaela Engelmann, *Pseudepigraphie und Verfasserfiktion in frühchristlichen Briefen* (WUNT 246; Tübingen: Mohr Siebeck, 2009).

2. Hindy Najman, "How Should We Contextualize Pseudepigrapha? Imitation and Emulation in 4 Ezra," in Najman, *Past Renewals: Interpretative Authority, Renewed Revelation and the Quest for Perfection in Jewish Antiquity* (JSJSup 53; Leiden: Brill, 2010) 235-43 (238). (Previously published in Anthony Hilhorst, Émile Puech, and Eibert Tigchelaar, eds.,

that in the minds of the later writers was full of divine access, prophecy and political independence."[3] She suggests, moreover, that "to attribute a text to a great figure of the past is to take that figure as a guide on the path of desire."[4] It reflects a desire not only to imitate (to be like) the pseudonymous hero but to emulate him (actually be the figure in question). Pseudepigraphy, on this account, effects "a metaphorical identification, pregnant with indeterminate implications."[5]

I will argue in this chapter that Najman's account of pseudepigraphy works well in the case of Enoch, but that the case of *4 Ezra* is more complex. There pseudepigraphy entails something other than straightforward identification with the pseudonymous hero, because it entails a radical revision of the persona of Ezra. A pseudepigraphic work, in short, can deconstruct and refashion its pseudonymous hero as well as emulate him, or, perhaps, as a pre-condition of emulating him. The figure of Enoch, as portrayed very briefly in Genesis, was congenial to apocalyptic revelation, because he was believed to have associated with *elohim* or angels and to have been taken up to heaven. The biblical Ezra, in contrast, was closely identified with the law and covenant of Moses and required revision if he was to become the purveyor of heavenly mysteries.

The comparison and contrast between Enoch and Ezra offer an interesting angle of vision on the workings of the apocalyptic genre. While *4 Ezra* is quite explicitly dependent on Daniel in chapters 11–13, it is not clear to me that the author was familiar with the books of Enoch at all. Nonetheless, Enoch provides a useful counterpoint to *4 Ezra*, involving both obvious differences in dominant motifs and, at a higher level of abstraction, shared assumptions about the world and human destiny that may reasonably be called a worldview. At issue here is the degree of coherence or variation that we may expect to find within literature that is usually, and I believe appropriately, classified together as apocalyptic.

Flores Florentino: Dead Sea Scrolls and Other Early Jewish Studies in Honor of Florentino García Martínez [JSJSup 122; Leiden: Brill, 2007] 529-36.)

3. Najman, "How Should We Contextualize Pseudepigrapha?" 238.

4. Najman, "The Quest for Perfection in Ancient Judaism," in Najman, *Past Renewals*, 219-34 (230). (Originally published as "La Recherche de la Perfection dans le Judaïsm Ancien," in Jean Riaud, ed., *Les Élites dans le Monde Biblique* [Bibliothèque d'Études Juives; Paris: Champion, 2006] 99-116.)

5. Najman, "How Should We Contextualize?" 240.

Emulating Enoch

It is not difficult to see why someone would look to Enoch as a source of revelation. His entire biography in the Bible is limited to a few sentences, but they are indeed "pregnant with indeterminate implications." Born in the seventh generation, he was son of Jared and father of Methuselah. Crucially, for the later tradition, he was said to "walk with *elohim*" after the birth of Methuselah for three hundred years. Then he was no more, because God took him" (Gen. 5:22-24). Whatever this elliptic statement may have meant in Genesis, in the Hellenistic period it was understood to mean that he had ascended to heaven and associated with the angels, and that at the end of his earthly life he had not died, but been taken up to heaven by God.[6]

The *Book of the Watchers*, which introduces the collection of writings that we know as *1 Enoch*, seems to situate Enoch a little later in history, after the Watchers, or sons of God, had descended to earth. In Genesis, the "sons of God" are introduced after the birth of Noah, and their careers are followed by the Flood. In the *Book of the Watchers*, however, they descend in the days of Jared, the synchronization being suggested by a play on the name. Consequently, their earthly careers are recounted before Enoch is introduced at all. In fact, the Watchers provide the occasion for Enoch's first ascent to heaven, in an intercessory role that is not suggested in Genesis. As Paolo Sacchi and others have noted, the sin of the Watchers provides the underlying problem to which Enoch's revelations respond.[7] Apocalypses, like Proppian folk-tales, require a *lack*, or a problem, to get the action started. In the Enoch tradition, this lack is supplied by the disruption of the earth by the fallen angels. It should be noted that this is, in principle, a problem for humanity at large, not only for Israel, although the later Enochic books narrow their focus to the chosen seed of Abraham, and even more so to the elect at the end of history.

The stories of the Watchers and of Enoch have no more than a jumping-off point in the text of Genesis.[8] The elaboration is a work of

---

6. On the figure of Enoch and its Mesopotamian associations, see James C. Vander-Kam, *Enoch and the Growth of an Apocalyptic Tradition* (CBQMS 16; Washington, DC: Catholic Biblical Association of America, 1984) 33-51; VanderKam, *Enoch: A Man for All Generations* (Columbia: University of South Carolina Press, 1995) 6-8.

7. Paolo Sacchi, *Jewish Apocalyptic and Its History* (JSPSup 20; Sheffield: Sheffield Academic Press, 1997) 72-87.

8. On the exegetical aspects of the Enoch legend, see James L. Kugel, *Traditions of the Bible* (Cambridge, MA: Harvard University Press, 1998) 172-79.

imagination. It is clear enough that the story of the Watchers serves as an allegory for a world gone awry, even if it resists simple decoding. Most readily, it evokes the culture shock induced by the spread of Hellenistic culture in the Near East, with its advanced technology and liberated attitude toward the human body.[9] It is brought to an end, initially, by a divine judgment that cleanses the earth (*1 Enoch* 10). But the book is clearly composite, and does not simply proceed in a unilinear way.[10] A more extensive counterpart to the story of the Watchers is supplied by the journeys of Enoch, in the company of an angel, to the ends of the earth. He sees and describes an ordered cosmos, which is in sharp contrast to the world disrupted by the Watchers. The contrast is drawn most pointedly with regard to the fate of the Watchers. In *1 Enoch* 15, the Lord directs Enoch to ask the Watchers:

> Why have you forsaken the high heaven, the eternal sanctuary,
> and lain with women and defiled yourselves with the daughters of
>   men,
> and taken for yourselves wives, and done as the sons of earth,
> and begotten for yourselves sons, giants?
> You were holy ones and spirits, living forever.
> With the blood of women you have defiled yourselves
> and with the blood of flesh you have begotten,
> and with the blood of men you have lusted,
> and you have done as they do —
> flesh and blood, who die and perish.
> Therefore I gave them women,
> that they might cast seed into them,
> and thus beget children by them,
> that nothing fail them on the earth.
> But you originally existed as spirits, living forever,
> and not dying for all the generations of eternity;
> therefore I did not make women among you.
> The spirits of heaven, in heaven is their dwelling.
>
> (*1 En.* 15:3-7, trans. Nickelsburg)

9. On the setting of the Watcher myth, see George W. E. Nickelsburg, *Jewish Literature between the Bible and the Mishnah* (2nd ed.; Minneapolis: Fortress, 2005) 49.

10. See George W. E. Nickelsburg, *1 Enoch 1: A Commentary on the Book of 1 Enoch, Chapters 1–36; 81–108* (Hermeneia; Minneapolis: Fortress, 2001) 129-332.

Enoch, in contrast, is a human being who ascends from the corruptible world of the flesh to associate with the holy ones of heaven in the spiritual realm and live forever. As such, he provides a model for the apocalyptic writer and his readers. An important place in Enoch's revelations is also occupied by the coming judgment, with its promise of access to the tree of life for the righteous (25:3) and an eternal curse for the wicked. Together, the spatial dualism of heaven and earth and the temporal dualism marked off by the judgment outline a quintessentially apocalyptic worldview, in which the human hope for salvation is based on the revelation of transcendent reality, beyond the bounds of earthly life.[11]

All of this goes far beyond what is said of Enoch in Genesis. The biblical text, however, provides an opening by claiming (or seeming to claim) that Enoch associated with the angels even in his lifetime, and was taken up alive to heaven. Hence he was in a position to have seen the heavenly tablets, where the course of history was already inscribed, and to know the mysteries of the cosmos. He could reveal mysteries that were hidden from the rest of humanity. Despite the initial use of Genesis, and occasional echoes of other biblical texts, Enoch's revelations have little to do with the Law of Moses. They are concerned with things that are not found in the Torah. It is true, of course, that since Enoch lived before the Flood, overt reference to Moses would be anachronistic, but this is hardly to the point. According to Moses, in Deuteronomy, God's revelation "is not in heaven, that you should say, 'who will go up to heaven for us, and get it for us so that we may hear it and observe it?'" (Deut. 30:12). In contrast, the essential presupposition of the Enoch literature is that the revelation necessary for salvation *is* in heaven, and that humanity *does* need someone who has gone up to heaven to reveal it. Fortunately, Enoch was such a person. This is not to say that the early Enoch literature is anti-Mosaic: it simply approaches religion differently from the Mosaic Torah.[12] As Nickelsburg has shown, "covenant" is not an important concept in these books.[13] There is some rapprochement with the Mosaic tradition in

11. Nickelsburg, *1 Enoch 1*, 37-41. Compare the definition of an apocalypse in my book, *The Apocalyptic Imagination* (2nd ed.; Grand Rapids: Eerdmans, 1998) 5.

12. See my essay, "How Distinctive Was Enochic Judaism?" in Moshe Bar-Asher and Emanuel Tov, eds., *Meghillot V–VI: A Festschrift for Devorah Dimant* (Jerusalem: Bialik, 2007) 17-34.

13. George W. E. Nickelsburg, "Enochic Wisdom: An Alternative to the Mosaic Torah?" in Jodi Magness and Seymour Gitin, eds., *Hesed Ve-Emet: Studies in Honor of Ernest S. Frerichs* (BJS 320; Atlanta: Scholars Press, 1998) 123-32, especially 129; Nickelsburg,

later Enochic books such as the *Animal Apocalypse*,[14] but the fundamental orientation of the Enoch literature is toward heavenly revelation, not toward a Torah that was already revealed.

It is reasonable to assume, with Najman, that the authors of the Enoch books identified with Enoch and put themselves imaginatively in his place. The reader was invited to do likewise. The profile of Enoch as the one taken up to heaven could be affirmed without reservation, and viewed as a model for what the righteous could hope to attain. Emulation, then, is the goal. The aspect of Enoch's career that provided the ultimate goal for his earthly followers was his ultimate assumption into heaven, a point made quite explicitly at the end of the *Similitudes of Enoch*: "and all will walk in your path since righteousness will never forsake you; with you will be their dwelling and with you their lot, and from you they will not be separated forever and forever and ever" (*1 Enoch* 71:16). The Enochic books certainly affirm the hope for the transformation of this world. Ultimately, however, the salvation of individual righteous people would be sought not in this world but in the "other" world of the angels.

The Profile of Ezra

The profile of Ezra in the Hebrew Bible is considerably more developed than that of Enoch. He is introduced in Ezra 7 as a priest who was "a scribe skilled in the law of Moses." He received permission from the Persian king to lead a group of Judeans from Babylon back to Judah, and allegedly to enforce the Law of Moses by royal authority.[15] Ezra is said to have revived the observance of various festivals (Nehemiah 8), but he is most vividly remembered for making Judeans who had married foreign women divorce them. When he first discovers the problem of mixed marriages, Ezra recites a confession of sin on behalf of the people. While the word "covenant" does not occur in the prayer in Ezra 9, the whole prayer is imbued with

---

"Enochic Wisdom and Its Relationship to the Mosaic Torah," in Gabriele Boccaccini and John J. Collins, eds., *The Early Enoch Literature* (JSJSup 121; Leiden: Brill, 2007) 81-94.

14. Andreas Bedenbender, *Der Gott der Welt tritt auf den Sinai. Entstehung, Entwicklung und Funktionsweise der frühjüdischen Apokalyptik* (Berlin: Institut Kirche und Judentum, 2000) 208-30; Bedenbender, "The Place of the Torah in the Early Enoch Literature," in Boccaccini and Collins, eds., *The Early Enoch Literature*, 65-79.

15. Ezra 7:26. The historical trustworthiness of the book of Ezra need not concern us here, only the form in which the book was known in the first century CE.

covenantal theology. (In his other long prayer, in Nehemiah 9, Ezra refers to God as "keeping covenant" in v. 32, and the people respond to his prayer in Ezra 10 by making a new covenant.) The logic of the prayer is that disaster is a punishment for failure to keep the covenantal laws: "From the days of our ancestors to this day we have been deep in guilt, and for our iniquities we, our kings, and our priests have been handed over to the kings of the lands, to the sword, to captivity, to plundering, and to utter shame, as is now the case" (Ezra 9:7). Ezra unquestioningly affirms the justice of God's punishments: "You have been just in all that has come upon us, for you have dealt faithfully and we have acted wickedly; our kings, our officials, our priests, and our ancestors have not kept your law or heeded the commandments and the warnings that you gave them" (Neh. 9:33-34).

In *4 Ezra*, however, Ezra has quite a different profile, one that is reminiscent of the biblical Job rather than the biblical Ezra.[16] In the opening dialogue, Ezra explicitly recounts the history of the covenant between God and Israel. The inhabitants of Jerusalem transgressed; therefore God delivered the city into the hands of its enemies. But the apocryphal Ezra does not accept the divine judgment as his biblical prototype had done. Rather, he complains: "Are the deeds of those who inhabit Babylon any better? Is that why she has gained dominion over Zion?" Rather, Ezra observes, God has spared those who act wickedly and preserved his enemies. He asks, bitterly, "Has another nation known thee besides Israel? or what tribe has so believed thy covenants as Jacob? Yet their reward has not appeared and their labor has borne no fruit" (*4 Ezra* 3:30-33). As Karina Hogan has observed, this first speech of Ezra (3:4-36) can be "read as a parody of the covenant *rîb* form, since Ezra uses a selective recital of Heilsgeschichte . . . to indict God, not Israel."[17] Again in the second dialogue Ezra accuses God of abandoning the covenant:

> from all the multitude of peoples you have gotten for yourself one people, and to this people whom you have loved you have given the Torah which is approved by all. But now, O Lord, why have you given over the one to the many, and dishonored the one root beyond the others, and scattered your only one among the many? And those who opposed your law have trodden down those who believed in your covenant. If

16. Michael A. Knibb, "Apocalyptic and Wisdom in 4 Ezra," *JSJ* 13 (1982) 56-74. Karina Martin Hogan, *Theologies in Conflict in 4 Ezra* (JSJSup 130; Leiden: Brill, 2008) 102.

17. Hogan, *Theologies in Conflict*, 103.

you did really hate your people, they should be punished at thy own hands. (*4 Ezra* 5:27-30)

The suggestion that God hates his people should be taken to mean that he has repudiated them, in accordance with the range of meaning of the Hebrew verb שנא. This possibility was envisioned as early as the prophet Hosea (chapter 2) and was in accordance with the provisions of the covenant. The novelty of *4 Ezra*'s complaint is that he questions the justice of God's strict enforcement of the provisions of the covenant, while "Babylon" suffers no immediate consequences of its actions.

Already in the opening dialogues, Ezra's concerns are not exclusively for Israel. He is also concerned for humanity as a whole, the children of Adam, who are afflicted with an "evil heart," or evil inclination, which is embedded in humanity from creation. Indeed, Israel's failure to keep the covenant is due to the fact that "you did not take away from them their evil heart, so that thy Torah might bear fruit in them" (3:20). In the third dialogue, he shifts his focus more to the fate of sinful humankind.[18] Nonetheless, he again questions the covenantal bond between God and Israel:

> All this I have spoken before thee, O Lord, because thou hast said that it was for us that thou didst create this world. But as for the other nations, which have descended from Adam, thou hast said that they are nothing, and that they are like spittle, and thou hast compared their abundance to a drop from a bucket. And now, O Lord, behold these nations, which are reputed as nothing, domineer over us and trample upon us. But we thy people, whom thou hast called thy firstborn, only-begotten kin and dear one, have been given into their hands. If the world has indeed been created for us, why do we not possess our world as an inheritance? How long will this be so?

Uriel replies to this that the punishment of Israel is justified:

> Let many perish who are now living rather than that the law of God which is set before them be disregarded. For God strictly commanded those who came into the world when they came what they should do to live and what they should observe to avoid punishment. Nevertheless they were not obedient. . . . They scorned his law and denied

18. Hogan, *Theologies in Conflict*, 109.

his covenants; they have been unfaithful to his statutes and have not performed his works. (7:20-24)

Ezra does not deny the prevalence of disobedience. His complaint is that humanity is not capable of keeping the law because of the evil heart, and that Israel is no better off than the rest of humanity in this respect. In a poignant passage, he seems to place the blame on Adam rather than on God: "O Adam, what have you done? For though it was you who sinned, the fall was not yours alone, but ours also who are your descendents" (7:118). But even Adam was a victim of the evil inclination. So all Ezra can do is pray for mercy in 8:20-36. Ed Sanders observed many years ago that *4 Ezra* accords exceptionally little space to mercy in his view of the covenant,[19] but it does not eliminate it entirely. The possibility of mercy, however, is not enough to overcome Ezra's conviction that the whole covenantal relationship is unsatisfactory, because of the inherent shortcomings of humanity, including Israel.

One can hardly imagine the biblical Ezra speaking of the covenant in this vein. The question then arises, why did the author of *4 Ezra* choose the famous devotee of the Law as the mouthpiece for his critique of the covenant? Unlike Enoch, Ezra had no particular qualification as an apocalyptic revealer. He had not ascended to heaven and was not known to have dreams or visions. He was above all a spokesman for the Law and the covenant. In *4 Ezra,* too, Ezra starts out from a position that has reasonably been called "ethnocentric covenantalism,"[20] a characterization that fits the biblical Ezra equally well. In *4 Ezra*, however, that theological position is no longer satisfactory, and it gives rise to bitter complaints on the part of Ezra.

Of course, Ezra is more positively associated with Law and covenant at the end of *4 Ezra*. In chapter 14, he is cast as a new Moses, summoned by a voice from a bush (14:1), and then inspired to dictate not only the twenty-four books of scripture that were to be made public but also seventy others, which were to be given to the wise among the people. As Stone comments, "the association with Moses is very clear."[21] Commentators typically cite rabbinic passages that show that Ezra was deemed worthy to receive the

19. E. P. Sanders, *Paul and Palestinian Judaism* (Philadelphia: Fortress, 1977) 409-18.

20. Bruce W. Longenecker, *Eschatology and the Covenant: A Comparison of 4 Ezra and Romans 1–11* (JSNTSup 57; Sheffield: JSOT, 1991) 34. On the ethnocentrism of *4 Ezra* see further my essay, "The Idea of Election in 4 Ezra," *JSQ* 16 (2009) 83-96.

21. Michael E. Stone, *4 Ezra* (Hermeneia; Minneapolis: Fortress, 1990) 410.

Torah in the same measure as Moses.[22] But the revelation that Ezra receives is much more than the Torah. The seventy esoteric books, which are reserved for the wise among the people, contain "the springs of understanding, the fountains of wisdom, and the river of knowledge" (14:47). So while the apocryphal Ezra takes over the role of lawgiver and revealer, in the manner of Moses and of the biblical Ezra, his role is by no means identical to theirs.

Why Ezra?

Theodore Bergren has suggested a few factors that may be relevant to the choice of Ezra as pseudonymous visionary in this apocalypse.[23] Insofar as Ezra was associated with the restoration of Judah after the destruction by the Babylonians, even if the historical Ezra lived three-quarters of a century after the initial restoration, he was a relevant figure for someone writing after the Roman destruction. Bergren suggests that the evocation of Ezra was a reminder that the people could and would rebound from disaster. More specifically, Ezra was associated with renewal through the Law: "Just as the biblical Ezra had promoted and embodied a renewal of the knowledge and observance of the Mosaic Law after the Babylonian destruction, so does the pseudepigraphic Ezra after the Roman destruction."[24] Bergren also notes that "the two Ezras have in common an extreme pitch of piety and devotion to God and the Law, manifested through fasting and other acts. Both are strong leaders of the Jewish community, both exercise an intercessory role between God and the community when the need arises, and both address heartfelt prayers of confession to God in this capacity."[25] Bergren also attaches significance to the fact that both Ezras were scribes. It should be noted that Enoch is also said to be a scribe in 1 Enoch 12:3-4. As Karina Hogan has noted, both Enoch and Ezra are bridge figures, who secure the transmission of tradition at times of great crisis — the Flood in the case of Enoch, and the Exile in the case of Ezra.[26]

---

22. Stone, 4 Ezra, 411.

23. Theodore A. Bergren, "Ezra and Nehemiah Square Off in the Apocrypha and Pseudepigrapha," in Michael E. Stone and Theodore A. Bergren, eds., Biblical Figures Outside the Bible (Harrisburg, PA: Trinity Press International, 1998) 340-63.

24. Bergren, "Ezra and Nehemiah," 360.

25. Bergren, "Ezra and Nehemiah," 360-61.

26. Karina Martin Hogan, "Pseudepigraphy and the Periodization of History," in

These points are all relevant to the choice of pseudonym, but knowledge and observance of the Mosaic Law are hardly Ezra's primary objectives in the apocryphal apocalypse. Consequently, the degree of identification with the biblical Ezra must be questioned.

For Najman, "pseudonymous attribution should be seen as a metaphorical device, operating at the level of the text as a whole, whereby the actual author emulates and self-identifies as an exemplar."[27] It is true that Ezra, in chapter 14, takes over the role of Moses, but he transforms that role so thoroughly that the disjunction is at least as striking as the continuity.

Here we must bear in mind that the generative problem in *4 Ezra* is not only the destruction of the temple or the displacement of the people, but includes the breakdown of the theology with which Ezra was traditionally associated. I would suggest that it is precisely for this reason that Ezra is chosen as pseudonymous hero. As representative of a failed theology, Ezra must be deconstructed and refashioned so that the law that he gives to the people is supplemented and to some degree superseded by apocalyptic revelations, for which the biblical Ezra felt no need. The biblical Ezra and his covenantal theology are not overtly rejected, and the attribution of the new revelations to "Ezra" is an affirmation of continuity with the past, but in fact Ezra and his theology are transformed, almost beyond recognition.[28]

The Transformation of Ezra

All commentators recognize that Ezra undergoes a transformation in the course of *4 Ezra*, and that this transformation comes about in the fourth vision, in the vision of a woman who is transformed into a city (9:26–10:59). Najman describes it as follows:

> By taking the role of an instructing angel, Ezra undergoes two transformations. First, he overcomes his individual sense of suffering, and identifies with the suffering of Zion. Then, on the basis of his identi-

---

Frey et al., eds., *Pseudepigraphie,* 61-83, especially 75-76 and 81. She notes that *1 Enoch* is concerned to establish a relationship between Enoch and his great-grandson, Noah, in order to account for the survival of Enoch's writings.

27. Najman, "How Should We Contextualize?" 241.

28. In contrast, the Deuteronomic theology associated with Ezra is vigorously defended in the contemporary apocalypse of *2 Baruch.* See Matthias Henze, *Jewish Apocalypticism in Late First Century Israel* (TSAJ 142; Tübingen: Mohr Siebeck, 2011) 218-30.

fication, he is able to express his sorrow in the form of a lament. And once he is able to pray, albeit in the form of a lament, he has turned towards God and is therefore able to receive mercy from God. Having undergone this transformation, Ezra is able, in the visions that follow, to accept — including, so it seems, his own death — as a rebirth for the righteous remnant.[29]

But in fact Ezra had already turned to God in 8:20-36 and prayed specifically for mercy. His lament for Zion in 10:19-24 is addressed not to God, but to the woman. It may be that the lament is a catalyst for his transformation, but prayer does not play such a role here.

Michael Stone, following Hermann Gunkel, has argued vigorously that this transformation should be understood in psychological terms: "Ezra changed radically, but that change is not a literary device designed to create a purified Ezra, worthy of receipt of revelation. It is a real change, an experience of religious conversion undergone by the author."[30] For Stone, the catalyst of the transformation is simply the role reversal:

This dynamic precipitated a very powerful religious experience in the course of which the seer received enlightenment and fell unconscious. This experience was one of religious conversion. In it, the values and ideas that had previously been externalized in the figure of the angel were internalized by the seer, while his pain was now outside him, seen as the woman, and she is wondrously transformed into the Heavenly Jerusalem! The theological arguments are never resolved theologically, because they are resolved by the conversion itself. In conversion, doubts and inner struggles become irrelevant.[31]

On Stone's interpretation, the eschatological information imparted by the angel in the course of the first three visions did not differ in its

---

29. Najman, "The Quest for Perfection," 233.

30. Michael E. Stone, "On Reading an Apocalypse," in John J. Collins and James H. Charlesworth, eds., *Mysteries and Revelations: Apocalyptic Studies since the Uppsala Colloquium* (JSPSup 9; Sheffield: JSOT, 1991) 74.

31. Stone, "On Reading an Apocalypse," 74. Similarly for Frances Flannery-Dailey, *Dreamers, Scribes, and Priests: Jewish Dreams in the Hellenistic and Roman Eras* (JSJSup 90; Leiden: Brill, 2004) 197, "it is his dream that provides him with access to otherworldly realms that occasions this emotional transformation, since he actually experiences future and heavenly dimensions of reality in a way that his former dialogue with Uriel was not able to accomplish."

conceptual content from the information revealed by means of the Dream Visions 5–6. Yet in Visions 1–3 that information did not satisfy or assuage Ezra's pain, while in Visions 5–6 it certainly did.[32] This is also Najman's assumption. Specifically, she points to the correspondence between the angel's teaching about what happens after death in 7:78-91 and Ezra's teaching to the people in 14:35: "For after death the judgment will come, when we shall live again, and then the names of the righteous will become manifest, and the deeds of the ungodly will be disclosed" (14:35). In the end, Ezra succumbs to the teaching of the angel, even if he has not been persuaded by argumentation. Stone, indeed, regards it as self-evident that "the views put by the angel/God cannot have been opposed by the author."[33]

This understanding of *4 Ezra* has been challenged by Karina Hogan, who finds in *4 Ezra* not two theological perspectives but three. On her reading, Ezra and the angel Uriel represent two distinct wisdom traditions, while the apocalyptic visions provide a third perspective. Ezra articulates the covenantal wisdom typified by Ben Sira, and Uriel the eschatologized wisdom typified by 4QInstruction. Ezra believes that the way of the Most High should be susceptible to reason and is frustrated to find that it is not. Uriel asserts that knowledge of God requires revelation, specifically revelation about eschatological events and the world to come.[34] Moreover, while Ezra starts out from a perspective of covenantal solidarity of the people of Israel, Uriel's eschatology is highly individualistic.[35] "The Most High made this world for the sake of many, but the world to come for the sake of only a few" (8:1). Membership in a covenant people does not compensate for lack of individual merits. Moreover, the statutes of the Lord that provide the criteria for judgment are not simply identical with the Law of Moses. Adam already transgressed God's statutes (7:11), and the nations are also chastised for failing to obey the divine law. Hogan concludes that "once Uriel's statements are distinguished from Ezra's, however, it becomes clear that Uriel is pushing Ezra toward an understanding of the Torah that is very abstract and universal, and not tied to God's covenant with Israel."[36]

Crucially, for Hogan, "Uriel's eschatology in the dialogues for the

---

32. Stone, "On Reading an Apocalypse," 74.

33. Stone, "On Reading an Apocalypse," 73.

34. Hogan, *Theologies in Conflict*, 123.

35. Compare Longenecker, *Eschatology and the Covenant,* 96: Uriel "with his rigid individualism undermines the basis of a covenantal conception of Israel."

36. Hogan, *Theologies in Conflict*, 140. See her reflections on the question whether Uriel's theology implies a kind of natural law (141).

most part lacks those themes of national-restoration eschatology that are also missing from 4QInstruction: the restoration of Zion and of the twelve tribes of Israel, the Messiah, and the eschatological war."[37] There are exceptions to this in 7:26-44, where Uriel spells out a full eschatological scenario. Yet it should be noted that even there the traditional "national" eschatology is not the end. After four hundred years, the messiah will die, and the world will be turned back to primeval silence. Then follows the judgment. The nations are rebuked for despising the commandments of God (7:37), but individuals are judged on their own merits. In light of this mention of a messianic reign, it is apparent that Uriel does not reject some kind of national restoration, but Hogan is surely right that by far the predominant emphasis in the angel's eschatology falls on individual judgment. In contrast, the visions in *4 Ezra* 11–13 are entirely concerned with the coming of the messiah and the restoration of Israel, and do not address the final judgment at all.

Hogan contends that the three symbolic visions succeed in consoling Ezra at least in part because they address his concerns about the fate of Israel in a way that the dialogues do not. Granted, their effectiveness is also due in part to their symbolic form. "They overpower Ezra's mind with powerful religious images, rather than providing intellectual answers to his questions."[38] She allows that Ezra's transformation can be compared to religious conversion, but she argues, reasonably, that "it also seems likely that the author had a purpose beyond portraying his own spiritual journey. He may have intended Ezra to serve as a model for others to overcome a crisis of faith by embracing an apocalyptic theology."[39] On this reading, Ezra does not simply accept the position that Uriel has been advocating all along, but is consoled by the affirmation of traditional Israelite hopes.

Whether Uriel's theology was already apocalyptic might be disputed. There is a difference between the eschatology articulated by Uriel and that of the fifth and sixth visions, but it is a difference of emphasis. Uriel affirmed at least a temporary messianic age. The visions focus on the coming of the messiah without reflecting on the duration of his reign. While the visions do not address the judgment of individuals, Ezra affirms, in the end, that "after death the judgment will come, when we shall live again;

37. Hogan, *Theologies in Conflict*, 151.

38. Hogan, *Theologies in Conflict*, 161. Compare Flannery-Dailey, *Dreamers, Scribes and Priests*, 218.

39. Hogan, *Theologies in Conflict*, 161.

and then the names of the righteous will become manifest, and the deeds of the ungodly will be disclosed" (14:34). It is not clear whether the messianic age is temporary, but since Uriel's account of the messianic age is never questioned, we should probably assume that it is of finite duration. In chapter 14, Ezra is told to "renounce the life that is corruptible and put away from you mortal thoughts; cast away from you the burdens of man and divest yourself now of your weak nature, and lay to one side the thoughts that are most grievous to you, and hasten to escape from these times" (14:13-15). In the end, in the Syriac and other versions except the Latin, Ezra is caught up and taken to the place of those who are like him, a destiny that has already been foretold in 14:9.[40]

But regardless of the relation between the theology of Uriel and that of the visions, there is no doubt that both perspectives contrast sharply with the ethnocentric covenantalism that provides Ezra's starting point. In the end, Ezra accepts an apocalyptic theology that is quite different from the tradition associated with the biblical Ezra.

A Common Apocalyptic Worldview

At this point the similarity between *4 Ezra* and *1 Enoch* becomes apparent. This similarity is not a matter of common traditions. Ezra displays little interest in the movements of the stars or the cosmological details that fascinate Enoch on his travels. Again, the accounts of the origin of sin in the two apocalypses are significantly different. *4 Ezra* has no role for fallen angels. *1 Enoch* assigns no role to the evil heart, or evil inclination, and assigns only a marginal role to the sin of Adam (*1 Enoch* 32:6).[41] But for Ezra as for Enoch, there is "not one world but two" (*4 Ezra* 7:50). In Enoch, the hidden world that is revealed is primarily vertical — the cosmology of the heavens or of the ends of the earth — but the different world of the future is also of fundamental importance. In Ezra, the other world is the world to come, and there is less interest in cosmology; but in the end, Ezra ascends to the heavenly world to be with those like him. The contrast between "the life that is corruptible" (14:13) and the world to come in *4 Ezra* is just

---

40. Stone, *4 Ezra*, 442.

41. See my essay, "Before the Fall: The Earliest Interpretations of Adam and Eve," in Hindy Najman and Judith H. Newman, eds., *The Idea of Biblical Interpretation: Essays in Honor of James L. Kugel* (Leiden: Brill, 2004) 293-308.

as sharp as that between the heavenly spiritual life and earthly defilement in *1 Enoch*. It is this conviction that this world is not the end or destiny of human beings, and the affirmation of the transcendence of death, that underpins the common apocalyptic worldview of *1 Enoch* and *4 Ezra*.[42]

42. See my essay, "Apocalyptic Eschatology as the Transcendence of Death," in my book, *Seers, Sibyls, and Sages in Hellenistic-Roman Judaism* (JSJSup 54; Leiden: Brill, 1997) 75-97. This is also true of the commonality of both the Enoch and the Ezra apocalypses with *2 Baruch,* which is far closer than either of them to the traditional Deuteronomic theology.

CHAPTER 15

Sibylline Discourse

Pseudepigraphy had many uses in the ancient world. It might be used to honor a teacher, to extend the discourse of a founding figure, to subtly subvert an authoritative figure and alter his legacy, or to re-create imaginatively what a great figure of the past might have said or experienced on a given occasion. Or it might have been used to falsify tradition, for purposes of propaganda or gain.[1]

In the context of ancient Jewish literature, works attributed to Gentile authors constitute a distinctive class. We have verses attributed to poets (Phocylides, Menander), tragedians (Sophocles), historians (Hecataeus), mythical figures (Orpheus), and even to an otherwise unknown courtier (Aristeas). The most prolific of these pseudonymous figures, however, was the Sibyl. The earliest Jewish Sibylline oracles can be dated to the second century BCE.[2] Three, possibly four, collections of Jewish oracles

1. B. M. Metzger, "Literary Forgeries and Canonical Pseudepigrapha," *JBL* 91 (1972) 3-24; W. Speyer, *Die Literarische Falschung im Heidenischen und Christlichen Altertum. Ein Versuch Ihrer Deutung* (Munich: Beck, 1971); N. Brox, ed., *Pseudepigraphie in der heidnischen und jüdisch-christlichen Antike* (Wege der Forschung 484; Darmstadt: Wissenschaftliche Buchgesellschaft, 1977); H. Najman, *Seconding Sinai: The Development of Mosaic Discourse in Second Temple Judaism* (JSJSup 77; Leiden: Brill, 2003) 1-16; M. Janssen and J. Frey, "Einführung," in J. Frey, J. Herzer, M. Janssen, and C. K. Rothschild, eds., *Pseudepigraphie und Verfasserfiktion in frühchristlichen Briefen* (WUNT 246; Tübingen: Mohr, 2009) 3-24; B. D. Ehrman, *Forgery and Counterforgery: The Use of Literary Deceit in Early Christian Polemics* (New York: Oxford University Press, 2013) 93-145.

2. J. J. Collins, "Sibylline Oracles," in J. H. Charlesworth, ed., *The Old Testament Pseudepigrapha*, vol. 1: *Apocalyptic Literature and Testaments* (New York: Doubleday, 1983) 317-472; Collins, "The Development of the Sibylline Tradition," *ANRW* 20.1 (1987) 421-59.

have survived almost intact,[3] while substantial parts of Jewish oracles are preserved in two books that are Christian in their present form.[4] The tradition continued down to the Middle Ages. The Sibyl, then, merits consideration as one of the major pseudonymic authors of ancient Jewish and early Christian literature.

There is one obvious consideration that applies to all the Gentile pseudonyms in Jewish literature. Famous, and even obscure, Gentile figures carried a certain authority as witnesses to the wisdom and ethical superiority of Judaism. They were presumably objective, disinterested witnesses, in a way that Jewish authorities were not. All the ostensibly Gentile Jewish pseudepigrapha seem to have originated in the Diaspora, most of them in Egypt, but some possibly in Asia Minor or Syria. They were composed in Greek, even in the rare case where they have survived in translation, as in the case of the *Words of the Wise Menander*. At one time, all this literature was routinely classified as apologetic. Victor Tcherikover famously argued that it was intended for Jewish rather than Gentile readers, and his argument has been universally accepted.[5] Nonetheless, the use of Gentile pseudonyms bespeaks an apologetic attitude, as it reflects a need for Gentile approval. The Jewish values propounded by Phocylides or Aristeas pose no obstacle to participation in Hellenistic society. On the contrary, they meet with the highest approval from distinguished Hellenes. These pseudonymous writings, then, show that it was possible to maintain a Jewish identity and still consider oneself to be authentically Hellenistic.[6]

The Sibyl

The Sibyl, however, had a profile different from that of Phocylides or Aristeas. To begin with, she was a prophetess, more specifically a prophetess of doom, noted for what H. W. Parke euphemistically called "her

---

3. Books 3, 4, and 5 are indisputably Jewish, despite the reservations of James R. Davila about Book 3 and especially Book 5, *The Provenance of the Pseudepigrapha: Jewish, Christian, or Other?* (JSJSup 105; Leiden: Brill, 2005) 180-89. Book 11 is less widely recognized as Jewish, but may well be so.

4. Books 1 and 2, which form a unity, and Book 8.

5. V. Tcherikover, "Jewish Apologetic Literature Reconsidered," *Eos* 48 (1956) 169-93.

6. See my essay, "Hellenistic Judaism in Recent Scholarship," in J. J. Collins, *Jewish Cult and Hellenistic Culture: Essays on the Jewish Encounter with Hellenism and Roman Rule* (JSJSup 100; Leiden: Brill, 2005) 1-20.

lack of charm."[7] Heraclitus, about 500 BCE, referred to her as a figure "with frenzied lips, uttering words without laughter and without charm of sight or scent," who "reaches a thousand years with her voice on account of the god."[8] Plato cites her in the same context as the Pythia as an example of inspired prediction: "Sibyl and others, who by practicing heavenly-inspired divination have foretold many future things accurately."[9] The oldest references assume that she was an individual woman of hoary antiquity. Pausanias preserves a tradition that she was of mixed human and divine descent, daughter of Zeus and Lamia, who in turn was the daughter of Poseidon.[10] According to Heraclides Ponticus (fourth century BCE), she was older than Orpheus.[11] Ovid says that she was granted by Apollo that she might live as many years as there were grains of sand on the seashore, but that she neglected to ask for youth, so she remained a shriveled, shrunken old woman.[12] A coin from Erythrea in Asia Minor refers to her as Thea Sibulla, the goddess Sibyl.[13] She was not then just a human prophetess, but, as Pausanias put it, "midway between mortal and god."

From the fourth century BCE on, "sibyl" became a generic name for female prophets associated with different locations. The most famous sibyls were those of Erythrea and Marpessus in Asia Minor, and of Cumae in Italy. Varro listed ten sibyls, beginning with a Persian one, "of whom Nicanor who wrote the deeds of Alexander of Macedon made mention."[14] Pausanias reduced the list to four.[15] The oldest sibyl was Libyan. The Delphic sibyl, also named Herophile and Artemis, lived before the Trojan War and prophesied about Helen. Herophile was also used as the name of the Erythrean sibyl. This sibyl, according to Pausanias, originated at

---

7. H. W. Parke, *Sibyls and Sibylline Oracles in Classical Antiquity* (ed. B. McGing; London: Routledge, 1988) 12.

8. Plutarch, *De Pythiae Oraculis* 6 (397A); Parke, *Sibyls and Sibylline Oracles*, 63.

9. Plato, *Phaedrus* 244B.

10. Pausanias 10.12.3; J. L. Lightfoot, *The Sibylline Oracles: With Introduction, Translation, and Commentary on the First and Second Books* (Oxford: Oxford University Press, 2007) 15-16; R. Buitenwerf, *Book III of the Sibylline Oracles and Its Social Setting, with an Introduction, Translation and Commentary* (SVTP 17; Leiden: Brill, 2003) 94.

11. Clement, *Strom.* 1.108.1.

12. Ovid, *Metamorphoses* 14.132.

13. M. Goodman, "Jewish Writings under Gentile Pseudonyms," in E. Schürer, *The History of the Jewish People in the Age of Jesus Christ*, vol. III.1 (rev. and ed. G. Vermes, F. Millar, and M. Goodman; Edinburgh: T&T Clark, 1986) 618-54 (619).

14. Lactantius, *Div Inst* 1.6; Parke, *Sibyls and Sibylline Oracles*, 30-31.

15. Parke, *Sibyls and Sibylline Oracles*, 37-45.

Marpessus in the Troad but was associated also with other sites, including Samos, because she had visited them. His third sibyl was the Cumean, while the fourth was "brought up in Palestine named Sabbe, whose father was Berossus and her mother Erymanthe. Some say she was a Babylonian, while others call her an Egyptian Sibyl."[16] This latter figure has no counterpart in Varro's list, and probably reflects some acquaintance with Jewish Sibylline oracles. Berossus was a Chaldean priest of the early Hellenistic period who wrote a history of Babylonia in Greek, and could hardly have been the father of the legendary sibyl, except metaphorically. Sibyls were widely known in the Hellenistic and Roman worlds, and the fame of the Sibyl was by no means confined to the areas in the Troad or Cumae, where she was associated with a shrine.

By the Hellenistic period, the identity of the Sibyl was somewhat variable. The Jewish sibyllists staked out their own position. At the end of the third book of *Sibylline Oracles* we read that the Sibyl left "the long Babylonian walls of Assyria, frenzied, a fire sent to Greece" (*Sib. Or.* 3:809-10). She goes on to dispute one common identification:

> throughout Greece mortals will say that I am of another country, a shameless one, born of Erythrae. Some will say that I am Sibylla born of Circe as mother and Gnostos as father, a crazy liar.

Instead, the Sibyl insists that she is "a prophetess of the great God" and goes on to identify herself as the daughter-in-law of Noah.[17] Jane Lightfoot comments that "the author wanted to exploit the associations of this famous sibyl, but without committing himself to the position that the oracle was genuinely her prophecy."[18] Momigliano noted that "Noah was not a Jew, but a respected ancestor to the Jews. His age was that of the Flood, an event recognized also by pagans. A non-Jewish daughter-in-law of Noah . . . offered the best of two worlds and maintained, indeed increased, the Sibyl's reputation for antiquity."[19] In fact, the Sibyl seems to reject the Erythrean identification in favor of Babylonian origin (hence Pausanias's

---

16. Parke, *Sibyls and Sibylline Oracles*, 41.

17. G. L. Watley, *Sibylline Identities: The Jewish and Christian Editions of Sibylline Oracles 1-2* (diss., University of Virginia, 2010) 72-81.

18. Lightfoot, *The Sibylline Oracles*, 5.

19. A. Momigliano, *From the Pagan to the Christian Sibyl: Prophecy as History of Religion,* in A. C. Dionisotti, A. Grafton, and J. Kraye, eds., *The Uses of Greek and Latin: Historical Essays* (London: Warburg Institute, University of London, 1988) 3-18 (11).

Babylonian, also known as Hebrew, sibyl). Nonetheless, the association of these oracles with the Erythrean sibyl persisted. Lactantius frequently cites the Erythrean sibyl, and the citations correspond to passages in *Sibylline Oracles* 3.[20]

At the beginning of the fourth book the Sibyl protests, "I am not an oracle-monger of false Phoebus, whom vain men called a god, and falsely described as a seer." Pausanias says that the Delphic sibyl claimed to be Artemis, sister of Apollo, and Lightfoot suggests that the Jewish Fourth Sibyl may be countering that claim.[21] Later Christian authorities would take the Sibyl as evidence that pagans as well as Israelites had foretold the messiah. The Jewish authors seem more ambivalent about the pagan character of the Sibyl. She is indeed the prophetess revered by Gentiles, but they do not know who she really is. Just as Plato had supposedly borrowed from Moses, so Greek prophecy was indebted to a figure rooted in biblical, if admittedly pre-Israelite, tradition. Her prophecy does not derive from Apollo, but from the true God.

Nonetheless, the advantage of using the Sibylline genre lay in the fact that it was familiar to Gentiles in the Greco-Roman world. In order to have their compositions pass for Sibylline oracles, the Jewish authors "had to assume the literary conventions expected of a sibyl."[22]

The Characteristics of Sibylline Oracles

The most obvious of these conventions was the use of epic hexameters, which required some sophistication in the use of the Greek language. Hexameters were traditional for all sorts of Greek oracles. The convention may have originated at Delphi, as early as the eighth century.[23] Unlike the oracles delivered at Delphi and other shrines, however, the Sibylline oracles were not responses to queries or consultations. In the words of Parke, "the pagan Sibyl's prophecies were discursive pieces of verse addressed to the world in general rather than to any particular enquirer."[24] The Cumean

---

20. Parke, *Sibyls and Sibylline Oracles*, 3.
21. Lightfoot, *The Sibylline Oracles*, 6.
22. Parke, *Sibyls and Sibylline Oracles*, 6; cf. Momigliano, *From the Pagan to the Christian Sibyl*, 10.
23. Parke, *Sibyls and Sibylline Oracles*, 6
24. Parke, *Sibyls and Sibylline Oracles*, 7.

sibyl in Virgil's *Aeneid* is an exception to this generalization, but she is unparalleled in the other references to ancient sibyls.

While sibyls were not generally available for consultation, there was a famous collection of Sibylline oracles in the temple of Jupiter Optimus Maximus on the Capitol in Rome.[25] A college of priests, the *quindecimviri*, was appointed to consult and interpret the books. Consultations were ordered by the senate. These books were consulted on more than fifty known occasions between 496 and 100 BCE. Unfortunately the words of the oracles are not quoted. Instead, there are only accounts of plagues, famines, or prodigies that led to the consultation, and some details of rituals that were prescribed. The only oracles cited verbatim from the collection are preserved in Phlegon's *Peri Thaumasion,* which was compiled in the reign of Hadrian.[26] One is an oracle that was read and expounded from the books in 125 BCE, on the occasion of the birth of an androgyne. It apparently consists of two older oracles that had been composed nearly a century earlier on the occasion of similar prodigies. Another oracle deals with the origin of the *Ludi Saeculares,* and shows how Sibylline oracles could be used to legitimize new rituals.[27] The temple of Jupiter was destroyed by fire in 83 BCE. Seven years later an attempt was made to replace the collection. A commission sent people to Erythrae, but these gathered only about one thousand verses. Further expeditions were sent to cities in Italy, Sicily, Samos, and northern Africa. The *decemviri* are said to have judged the authenticity of the collected oracles by their use of an acrostic pattern. Later Augustus transferred the oracles to a new temple of Apollo on the Palatine.[28]

There were obviously far more Sibylline oracles in circulation than were collected in Rome, and some of these bear a closer analogy to the Jewish oracles than do the Roman texts. Already in the fifth century Aristophanes lampooned the style of oracular sources such as the Sibyl and Bakis: "O mortals, wretched and foolish . . . men who in your senselessness, not understanding the minds of the gods. . . . For as long as the

25. See Parke, *Sibyls and Sibylline Oracles,* 190-215; H. Cancik, "Libri Fatales: Römische Offenbarungsliteratur und Geschichtstheologie," in D. Hellholm, ed., *Apocalypticism in the Mediterranean World and the Near East* (Tübingen: Mohr Siebeck, 1983) 549-76.

26. FGH 257 F 37; H. Diels, *Sibyllinischer Blätter* (Berlin: Reimer, 1890); L. Breglia Pulci Doria, *Oracoli Sibillini tra Rituali e Propaganda* (Studi su Flegonte di Tralles; Naples: Liguori, 1983).

27. So Buitenwerf, *Book III of the Sibylline Oracles,* 102.

28. Parke, *Sibyls and Sibylline Oracles,* 141.

root-beetle in fleeing emits a fart most foul and Acalanthis hurries on her birthpangs and brings forth blind offspring, so long is it not yet right for peace to be made."[29] Some of the surviving, scattered oracles deal with natural disasters. Pausanias speaks of an earthquake that shook the island of Rhodes so severely that it appeared that a Sibylline oracle had been fulfilled.[30] Strabo cites an oracle about the Pyramus river silting up its beach and reaching to Cyprus.[31] Others were predictions of warfare. Plutarch reports an oracle related to the battle of Chaeronea in the fourth century: "As for the battle on Thermodon, may I be far away from it as an eagle in the clouds and the upper air, to behold it only. The vanquished weeps, but the victor is destroyed."[32] Another oracle cited by Pausanias refers openly to the Second Macedonian War.[33] Sometimes these oracles could be used for subversive purposes. When Lentulus was charged with conspiracy against the Roman republic in 63 BCE, it was reported that he had claimed that his rule was predicted in a Sibylline oracle: three Cornelii were to rule the city, and he was to be the third.[34] Lucan laments that "the dreadful lays of the Cumean seer are spread among the people," on the eve of the civil war. Cassius Dio reports that in 19 CE the consuls were worried by a Sibylline oracle: "When thrice three hundred revolving years have run their course, civil strife shall bring destruction upon Rome."[35] Tiberius declared the oracle false. The oracle was invoked again, however, in 64 CE when a large part of Rome was destroyed by fire. Nero pointed out that the oracle was not found in the sacred books, but then another oracle began to circulate: "Last of the sons of Aeneas, a mother-slayer will govern."[36] The latter was a pointed prophecy of the downfall of Nero himself.[37] Both Augustus and Tiberius undertook to examine oracles in popular circulation and destroy those that were deemed inauthentic.[38]

Natural disasters could easily be combined with predictions of war.

---

29. Aristophanes, *Peace,* 1095, 1116, cited by Buitenwerf, *Book III of the Sibylline Oracles,* 94.

30. Pausanias 2.7.1.

31. Strabo 1.3.8; 12.2.4.

32. Plutarch, *Demosthenes* 19.1; Parke, *Sibyls and Sibylline Oracles,* 119.

33. Pausanias 7.8.9; Parke, *Sibyls and Sibylline Oracles,* 132.

34. Parke, *Sibyls and Sibylline Oracles,* 140.

35. Cassius Dio 57.18.5.

36. Cassius Dio 62.18.4.

37. Parke, *Sibyls and Sibylline Oracles,* 142-43; Buitenwerf, *Book III of the Sibylline Oracles,* 97.

38. Parke, *Sibyls and Sibylline Oracles,* 142.

So Tibullus says that "[The Sibyls] told that a comet would be the evil sign of war, and how plenty of stones would rain down on the earth. They say that trumpets have been heard and weapons clashing in the sky, and that groves have prophesied defeat."[39]

With the exception of the Roman Sibyllina, the pagan oracles are generally brief predictions of wars, political events, and natural disasters. Occasionally, they strike a moral tone. At the pyre of Croesus, the Sibyl "was seen to descend from a height so that she herself might observe the happenings. . . . After a short pause she shouted vehemently, 'Miserable men, why do you pursue what is impious? . . . But obey the undeceiving oracles of my words, lest you perish by an evil fate for your folly against God.' "[40] More typically, however, she simply predicts disasters.

Only rarely can we identify a pagan oracle that is incorporated in the Jewish Sibylline books. *Sibylline Oracles* 3:736, "do not disturb Camarina, for it is better undisturbed," is one example. *Sibylline Oracles* 4:97-98, about the silting up of the Pyramis, is another. But all the Jewish books contain plenty of material of this general type, and much of it could well be derived from pagan sources. Especially notable is a block of material in the middle of *Sibylline Oracles* 3:295-544. Apart from a long and passionate oracle against Rome in verses 350-80, this section is a concatenation of very brief pronouncements of doom against a wide range of people, many of them in Asia.[41] The only reference to Jewish history is in an oracle against Babylon at the beginning of the section. There is also a reference to Gog and Magog in verse 319. Verses 401-88, in particular, are brief oracles of destruction against specific places that have no bearing on Jewish history. They include a prophecy of the Trojan War and a diatribe against Homer: "a certain false writer, an old man, of falsified fatherland . . . He will call himself a Chian and write the story of Ilium, not truthfully but cleverly. For he will master my words and meters" (*Sib. Or.* 3:419-24). In the list of sibyls attributed to Varro and quoted by Lactantius, it is the Erythrean sibyl who calls Homer's writings lies. If these verses are indeed taken from the Erythrean sibyl, this might explain why Lactantius attributes verses from the Third Sibyl to the Erythrean, and why the Sibyl has to insist that the

39. Tibullus 2.5.71-80; Parke, *Sibyls and Sibylline Oracles*, 210.

40. Heraclides Ponticus, cited by Parke, *Sibyls and Sibylline Oracles*, 60.

41. Buitenwerf, *Book III of the Sibylline Oracles*, 132-33, argues on the basis of this material that the Third Sibyl originated in Asia Minor, but in fact this section is rather atypical of the book. See my essay, "The Third Sibyl Revisited," in Collins, *Jewish Cult and Hellenistic Culture*, 82-98, especially 86-87.

Erythrean identification is false. It is possible, however, that the attribution of the verses about Homer was added by Lactantius, and presupposes the identification of the Third Sibyl with the Erythrean. In any case this whole section of the book appears to be inserted to establish the author's Sibylline credentials. It is on the basis of this material that anyone familiar with Sibylline oracles might be expected to accept the Jewish book as an authentic representative of the genre.

There was an obvious Jewish analogue for oracles of this type, in the oracles against the nations in the Hebrew prophets. The Hebrew oracles are often lengthier, and interspersed with expressions of divine judgment for the moral failings of the nations in question. The motif of judgment is often found in the Sibyl, too, but verses 401-88 consist of simple factual pronouncements. Nonetheless, there is an obvious affinity between the two sets of oracles.

The problem is that the Jewish and Christian *Sibylline Oracles* as a whole are characterized by much lengthier discourses and have a more sustained literary character. There are enough short oracles of destruction to suggest continuity with the pagan Sibylline oracles, but the genre as a whole is refashioned to allow for longer prophetic speeches. While some books, especially the fifth, are consistently negative in tone, book 3, which contains the earliest Jewish Sibylline oracles, is much more nuanced. The use of Greek hexameters, and even the choice of the Sibyl as pseudonym, bespeaks a fairly high level of acculturation, and so the question arises why the author chose a genre that is usually identified with oracles of doom.

Lengthy Discourses

One of the more obvious ways in which the Jewish Sibylline oracles differ from their pagan counterparts is that they typically survey a wide sweep of history.[42] This is especially prominent in book 4 and the Jewish substratum of books 1-2, which date from the late first century CE.[43] In those books

42. On the Jewish adaptation of the genre, see my essay, "The Jewish Transformation of Sibylline Oracles," in J. J. Collins, *Seers, Sibyls and Sages in Hellenistic-Roman Judaism* (JSJSup 54; Leiden: Brill, 1997) 181-97.

43. For the date of *Sibylline Oracles* 4, see Collins, "Sibylline Oracles," 382. For the Jewish substratum of *Sibylline Oracles* 1-2 see O. Wassmuth, *Sibyllinische Orakel 1-2. Studien und Kommentar* (Leiden: Brill, 2011) 486-87. Lightfoot, *The Sibylline Oracles*, 148-50, questions, unconvincingly, whether there was a distinct Jewish composition in Books 1-2.

the succession of generations serves to structure the entire oracles. Book 4 divides history, beginning with the Assyrians, into four kingdoms and ten generations. This is followed by the rise of Rome, outside the numerical sequence, and then by conflagration, resurrection, and judgment. The Jewish oracle underlying books 1 and 2 begins with creation and divides all history into ten generations, although the sequence is interrupted by a lengthy Christian interpolation in the seventh generation. The earliest Jewish Sibylline book, the third, is not so systematic, but it includes a euhemeristic account of primeval history, followed by a list of kingdoms (*Sib. Or.* 3:97-161). The succession of kingdoms is a major concern throughout the book. A passage in *Sibylline Oracles* 3:248-81 "predicts" the history of Israel, from the Exodus to the Babylonian exile. Some other ostensible predictions, such as the rise of Rome (3:175-93), are also after the fact.

There is little precedent for this kind of historical schematization in the extant pagan Sibylline oracles. There are certainly some instances of *ex eventu* prophecy. If the Erythrean sibyl prophesied about Homer, this was surely after the fact. A Sibylline oracle cited by Pausanias with reference to the defeat of Athens in the Peloponnesian War may well have been composed after the event,[44] and this is also true of the oracle about the battle of Chaeronea and Philip of Macedon.[45] But the extant Sibylline verses deal with single occurrences, not with the sweep of history. There is only one passage in a pagan source that suggests otherwise. This is the famous opening line in Virgil's *Fourth Eclogue:* "ultima Cumaei venit iam carminis aetas" — the final age of the Cumean's song has now come. Virgil went on to speak of a new world order, the end of the iron generation and the rise of a golden race. The grammarian Servius, writing about 400 CE, explained that the Cumean sibyl divided the *saecula* according to metals, said who would rule over each *saeculum,* and predicted that the Sun, identified with Apollo, would rule over the tenth and that everything would be renewed when the *saecula* had run their course.[46]

Servius's interpretation was not necessarily entailed by Virgil's poem, but some scholars have speculated that Virgil was referring to a little-known Sibylline oracle that predicted a golden age.[47] Others have

44. Pausanias 10.9.11; Parke, *Sibyls and Sibylline Oracles,* 105.

45. Plutarch, *Demosthenes* 19; Parke, *Sibyls and Sibylline Oracles,* 119-20.

46. G. Thilo, ed., *Servii Grammatici qui feruntur in Vergilii Bucolica et Georgica Commentarii* (Leipzig: Teubner, 1887) 44-45.

47. G. Jachmann, "Die Vierte Ekloge Vergils," *Annali della Scuola Normale Superiore di Pisa* 21 (1953) 13-62; G. Williams, *Tradition and Originality in Roman Poetry* (Oxford:

speculated that he may have been influenced by the Jewish Sibyl. Alexander Polyhistor had cited the Third Sibyl a generation before Virgil. The visit of Herod to Rome in 40 BCE and the decree of the senate proclaiming him king of Judea occurred in the consulship of Asinius Pollio, who is addressed in the Fourth Eclogue.[48] Parke, the foremost authority on the pagan sibyls, thought that "Vergil not merely presupposes the immediate advent of the Golden Age, but also endows it with some of the special features of the Jewish Sibyllines."[49] Virgil's poem recalls Isaiah chapters 7 and 11, by the motifs of the birth of a child and the idyllic transformation of nature. The Sibyl also evokes Isaiah in *Sibylline Oracles* 3:785ff.: "Rejoice, maiden, and be glad, for to you the one who created heaven and earth has given the joy of the age. . . . Wolves and lambs will eat grass together . . . the flesh-eating lion will eat husks at the manger like an ox, and mere infant children will lead them . . . serpents and asps will sleep with babies and will not harm them." The Sibylline passage does not speak of the birth of a child, and defenders of Sibylline influence on Virgil have to suppose that he knew a different version of the oracle.

To reconstruct a Sibylline oracle on the basis of Virgil's verse, however, seems a hazardous undertaking. The division of history into *saecula* had a native Italian background in Etruscan tradition, which held that the Etruscan name would disappear after ten *saecula,* and some thought that the final *saeculum* was at hand in the first century BCE. Either the Cumean sibyl or Virgil himself may have picked up the theme from an Etruscan source. Virgil does not number the generations or suggest that the Sibyl prophesied about all of history.

Jane Lightfoot has recently suggested that "the structure of the historical review in *Or. Sib. 1–2* is owed to a Jewish text," specifically the *Apocalypse of Weeks* in *1 Enoch,* which also lists ten periods ("weeks") and has a break in the seventh period.[50] (In the Sibyl, however, the break is caused by a Christian redactor.) It is certainly true that the Sibylline oracles of the late first century CE (*Sibylline Oracles* 4 and *Sibylline Oracles* 1–2) are influenced by apocalyptic traditions, especially in the matter of the final judgment. The earliest Jewish Sibylline oracles in book 3, however,

---

Oxford University Press, 1968) 274-84; W. Clausen, "Virgil's Messianic Eclogue," in J. L. Kugel, ed., *Poetry and Prophecy: The Beginnings of a Literary Tradition* (Ithaca, NY: Cornell University Press, 1990) 65-74.

48. Josephus, *Antiquities* 14.377-89.

49. Parke, *Sibyls and Sibylline Oracles*, 146.

50. Lightfoot, *The Sibylline Oracles*, 111-13.

differ from the contemporary apocalypses in significant ways.[51] Not only is the medium of revelation different, but there is no role for angelic powers, and no resurrection or judgment after death (although these appear prominently in books 1–2 and 4). The retelling of primeval history in book 3 has no place for the descent of the Watchers, although they could have been accommodated to the Titans, as they are later, in book 1. So despite the common use of pseudepigraphy and long-term prophecy, *Sibylline Oracles* 3 does not share the apocalyptic worldview that crystallized in *1 Enoch* and Daniel. There is one allusion to the Book of Daniel in *Sibylline Oracles* 3:396-400, which speaks of ten horns and a horn growing on the side, but this appears to be an independent oracle of uncertain provenance. In any case, its use of Daniel is limited to one motif. It does not extend to the four-kingdom schema that figures so prominently in Daniel 2 and 7. Notably, when that schema appears in *Sibylline Oracles* 4, the first kingdom is identified as Assyria rather than Babylon, indicating that the Sibyl was not following Daniel's version of the schema.

In fact, the discourse of the Sibyl is closer to that of the classical prophets than to that of Daniel or Enoch. We have already noted the use of Isaiah in *Sibylline Oracles* 3:785ff. This passage represents the culmination of history in the perspective of *Sibylline Oracles* 3. It is noteworthy for its earthly character and its focus on the temple. The "prophecy" of Israelite history in verses 248ff. recounts the Babylonian exile as punishment for idolatry. "Therefore for seven decades of times all your fruitful earth and the wonders of the temple will be desolate" (vv. 280-81). But a good end and great glory await. God will send a king, and the "royal tribe will begin to raise up a new temple" (v. 290). In this case, the king sent by God is Cyrus of Persia, in accordance with Isaiah 44:28 and 45:1. The later oracles in the book look to a more definitive restoration. The temple, we are told, will be laden with wealth and will arouse the envy of nations, an echo perhaps of the story of Heliodorus in 2 Maccabees 3. Then "the kings of the peoples will launch an attack together against this land, bringing doom upon themselves, for they will want to destroy the temple of the great God" (vv. 664-65). But then judgment will come upon them, and all will perish at the hand of the immortal. This is the old myth of the inviolability of Zion, familiar from Psalms 2 and 48, and from the story of Sennacherib's

---

51. See my essay, "The Sibyl and the Apocalypses," in D. Aune and F. E. Brenk, eds., *Greco-Roman Culture and the New Testament: Studies Commemorating the Centennial of the Pontifical Biblical Institute* (NTSup 143; Leiden: Brill, 2012) 185-202.

abortive assault on Jerusalem in Isaiah and 2 Kings. In the Hebrew Bible, this myth was part of the royal ideology of Judah. The Sibyl, however, does not envision a restoration of the line of David, but rather looks for "a king from the sun" (v. 652), who should be understood as a Ptolemaic king, who would play a role analogous to that of Cyrus in the earlier oracle.[52] After the defeat of the nations, "the sons of the great God will all live peacefully around the temple" (vv. 702-3).

The reviews of history are interspersed with speeches where the Sibyl addresses her audience directly. Some of these are eulogies of the Jews, others are appeals to the Greeks. In verses 218-64, she digresses to extol "a race of most righteous men" who originate from Ur of the Chaldees. There is no attempt to disguise the identity of this race — Moses is mentioned by name, and there is clear reference to the Exodus and the giving of the Law on Mount Sinai. This passage is perhaps the clearest indication that the book was intended primarily for Jewish readers. It is difficult to imagine that any Gentile would have accepted this passage as an authentic oracle of the Sibyl. There is another eulogy of the Jews in verses 573-600.

The Sibyl also addresses the Greeks, however, in verses 545-72, 624-34, and 732-40. The tone of these addresses vacillates between scolding and pleading, not unlike the speeches of the biblical prophets:

> Greece, why do you rely on mortal leaders who are not able to flee the end of death? To what purpose do you give vain gifts to the dead and sacrifice to idols? Who put error in your heart that you should abandon the face of the great God and do these things? (vv. 545-49)

The Sibyl has a simple recommendation for the Greeks:

> Greece, also, by offering the holocausts of oxen and loud-bellowing bulls, which she has sacrificed, at the temple of the great God, will escape the din of war and panic and pestilence and will again escape the yoke of slavery.

In short, Greece must acknowledge the true God and worship at his temple. The Sibyl concedes that "you certainly will not sacrifice to God until everything happens," but adds, "what God alone has planned will not go

---

52. See my essay, "The Sibyl and the Potter: Political Propaganda in Ptolemaic Egypt," in Collins, *Seers, Sibyls and Sages,* 199-210.

unfulfilled" (vv. 570-71). The appeal to send offerings to the true God is repeated in verses 624-34. Then, after the final assault on Jerusalem by the nations, the Greeks will see the error of their ways and resolve to make amends:

> Come let us all fall on the ground and entreat the immortal king, the great eternal God. Let us send to the Temple, since he alone is sovereign, and let us all ponder the Law of the Most High God. (vv. 716-19)

The vision, then, is of a utopian future similar to what we find in Deutero-Isaiah, when the nations would stream to Mount Zion, bringing offerings to the temple of the true God.

Why the Sibyl?

Why use the name of the Sibyl to convey this message? "One did not consult the sibyl for entertainment," writes John Barclay. "Her predominant mood was despair, and she larded her doleful predictions of natural and political disaster with contemptuous comments on the follies of humanity."[53] Accordingly, Barclay classifies the Third Sibyl as a work of "cultural antagonism." "Adopting the scornful Sibylline mask," he writes, "allows these Jewish oracle-mongers to launch a vigorous attack on other nations. Their sins and follies are amply recounted, most often . . . in the categories of 'idolatry' and moral licence. . . . Such social alienation is writ large across every page of these doom-laden oracles. . . . If this is propaganda, it represents a proselytization by fear."[54]

There is antagonism to the Gentile world to be found in the *Sibylline Oracles,* most obviously in *Sibylline Oracles* 5, which has nothing good to say about any people except the Jews. There are passionate anti-Roman oracles in book 3, notably in verses 350-80, but they do not belong to the original core oracles. But Barclay's characterization of book 3 is a serious misreading of the oracle. He grants, but dismissively, that "the adoption of the Sibylline genre form indicates some degree of acculturation,"[55] and that

---

53. J. M. G. Barclay, *Jews in the Mediterranean Diaspora: From Alexander to Trajan (323 BCE–117 CE)* (Edinburgh: T&T Clark, 1998) 217.

54. Barclay, *Jews in the Mediterranean Diaspora,* 222.

55. Barclay, *Jews in the Mediterranean Diaspora,* 224.

"the final oracle includes a vision of world-wide repentance and the worship of all nations at the temple of God."[56] But these concessions should give pause about his unqualified negative reading of the book. A more sensitive reading is offered by Erich Gruen:

> Whereas the oracle mounts a heavy assault upon Roman wickedness, no comparable attacks are leveled at the Greeks. To the contrary. The Sibyl reaches out to the Hellenic world, exhorting its people to repentance, urging acknowledgment of the true God, and offering hope of salvation. . . . Insofar as the Third Book contains negative aspersions upon Greeks, it includes them among wayward peoples whose failure to see the truth has led them into arrogance, impiety, and immorality, thus provoking divine vengeance. But Greeks alone are singled out for encouragement to enter the fold of the true believers.[57]

This is not to deny that the Sibyl is uncompromising in her insistence on the superiority of Judaism and the folly of idolatry. The same could be said of nearly every surviving piece of literature from Egyptian Judaism, including such "culturally convergent" works as the *Letter of Aristeas* and Philo. All these works insist on the distinctive identity, and on the superiority, of Judaism.[58]

Barclay tries to dissociate the Sibyl from authors like Aristobulus and Aristeas, and associate her with "lower-class Alexandrian Jews" who were involved in conflict with Alexandrians in the early Roman era, arguing that "the natural milieu of Sibylline oracles is the street, not the academy."[59] But it is unlikely that many lower-class Jews in Alexandria would have read epic hexameters. Brief oracles of a line or two, such as we find in the extant pagan oracles, might have circulated easily enough, but the Jewish *Sibyllina* are long, literary works. Like the other Jewish works written in Greek, the Oracles presuppose a considerable Hellenistic education. The hectoring tone no more implies alienation from the Hellenistic world than the sharp rebukes of Jeremiah and Ezekiel implied alienation from Judah. By adopting the voice of the Sibyl, the author took a stand within the Hellenistic world, even as he attempted to reform it in the likeness of Judaism.

56. Barclay, *Jews in the Mediterranean Diaspora*, 222.

57. E. S. Gruen, *Heritage and Hellenism: The Reinvention of Jewish Tradition* (Berkeley: University of California Press, 1998) 287.

58. See further my essay, "Hellenistic Judaism in Recent Scholarship."

59. Barclay, *Jews in the Mediterranean Diaspora*, 224.

The appeal of the Sibyl for a Jewish author was that she was the preeminent prophetic voice in the Hellenistic world. She provided license for the sharp rebukes of Hellenistic mores, while she still, in theory, commanded the respect of the pagan world. This kind of ambivalence toward the dominant culture is a common feature of colonial societies, as postcolonial theorists have emphasized in recent years. On the one hand, there is a measure of resentment and even anger toward the dominant culture. On the other hand, that culture is internalized so that even those who are critical of it seek approval by its standards.

Forgery or Literary Convention?

It is unlikely that any non-Jewish reader would have been impressed by these Sibylline utterances. Forgery of oracles was commonplace in antiquity, and while the masses may have been gullible, the elites were not. Herodotus tells of a forger who was exiled from Athens for interpolating the oracles of Musaeus.[60] Augustus and Tiberius instituted examinations of Sibylline verses to establish their authenticity. To be sure, they were probably more concerned with the content and subversive potential of oracles than authenticity in the strict sense, but the possibility of forgery was obvious and well known.[61]

Whether the Jewish authors expected their work to be viewed as genuine utterances of an ancient prophetess, or rather regarded Sibylline verse as a literary convention, is more difficult to say. Lightfoot has argued that "none of the cultures in which Sibylline oracles were produced supported pseudepigraphy just for the sake of literary fiction. For pagan oracles, at least, there was a notion that they were not shapeless drifting masses of verbiage; either they belonged to the person to whom they were ascribed, or at least they seemed to come from the mists of time, and if that illusion was dispelled, their authority dwindled or disappeared."[62] Similarly, John Barton argues that "there can have been little point in pseudepigraphy unless one's probable readers could understand a claim to authorship and thought that it mattered who the author of a book was."[63] In the case of

---

60. Herodotus 7.6.
61. See especially Ehrman, *Forgery and Counterforgery*, 78-85.
62. Lightfoot, *The Sibylline Oracles*, 54.
63. J. Barton, *Oracles of God: Perceptions of Ancient Prophecy in Israel after the Exile* (London: Darton, Longman and Todd, 1986) 211.

oracles, these statements must be qualified somewhat. Many oracles circulated without attribution, and hexameters that were originally ascribed to one source could easily be transferred to another. So, for example, an oracle that appears in *Sibylline Oracles* 3:736, "do not disturb Camarina, for it is better undisturbed," was originally attributed to the Pythia. Several oracles now incorporated in the Third Sibyl may have been anonymous to begin with. The longer compositions, however, such as the core of book 3,[64] book 4, and book 5 surely were circulated as words of the Sibyl and acquired their authority from that association.

In the case of the later Sibylline books, it is easy enough to see that the authors were following literary convention. The author of the Third Sibyl, however, and arguably also the authors of the fourth and first and second books, constructed a new persona for the Sibyl. While the psychology of pseudonymous writing remains obscure to us, these Jewish authors were not honoring a founder, or modestly attributing their work to a teacher. The constant moral invective makes it unlikely that the composition of these Sibylline oracles was a playful literary exercise, as might be supposed in the composition of epics and tragedies by Jewish authors in the Hellenistic Diaspora.[65] These works can reasonably be described as forgery, with an intent to deceive, however noble one deems their intent of boosting Jewish self-esteem in a Gentile environment.[66] They had little success with their Greek neighbors in Egypt. They appear to have had modest success with their fellow Jews, enough, at least, to ensure the survival of the oracles. They had considerably more success with later Christians, who transformed the Sibyl into a prophetess who foretold Christ. Her reputation earned her a place on the ceiling of the Sistine chapel, and her denunciations of idolatry gained her admittance to Augustine's *City of God*.[67] It was left to the cold light of the Enlightenment to finally banish her to the status of literary fiction.

---

64. I assume that an original core can be identified in *Sibylline Oracles* 3, consisting of vv. 97-349 and 489-829. See Collins, "Sibylline Oracles," 354-55, and "The Third Sibyl Revisited," 83-87.

65. This possibility was suggested to me by Johannes Magliano-Tromp at the Leuven meeting.

66. Compare the judgment of Ehrman on the Christian Sibylline as "apologetic forgeries" (*Forgery and Counterforgery*, 513-18).

67. Parke, *Sibyls and Sibylline Oracles*, 170.

PART V

Ethics and Politics

CHAPTER 16

Ethos and Identity in Jewish Apocalyptic Literature

Apocalyptic literature is not all of a piece. The genre is defined by a combination of literary forms and characteristic motifs, and these can be pressed into service by people of different ideological persuasions. Moreover, there are significant differences between different kinds of apocalypses, such as the "historical" apocalypses that focus on historical crises, on the one hand, or the more cosmically or even mystically oriented ascent apocalypses on the other. If we wish to discuss the question of ethos and identity in the apocalyptic literature, then, we must allow for some variation. In light of this variation, it is even reasonable to ask whether there is any correlation between the literary form of an apocalypse and ethos or identity at all. I will argue that there is a correlation, although it can play out in various ways, and can, like any literary form, be subverted by an ironic writer. It is important, however, that we consider specific cases, so that we can do justice both to the variation and to the commonality within the genre.

Our discussion may be framed by two contrasting scholarly judgments about the literature attributed to Enoch. E. P. Sanders finds in *1 Enoch* "much the same pattern of religion as we found in the Rabbis ... salvation depends on election and that which is necessary to *maintain* the elect state — to be righteous — is to maintain loyalty and obedience to God and his covenant."[1] Sanders calls this pattern of religion "covenantal nomism" and claims that it is ubiquitous in early Judaism. He recognizes that there is a tendency to sectarianism in the Enoch literature, but argues that "it is more likely that the righteous of the various parts of 1 Enoch did not see themselves as members of a sect *within* Israel, but as the *only true*

---

1. E. P. Sanders, *Paul and Palestinian Judaism* (Philadelphia: Fortress, 1977) 362.

Israelites. It seems that in 1 Enoch the righteous *are* the elect and that all others are apostates or heathen."[2] In short, the understanding of what it means to be an Israelite is not unusual, but only a small group is thought to qualify. For Gabriele Boccaccini, in contrast, "1 Enoch is the core of an ancient and distinct variety of second temple Judaism."[3] Following his teacher, Paolo Sacchi, he argues that "its generative idea . . . can be identified in a particular conception of evil, understood as an autonomous reality antecedent to humanity's ability to choose, the result of "a contamination that has spoiled [human] nature," an evil that "was produced before the beginning of history."[4] This branch of Judaism, we are told, "arose out of anti-Zadokite priestly circles that opposed the power of the priestly Zadokite establishment."[5] Its attitude is "at once critical of the reality it sees in the temple and deeply devoted to the ideal of the temple understood in a quite concrete way."[6] None of this is necessarily incompatible with covenantal nomism, but in fact covenant is not a central category in the Enoch literature. The concerns of that literature are different, and in this respect Boccaccini is surely right. The ideas of covenant and the Mosaic law are central in some other apocalypses, such as *4 Ezra* and *2 Baruch,* and in some apocalyptic literature in a broader sense, such as *Jubilees* and the sectarian scrolls from Qumran, but even in these cases the apocalyptic perspective makes a difference to the pattern of covenantal nomism, which distinguishes this literature from that later produced by the rabbis.

Sectarian Identity

To begin with the most distinctive cases, a number of apocalypses refer to distinct movements or groups whose identity is more specific than that of Israelite or Jew.[7] According to the *Apocalypse of Weeks* in *1 Enoch,* the

2. Sanders, *Paul and Palestinian Judaism,* 361.

3. G. Boccaccini, *Beyond the Essene Hypothesis* (Grand Rapids: Eerdmans, 1998) 12.

4. Boccaccini, *Beyond the Essene Hypothesis,* 12-13. See P. Sacchi, *Jewish Apocalyptic and Its History* (Sheffield: Sheffield Academic Press, 1997).

5. Boccaccini, *Beyond the Essene Hypothesis,* 77.

6. So M. Himmelfarb, *Ascent to Heaven in Jewish and Christian Apocalypses* (New York: Oxford University Press, 1993) 27, cited by Boccaccini, *Beyond the Essene Hypothesis,* 78.

7. For recent discussion of these groups see J. J. Collins, "Pseudepigraphy and Group Formation in Second Temple Judaism," in E. G. Chazon and M. Stone, with A. Pinnick, eds,

seventh week, which is the post-exilic generation, will be dominated by an apostate generation, but at its end "the chosen righteous from the eternal plant of righteousness will be chosen" (93:10). The "plant of righteousness" is introduced earlier in the apocalypse, where it refers to the descendants of Abraham. The chosen righteous are evidently a distinct group, singled out from that line. They are given "sevenfold teaching" concerning all creation, and are given a sword to execute righteousness. They eventually acquire houses because of their righteousness, before this world is destroyed and replaced by a new creation. Similarly, in the *Animal Apocalypse* (*1 Enoch* 85–90) the offerings in the second temple are said to be corrupt (89:73), but a group described as "small lambs" begin to open their eyes and see (90:6). They too become militant; they grow horns and find a leader who is described as a sheep with a big horn. They are vindicated in a judgment when God comes down to intervene.

Since the *Apocalypse of Weeks* and *Animal Apocalypse* are both ascribed to Enoch and are otherwise closely related, it is reasonable to assume that the small lambs and the chosen righteous are one and the same, and that the authors of the apocalypses belonged to this group. Whether they can be described as sectarian is debatable. We know nothing of their organization, and at least the *Animal Apocalypse* appears to support Judas Maccabee (the sheep with the big horn),[8] and the *Apocalypse of Weeks* also endorses the use of the sword. They are often identified with the Hasidim of the Maccabean period, who were also supporters of the Maccabees, but we know too little about the Hasidim to make the identification with confidence.[9] They do not deny (at least in these texts) that other Jews belong to Israel, but in the *Animal Apocalypse* "blind sheep" (Jews who are judged by the author to be in error) are burnt in an abyss of fire (90:26). The elect group is the seed for Israel as it will be in the eschatological age.

The Enoch Tradition

The distinction between this elect group and the rest of Israel is grounded in a claim of a new revelation. The revelation is allegedly given to Enoch

---

Pseudepigraphic Perspectives: The Apocrypha and Pseudepigrapha in Light of the Dead Sea Scrolls (Leiden: Brill, 1999) 43-58, and the literature there cited.

8. P. A. Tiller, *A Commentary on the Animal Apocalypse of 1 Enoch* (Atlanta: Scholars Press, 1993) 62-63.

9. See the discussion by Tiller, *A Commentary on the Animal Apocalypse,* 109-15.

in primeval times, long before the revelation to Moses. There is no obvious reason why Enoch should be chosen as the spokesman for a militant group. Many more appropriate pseudonyms were available, such as Joshua or Elijah. Presumably, Enoch was chosen because there was already a tradition of revelatory works in his name. We cannot be sure whether this tradition was transmitted by one group, although this seems an attractive hypothesis. But there is at least a literary tradition wherein Enoch was established as an authoritative mediator of revelation. The associations of Enoch are primarily with figures of Mesopotamian primeval lore.[10] As seventh from Adam, he has been compared with the seventh king of the Sumerian king list, Enmeduranki king of Sippar. Sippar was a center of the cult of Shamash, the sun god. Enoch is associated from the beginning with a solar calendar; his age is given in Genesis as 365 years. Enmeduranki was founder of a guild of diviners, and he had allegedly been taken into the divine assembly and shown the tablet of the gods and the secret of heaven. The number seven is also associated with Utuabzu, the seventh sage, who was said to have been taken up to heaven. Utnapishtim, the flood hero in the *Epic of Gilgamesh,* was taken away to live with the gods. The biblical counterpart of Utnapishtim is Noah, but it is Enoch who is "taken" by God. Enoch seems to have picked motifs that were associated with various Mesopotamian heroes. There can be little doubt that the legend of Enoch first developed in Babylon and was an exercise in what might be called "competitive mythology." Several parallels for this phenomenon can be found, somewhat later, in Hellenistic Jewish literature, where Abraham and Moses are often portrayed as culture heroes who outshine the heroes of Egyptian and other Gentile tradition. The legend of Enoch supplied Jewish exiles with an ancestor who could be compared favorably with Enmeduranki or Utnapishtim in antiquity and status, and might even be said to surpass any of them. Such a figure could bolster Jewish pride and strengthen Jewish identity, but he would seem to have little relevance to the idea of a covenant between God and Israel.

In fact, the earliest Enochic writings are conspicuous for their lack of reference to the Mosaic covenant. The absence of such references cannot be fully explained by the fact that Enoch belongs to an earlier era, so that

10. See especially J. C. VanderKam, *Enoch and the Growth of an Apocalyptic Tradition* (Washington, DC: Catholic Biblical Association Press, 1984) 33-51; idem, *Enoch: A Man for All Generations* (Columbia: University of South Carolina Press, 1995) 6-8. Also H. S. Kvanvig, *Roots of Apocalyptic: The Mesopotamian Background of the Enoch Figure and of the Son of Man* (Neukirchen-Vluyn: Neukirchener Verlag, 1988) 160-213.

explicit reference to Moses would be anachronistic. The Book of *Jubilees* also describes a time before Moses, but nonetheless insists that the patriarchs acted in conformity with the Law. The interests of the earliest Enoch books are different. The *Astronomical Book* (*1 Enoch* 73–82) is introduced as "the book of the revolutions of the lights of heaven, each as it is, according to their classes, according to their period of rule and their times, according to their names and their places of origin and according to their months, which Uriel, the holy angel who was with me and is their leader, showed to me" (*1 En.* 72:1). Enoch apparently received his astronomical education from Uriel in the course of a journey or series of journeys in which he is taken to the ends of the earth (cf. 76:1). The main body of the text, up to chapter 79 where the discourse is pronounced complete, is an instruction by Enoch to his son Methusaleh about "the whole law of the stars of heaven." As M. Albani has shown, it presupposes an astronomical system that is found in the Akkadian text MUL.APIN.[11] The antiquity of this system is disputed, but it certainly predates the Babylonian exile of the Jews. Albani suggests that some Jewish exiles or their descendants, possibly in the Persian period, had access to scribal schools, where they could have encountered such a text. (Compare the admittedly fictional story of the education of Jewish youths in the Book of Daniel.) In any case, the fact that the Jewish author was acquainted with the Akkadian system is beyond reasonable doubt. This fact explains one of the most puzzling aspects of the *Astronomical Book*. It is a major contention of the book that "the year amounts to exactly three hundred and sixty-four days" (72:32). It does not, however, polemicize against the 354-day lunar calendar, which at least in later times was the normative cultic calendar of Judaism. Neither does it discuss the dates of the Jewish festivals. Instead it attacks a 360-day calendar, which fails to add the four additional days (75:1-2; 82:4-6), although we know of no such calendar in Jewish tradition.[12] In the Akkadian text, the length of the year is given as 360 days. It appears, then, that the *Astronomical Book* was not composed to address an inner-Jewish dispute about the calendar (such as we find reflected in *Jubilees* and the Dead Sea Scrolls). It was rather a correction of its Akkadian prototype. Despite the correction, the astronomy of the *Astronomical Book* remains archaic. The

---

11. M. Albani, *Astronomie und Schöpfungsglaube. Untersuchungen zum astronomischen Henochbuch* (Neukirchen-Vluyn: Neukirchener Verlag, 1994); A. Bedenbender, *Der Gott der Welt tritt auf den Sinai. Entstehung, Entwicklung und Funktionsweise der frühjüdischen Apokalyptik* (Berlin: Institut Kirche und Judentum, 2000) 157-58.

12. Albani, *Astronomie und Schöpfungsglaube*, 160-61.

author was not abreast of the Babylonian science of the Persian or Hellenistic periods. What the author had absorbed from his Akkadian learning,
such as it was, was a sense of the importance of the stars and the heavens
as manifestations not only of the glory of God but of the regulated order
of the universe. The discourse of Enoch to Methusaleh, then, is a kind of
wisdom instruction, but an unusual one insofar as it presupposes angelic
revelation and has a highly technical character. It should also be noted that
it speaks of the stars as living beings, in the idiom of mythology rather than
that of science.

Two chapters of the *Astronomical Book,* 80 and 81, have a quite different character from this astronomical instruction, and accordingly are often
regarded as secondary additions. Chapter 80 narrates a supplementary
instruction by Uriel: "But in the days of the sinners the years will become
shorter, and their seed will be late on their land on their fields, and all
things on the earth will change, and will not appear at their proper time"
(80:2). Then "the entire law of the stars will be closed to the sinners, and
the thoughts of those who dwell upon the earth will go astray over them,
and they will turn from all their ways, and will go astray, and will think
them gods. And many evils will overtake them, and punishment will come
upon them to destroy them all" (80:7-8). For our present discussion, the
important point is that the ethos implied in this passage is also implied in
the preceding astronomical instruction: people should live in accordance
with the laws of nature. Sinners are people who fail to understand these
laws. Here again there is a strong similarity to the wisdom tradition, although the astronomical interest is not prominent in the wisdom books.
Chapter 81 is more clearly discontinuous with the rest of the book. Here
Enoch is said to have derived his wisdom from the heavenly tablets rather
than from Uriel. His learning is not especially cosmological but concerns
the judgment of human beings after death. Even in chapter 81, however, it
is not clear just what constitutes righteous conduct, and there is no reference to a covenant or to a special law for Israel.

The *Book of the Watchers*

The *Astronomical Book* may well contain the oldest stratum of the Enochic
tradition. Its reliance on (outdated) Babylonian astronomy is most easily
explained in a Babylonian context, although we have no clear evidence
for its actual provenance. The other early book of Enoch, the *Book of the*

Watchers (*1 Enoch* 1–36), is more easily explained in a Palestinian setting. The central revelatory experience is located at Tel Dan, by the waters of the Jordan.[13] Like the *Astronomical Book,* much of it is concerned with the journeys of Enoch, under the guidance of an angel. But the *Book of the Watchers* also contains a vivid narrative about the Fall of the Watchers, which P. Sacchi and G. Boccaccini take as the constitutive core of the Enochic tradition. The sin of the Watchers has two aspects. The first is emphasized in the divine judgment, pronounced in chapter 15: "Why have you left the high, holy and eternal heaven, and lain with the women and become unclean with the daughters of men, and taken wives for yourselves? . . . And you were spiritual, holy, living an eternal life, but you became unclean upon the women . . . and produced flesh and blood as they do who die and are destroyed." The second is elaborated in chapters 7 and 8, which tell how the Watchers imparted forbidden knowledge to humanity — the making of charms and spells, swords and daggers, jewelry and ornamentation. As a result "the world was changed, and there was great impiety and much fornication" (8:2). Implicit in this narrative is the judgment that cultural innovation is bad, especially when it is accompanied by fornication. These chapters are often, plausibly, read as an indirect expression of the author's reaction to the novelties of the Hellenistic age, which was marked by technological progress, on the one hand, and exposure to Greek attitudes to the human body and sexuality, on the other.[14] The ethic of the *Book of the Watchers* can reasonably be described as reactionary, just as the *Astronomical Book* was reactionary in clinging to an outdated cosmology. Whether there was social or historical continuity between the authors of the two books is open to question. The improper knowledge imparted by the Watchers includes astrology and the path of the moon. While the path of the moon may be regarded as an improper subject because of the author's preference for a solar calendar, the fact remains that there is an account of the moon in the *Astronomical Book,* in chapter 78.

The *Book of the Watchers* provides a much more vivid account of the disruption of the cosmos than anything found in the *Astronomical Book*. At the heart of this account is the antithesis between the high, holy, heaven, where angels enjoy eternal life, and the earthly world of begetting, corruption, and death. The fall of the Watchers is not only an explanation of the

---

13. See G. W. Nickelsburg, "Enoch, Levi and Peter: Recipients of Revelation in Upper Galilee," *JBL* 100 (1981) 575-600.

14. G. W. Nickelsburg, "Apocalyptic and Myth in 1 Enoch 6–11," *JBL* 96 (1977) 383-405.

origin of sin. It is also a paradigm of mistaken values. In contrast, Enoch is a human being who ascends to heaven, and is thereby paradigmatic of the exaltation possible for at least some human beings. The ideal of living an angelic life may not be a constant factor in all apocalyptic literature, but it is prominent in much of it, especially in the earliest, pre-Christian Jewish apocalypses. This ideal lends itself to a negative view of sexuality, the medium by which corruptible life is transmitted, and a general devaluation of the pleasures and successes of this world.

The story of the fallen angels is often taken as a thinly veiled polemic against the Jerusalem priesthood in the period before the Maccabean revolt.[15] Angels were the priests of the heavenly temple. The Watchers are told that they should have petitioned on behalf of human beings, not vice versa. Enoch is pointedly described as a righteous scribe (*1 En.* 12:4), not as a priest. (Enoch is given a priestly role in *Jub.* 4:26, where he is said to burn the incense of the sanctuary, but this is a later text that tries to harmonize the Enoch tradition with Mosaic Judaism.) It may well be, then, that there is here a polemic against the Jerusalem priesthood, although it is expressed indirectly. As we have seen, the *Animal Apocalypse* regarded the offerings of the second temple as impure. But the *Book of the Watchers* is not only a polemic against the priesthood; it is a contrast of two value systems and styles of life. The travels of Enoch, in chapters 17–36, probably represent a number of discrete expansions of the book. They continue the interest of the Enoch tradition in cosmological lore, although they do not engage in the kind of quasi-scientific speculation found in the *Astronomical Book*. They also show Babylonian influence at some points — the abode of the dead is located inside a mountain in *1 Enoch* 22.[16] But these chapters also draw on traditions known to us from the Bible. They envision a mountain with the house of the Lord and the fragrant tree of life (chapter 25). They incorporate the story of Adam and Eve (32:6), although the story of the Watchers seems to provide the paradigm of the origin of sin. They seem to draw on a richer mythology than what is now found in the Bible. They speak of a prison where stars are punished,[17] because they failed to come out at the right time (18:14-16), and of an abyss of fire (18:11; 21:7). The tree of life flourishes on the high mountain where God will visit the earth for

15. See especially D. W. Suter, "Fallen Angel, Fallen Priest: The Problem of Family Purity in 1 Enoch 6–16," *HUCA* 50 (1979) 115-35.

16. See the detailed treatment of this passage by M.-T. Wacker, *Weltordnung und Gericht. Studien zu 1 Henoch 22* (Würzburg: Echter, 1982).

17. Compare the prison for the host of heaven in Isaiah 24:22.

good. Many of these chapters deal with the theme of judgment. Yet they make no allusion to Mosaic Law or to the election of Israel. This does not necessarily mean that the authors did not know or observe the Law of Moses, but it does not seem to be central to their identity, insofar as that identity can be inferred from the text.

The Ethos of the Enoch Tradition

It would seem, then, that the tradents of the Enoch literature originally had an identity that was not grounded in the Mosaic Torah, or in what we know as the canonical scriptures. At some point, however, there was a rapprochement between the Enochic and Mosaic traditions. The *Animal Apocalypse* and the *Apocalypse of Weeks* show a knowledge of, and interest in, the history of Israel that is not hinted at in the *Astronomical Book* or the *Book of the Watchers*. Insofar as these apocalypses show a pattern of sin and deliverance in history, they are surely influenced by the Deuteronomic tradition.[18] Yet the chosen righteous are a group set apart, and they appeal to an authority older than Moses. Again, the first five chapters of *1 Enoch*, which appear to have been added relatively late as an introduction, are replete with biblical allusions.[19] They begin with an account of a theophany on Mount Sinai, although it may be significant that the Lord is said to come to, rather than from, Mount Sinai. But the following chapters emphasize the order of nature as the model for understanding the Law of the Lord, just as was the case in the *Astronomical Book*. It is possible that the author identified the Law of Moses with the Law of cosmic wisdom, as Ben Sira did,[20] but Enoch does not make this identification explicit.

18. See especially Bedenbender, *Der Gott der Welt*, 206-7, building on the older work of O. H. Steck, *Israel und das gewaltsame Geschick der Propheten* (Neukirchen-Vluyn: Neukirchener Verlag, 1967). David Bryan has argued that the imagery of the *Animal Apocalypse* shows the seer "as one whose mentality was shaped and fully governed by the world-view and inherent symbolism of the kosher rules" (*Cosmos, Chaos and the Kosher Mentality* [Sheffield: Sheffield Academic Press, 1995] 169). This is an intriguing suggestion, which is plausible enough in the context of the Antiochan persecution, but it must be weighed against the lack of explicit reference to kosher rules in the Apocalypse — e.g., the Israelites are never accused of sinning by their dietary habits.

19. See especially L. Hartman, *Asking for a Meaning: A Study of 1 Enoch 1–5* (Lund: Gleerup, 1979); Bedenbender, *Der Gott der Welt*, 215-30.

20. Sirach 24:23. See J. J. Collins, *Jewish Wisdom in the Hellenistic Age* (Louisville: Westminster John Knox, 1997) 42-61.

At no point are we told much about the actual practices of the chosen righteous. They support the Maccabees (at least in the case of the *Animal Apocalypse*), and they are willing to resort to violence. They hope to acquire houses when the wicked are overthrown. If the *Book of the Watchers* is still representative of this group in the Maccabean era, however, we should expect a more otherworldly piety that aspires to contemplation of the divine throne and life with the angels. We should not assume too hastily that concern for justice (or even property) on earth is incompatible with mystical inclinations. The *Epistle of Enoch,* the longer work in which the *Apocalypse of Weeks* is now embedded, is vitally concerned with social justice and pronounces woes against sinners whose riches make them appear righteous.[21] The hope of the righteous, however, is fellowship with the angels in heaven. They are told: "you will shine like the lights of heaven and will be seen, and the gate of heaven will be opened to you . . . for you shall be associates of the host of heaven" (*1 En.* 104:2, 6). This is also true in the *Similitudes of Enoch,* which cries out for the overthrow of the kings and the powerful, but looks for a future when the righteous will become angels in heaven (51:4) and share in the lot of the figure called "that Son of Man" (72:16-17).[22] The interest in the angelic world is pervasive in the Enoch literature. At the root of the tradition is the report that Enoch walked with *'elohîm,* which may be, and often was, taken in its plural sense as "heavenly beings." It is from angels that Enoch receives his revelations. It is not surprising, then, that several works attributed to Enoch express the hope of eternal life in the angelic world, a fate already supposedly enjoyed by Enoch himself. While this hope could be combined with elements of Deuteronomic theology, it was fundamentally different from the traditional Deuteronomic hope for long life and abundant progeny in the land, and it implied a different, more spiritual, ethos.

Daniel

The Book of Daniel also knows of an elite group, the wise or *maskilim,* who come to the fore in the time of persecution. Like the elect righteous in the

21. See G. W. Nickelsburg, "Riches, the Rich and God's Judgment in 1 Enoch 92–105 and the Gospel according to Luke," *NTS* 25 (1979) 324-44.

22. On the *Similitudes of Enoch* see further J. J. Collins, *The Apocalyptic Imagination* (2nd ed.; Grand Rapids: Eerdmans, 1998) 177-93.

Enoch books, they are distinguished by their wisdom, but unlike them they have little regard for the Maccabees or their methods. They cannot be collapsed into the same movement.[23] The *maskilim* have not rejected the remainder of Israel. They are said to instruct the *rabbim,* the common people, to make them understand, even though some of them fall, to purify them and to make them white. The nature of the instruction is not spelled out, but it seems reasonable to assume that it corresponds to the wisdom disclosed in the Book of Daniel itself.

Like the books of Enoch, Daniel contains within itself evidence of the growth of a tradition. The Aramaic court tales in chapters 2–6 are generally regarded as older than the visions in chapters 7–12. The tales provide narratives of human conduct, and so illustrate ethos to a greater degree than is usual in apocalypses. John Barton has argued that the piety reflected in these narratives is "normal" Jewish piety.[24] Daniel and his friends are fastidious about their food, lest they be defiled, and refuse to participate in idolatry. Daniel prays toward Jerusalem three times a day, even in defiance of a royal command. At the same time, they function quite well as loyal servants of Gentile kings. None of this is peculiarly apocalyptic. Indeed. To paraphrase George Bernard Shaw, nobody is apocalyptic all the time.[25] But the distinctively apocalyptic part of Daniel is not found in the tales, but in the visions, and the ethos it entails is well illustrated in the brief discussion of the *maskilim.* This discussion occurs as part of a lengthy revelation. The angel discloses to Daniel that there is a struggle in heaven between the angels Gabriel and Michael on the one hand and the princes of Persia and Greece on the other. This is the heavenly backdrop of the wars on earth. In the end, the rampaging "king of the north" (Antiochus Epiphanes) will be destroyed. Then "Michael, the great prince, the protector of your people, shall arise." Then the dead will be raised, some to shame and contempt and some to everlasting life. The wise *maskilim* "will shine like the splendor of the firmament and those who lead the many to righteousness will be like the stars for ever and ever" (Dan. 12:3). To shine like the stars means to become companions to the host of heaven, the destiny of the righteous also in the *Epistle of*

---

23. Despite numerous attempts to subsume them all under the Hasidim. See J. J. Collins, *Daniel* (Hermeneia; Minneapolis: Fortress, 1993) 66-69.

24. J. Barton, "Theological Ethics in the Book of Daniel," in J. J. Collins and P. W. Flint, eds., *The Book of Daniel: Composition and Reception* (Leiden: Brill, 2001) 661-70.

25. "I don't think anybody can be a Christian all the time. Every now and then one forgets, and something comes out quite naturally" (G. B. Shaw, in *Androcles and the Lion*).

Enoch.[26] This revelation equips the *maskilim* with an understanding over and above what is provided by the Mosaic Torah. In traditional Deuteronomic theology, those who kept the law were promised long life in the land, and hoped to see their children to the third generation. This theology was put in question by the persecution, when people were put to death for keeping the law. Daniel's revelation explained how fidelity still made sense. There is another world, the world of angelic powers disclosed in the visions. The hope of the righteous is not for future generations but for life with the angels after death, and this makes an enormous difference for the kind of conduct that makes sense in the present.

The apocalypses of Enoch and Daniel differ in many respects. Daniel lacks Enoch's interest in cosmology and makes no appeal to the law of nature. He expresses no criticism of the temple and is greatly disturbed by its defilement under Antiochus Epiphanes. Observance of the Mosaic Law receives little explicit attention, but is probably assumed throughout, in view of the resistance of the *maskilim* to the persecution. But like Enoch, Daniel is built on the assumption that a higher revelation is needed. This higher revelation is not opposed to the Mosaic Law in either book, but it is a necessary complement. Enoch and Daniel reject, in effect, the old Deuteronomic dictum that the word of God is "not in heaven, that you should say: 'who will go up to heaven for us to get it for us that we may hear it and observe it?'" (Deut. 30:11). The need for higher revelation goes hand in hand with a new spirituality that focuses on the heavenly world and looks for salvation after death, with the angels.

Apocalypticism and Torah-Piety

In the generation after the Maccabean era, however, the Mosaic Torah becomes more central and prominent in works that are apocalyptic, at least in a broad sense. We have seen that already in the Enoch literature a rapprochement was effected between the Enochic and the Deuteronomic traditions. This becomes evident in the summaries of Israelite history in the apocalypses of the Maccabean era. It may be that the attempt to suppress the Torah in the reign of Antiochus Epiphanes had the effect of heightening its importance for Jews who resisted the persecution. But even apart from the persecution, the Torah became increasingly central in Jewish

26. Collins, *Daniel*, 393-94.

life in this period — witness the identification of Wisdom with the Torah in Ben Sira, a few decades earlier, which also brought a tradition that was essentially independent of Mosaic authority under the aegis of the Torah.[27] In any case, we find a blend of Torah-centered piety and apocalyptic revelation in the Book of *Jubilees* and in the sectarian scrolls from Qumran.

Jubilees has the form of an angelic discourse, but it is essentially a paraphrase of the Book of Genesis and part of Exodus. In chapter 23, however, there is a prediction of coming travails, which includes the emergence of a pious group, analogous to the elect righteous in the Enoch literature. In this case, however, the characterization of the group is different: "the children will begin to study the laws, and to seek the commandments, and return to the path of righteousness" (*Jub.* 23:26). It is not clear whether this passage is a prophecy after the fact or a genuine prediction of something that was to happen in the eschatological age. There is no doubt, however, that the ethos promoted by the Book of *Jubilees* is focused on the study of the Torah.

The same is true of the ethos of the Dead Sea sect. There is no clear case of an apocalypse that was composed within the sect, although both the genre and the provenance of some fragmentary works are unclear. There was, however, a strong interest in apocalyptic matters at Qumran, as can be seen from the multiple copies of the books of both Enoch and Daniel that were preserved there. Moreover, Qumran is often, justifiably, called an apocalyptic community because of the prominence of apocalyptic themes (cosmic warfare, calculation of an "end," interest in the heavenly world) in the sectarian texts.[28] There is also in the Scrolls a claim of higher revelation. God revealed to his chosen ones "hidden matters in which all Israel had gone astray; his holy sabbaths and his glorious feasts, his just stipulations and his truthful paths, and the wishes of his will which man must do in order to live by them" (CD 3:13-16). The revelations largely concern issues of calendar and law. It is clear from 4QMMT that the sectarians held the same Torah as other Jews of their time, but interpreted it differently.[29] They held their interpretation, however, as itself revealed, mediated through the Teacher of Righteousness, the authoritative "Interpreter of the Law" (CD 6:7) to whom God also disclosed the secrets of the

---

27. See Collins, *Jewish Wisdom*, 1-20.

28. For an extended treatment, see J. J. Collins, *Apocalypticism in the Dead Sea Scrolls* (London: Routledge, 1997).

29. 4QMMT C 10–11. The writer invites the addressee to consider the books of Moses and the Prophets.

prophetic writings (1QpHab 7:4-5). The status of the Teacher may be one reason why the sectarians did not compose apocalypses in the name of ancient worthies like Enoch. Another reason may be their conviction that all truth was already revealed in Scripture, and so their revelation takes the form of interpretation rather than of new visions.[30]

The Dead Sea sect, as described in the *Damascus Document,* clearly saw itself as heir to God's covenant with Israel. It is the plant root sprung from Aaron and Israel. It does not follow that it denied that its opponents also belonged to Israel. If 4QMMT is indeed addressed to a non-sectarian ruler, as is generally supposed, then Israel is still recognized as a wider entity.[31] Similarly the Prayer for King Jonathan assumes that Israel is the entity over which the king rules, not just the community of the new covenant. Again, when Belial is said to be sent against Israel in CD 4:13, the reference seems to be to the wider Jewish people. But the community is, so to speak, the seed for Israel at the end of days. Others may join it for a time, but eventually that possibility will be denied (CD 4:10-11). In the eschatological time, the distinction between the community and Israel will collapse, as can be seen in the *Messianic Rule* (1QSa).[32] The higher revelation to which the community is privy is complementary to the Torah, not an alternative to it.

There is, however, another aspect to the identity of the Qumran sect. The sectarians are also Sons of Light, whereas their opponents are Sons of Darkness. This opposition is fundamentally different from the opposition between Israel and the nations, which is also maintained in the Scrolls. It provided a way of explaining why so much of Israel deviated from the way of truth, and it seriously relativizes the importance of "Israel" as the vehicle of salvation. However, the identity of the sectarians was deeply rooted in the traditions of Israel, and consequently the dualism of light and darkness has only an occasional and subordinate role in the Scrolls.

The ethos of the Dead Sea sect was regulated to a great degree by their strict interpretation of the Torah. There are at least two respects, however, in which it was shaped distinctively by the apocalyptic heritage

---

30. See further Collins, "Pseudepigraphy and Group Formation," 55-58.

31. See, however, the interesting arguments of Steven Fraade, "To Whom It May Concern: 4QMMT and Its Addressee(s)," *RevQ* 19 (2000) 507-26. Fraade argues that 4QMMT is an instructional document for use within the sect.

32. See Sanders, *Paul and Palestinian Judaism,* 247. H. Stegemann, "Some Remarks to *1QSa,* to *1QSb* and to Qumran Messianism," *RevQ* 17 (1996) 494, argues that 1QSa addresses the present time, but this view is problematic in view of the presence of the messiah.

of the sect. One concerns the claim, found especially in the Hodayot, that the members of the community are already living an exalted life "on the height": "The corrupt spirit you have purified from great sin so that he can take his place with the host of the holy ones and can enter into communion with the congregation of the sons of heaven" (1QH 3:23). Life with the angels was the Enochic ideal, shared also by Daniel after the resurrection. The sectarians (or some of them) appear to claim that they enjoyed it already in the present. Angelic life, however, imposes some restrictions on human behavior. According to the *Messianic Rule* (1QSa 2:3-9), no one with any impurity may enter the congregation, "for the angels of holiness are among their congregation." Women and boys are barred from the army of the Sons of Light on the day of battle for the same reason (1QM 7). This ideal of angelic life bears directly on the much-disputed question of celibacy at Qumran. According to Pliny, Josephus, and Philo, the Essenes were celibate, although one branch of the sect allowed marriage.[33] The sectarian Scrolls never demand celibacy explicitly, and the *Damascus Document* legislates for women and children. It is difficult to see, however, how the so-called "men of perfect holiness," who aspired to live like the angels, could have engaged in sexual activity. I suspect, then, that the report in the Greek sources has a basis in the practice of the Dead Sea sect, although it may not be completely accurate. (Married people, with children, may have been allowed to join the sect on condition of future celibacy, or the celibate wing of the Essene movement may have been in the minority.)[34]

The second issue concerns the attitude of the sect to violence. "I shall not repay anyone with an evil reward; with goodness I shall pursue the man. For to God (belongs) the judgment of every living being, and it is he who pays man his wages," says the hymn at the end of the *Community Rule* (1QS 10:17-18). The logic of this position is familiar from some apocalyptic writings. In the *Assumption of Moses*, Taxo and his sons respond to persecution by purifying themselves by fasting, and then going into a cave in the field, to die rather than transgress the commandments: "For if we do this and die, our blood will be avenged before the Lord" (*Ass. Mos.* 9:7).[35] The

33. For the sources, see G. Vermes and M. Goodman, eds., *The Essenes according to the Classical Sources* (Sheffield: JSOT, 1989).

34. Among the many articles on celibacy and the scrolls, see especially J. M. Baumgarten, "The Qumran-Essene Restraints on Marriage," in L. H. Schiffman, ed., *Archaeology and History in the Dead Sea Scrolls* (Sheffield: JSOT, 1990) 13-24.

35. See J. Licht, "Taxo, or the Apocalyptic Doctrine of Vengeance," *JJS* 12 (1961) 95-103.

maskilim in Daniel, too, expected God to exact the vengeance from which they refrained. The Qumranian sectarians are distinctive insofar as their restraint is temporary: they will not engage with the men of the pit until "the day of wrath." It may indeed have been the tragedy of the community that they thought the day of wrath had come when the Roman army arrived at Qumran in 68 CE. An apocalyptic worldview does not necessarily lead to a quietistic stance in this way. We have seen that the Enoch apocalypses endorse the militancy of the Maccabees. But an apocalyptic worldview could easily lend support to a quietistic stance, since it allowed for retribution in the next life if one refrained from seeking it in this one.

Later Developments

I have restricted my comments to apocalyptic writings from the pre-Christian period. If we were to extend our review into the Common Era we would find a few more variations on identity and ethos in apocalyptic literature. Let me cite briefly a couple of examples.[36] The apocalypses of *4 Ezra* and *2 Baruch,* written at the end of the first century CE, focus to a great degree on questions of theodicy and the efficacy of the Law. *4 Ezra* is skeptical, since most people fail to keep the Law and are doomed to perdition. At the end of the book (2 Esdras 14), Ezra is given a new revelation to replace the Law that has been burned. He is inspired, however, to dictate not just the twenty-four books of the Hebrew Bible, but also seventy others, which he should not make public but give only to the wise among his people, "for in them is the spring of understanding, the fountain of wisdom, and the river of knowledge" (14:47). Here we find the classic apocalyptic understanding of revelation, which does not repudiate the Law of Moses, but relativizes it by insisting on the need for something more. *2 Baruch,* in contrast, feels no such need. Baruch tells the people: "Only make up your minds to obey the law and be subject to those who, in fear, are wise and understanding, and determine that you will never depart from them. For if you do this, the good things I told you about before will come to you, and you will escape the punishment" (*2 Bar.* 46:5-6). In *2 Baruch,* the claim of higher revelation serves to reinforce the covenantal nomism of the Mosaic Torah.

36. For more extensive discussion of these texts, see Collins, *The Apocalyptic Imagination*, 194-232, 248-51.

4 Ezra and *2 Baruch* operate entirely within the horizons of the people of Israel. A quite different use of apocalypticism is found in the Hellenistic Diaspora. In *3 Baruch,* the seer begins in a state of distress over the destruction of Jerusalem. An angel, however, tells him to stop worrying over Jerusalem and to come see the mysteries of God. He is taken on a tour of the heavens that culminates in a vision of individual retribution. The implication is that God ultimately judges individuals. The fate of Jerusalem is not of ultimate concern. Here we have a use of the apocalyptic form by a radical wing of Diaspora Judaism that sought to separate its religion from the fate of the homeland and sanction this separation by the authority of angelic revelation.

Conclusion

In conclusion, I return to the issue posed by the divergent assessments of the Enoch literature by E. P. Sanders and G. Boccaccini. Was there an apocalyptic religion in ancient Judaism? Clearly not. Apocalypse was a literary form that could be used by people of various ideological persuasions. Even apocalypticism as a worldview could be adapted to support various commitments. But nonetheless, both the genre and the worldview carried with them some implications that were more amenable to some positions than to others and that distinguish most apocalyptic literature quite clearly from the covenantal nomism of the rabbis. (*2 Baruch* is arguably an exception.) An apocalypse reveals a world beyond this one, either the heavenly world in the present, or the eschatological future, or both. This revelation tends to relativize the values of this world. So, for example, celibacy may make sense if one wants to enjoy eternal life like the angels, or martyrdom may make sense since the future is not of this world. Accordingly, much, though not all, apocalyptic literature has a somewhat otherworldly ethos, although, again, there are significant differences in degree. More fundamentally, however, an apocalypse is always the revelation of something more than what is found in the publicly available Torah of Moses. The something more may support and confirm the Mosaic Law, as in *2 Baruch,* but most often it supplements it in some way, and in the case of the Enoch literature it may provide a quite different point of view. The claim of a special revelation is often, though not always, the basis for a distinct identity. Those who base their lives on the revelation of Enoch thereby distinguish themselves from those who live by the Law of Moses, although the sharpness of the distinction may vary. Those who accepted the authority of the Teacher found it necessary to separate themselves from those who did not. It is the claim to have a higher revelation, however, that provides the basis for distinct identity and explains why apocalypticism is so often associated with a tendency to sectarianism.

CHAPTER 17

Apocalypse and Empire

The idea that apocalypses are a form of resistance literature is not new. One thinks of Samuel K. Eddy's book, *The King Is Dead*, from fifty years ago, which postulated widespread resistance to Hellenistic rule throughout the Near East, expressed in apocalyptic writings as well as in other genres.[1] More recently Rainer Albertz has written of "a new apocalyptic theology of resistance" that transforms the old Israelite theology of liberation into "an eschatological religion of redemption."[2] Many other names could be added.[3]

In recent years there has been an upsurge of interest in this aspect of apocalyptic literature, prompted in part by the currently fashionable interest in postcolonial theory. Recent studies have ranged from the crudely simplistic[4] to the methodologically sophisticated,[5] and have also varied in their appreciation of the nuances of apocalyptic literature. Richard Hors-

---

1. Samuel K. Eddy, *The King Is Dead: Studies in Near Eastern Resistance to Hellenism, 334–31 B.C.* (Lincoln: University of Nebraska Press, 1961).

2. Rainer Albertz, *A History of Israelite Religion in the Old Testament Period*, vol. 2: *From the Exile to the Maccabees* (trans. John Bowden; Louisville: Westminster John Knox, 1994) 564.

3. See already John J. Collins, *The Apocalyptic Vision of the Book of Daniel* (HSM 16; Missoula, MT: Scholars Press, 1977) 191-218. See more recently my essay, "Temporality and Politics in Jewish Apocalyptic Literature," in Christopher Rowland and John Barton, eds., *Apocalyptic in History and Tradition* (JSPSup 43; Sheffield: Sheffield Academic Press, 2002) 26-43.

4. Richard A. Horsley, *Scribes, Visionaries and the Politics of Second Temple Judea* (Louisville: Westminster John Knox, 2007); *Revolt of the Scribes: Resistance and Apocalyptic Origins* (Minneapolis: Fortress, 2010).

5. Stephen D. Moore, *Empire and Apocalypse: Postcolonialism and the New Testament* (Sheffield: Sheffield Phoenix, 2006); Anathea Portier-Young, *Apocalypse against Empire: Theologies of Resistance in Early Judaism* (Grand Rapids: Eerdmans, 2011).

ley, probably the most prolific writer on the subject of empire in relation to ancient Judaism and early Christianity, does not recognize a distinct apocalyptic genre, or a distinctive apocalyptic worldview, at all, and finds "no defined boundaries between texts and other cultural expressions previously categorized as either apocalyptic or sapiential."[6] For Horsley, the (only?) important feature of these texts is that they are struggling with oppressive violence by foreign imperial powers, and their religious ideas are to be understood in "down-to-earth" political-economic terms.[7] In contrast, Anathea Portier-Young argues that the characteristic features of the sub-genre "historical apocalypse,"

> including such elements as the prophetic review of history, narrative frame, angelic mediation, and revered human recipient of revelation, all play a crucial role in how the text functions as resistant discourse and how the text presents its program of resistance.[8]

Moreover, while Stephen Moore writes about New Testament texts rather than those of Hellenistic-era Judaism, his reading of these texts in light of postcolonial theory leaves him unconvinced by attempts of scholars like Horsley to read them as "unequivocal anti-imperial resistance literature."[9] Moore does not, of course, deny that some resistance to Rome is entailed, most explicitly in Revelation, but he finds a great deal more ambiguity in these texts than is suggested by the simple characterization as "resistance to empire."

Much of the recent discussion of Jewish apocalyptic texts in relation to empire has focused, naturally enough, on the Book of Daniel, but also on the early Enoch literature, especially the *Book of the Watchers*. These texts have the advantage that they can be related to the rule of the Hellenistic empires, especially the Seleucids. There are of course many later apocalyptic texts that address the Roman empire, notably the apocalypses of *4 Ezra* and *2 Baruch*. For the present, we will focus on the apocalypses of the Hellenistic period, since these also provide an opportunity to assess the novelty of the apocalyptic worldview. That Daniel and the *Book of the Watchers* each entails resistance to empire is not in dispute. What we want

6. Horsley, *Scribes, Visionaries*, 4. Compare in the same volume 193-206; *Revolt of the Scribes*, 193-207.

7. See, e.g., Horsley, *Scribes, Visionaries*, 5.

8. Portier-Young, *Apocalypse against Empire*, xiii.

9. Moore, *Empire and Apocalypse*, 122.

to consider is whether we can move beyond that elementary observation and see whether the apocalyptic articulation of resistance is distinctive. In pursuing this question it would be helpful to comment on the social location of the apocalyptic authors (on which we have scarcely any information) and the circumstances in which they wrote, to determine what elicited the resistance and consider what kind of alternative to the current empire was proposed. It is important to appreciate both the common elements that determine an apocalyptic response and the variation that is inevitable between any two specific texts.

The Court-Tales in Daniel

The Book of Daniel is a hybrid composition. Its hybridity is manifest in literary genre (the contrast between tales and visions) but also in language. Although scholars of an earlier generation, most notably H. H. Rowley,[10] sometimes argued for the unity of the book, in recent decades it has been generally accepted that the Aramaic tales in Daniel 2-6 are older than the apocalyptic visions in the second half of the book, and date from a period earlier than the Maccabean revolt.[11] Consequently, the presence of two languages in the book lends itself to a diachronic explanation. Daniel's first vision, in chapter 7, is composed in Aramaic, which was probably the author's first language, to maintain continuity with the tales. The later visions, however, are composed in Hebrew, presumably because of the nationalistic fervor around the time of the Maccabean revolt. On this hypothesis, Daniel 1, which is primarily an introduction to the tales and for that reason is likely to have been composed in Aramaic, was translated into Hebrew to form an *inclusio* with the Hebrew chapters at the end of the book.[12] The book as it stands is not just a collection of materials composed at different times but reflects some editorial intentionality.

10. H. H. Rowley, "The Unity of the Book of Daniel," in idem, *The Servant of the Lord and Other Essays on the Old Testament* (London: Lutterworth, 1952) 237-68.

11. John J. Collins, *Daniel* (Hermeneia; Minneapolis: Fortress, 2003) 24-38. More complex developmental theories are offered by Reinhard Gregor Kratz, *Translatio imperii. Untersuchungen zu den aramäischen Daniel-erzählungen und ihrem theologiegeschichtlichen Umfeld* (WMANT 63; Neukirchen-Vluyn: Neukirchener Verlag, 1987) 11-76; Agus Santoso, *Die Apokalyptik als jüdische Denkbewegung. Eine literarkritische Untersuchung zum Buch Daniel* (Marburg: Tectum, 2007).

12. Collins, *Daniel*, 35.

Some recent studies further accentuate the editorial intentionality. Anathea Portier-Young argues, rightly, that the use of Hebrew in the opening chapter "establishes Hebrew as the matrix, the mother tongue of the faithful, and the 'base language' for the book's multilingual discourse."[13] She further argues, more questionably, that the use of Hebrew here and in the later chapters "establishes a covenant framework for the book as a whole."[14] In any case, the linguistic situation is complicated already in chapter 1 by the frequent use of loanwords and the fact that Daniel and his companions must learn the language and literature of the Chaldeans.[15] Aramaic functions as the language of empire in chapters 2 to 6. In chapter 7, however, the context is different. "At this moment," writes Portier-Young, "Aramaic loses its power as language of empire, because empire itself is stripped of all claims to authority."[16] The switch back to Hebrew in 8:1

> constructs a new context again, in which the empire makes no further claim on the reader. The authors of Daniel now ask their readers to disidentify with the earlier claims of the empire and make the unexpected — and difficult — identification with a people bound in covenant to God alone.[17]

In fact, the context of Daniel 8 is scarcely different from that of chapter 7, but Portier-Young is right that the switch back to Hebrew reflects a repudiation of the imperial context that dominated the tales, and that chapter 7 serves as a transitional chapter in the book.

Scholarship on the tales in Daniel 1–6 in the last forty years or so has generally followed the lead of W. Lee Humphreys and seen the tales as proposing "a life-style for the Diaspora."[18] The Gentile rulers, with occa-

---

13. Anathea Portier-Young, "Languages of Identity and Obligation: Daniel as Bilingual Book," *VT* 60 (2010) 110.

14. Portier-Young, "Languages of Identity," 110. The concept of covenant is used in chapter 11 to characterize the faithful life, but it is not explicit in the tales. Some kind of covenantal relationship would seem to be implied, but whether this should be understood in terms of the Sinai covenant may be debated.

15. Portier-Young, "Languages of Identity," 109, seems to identify the language of the Chaldeans as Aramaic. While it is true that the Chaldeans speak Aramaic, the language of the specialized Chaldean literature is far more likely to be Akkadian.

16. Portier-Young, "Languages of Identity," 112.

17. Portier-Young, "Languages of Identity," 113.

18. W. Lee Humphreys, "A Life-Style for the Diaspora: A Study of the Tales of Esther

sional exceptions, are benign. Daniel and his companions succeed in the service of the empire and rise to the highest levels of its administration. They do this without compromising their allegiance to their God or their traditional observances. Tensions arise, to be sure, but they are resolved. There is no hint of rebellion in these stories. Eschatological hope for the kingdom of God is still maintained, but it is deferred. It has been conjectured that these stories reflect, however obliquely, the interests and concerns of Judeans who actually worked in the service of foreign kings, but this remains hypothetical.[19]

In recent years, several scholars have read the tales in Daniel quite differently.[20] Daniel Smith-Christopher emphasizes their potential "as stories of resistance to cultural and spiritual assimilation of a minority by a dominant foreign power."[21] "The perspective of the book of Daniel toward foreign conquerors," writes Smith-Christopher, "even in the first six chapters, is not nearly so benign as is often thought; in fact, it is openly hostile to their authority."[22] Shane Kirkpatrick uses social-scientific models to show "how these tales could have been read as literature of resistance by second-century Judeans."[23] In his reading, "the honor-laden relationship of patronage between the Judean people and their God is compared to the imposed heritage of the foreign oppressors," to the detriment of the latter.[24] For Portier-Young, while the stories in Daniel 1 and 3 were probably not

---

and Daniel," *JBL* 92 (1973) 211-23. See Lawrence M. Wills, *The Jew in the Court of the Foreign King: Ancient Jewish Court Legends* (Minneapolis: Fortress, 1990); Collins, *Daniel*, 38-52.

19. Collins, *Daniel*, 47-50; Robert R. Wilson, "From Prophecy to Apocalyptic: Reflections on the Shape of Israelite Religion," *Semeia* 21 (1981) 79-95. Karel van der Toorn, "Scholars at the Oriental Court: The Figure of Daniel against Its Mesopotamian Background," in John J. Collins and Peter W. Flint, eds., *The Book of Daniel: Composition and Reception* (VTSup 83; Leiden: Brill, 2001) 1.37-54, argues that "the tales about Daniel preserve the atmosphere of the oriental court as it can be reconstructed from the letters of Assyrian and Babylonian scholars" (41).

20. Daniel Smith-Christopher, "The Book of Daniel," in *The New Interpreter's Bible* (Nashville: Abingdon, 1996) 17-194; David Valeta, *Lions and Ovens and Visions: A Satirical Reading of Daniel 1-6* (Sheffield: Sheffield Phoenix, 2006); Shane Kirkpatrick, *Competing for Honor: A Social-Scientific Reading of Daniel 1-6* (Leiden: Brill, 2005); Portier-Young, *Apocalypse against Empire*, 223-26. Note also, from outside the world of academic scholarship, Daniel Berrigan, *Daniel under the Siege of the Divine* (Farmington, PA: The Plough Publishing House, 1998).

21. Smith-Christopher, "The Book of Daniel," 20.

22. Smith-Christopher, "The Book of Daniel," 21.

23. Kirkpatrick, *Competing for Honor*, 145.

24. Kirkpatrick, *Competing for Honor*, 145-46.

composed during the Antiochan persecution, they "demonstrate specific modes of nonviolent resistance."[25] For Horsley, the tales portray entirely a situation of conflict and are characterized by "ominous anti-imperial pronouncements."[26] In his view, these tales "would surely have prepared Judean intellectuals for potential resistance to measures and institutions intended to cultivate and enforce loyalty to the empire."[27]

The argument that the tales in Daniel 1–6 express resistance to the demands of empire offers a useful corrective to the more benign reading of the tales, but the pendulum has swung too far. Horsley, who offers the most extreme anti-imperial reading of these stories, simply misreads the text at many points. He declares that the idea that religious fidelity was compatible with royal service and could lead to advancement is "a modern Western theological interpretation that assumes the separation of religion and politics."[28] But in fact these stories typically end with the promotion or validation of Daniel and his companions (2:48-49; 3:30; 6:28). Horsley also denies that they envision the conversion of the Gentile king, despite the declaration of Nebuchadnezzar that Daniel's God is "God of gods and Lord of kings" (2:47) and his confession of the sovereignty of the Most High at the end of Daniel chapter 4. In fact, the attitude of the Judean exiles to the king is far from open hostility, but rather one of client to patron. God is not the only patron of the Judeans in these stories.[29]

The relation of Daniel and his companions to the empire can be elucidated with the help of some recent postcolonial theory. On the one hand, the stories can be read as "hidden transcripts," to use the terminology popularized by James C. Scott.[30] While Daniel and his companions are outwardly deferential, even obsequious, to the pagan kings, the stories reflect subversive attitudes that mock these kings in various ways and predict the ultimate demise of all Gentile kingdoms. So for example Daniel prefaces his interpretation of Nebuchadnezzar's dream by saying, "My Lord, may the dream be for your enemies, and its interpretation for your adversaries!" although it is quite clear that it applies to the king him-

---

25. Portier-Young, *Apocalypse against Empire*, 262.

26. Horsley, *Revolt of the Scribes*, 34.

27. Horsley, *Revolt of the Scribes*, 40.

28. Horsley, *Revolt of the Scribes*, 213 n. 16.

29. The ambiguity and irony of these stories is emphasized by Danna Nolan Fewel, *Circle of Sovereignty: Plotting Politics in the Book of Daniel* (Nashville: Abingdon, 1991).

30. James C. Scott, *Domination and the Arts of Resistance: Hidden Transcripts* (New Haven: Yale University Press, 1990).

self.[31] The relevance of Scott's work on "hidden transcripts" is noted by Horsley,[32] who nonetheless concludes that Daniel is "a model of 'speaking truth to power,' even under threat of punishment or death."[33] But the idea of "speaking truth to power" brings to mind rather a prophet like Amos, whose transcripts were not hidden at all, and misses the double-speaking, irony, and ambiguity that characterize "hidden transcripts" in Scott's work.[34]

Even more illuminating for the tales in Daniel 1–6 is the work of Homi Bhabha.[35] In the words of Stephen Moore:

> For Bhabha, colonial discourse is characterized above all by *ambivalence*. It is riddled with contradictions and incoherences, traversed by anxieties and insecurities, and hollowed out by originary lack and internal heterogeneity. For Bhabha, moreover, the locus of colonial power, far from being unambiguously on the side of the colonizer, inheres instead in a shifting, unstable, potentially subversive, "in-between" or "third" space between colonizer and colonized, which is characterized by *mimicry*, on the one hand, in which the colonized heeds the colonizer's peremptory injunction to imitation, but in a manner that constantly threatens to teeter over into mockery; and by *hybridity*, on the other hand, another insidious product of the colonial encounter that further threatens to fracture the colonizer's identity and authority.[36]

While Bhabha is primarily concerned with the identity of the colonizer, his work also has implications for the hybrid identity of the subject people. Daniel's deference to Nebuchadnezzar is not simply a mocking strategy. He is indeed the king's loyal subject, who does his bidding and accepts his honors. The hybridity of the characters is reflected in their double names, Daniel/Belteshazzar, etc. The stories reflect evident pride in the success of Daniel and his companions at the Gentile courts. Even while the kings are ridiculed by the exaggerated depictions of their behavior, there is evident

---

31. Daniel 4:19.

32. Horsley, *Revolt of the Scribes*, 213-14.

33. Horsley, *Revolt of the Scribes*, 45.

34. There is some variation within the tales in Daniel in this regard. In chapter 5, Daniel's tone is more denunciatory than in the other tales.

35. Homi K. Bhabha, *The Location of Culture* (London: Routledge, 1994).

36. Moore, *Empire and Apocalypse*, 90.

mimicry of the Gentile court in the acceptance of royal office. There is an overtone of eschatological judgment, at least in Daniel 2, but the eschatology is deferred. Even the way the kingdom of God is conceived entails a measure of mimicry of the Babylonian kingdom.

When conflict arises in these tales, it is worthwhile to reflect on the issues that cause it. In Daniel 3, certain Chaldeans denounce the Judean courtiers: "These pay no heed to you, O King. They do not serve your gods and they do not worship the golden statue that you have set up" (Dan. 3:12). The reader may suspect that the Chaldeans are motivated by envy, but the complaint is formulated in relation to worship. In Daniel 6, the motif of envy is explicit. The other imperial officials seek to find grounds for complaint against Daniel but fail to do so, and conclude that "We shall not find any ground for complaint against this Daniel unless we find it in connection with the law of his God" (Dan. 6:5). Accordingly they induce the king to establish an ordinance that no one should pray to anyone but him, on pain of being thrown into the lions' den. In each case, the ground for complaint against the Judeans is their worship of their God.

It is commonplace in modern scholarship to say that the distinction between religion and politics is a modern anachronism when applied to the ancient world.[37] But Judeans under Gentile rule routinely made precisely this distinction. Daniel is unimpeachable as a servant of the king, except in the matter of the law of his God. Herein lies his *hybridity:* loyal subject and servant, except when a crucial issue is involved. (We might compare the much later case of St. Thomas More in Reformation England.) Daniel's stance here is typical of Diaspora Judaism, also in the Hellenistic period. The complaint of Apion against the Judeans of Alexandria was that they did not worship the same gods as the Alexandrians.[38] Even in Jerusalem, the revolt against Antiochus Epiphanes was triggered primarily by the king's offensive against the traditional cult.[39] Daniel and his companions have no problem in adopting the language of the empire, or indeed in seeking promotion and honor in the imperial system. But they draw a line in the sand when the worship of their God is involved.

---

37. E.g., Horsley, *Revolt of the Scribes*, 39.

38. Josephus, *Against Apion*, 2.66.

39. See my essay, "Cult and Culture: The Limits of Hellenization in Judea," in my book, *Jewish Cult and Hellenistic Culture: Essays on the Encounter with Hellenism and Roman Rule* (JSJSup 100; Leiden: Brill, 2005) 21-43.

The Visions in Daniel 7-12

The ambivalence that characterizes the tales in Daniel 1-6 disappears, however, in the properly apocalyptic visions of Daniel 7-12. Even though Daniel 7 is in Aramaic, any hint of deference or obligation to empire is withdrawn, as Portier-Young has rightly noted. Daniel is no longer depicted as interpreting the dreams of the king, but as the recipient of his own revelations, which are interpreted for him by an angel. There is no occasion, then, for formulaic wishes that the king live forever or that the vision apply to his enemies. The visions foretell unequivocally the end of Gentile, imperial, rule.

The reasons for the change in attitude are not difficult to fathom. According to Daniel 7, the fourth beast, which represents the Greek kingdom, is far more violent and destructive than those that preceded it. Even more offensive to Daniel, however, is the fact that the little horn (representing Antiochus Epiphanes) speaks words against the Most High and attempts to change the cultic calendar and the law (Dan. 7:25). Subsequent chapters focus especially on the desecration of the temple as the event that puts the Gentile empire beyond redemption. Judeans had borne the rapaciousness of several imperial rulers since the Babylonian exile. Only the disruption of the cult, however, rendered imperial rule finally intolerable.

But while the visions leave no doubt as to their judgment on the empires, they do not announce it in plain prose. The visions of chapters 7 and 8 are presented in symbolic language, often described as "baroque," and often a source of confusion to modern readers unfamiliar with the ancient myths from which the symbols are drawn.[40]

These are not, of course, the first symbolic visions in the Hebrew Bible, but they are considerably more elaborate and sustained than what we find in the prophets.[41] Even Daniel 10-12, which does not describe the actual vision but only gives the interpretation, veils its historical references, if only lightly, in an enigmatic discourse about kings of the north and kings of the south. The introduction to this revelation by the angel Gabriel, in Daniel

---

40. Compare Santoso, *Die Apokalyptik*, 1: "stösst man auf viele Darstellungen, die sehr seltsam oder geheimnisvoll sind."

41. See Susan Niditch, *The Symbolic Vision in Biblical Tradition* (HSM 30; Chico, CA: Scholars Press, 1983); Klaus Koch, "Vom profetischen zum apokalyptischen Visionsbericht," in David Hellholm, ed., *Apocalypticism in the Mediterranean World and the Near East: Proceedings of the International Colloquium on Apocalypticism, Uppsala, August 12-17, 1979* (Tübingen: Mohr Siebeck, 1983) 387-411.

10:12-14, 20-21, reveals much about the worldview of the book. Rather than speak directly about human conflicts, between Judeans and Persians or Judeans and Greeks, Gabriel tells how he has been opposed by the (angelic) "prince of Persia," and how "when I am through with him the prince of Greece will come." The point of the vision is that it discloses a view of reality different from what is commonly assumed. As Jin Hee Han recently put it, the apocalyptic vision facilitates "an alternative experience of reality."[42] To be sure, the Hebrew prophets, too, had provided glimpses of the alternative reality of the heavenly world, but no earlier prophet was concerned with the heavenly backdrop of human affairs in such a sustained way.

In the last section of the book, the heroes in time of persecution are described as "the people who know their God," who stand firm and take action. Despite occasional suggestions to the contrary, there is little reason to find here a reference to military action.[43] The only explicit indication of their activity is that they "give understanding to the many" (ישכילו לרבים); they themselves are characterized as *maskilim*, wise, a term that recalls the characterization of Daniel and his companions at the beginning of the book as משכילים בכל חכמה — versed in all wisdom. The nature of their instruction is not specified, but there can be little doubt that it is typified by the revelations in the Book of Daniel itself. The fact that they are contrasted with those who betray the covenant (מרשיעי ברית) in Daniel 11:32 gives substance to the view that they are in some sense teachers of covenantal lore, but this does not necessarily mean that they were expounding Deuteronomy. As Carol Newsom has pointed out:

> In second century Judaism terms such as "torah," "Israel," "covenant," "righteousness," "what is good in his eyes," and many others were precisely the sort of terms that became ideological signs. But as each group used those terms they did so with a different "accentuation." "Torah" has a different flavor in the Maccabean slogan than it does when the Qumran community speaks of "those who do torah." . . . Simply put, every ideological sign is the site of intersecting accents. It is "socially multiaccentual."[44]

42. Jin Hee Han, *Daniel's Spiel: Apocalyptic Literacy in the Book of Daniel* (Lanham, MD: University Press of America, 2008) 29. Han emphasizes the importance of apocalyptic language in constructing an alternative view of reality.

43. See the thorough analysis of the terminology by Portier-Young, *Apocalypse against Empire*, 235-42.

44. Carol A. Newsom, *The Self as Symbolic Space: Constructing Identity and Commu-*

In fact, Torah is mentioned in the Book of Daniel only in the prayer in chapter 9, which is most probably secondary, and the book shows little if any interest in halachic matters.[45]

It is now generally agreed that the authors of Daniel, and of the other apocalypses, were scribes, who were learned in some way.[46] They were not marginal in their society; they belonged to the small literate elite. If they adopt a stance of marginality, they do so deliberately, in relation to the regnant empire.[47] We get some sense of the range of interests of scribes in early second-century BCE Jerusalem from Ben Sira, chapter 39, who describes how the scribe "seeks out the wisdom of all the ancients," in all its forms, and even "travels in foreign lands" to learn what is good and what is evil.[48] It would be ridiculous, however, to suppose that all scribes necessarily had the same interests as Ben Sira, or indeed that all had the same social location. While we have a good idea how Ben Sira made his living, as a retainer for the ruling priestly class in Jerusalem, we have no reliable evidence of the daily occupation of the *maskilim*. Horsley's claim that they "had devoted their lives to learning Mosaic covenantal Torah"[49] is gratuitous. Not all scribes were halachic specialists. The scribes behind the Book of Daniel were evidently interested in myths and prophecies. While they were certainly familiar with the materials we know as biblical, they were not primarily interpreters of Torah. Rather, they were creative visionaries, who were engaged in constructing a symbolic universe that posed an alternative not only to the Seleucid empire but also to some of the more mundane forms of Judaism, including the practical militancy of the Maccabees.

Perhaps the most striking instance of the contrast between the symbolic universe of Daniel and that of traditional Judaism is the ultimate goal of the *maskilim*. At the end of the crisis, when the archangel Michael arises

---

nity at Qumran (STDJ 52; Leiden: Brill, 2004) 10-11. Arie van der Kooij, "The Concept of Covenant *(Berît)* in the Book of Daniel," in A. S. van der Woude, ed., *The Book of Daniel in the Light of New Findings* (BETL 106; Leuven: Peeters, 1993) 495-501, is perhaps too restrictive when he argues that "covenant" in Daniel is concerned only with the cult.

45. Compare Newsom, *The Self as Symbolic Space,* 42, 47; Portier-Young, *Apocalypse against Empire,* 244.

46. See, e.g., Philip R. Davies, "The Scribal School of Daniel," in Collins and Flint, eds., *The Book of Daniel,* 1.247-65.

47. Newsom, *The Self as Symbolic Space,* 48.

48. Horsley, *Scribes, Visionaries,* 12, describes this as "the full repertoire of Judean culture."

49. So Horsley, *Revolt of the Scribes,* 31.

in victory, "many of those who sleep in the dust of the earth will awake, some to everlasting life and some to shame and everlasting contempt" (Dan. 12:2). The *maskilim*, however, will shine with the brightness of the sky and will be like the stars forever and ever. This is not mere metaphor. The stars were the heavenly host, and the significance of the imagery is made clear in near-contemporary *Epistle of Enoch*, which promises the righteous that "you will shine like the lights of heaven, and will be seen, and the gate of heaven will be opened to you . . . for you will be associates of the host of heaven."[50] The ultimate goal of life, then, was not to live long in the land and see one's children's children, as it had been for traditional Judaism, but fellowship with the angels in eternal life.

Horsley denies that the belief in resurrection constitutes a basic shift in worldview.[51] He dismisses the idea of resurrection as "vague and elusive."[52] But here again he shows his failure to grasp the logic of Daniel in his zeal to reduce everything to political and economic terms. For it is precisely the hope of resurrection and exaltation that makes it possible for the *maskilim* to lay down their lives rather than submit to the demands of the king.[53] In the traditional Mosaic covenant, those who kept the law were supposed to prosper and enjoy life in this world. The persecution of Antiochus Epiphanes created cognitive dissonance in this regard, because now those who were faithful to law and tradition were the ones who lost their lives. This dissonance was relieved by the prospect of reward, or punishment, after death. The hope of resurrection did not mean a complete break with the past. Daniel also hoped that "the people of the holy ones of the Most High" would enjoy "the greatness of the kingdoms under the whole heaven" (Dan. 7:27) — a hope that was itself shaped by colonial mimicry. But the hope for fellowship with the angels bespoke a new set of values that did not require long life in the land and was not concerned only with material reality.

It remains true that Daniel is fundamentally resistance literature — the articulation of a stance of refusal toward the demands of the Seleucid empire. To say only that much, however, fails to distinguish between the

---

50. *1 Enoch* 104:2, 6. See George W. E. Nickelsburg, *Resurrection, Immortality, and Eternal Life in Intertestamental Judaism and Early Christianity* (HTS 56, expanded ed.; Cambridge, MA: Harvard University Press, 2006) 152.

51. Horsley, *Scribes, Visionaries*, 199.

52. Horsley, *Scribes, Visionaries*, 250 n. 54.

53. See my essay, "Apocalyptic Eschatology as the Transcendence of Death," *CBQ* 36 (1974) 21-43, reprinted in my book, *Seers, Sibyls and Sages in Hellenistic-Roman Judaism* (JSJSup 54; Leiden: Brill, 1997) 75-97.

stance of the visions and that of tales, which as we have seen was much more nuanced and ambivalent, and also between the stance of Daniel and that of the Maccabees, who are characterized as at most "a little help" in Daniel 11:34. It fails to appreciate the modality of Daniel's resistance, which is primarily a matter of vision, of seeing the world in a different way.[54] The prophets of old had mainly relied on direct exhortation to convey their message. Daniel does not engage in direct exhortation at all. Rather, the focus is on understanding the vision. Right action will presumably follow from right understanding. But the overthrow of empires is not to be accomplished by human means, and the Book of Daniel is not a call to militancy. Rather, it is a call to understanding and endurance in expectation of divine deliverance.

The *Book of the Watchers*

Daniel, then, is resistance literature in a distinctive key, but it is indubitably resistance literature. This is also true of several other apocalypses — think, for example, of the powerful critique of Rome in *4 Ezra* 12 and in the Book of Revelation. Should we conclude that resistance to empire is an intrinsic aspect of the apocalyptic genre?

An interesting test-case is provided by the Enochic *Book of the Watchers*, which is arguably the earliest apocalypse of all, certainly one of the earliest. Unlike some other sections of *1 Enoch,* such as the *Animal Apocalypse* and the *Apocalypse of Weeks,* the *Book of the Watchers* does not speak explicitly of the overthrow of earthly powers, and its discourse is not about kingdoms. Instead, the literary and conceptual context of the book is provided by the myth of the fallen "sons of God," which is preserved in very terse form in Genesis 6, according to which the sons of God had intercourse with human women and begat a race of giants on earth, called Nephilim. In the *Book of the Watchers*, this story is greatly expanded.[55] The sons of God explicitly recognize that they are committing sin and bind each other by oath for mutual support. Not only do they have intercourse with human

---

54. Compare Stefan Beyerle, "Daniel and Its Social Setting," in Collins and Flint, eds., *The Book of Daniel,* 1.221: "the transcendent character of Dan 12:1-3 only comes to light in the context of a vision-like reality that discloses a heavenly salvation."

55. On the growth of traditions in *1 Enoch* 6–11 see George W. E. Nickelsburg, *1 Enoch 1: A Commentary on the Book of 1 Enoch, Chapters 1–36; 81–108* (Hermeneia; Minneapolis: Fortress, 2001) 165-72; Siam Bhayro, *The Shemihazah and Asael Narrative of 1 Enoch 6–11* (AOAT 322; Münster: Ugarit-Verlag, 2005).

women, but they proceed to impart forbidden knowledge to humanity, as Prometheus had done in Greek myth. Asael teaches men to make swords of iron and weapons of war, and also teaches them metallurgy and the making of jewelry. Shemihaza and other Watchers teach spells, sorcery, and astrology. Moreover, the giants born of them devour the products of human labor. "And they began to sin against the birds and beasts and creeping things and the fish, and to devour one another's flesh, and they drank the blood" (*1 En.* 7:3). And so the earth cried out to God for deliverance.

It is very likely that the story of the Watchers reflects concerns of the time when the book was composed, but the story resists simple decoding as allegory. The Watchers have variously been thought to represent the Diadochi, the successors of Alexander,[56] or the Jerusalem priesthood,[57] but it is in the nature of a mythic story such as this that it is multivalent.[58] For Horsley, predictably, "the driving concern of the story of the watchers' rebellion is to explain the origin of imperial military violence that destroys human life and leads to the devouring of people's produce."[59] This is, perhaps, one possible application of the story, but the myth is more complicated than that. Horsley ignores one of the two major motifs, the imparting of forbidden knowledge. Yet, if we do read the story as an allegory for colonial expansion, the motif of forbidden knowledge entails much of the ambivalence noted by postcolonial theorists. Was there no positive aspect to the increase of knowledge? Would humanity have really been better off without metallurgy? And for that matter, were the invention of jewelry and eye-shadow such unmitigated disasters? An anti-imperial reading of the story of the Watchers is one possible allegorical interpretation, but requires more nuance than Horsley allows. More reasonable is Nickelsburg's judgment that the story displays "antipathy to Hellenistic culture," although he also notes that it employs elements of the religion and culture from the Gentile environment, in good postcolonial fashion.[60]

The story of the Watchers, and their eventual imprisonment under the earth, is not, however, the ultimate focus of the *Book of the Watchers*. Only in chapter 12, after the destruction of the Watchers has been nar-

56. So Nickelsburg, *1 Enoch 1*, 170.

57. David Suter, "Fallen Angel, Fallen Priest: The Problem of Family Purity in 1 Enoch 6–16," *HUCA* 50 (1979) 115-35.

58. John J. Collins, *The Apocalyptic Imagination* (2nd ed.; Grand Rapids: Eerdmans, 1998) 51-52.

59. Horsley, *Revolt of the Scribes*, 55.

60. Nickelsburg, *1 Enoch 1*, 62.

rated, is the figure of Enoch introduced, although he is retrojected into the Watchers' career. They approach Enoch, "the righteous scribe," and ask him to write a petition for them and convey it to the Most High. Enoch complies and ascends to heaven on a cloud. The petition is rejected, but it provides an occasion to highlight the contrasting paradigms of the Watchers and Enoch. He is told to say to the Watchers:

> You should petition in behalf of humans, and not humans in behalf of you. Why have you forsaken the high heaven, the eternal sanctuary; and lain with women, and defiled yourselves with the daughters of men and taken for yourselves wives, and done as the sons of earth; and begotten for yourselves sons, giants? . . . But you originally existed as spirits, living forever, and not dying for all the generations of eternity; therefore I did not make women among you. The spirits of heaven, in heaven is their dwelling. (*1 En.* 15:2-10)

The issue here is not socio-economic exploitation, although that was undoubtedly a fact of imperial rule, but misplaced priorities. The Watchers originally enjoyed the ideal life in heaven, in the divine presence, but they gave up heaven for sex. Enoch, in contrast, is born on earth but ascends to heaven, and becomes the paradigm of upward mobility that would inspire both the sectarians known from the Dead Sea Scrolls and generations of Christian monks who aspired to the angelic life.[61]

The remainder of the *Book of the Watchers* is concerned with Enoch's tours of the ends of the earth, places beyond normal human access. He sees the place of the luminaries, the treasuries of the stars and the winds, and the foundations of the earth. But a great deal of what he sees has to do with places of divine judgment. In 18:14, he sees a place that is the end of heaven and earth, which is a prison for the stars and the hosts of heaven. Chapter 21 expands this vision of a burning abyss. In chapter 22, he sees the abodes of the dead inside a mountain, where they await the final judgment. Chapters 25 and 26 describe the place in the middle of the earth where God will sit when he descends to visit the earth, and also the tree of life whose fruit will be given to the righteous. Then he proceeds to the paradise of righteousness, in chapter 28.

---

61. See my essay, "The Life Angelic," in Turid Karlsen Seim and Jorunn Økland, eds., *Metamorphoses: Resurrection, Body and Transformative Practices in Early Christianity* (Ekstasis 1; Berlin: de Gruyter, 2009) 291-310.

Horsley objects that because the *Book of the Watchers* is usually classified as an apocalypse, "interpreters often overplay the 'eschatology' of the book," which, in his view, lacks eschatological urgency and has *only* "an eschatological *perspective*."[62] But the eschatological perspective is the whole point of the book. If the story of the Watchers is taken as in some sense an allegory for the world gone awry, the visions of Enoch serve to put it in perspective. These visions disclose "an alternative universe," in thick cosmological detail. The details of the visions assure the reader that the places of judgment and the rewards and punishments to follow are already prepared, and endow them with a sense of realism. This alternative world exists in the present, but is also the world to come. As a later apocalypse would put it, "the Most High has made not one world, but two" (*4 Ezra* 7:49). While the story of the Watchers ends with the renewal of the earth, in chapters 10 and 11, the ultimate hope of the righteous is for eternal life in a world transformed.

Both Enoch and Daniel were, of course, pseudonyms for the real authors of the apocalypses. In the case of Daniel, the name was probably chosen because of the stories about Daniel at the Babylonian and Persian courts, which made him a witness to the rise and fall of empires. In the case of Enoch, we are told in Genesis that he "walked with *elohim*," which should probably be understood as angels (Gen. 5:22).[63] This gives rise to the stories of his ascent to heaven.[64] He becomes paradigmatic for the aspiration to ascend and commune with the angels. He is identified as a scribe, and the books of Enoch are scribal products. Here again, being a scribe does not necessarily mean being a student of covenantal Torah. As Nickelsburg has pointed out, "to judge from what the authors of 1 Enoch have written and not written, the Sinaitic covenant and Torah were not of central importance to them."[65] To be sure, some scholars find it difficult to

62. Horsley, *Revolt of the Scribes*, 61; *Scribes, Visionaries*, 162.

63. James C. VanderKam, *Enoch and the Growth of an Apocalyptic Tradition* (CBQMS 16; Washington, DC: Catholic Biblical Association of America, 1984), 31.

64. Horsley, *Scribes, Visionaries*, 199, dismisses the characterization of Enoch's ascent as an otherworldly journey, on the grounds that it entails a prophetic commissioning, as if the novelty of the account of the ascent were thereby negated!

65. G. W. E. Nickelsburg, "Enochic Wisdom: An Alternative to the Mosaic Torah?" in Jodi Magness and Seymour Gitin, eds., *Hesed ve-emet: Studies in Honor of Ernest S. Frerichs* (Atlanta: Scholars Press, 1998) 123-32. See also Nickelsburg, "Enochic Wisdom and Its Relationship to the Mosaic Torah," in Gabriele Boccaccini and John J. Collins, eds., *The Early Enoch Literature* (JSJSup 121; Leiden: Brill, 2007) 81-94; Andreas Bedenbender, "The Place of the Torah in the Early Enoch Literature," in Boccaccini and Collins, eds., *The Early Enoch*

accept the idea that the Torah was not always central to all forms of Judaism. They point out that there are many allusions to the "books of Moses" in the Enochic literature and that it would be anachronistic for Enoch to refer openly to the covenant.[66] But the Book of *Jubilees,* in which the covenant and Torah are indeed central, retrojects the laws of the Torah into primeval history, and the *Book of the Watchers* could have done so, too, if it were Torah-centric. Moreover, the choice of pseudonym is significant. It is unlikely that an author for whom the Torah was central would take as his pseudonym a figure who lived before the Flood. Enoch was chosen because he supposedly had access to arcane lore that was not revealed in the Torah of Moses. To this degree, at least, Gabriele Boccaccini is right to argue that "Enochic Judaism" was a distinct phenomenon, even if it was not necessarily opposed to Mosaic or "Zadokite" Judaism, as he supposes.[67]

The *Book of the Watchers* offers a description of the world that is quite novel in the Jewish literature that has come down to us from antiquity.[68] Not only was the cosmology novel, with its description of the abodes of the dead, the places of punishment, and the geography of paradise. It also offered a new, negative evaluation of human culture as it had evolved in the Hellenistic age. The new knowledge and technological prowess were not the benefactions of kings who deserved divine honors, but rather the fruits of sinful rebellion by fallen angels. The myth of the Watchers can be applied to the Hellenistic empires, although it does not address them overtly. The concern of this apocalypse, however, is not with empire as such, but rather with cultural innovation, which is often a by-product of foreign hegemony.

Literature, 65-79. Bedenbender allows for a rapprochement between Enoch and the Torah in the Maccabean era.

66. See, e.g., Mark Adam Elliott, "Covenant and Cosmology in the Book of the Watchers and the Astronomical Book," *Henoch* 24 (2002) 23-38. The issues are reviewed by Portier-Young, *Apocalypse against Empire,* 295-302.

67. See further my essays, "How Distinctive Was Enochic Judaism?" in *Meghillot* 5-6 (2007) 17-34 (Fs. Devorah Dimant), and "Enochic Judaism: An Assessment," in Adolfo Roitman, ed., *The Dead Sea Scrolls and Contemporary Culture* (Leiden: Brill, 2010) 219-34. For Boccaccini's views see his *Beyond the Essene Hypothesis: The Parting of the Ways between Qumran and Enochic Judaism* (Grand Rapids: Eerdmans, 1998); *Roots of Rabbinic Judaism: An Intellectual History from Ezekiel to Daniel* (Grand Rapids: Eerdmans, 2002). Boccaccini's characterization of Enochic Judaism and of "Zadokite" Judaism, and the supposed relation to the Dead Sea Scrolls, are all highly controversial.

68. On the cosmology of the *Book of the Watchers,* see Kelley Coblentz Bautch, *A Study of the Geography of 1 Enoch 17–19: No One Has Seen What I Have Seen* (JSJSup 81; Leiden: Brill, 2003).

It also denounces rapaciousness and violence, but these are not the only concerns. There is also the rejection of knowledge perceived as false, and a sense that the actions of the Watchers lead to defilement. The stance of the book may well be described as resistance, insofar as it condemns the new cultural values. The alternative that is affirmed includes the restoration of the earth, but is primarily concerned with ending defilement and living an angelic life. The slightly later Enochic books, the *Animal Apocalypse* and the *Apocalypse of Weeks*, are more directly concerned with the overthrow of foreign rule, but these apocalypses, like Daniel 7–12, date from the Maccabean era, after the attack on the Jerusalem cult by Antiochus Epiphanes. The *Book of the Watchers*, however, is primarily concerned with inculcating a new way of seeing the world. Like Daniel, it relies on description rather than exhortation. The goal is understanding. Right action will follow. In this sense it is a kind of wisdom, but the understanding of the world is vastly different from that of Proverbs or Ben Sira.

Conclusion

Richard Horsley has claimed that "both Daniel and sections of *1 Enoch* . . . state clearly that the principal problem with which they are struggling is oppressive violence by foreign imperial rulers."[69] He further claims that "no Second Temple Judean text classified as 'apocalyptic' has survived that does not focus on imperial rule and the opposition to it."[70] Opposition to imperial rule is certainly a factor in the great majority of apocalypses, but to define the central focus of these works simply as "opposition to empire" is simplistic and misses the nuances of the mode of resistance that is characteristic of apocalypses. These texts are not generally a call to militant uprising, such as we find in 1 Maccabees. Rather, they are concerned with vision and understanding. In the words of Anathea Portier-Young, "apocalyptic faith maintained that what could be seen on the surface told only part of the story."[71] Precisely the part of the story that was not seen on the surface was most important. Moreover, while the apocalyptic writers sought relief and deliverance from state terror and economic exploitation, they were often even more concerned with defilement and right worship.

69. Horsley, *Scribes, Visionaries*, 5.
70. Horsley, *Revolt of the Scribes*, 3.
71. Portier-Young, *Apocalypse against Empire*, 389.

The solution they sought might include a restored earth, but it also looked for life beyond this world in the company of angels. Rightly or not, they did not see the world in Marxist terms. In their view of the world, human welfare was inextricably bound up with right worship, and this took precedence over material concerns, although the latter were by no means negligible. Moreover, it should be said that in many apocalypses, especially those composed after 70 CE, resistance is muted by resignation, and the focus is on mourning and consolation.[72]

Horsley's simplistic reading of these texts as exclusively concerned with "resistance to empire" also obliterates generic distinctions that are essential for nuanced interpretation. He sees no difference between the apocalypses and earlier prophetic texts, despite the manifest shift in mode of presentation, from proclaiming the word of the Lord in prophetic oracles to description of veiled realities in the apocalypses.[73] Most glaringly, he fails to see the significance of the belief in resurrection and the new value placed on individual salvation, which had only exceptional precedents in the biblical world, in figures such as Enoch and Elijah. But in fact this belief was the underpinning of a new form of resistance, that of the martyrs, which would henceforth play a prominent role in both Jewish and Christian resistance to imperial demands. It remains true that the apocalypses are concerned with resistance to imperial oppression, but their resistance was grounded in a view of the world that diverged from the traditional covenantal Judaism and was not shared by all Judeans in the Hellenistic and Roman periods.

The faith of the apocalyptic writers was not simply an expression of the traditional covenantal religion of the Torah. This is not to suggest that it was in conflict with covenantal religion. Daniel denounces "those who violate the covenant," although he shows little halachic concern. Later apocalypses, such as *4 Ezra* and *2 Baruch*, would give the Torah a more central place. But in all the apocalypses, there is an appeal to a further, higher revelation, as "the spring of understanding, and the river of knowledge," in the words of *4 Ezra*. It is the "alternative universe" disclosed in these higher revelations that provides the ultimate grounding for resistance to all earthly empires in the apocalyptic literature.

72. See Dereck Daschke, *City of Ruins: Mourning the Destruction of Jerusalem through Jewish Apocalypse* (Leiden: Brill, 2010).

73. In part, the problem is his failure to consider the overall shape of literary works. The fact that motifs characteristic of apocalyptic literature may also be found in prophetic works does not mean that there is no significant difference in proportion.

CHAPTER 18

Cognitive Dissonance and Eschatological Violence: Fantasized Solutions to a Theological Dilemma in Second Temple Judaism

The possibility that there is an intrinsic link between religion, specifically monotheistic religion, and violence has haunted much of the world since the attacks on the United States by Muslim terrorists on September 11, 2001. Remarkably enough, the same possibility had been raised forcefully four years earlier in two quite different books dealing with the biblical tradition, *Moses the Egyptian: The Memory of Egypt in Western Monotheism,* by the German Egyptologist Jan Assmann, and *The Curse of Cain: The Violent Legacy of Monotheism,* by the American literary critic Regina Schwartz. Neither of these authors used the word "monotheism" in a strict, ontological sense. Schwartz, in fact, declares that strictly speaking there is no such thing as monotheism in the Hebrew Bible. "Monotheism would make an ontological claim that only one god exists. *Monolatry* or *henotheism* would better describe the kind of exclusive allegiance to one deity (from a field of many) that we find in, say, Deuteronomy."[1] Assmann, for his part, is concerned with the antagonism between true and false religion, which he calls "the Mosaic distinction": "Monotheistic religions structure the relationship between the old and the new in terms not of evolution but of revolution, and reject all older and other religions as 'paganism' or 'idolatry.' . . . There is no natural way leading from the error of idolatry to the truth of monotheism."[2] Both are concerned with the role of monotheistic,

1. Regina Schwartz, *The Curse of Cain: The Violent Legacy of Monotheism* (Chicago: University of Chicago Press, 1997) 17. She refers specifically to the warning against following other gods in Deuteronomy 28:14.

2. Jan Assmann, *Moses the Egyptian: The Memory of Egypt in Western Monotheism* (Cambridge, MA: Harvard University Press, 1997) 7.

or henotheistic, belief in identity formation. According to Schwartz, "as a cultural formation, monotheism is strikingly tenacious. Its tenet — one God establishes one people under God — has been translated from the sphere of the sacred to nationalism, and hence to other collective identities."[3] Both see monotheism, loosely defined, as fostering antagonism, although Schwartz insists that the relation between monotheism and the social order can be variously conceived, and is sometimes conceived in the Bible in ways that are not antagonistic.[4] "Cultural or intellectual distinctions such as these," writes Assmann, "construct a universe that is not only full of meaning, identity, and orientation, but also full of conflict, intolerance, and violence."[5]

In my own view, it is probably better to reserve the word "monotheism" for material that is informed by philosophical reflection. Such material first appears in the Jewish tradition in the Hellenistic era, and then only rarely.[6] This is not to deny that we find material with implications for the development of monotheism at an earlier time, notably in the Priestly account of creation and in Second Isaiah. Even earlier, we find strong affirmations that the God of Israel is the supreme God to whom the whole world owes fealty. It is this belief in the supremacy of the national God of Israel that concerns me here. There can, of course, be no question of imputing the origin of violence to this belief. Violence had been endemic in the ancient Near East, and probably in all societies, long before Israel emerged at all. Moreover, the belief that various peoples could worship the same "God of heaven," whether they called him Yahweh or Ahura Mazda or Zeus, is potentially a force for peace and harmony between peoples. Monolatry has certainly been implicated in violence on occasion — the examples of Akhenaten, Elijah, and Josiah come to mind, not to mention the numerous cases of religious persecution in the last two millennia. My concern in this chapter, however, is not with actual historical violence but with a phenomenon that is very characteristic of Second Temple Judaism — violent rhetoric, projected into the eschatological future. What bearing does this material have on the relation between monotheism and violence?

---

3. Schwartz, *The Curse of Cain*, 16. Compare Assmann, *Moses the Egyptian*, 2.

4. Schwartz, *The Curse of Cain*, 16.

5. Assmann, *Moses the Egyptian*, 1.

6. See my earlier reflections, "Jewish Monotheism and Christian Theology," in Hershel Shanks and Jack Meinhardt, eds., *Aspects of Monotheism: How God Is One* (Washington, DC: Biblical Archaeology Society, 1997) 81-105.

Cognitive Dissonance

The basic problem that gave rise to this phenomenon might be described as cognitive dissonance.[7] The dissonance in this case was between what was affirmed by religious belief and what was empirically the case. It is expressed most poignantly in *4 Ezra,* an apocalypse from the end of the first century CE, in the aftermath of the destruction of Jerusalem by the Romans. Ezra complains:

> All this I have spoken before thee, O Lord, because thou hast said that it was for us that thou didst create this world. As for the other nations which have descended from Adam, thou hast said that they are nothing, and that they are like spittle, and thou hast compared their abundance to a drop from a bucket. And now, O Lord, behold, these nations, which are reputed as nothing, domineer over us and devour us. But we thy people, whom thou hast called thy first-born, only begotten, zealous for thee, and most dear, have been given into their hands. If the world has indeed been created for us, why do we not possess our world as an inheritance? How long will this be so? (*4 Ezra* 6:55-59)

To be sure, the problems of the Judean community in the Second Temple period were not entirely theological. Domination by foreign powers had social and economic implications that were all too real, even apart from the occasional episodes of military suppression, which reached their climax with the destruction of Jerusalem.[8] But these problems are very often formulated in theological terms. As the psalmist already put it in the time of the exile: "why should the nations say, where is their God?" (Pss. 79:10; 115:2). The loss of dignity and respect that came with foreign occupation was all the more acute for people who believed, and amazingly continued to believe, that their God was the master of the universe.

---

7. The phrase "cognitive dissonance" was coined by Leon Festinger in *When Prophecy Fails: A Social and Psychological Study of a Modern Group That Predicted the Destruction of the World*, by Leon Festinger, Henry Riecken, and Stanley Schachter (Minneapolis: University of Minnesota Press, 1956). See also Festinger, *A Theory of Cognitive Dissonance* (Stanford, CA: Stanford University Press, 1957).

8. See, e.g., the discussion of Seleucid state terror by Anathea Portier-Young, *Apocalypse against Empire: Theologies of Resistance in Early Judaism* (Grand Rapids: Eerdmans, 2011) 140-75.

Violent Fantasy

The dissonance between the belief in the supremacy of YHWH and the actual political order is most frequently relieved by appeal to eschatology. In the great majority of cases, this involves fantasies of violence. The vision of cosmic harmony in Isaiah 11 stands out as exceptional, but it may well date from the monarchic period.[9] There are also peaceful fantasies of the nations flocking to Mount Zion in Second and Third Isaiah: "nations will come to your light and kings to the brightness of your dawn" (Isa. 60:3), but the optimism of the early Second Temple period soon faded. Already Isaiah 63 conjures up the image of a blood-stained divine warrior:

> I have trodden the wine press alone,
> and from the peoples no one was with me;
> I trod them in my anger
> and trampled them in wrath; their juice spattered on my garments
> and stained all my robes.
> For the day of vengeance was in my heart,
> and the year of my redeeming work had come. (vv. 3-4)[10]

More typical of the later prophetic books are passages such as Ezekiel 38–39, where "Gog from the land of Magog" is driven forward against the mountains of Israel, only to fall there and be left for the birds of prey and the wild animals to devour (Ezek. 39:4), or Zechariah 14, where the Lord gathers all the nations against Jerusalem for battle, and takes his stand against them on the Mount of Olives. The people will then be afflicted by a plague: "their flesh shall rot while they are still on their feet; their eyes shall rot in their sockets and their tongues shall rot in their mouths" (Zech. 14:12).

Many of these passages evoke the old myth of the assault of the nations on Mount Zion, familiar from Psalm 2. The psalm, which I would date to the Assyrian period, is monarchical rather than monotheistic.[11] Yahweh

---

9. There is no consensus on the date of Isaiah 11:1-9. For the range of opinion, see Hans Wildberger, *Isaiah 1–12* (Minneapolis: Fortress, 1991) 465-69; Joseph Blenkinsopp, *Isaiah 1–39* (AB 19; New York: Doubleday, 2000) 263-64.

10. See Paul D. Hanson, *The Dawn of Apocalyptic: The Historical and Sociological Roots of Jewish Apocalyptic Eschatology* (Philadelphia: Fortress, 1975) 203-8.

11. Adela Yarbro Collins and John J. Collins, *King and Messiah as Son of God: Divine,*

has set his king on Zion his holy mountain. As Yahweh is to the other gods, so is the king of Judah to the kings of the earth. This psalm was no doubt counter-factual in its original setting, and lent itself to an even more counter-factual interpretation in the Second Temple period, when there was no longer a king on Mount Zion.[12] The psalm is used in messianic prophecies, which envision a restoration of the house of David, although not as frequently as we might expect.[13] The description of the messiah in the *Psalms of Solomon* (mid-first century BCE) draws heavily on Psalm 2:

> in wisdom and righteousness to drive out sinners from the
>   inheritance;
> to smash the arrogance of sinners like a potter's jar;
> to shatter all their substance with an iron rod;
> to destroy the unlawful nations with the word of his mouth;
> At his warning the nations will flee from his presence. (*Pss. Sol.*
>   17:23-24; compare Ps. 2:8-9)

In the background of the whole passage is the motif of the assault of the nations on Jerusalem, as envisioned in Psalm 2. The use of the plural "nations" echoes the psalm, and their discomfiture and flight allude to a related formulation of the mythology of Zion in Psalm 48. Finally, the statement in *Psalms of Solomon* 7:32, "and their king shall be the Lord messiah," which

---

Human, and Angelic Messianic Figures in Biblical and Related Literature (Grand Rapids: Eerdmans, 2008) 10-15, and especially Eckart Otto, "Psalm 2 in neuassyrischer Zeit. Assyrische Motive in der judäischen Königsideologie," in Klaus Kiesow and Thomas Meurer, eds., *Textarbeit. Studien zu Texten und ihrer Rezeption aus dem Alten Testament und der Umwelt Israels. Festschrift für Peter Weimar* (AOAT 294; Münster: Ugarit-Verlag, 2003) 335-49.

12. Several German scholars date the psalm to the postexilic period, but it is highly unlikely that such an exalted view of the Davidic monarchy would have arisen when it no longer existed. See, e.g., Erhard S. Gerstenberger, *Psalms: Part One, with an Introduction to Cultic Poetry* (FOTL 14; Grand Rapids: Eerdmans, 1988) 48.

13. Annette Steudel, "Psalm 2 im antiken Judentum," in Dieter Sänger, ed., *Gottessohn und Menschensohn. Exegetische Paradigmen biblischer Intertextualität* (Neukirchen-Vluyn: Neukirchener Verlag, 2004) 189-97, acknowledges only three texts among the Pseudepigrapha that make use of the psalm: *Psalms of Solomon* 17, *Sibylline Oracles* 3:664-68, and *Testament of Levi* 4:2, but she overlooks important passages in *1 Enoch* 48:10 and *4 Ezra* 13. Psalm 2 is also cited in 4Q174, the *Florilegium*. The passage in *Sibylline Oracles* 3 speaks of an attack of the nations on Jerusalem and the temple but not of a messianic figure. See further my article "The Interpretation of Psalm 2," in Florentino García Martínez, ed., *Echoes from the Caves: Qumran and the New Testament* (STDJ 85; Leiden: Brill, 2009) 49-66.

should probably be emended to "the Lord's messiah,"[14] also echoes the reference to "the Lord and his anointed" in Psalm 2:2.

The role of the messianic king, however, is variable in Second Temple texts. For much of this period, messianic expectation is absent.[15] It reappears in the mid-first century BCE, in the *Psalms of Solomon* and in the Dead Sea Scrolls, in reaction both to the Hasmonean kingship, which was viewed as illegitimate, and to the Roman conquest. In the first century CE, it is given an apocalyptic twist.[16] *4 Ezra* 13 reports that "after seven days I had a dream in the night. I saw a wind rising from the sea that stirred up all its waves. As I kept looking, that wind brought up out of the depths of the sea something resembling a man and that man was flying with the clouds of heaven."

The image of the man flying with the clouds of heaven is a clear allusion to Daniel 7. But the figure is filled out with allusions to Psalm 2. A great host comes to make war on the man. He carves out a mountain for himself and takes his stand upon it. Then he destroys the onrushing multitude with the breath of his lips. The onslaught of the multitude recalls Psalm 2. The mountain is Zion, the holy mountain (Ps. 2:6). The breath of his lips is the weapon of the messianic king in Isaiah 11:4. Taken together, these allusions suggest that the man from the sea has taken on the role traditionally ascribed to the messianic king, although he is clearly a heavenly, transcendent figure.

The use of the traditional myth of the assault of the Gentiles on Mount Zion asserts the universal sovereignty of the God of Israel. The myth is agonistic, and antagonistic to the other nations. While it is a reactive myth, responding to the encroachments of the nations on Israel, the antagonism is not purely reactive. It projects the offences of some nations onto the nations in general. The Book of Joel complains of those who have sold the people of Judah and Jerusalem to the Greeks, but it summons *all* the nations for judgment to the valley of Jehoshaphat (Joel 3:1-3). The figure of Gog in Ezekiel 38–39 is probably based on Gyges of Lydia,[17] who had no contact whatsoever with Judah, but who is summoned to his fate on

---

14. See H. E. Ryle and M. R. James, *Psalms of the Pharisees: Commonly Called the Psalms of Solomon* (Cambridge: Cambridge University Press, 1891) 141-43. The phrase occurs again in *Psalms of Solomon* 18:7.

15. John J. Collins, *The Scepter and the Star: Messianism in Light of the Dead Sea Scrolls* (2nd ed.; Grand Rapids: Eerdmans, 2010) 21-51.

16. Collins, *The Scepter and the Star*, 205-14.

17. Walther Zimmerli, *Ezekiel 2* (Hermeneia; Philadelphia: Fortress, 1983) 301.

the mountains of Israel simply by virtue of being an eminent Gentile. The antagonism in these cases can reasonably be linked to monotheism, in the loose sense of belief in the supremacy of one God, which underlies these texts. This belief has ancient roots in the history of Israel, and, as Schwartz and Assmann have argued, it is closely bound up with the identity of the people of Israel. "Who is like thee among the gods?" asked the song of Moses in Exodus 15:11.

But not all eschatological fantasy is monotheistic even in this diluted sense. Arguably, the most distinctive development in the eschatology of Second Temple Judaism is the tendency toward dualism. Antagonism toward other people is all the greater when these people, too, have a representative in the supernatural realm. To be sure, dualism in the Israelite/Judean tradition is always qualified. Yahweh remains the supreme God. But the connection between the supreme God and violence cannot be understood without an appreciation of the adversarial role attributed to other supernatural forces.

The dualism of Second Temple eschatology is found especially in apocalyptic texts, and it takes two forms. One of these forms is rooted in the *Chaoskampf,* which plays a prominent role in the creation myths of the ancient Near East.[18] The other is a more measured dualism, found primarily in the Dead Sea Scrolls, and indebted unmistakably to Persian traditions.[19]

Combat Myths

Combat myths in the ancient Near East are associated especially with creation or cosmogony. The Akkadian *Enuma Elish* is a classic example. Even

---

18. The classic study of Hermann Gunkel, *Schöpfung und Chaos in Urzeit und Endzeit. Eine religionsgeschichtliche Untersuchung über Gen 1 und Ap Joh 12,* by Hermann Gunkel, with contributions by Heinrich Zimmern (Göttingen: Vandenhoeck & Ruprecht, 1895; ET *Creation and Chaos in the Primeval Period and in the Eschaton* [trans. William Whitney; Grand Rapids: Eerdmans, 2006]), was written before the discovery of the Ugaritic texts. On the latter see John Day, *God's Conflict with the Dragon and the Sea: Echoes of a Canaanite Myth in the Old Testament* (Cambridge: Cambridge University Press, 1985).

19. G. Widengren, M. Philonenko, and A. Hultgård, *Apocalyptique Iranienne et Dualisme Qoumrânien* (Paris: Maisonneuve, 1995); Albert de Jong, "Iranian Connections in the Dead Sea Scrolls," in T. H. Lim and J. J. Collins, eds., *The Oxford Handbook of the Dead Sea Scrolls* (Oxford: Oxford University Press, 2010) 479-500.

when they do not refer to the construction of the cosmos, as in the case of the Ugaritic Baal myth, they still describe the origin of cosmic order. These myths typically relate how the good god, Marduk or Baal, overcomes a chaos monster, Tiamat, Mot, or Yamm. There are several allusions to such a cosmogonic myth in the Hebrew Bible, although the story is never fully narrated. "By his power he stilled the Sea, by his understanding he struck down Rahab" (Job 26:12); "Was it not you who hacked Rahab in pieces? Who pierced the dragon? Was it not you who dried up the sea, the waters of the great deep?" (Isa. 51:9-10). But the victory is not once and for all, and chaos is not obliterated. The sea is confined by bars and doors (Job 38:8-11). Leviathan still sports in the deep (Job 41). As Jon Levenson has written:

> The survival of the tamed agent of chaos, whether imagined as the Sea, Leviathan, or whatever, points to an essential and generally overlooked tension in the underlying theology of these passages. On the one hand, YHWH's unique power to defeat and subjugate his adversary and to establish order is unquestioned. On the other hand, those passages that concede the survival of the defeated enemy raise obliquely the possibility that his defeat may yet be reversed.[20]

In the Second Temple period, on several occasions it did indeed appear as if YHWH's primordial victory was reversed, and the cosmogonic battle had to be fought all over again. As Gunkel famously observed more than a century ago, *Endzeit gleicht Urzeit*, "the things of the end time will be similar to those of the primal time."[21]

One illustration of the need to reconquer chaos can be found in the so-called "Apocalypse of Isaiah," in Isaiah 24–27.[22] These chapters certainly

---

20. Jon D. Levenson, *Creation and the Persistence of Evil: The Jewish Drama of Divine Omnipotence* (San Francisco: Harper, 1988) 18.

21. Gunkel, *Creation and Chaos*, 233, citing *Epistle of Barnabas* 6:13, "behold I make the last things like the first."

22. See W. R. Millar, *Isaiah 24–27 and the Origin of Apocalyptic* (Cambridge, MA: Harvard University Press, 1976); Dan G. Johnson, *From Chaos to Restoration: An Integrative Reading of Isaiah 24–27* (JSOTSup 61; Sheffield: JSOT, 1988); Donald C. Polaski, "Destruction, Construction, Argumentation: A Rhetorical Reading of Isaiah 24–27," in G. Carey and L. G. Bloomquist, eds., *Vision and Persuasion: Rhetorical Dimensions of Apocalyptic Discourse* (St. Louis: Chalice, 1999) 19-39; John J. Collins, "The Beginning of the End of the World," in John J. Ahn and Stephen L. Cook, eds., *Thus Says the Lord: Essays on the Former and Latter Prophets in Honor of Robert R. Wilson* (New York and London: T&T Clark, 2009) 137-55.

date to the Persian period, although we can only guess at the exact occasion of their composition. While Baal in the Ugaritic myth had swallowed death in primeval times, the Judean prophet looks forward to the day when YHWH will swallow Death forever (Isa. 25:8). Equally, although Leviathan and the Dragon had supposedly been killed in primeval times, we now read that "on that day the Lord with his cruel and great and strong sword will punish Leviathan the fleeing serpent, Leviathan the twisting serpent, and he will kill the dragon that is in the sea" (Isa. 27:1). The implication is that these forces of chaos are in the ascendancy in the present. This is not a world that is fully under the control of one supreme God. There are primordial forces that can be subjugated but not eradicated, and that burst forth into the world from time to time. To be sure, these forces are not ultimately on a par with the Most High, but they are not negligible, and they seriously qualify the supposed monotheism of the biblical texts.

An even more celebrated instance of the eruption of chaos is found in Daniel 7, where four great beasts arise from the turbulent sea.[23] In this case we know the occasion of composition, the suppression of the traditional cult in Jerusalem by Antiochus IV Epiphanes. The beasts, we are told, are four Gentile kingdoms, which can be identified in the context of Daniel as the Babylonians, the Medes, the Persians, and the Greeks. The fourth beast, the most terrible of all, has a little horn, symbolizing Antiochus IV Epiphanes, whose attempt to suppress the traditional cult in Jerusalem is the occasion of the vision. It would be a great mistake, however, to dismiss the mythological symbolism as "mere" metaphor, or to suppose that the angel's interpretation of the vision rendered the imagery dispensable. Rather, the vision expresses an understanding of the historical crisis as a struggle between supernatural powers. In Daniel 7, the crisis is resolved by a judgment rather than by a battle, but the motif of combat persists in the struggle between Michael and Gabriel, on the one hand, and the "princes" of Persia and Greece in Daniel 10–12. The condemnation of the fourth beast to be burned in fire in Daniel 7:11 is not less violent for the fact that it is the outcome of a judgment. The same mythological imagery of beast from the sea and chaos-dragon recur in the New Testament in the Book of Revelation, the text that inspired Gunkel's classic study of the role of chaos in creation.[24]

23. John J. Collins, *Daniel* (Hermeneia; Minneapolis: Fortress, 1993) 274-324; idem, "Stirring Up the Great Sea: The Religio-Historical Background of Daniel 7," in *Seers, Sibyls and Sages in Hellenistic-Roman Judaism* (JSJSup 54; Leiden: Brill, 1997) 139-55.

24. See Adela Yarbro Collins, *The Combat Myth in the Book of Revelation* (Missoula, MT: Scholars Press, 1976).

The motif of the *Chaoskampf* is well known and has often been studied. What has not received sufficient attention, I would suggest, is the degree to which it qualifies the supposed monotheism of the biblical tradition. The Priestly account in Genesis 1 was no doubt a reaction against this view of creation (Tiamat is reduced to inanimate *Tehom*), but it did not succeed in eliminating the vitality of chaos. Historical experience did not show creation to be good without qualification. Life is conflictual, and violence, on some level, remains necessary if good is to prevail.

The traditional combat myth embodies a qualified dualism, in the sense that the world is perceived as an arena where opposing powers are in conflict, even if they are not evenly matched. Such dualism was often accepted as an inherent part of creation in the ancient Near East. This kind of dualism is sometimes characterized as "complementary" or "dialectical" dualism, to distinguish it from eschatological dualism, which envisions a struggle in which the forces of evil will be eliminated.[25] In Second Temple Judaism, dualism is decidedly eschatological. It was often invoked to explain the deterioration of order on earth, and viewed as the prelude to a decisive eschatological battle.

Light and Darkness

A more systematic form of dualism is found in the Dead Sea Scrolls. According to the Discourse on the Two Spirits in the *Community Rule,* God created two spirits for people to walk in, spirits of truth and deceit, light and darkness. People are guided by a Prince of Light or an Angel of Darkness, and share in the opposing spirits to different degrees. God, we are told, has sorted them into equal parts until the last time (1QS 4:16-17). But then, "God, in the mysteries of his knowledge and in the wisdom of his glory, has determined an end to the existence of injustice and on the appointed time of the visitation he will obliterate it forever" (1QS 4:18-19).[26] The final obliteration of evil is the subject of the *War Scroll.* This remarkable document outlines a final war between the Sons of Light, under the leadership of the archangel Michael, and the Sons of Darkness, led by Belial.

25. See the discussion by P. Kyle McCarter, "Dualism in Antiquity," in Armin Lange, Eric M. Meyers, Bennie H. Reynolds, and Randall Styers, eds., *Light against Darkness* (Göttingen: Vandenhoeck & Ruprecht, 2011) 19-35.

26. Translations of the Dead Sea Scrolls are taken from F. García Martínez and E. J. C. Tigchelaar, *The Dead Sea Scrolls Study Edition* (Leiden: Brill, 1997).

> On this (day), the assembly of the gods and the congregation of men
> shall confront each other for great destruction. . . . In the war, the sons
> of light will be the strongest during three lots, in order to strike down
> wickedness; and in three (others) the army of Belial will gird them-
> selves in order to force the lot of [light] to retreat. (1QM 1:10, 13)

From later columns in the Scroll, it is apparent that each side prevails in
successive lots. But "in the seventh lot, God's great hand will subdue [Be-
lial and all] the angels of his dominion and all the men of [his lot]" (1QM
1:15). Here again, the supremacy of the God of Israel is confirmed, but Belial fights Michael to a stalemate, indicating a degree of parity between the
forces of good and evil that is without precedent in the biblical tradition.

There can be little doubt that the dualism of the two spirits is indebted to Zoroastrianism, even though we cannot trace the channels
through which it was transmitted.[27] In the *Gathas,* which are often ascribed
to Zoroaster himself, the two spirits are the twin children of Ahura Mazda,
the wise Lord.[28] Later the good spirit is identified with Ahura Mazda, and
the evil one is thought to be primordial. These spirits were associated with
light and darkness from an early time. According to Plutarch, who cites
Theopompus (c. 300 BCE) as his source,

> Horomazes is born from the purest light and Areimanius from dark-
> ness, and they are at war with one another. . . . Theopompus says that,
> according to the Magians, for three thousand years alternately the one
> god will dominate the other and be dominated, and that for another
> three thousand years they will fight and make war, until one smashes
> up the domain of the other.[29]

Plutarch's account is problematic in various ways, and it does not correspond in detail to the accounts of Zoroastrian thought preserved in the
much later Pahlavi literature.[30] But the similarity to what we find in the
Scrolls is striking: supernatural forces of light and darkness are engaged in

27. See further de Jong, "Iranian Connections."

28. R. C. Zaehner, *The Dawn and Twilight of Zoroastrianism* (London: Weidenfeld
& Nicholson, 1961) 50-51.

29. Plutarch, *On Isis and Osiris* 47. Trans. J. Gwyn Griffiths, *Plutarch's De Iside et
Osiride* (Cardiff: University of Wales Press, 1970) 46-47.

30. See Albert de Jong, *Traditions of the Magi: Zoroastrianism in Greek and Latin
Literature* (Leiden: Brill, 1997) 200-201.

a struggle in which each prevails in turn, until the forces of light eventually prevail.[31]

Our present concern, however, is not so much with the provenance of this dualistic thought system as with its implications for the supposed monotheism of Judaism in the Second Temple period. We do not know how widely such a dualistic account of the world was accepted. Both the *Community Rule* and the *War Scroll* were found in Qumran Cave 1, and were among the first scrolls published. Initially, the dualism of light and darkness was thought to be the very heart of sectarian thought.[32] When the full corpus came to light, however, it became apparent that this dualism was rather sparsely represented. The Discourse on the Two Spirits is not found in all copies of the *Community Rule,* and seems to have originated as a distinct composition. Some scholars believe it was a pre-sectarian text, although that position seems rather counterintuitive.[33] The dualism of the Discourse did, in any case, influence other parts of the *Community Rule,* and is also echoed in the *Damascus Document,* even though it plays a minor role there.[34]

It is easy enough to see why such a dualistic system would have been attractive to a separatist sect, such as the one described in the Scrolls. It provided an explanation for the rejection of the sect's teachings by other Judeans, despite what seemed to the sectarians to be their manifest truth. But the appeal of such a binary view of the world was limited. Even within the sectarian writings it does not serve very often as the frame of reference. It does, however, shape the conception of the final war, and provides ready justification for hating the forces of darkness, especially the Kittim, or Romans, and promises their final annihilation.

The thrust of my comments so far is that it is somewhat misleading to attribute the fantasies of eschatological violence in Second Temple Judaism to the influence of monotheism. To be sure, they all affirm the ultimate

31. See further John J. Collins, *Apocalypticism in the Dead Sea Scrolls* (London: Routledge, 1997) 102-3.

32. So, e.g., Devorah Dimant, "Qumran Sectarian Literature," in M. E. Stone, ed., *Jewish Writings of the Second Temple Period* (Compendia Rerum Iudaicarum ad Novum Testamentum 2.2; Philadelphia: Fortress, 1984) 483-550, especially 532-33.

33. E.g., Armin Lange, *Weisheit und Prädestination. Weisheitliche Urordnung und Prädestination in den Textfunden von Qumran* (Leiden: Brill, 1995) 126-32.

34. Lange, *Weisheit und Prädestination,* 165-70; Charlotte Hempel, "The Treatise on the Two Spirits and the Literary History of the Rule of the Community," in Géza G. Xeravits, ed., *Dualism in Qumran* (London and New York: T&T Clark, 2010) 102-20.

triumph of one God. But some of the most violent fantasies incline strongly to dualism. The need for divine intervention, and even for divine violence, is all the greater when the forces of darkness are thought to be supported by supernatural forces of their own.

Fantasy and Violence

But are these texts, which imagine divine violence at the end of history, conducive to actual violence by human agents? There have been scattered examples through history of people, such as Thomas Müntzer and John of Leiden in the sixteenth century, who resorted to violence in pursuit of the millennium. In the Second Temple period, the *Animal Apocalypse* in *1 Enoch* is generally thought to be supportive of the Maccabees, but even that is disputed.[35] But these are exceptional. The violence of the Maccabees cannot be attributed to the "wise teachers" of Daniel, who regarded it as at most "a little help" (Dan. 11:34), and more probably regarded it as counter-productive. One may argue, in fact, that Daniel's apocalyptic vision was presented as an alternative to the Maccabees, a way to remain faithful in a time of persecution without the compromise and bloodshed that armed revolt inevitably entailed. Since the wise *maskilim* in Daniel hoped to be elevated to the stars after death, they could afford to lose their lives in this world.[36] The logic of apocalyptic quietism is spelled out in the *Testament* (or *Assumption*) *of Moses,* a text close in time to the Book of Daniel, where a man named Taxo takes his sons into a cave in the field to purify themselves and die, in confidence that "the Lord will avenge the blood of his servants," as promised in Deuteronomy 32:43.[37] Then God's kingdom would appear before all creation, and Israel would be exalted to the stars. Equally, the people of the Dead Sea Scrolls vowed to avoid conflict with "the men of the Pit" until the day of wrath, although they made provision for that day in a detailed Rule for the eschatological war, for "to God belongs the judgment" (1QS 10:18). " 'Vengeance is mine,' saith the Lord" (Deut. 32:35). It is precisely the belief that the Lord will exact

35. For the dissenting view, see Daniel Assefa, *L'Apocalypse des animaux* (*1 Hen 85–90*). *Une propagande militaire* (JSJSup 120; Leiden: Brill, 2007) 207-21.

36. John J. Collins, "Apocalyptic Eschatology as the Transcendence of Death," in idem, *Seers, Sibyls and Sages,* 75-97.

37. Jacob Licht, "Taxo, or the Apocalyptic Doctrine of Divine Vengeance," *JJS* 12 (1961) 95-103.

vengeance with ultimate ferocity that enables such groups to refrain from violent action in the present. As the late Krister Stendahl put it: "With the Day of Vengeance at hand, the proper and reasonable attitude is to forego one's own vengeance and to leave vengeance to God. Why walk around with a little shotgun if the atomic blast is imminent?"[38] Similarly, the Book of Revelation undeniably indulges in extremely violent fantasies and has been accused of "brutality, misogyny and vengeance," in the words of David Frankfurter.[39] Yet it is explicitly a call for nonviolent endurance: "if you are to be taken captive, into captivity you go; if you kill with the sword, with the sword you must be killed" (Rev. 13:10).[40] In this case, too, it is precisely the hope for violent divine vengeance, vividly imagined as the overthrow of the whore of Babylon and as a grizzly feast for the birds of heaven, that undergirds the appeal for nonviolent endurance in the present.

Apocalyptic literature is often assumed to be revolutionary, but one could very well argue that it is counter-revolutionary in many cases. By enabling people to let off steam by fantasizing divine vengeance, it relieves the pressure toward action in the present and enables people to accommodate themselves to the status quo for the present.

Nonetheless, the suspicion remains that violent fantasies are conducive to violent action. Mark Juergensmeyer, in his study of religion and terrorism in the contemporary world, argues that many activists who have turned to terror are driven by an image of cosmic war: "What makes religious violence particularly savage and relentless is that its perpetrators have placed such religious images of divine struggle — cosmic war — in the service of worldly political battles. For this reason, acts of religious terror serve not only as tactics in a political strategy but also as evocations of a much larger spiritual confrontation."[41] The argument here is that even if an apocalyptic writing does not explicitly preach violence, it nonetheless

---

38. Krister Stendahl, "Hate, Non-Retaliation, and Love: 1QS X, 17–20 and Rom 12:19–21," *Harvard Theological Review* 55 (1962) 343-55 (citation from 344-45).

39. David Frankfurter, "The Legacy of Sectarian Rage: Vengeance Fantasies in the New Testament," in David A. Bernat and Jonathan Klawans, eds., *Religion and Violence: The Biblical Heritage* (Sheffield: Sheffield Phoenix, 2007) 114-28.

40. Adela Yarbro Collins, "Persecution and Vengeance in the Book of Revelation," in David Hellholm, ed., *Apocalypticism in the Mediterranean World and the Near East* (Tübingen: Mohr, 1983) 729-49.

41. Mark Juergensmeyer, *Terror in the Mind of God: The Global Rise of Religious Violence* (Berkeley: University of California Press, 2003) 148-49.

foments an attitude of violent antagonism. As Scott Appleby has written about modern apocalypticism: "Fundamentalists, who seek to create an alternative social and political order 'for the long run' are in the impossible situation of wanting to constrain apocalyptic violence after they have set loose its agents and unleashed its dynamics!"[42]

It is a matter of debate whether apocalyptic hopes were a factor in the Jewish revolt against Rome in the late first century BCE. Josephus assigns a measure of responsibility to a series of figures whom we might describe as apocalyptic prophets. After describing the activities of the *sicarii,* or daggermen, he goes on:

> Besides these there arose another body of villains, with purer hands but more impious intentions, who no less than the assassins ruined the peace of the city. Deceivers and impostors, under the pretence of divine inspiration fostering revolutionary changes, they persuaded the multitude to act like madmen, and led them out into the desert under the belief that God would give them tokens of deliverance. Against them, Felix, regarding them as but the preliminary insurrection, sent a body of cavalry and heavy-armed infantry, and put a large number to the sword. (*Jewish War* 2.259-60)

There was a succession of such sign prophets in the first century CE.[43] Josephus admits that the movements they led were not violent, but were inspired by the hope of miraculous divine intervention. But he blames them nonetheless for disturbing the peace of the city and creating an atmosphere congenial to rebellion. He also claims that the rebels were inspired by an "ambiguous oracle, which was found in the sacred texts" (*Jewish War* 6.312-15) more than by any other one thing. We do not know which oracle that was. Possibilities include Daniel 7 (the "one like a son of man") or Balaam's prophecy of the scepter and the star in Numbers 24:17. Josephus gives an unsympathetic account of the revolt, but he must be credited with insight into the workings of prophecy, ambiguous or otherwise. If people are told to expect a heavenly deliverer on a white horse who will annihilate their

---

42. Scott Appleby, "The Unholy Uses of Apocalyptic Imagination: Twentieth Century Patterns," in Abbas Amanat and John J. Collins, eds., *Apocalypse and Violence* (New Haven: Yale Center for International and Area Studies and the Council on Middle East Studies, 2007) 69-87 (citation from 77).

43. Richard A. Horsley and John S. Hanson, *Bandits, Prophets and Messiahs* (Minneapolis: Winston, 1985); Collins, *The Scepter and the Star,* 216-19.

enemies, it may be difficult for them to restrain themselves from giving him a helping hand.

I do not mean to imply that violence is always necessarily bad. It can be justified as a means of attaining justice, and there were certainly legitimate grievances that led to the Jewish revolt against Rome. But the outcome of that revolt is a sobering reminder of the perils of violence.

What Do These Fantasies Achieve?

Apocalyptic fantasies, in any case, contribute only indirectly to revolution and provide alternatives to violent action more often than not. What, then, can this kind of literature be said to accomplish?

It seems to me that this question may be answered in two ways that go some way toward explaining the enduring popularity of the genre. On the one hand, it enables people to dissent from a culture that they find oppressive or otherwise unacceptable, when they lack the practical means to change it. The people of Judea could not bring about the destruction of Babylon or Rome, but they could imagine it, and the fantasy afforded some satisfaction. In theological terms, it also relieved the dissonance between the supremacy of their God and the subordination of his people. The violence of the destruction is an expression of power on the part of the powerless, and serves to clear a way for a new beginning. All this literature expresses resistance to the present order, which is deemed unsatisfactory and worthy of destruction. The potential for resistance is increased in the apocalyptic literature, which imagines an alternative universe more fully than do the late prophetic texts, and hold forth the prospect of life in another world after death. This kind of resistance does not necessarily lead to violent revolution, but it shapes minds and preserves values, and its long-term effectiveness should not be underestimated. While the violent and vengeful imagery may be distasteful to modern Christians, we should be mindful of Elisabeth Schüssler Fiorenza's caution that those who are critical of apocalyptic violence "do not suffer unbearable oppression and are not driven by the quest for justice."[44] "Unbearable oppression," admittedly, may be in the eye of the oppressed, but it is deemed unbearable by those who indulge in apocalyptic fantasies.

---

44. Elisabeth Schüssler Fiorenza, *Invitation to the Book of Revelation* (New York: Doubleday, 1981) 84-85.

On the other hand, imagining an alternative universe can be therapeutic in times of crisis.[45] Wolfgang Schivelbusch has written of a "culture of defeat" that affects the victims of military conquest: "Defeat follows war as ashes follow fire. At the heart of both . . . lies the threat of extinction, a threat that resonates long past the cessation of hostilities."[46] He continues: "Every society experiences defeat in its own way. But the varieties of response within vanquished nations — whether psychological, cultural or political — conform to a recognizable set of patterns or archetypes that recur across time and national boundaries. A state of unreality — or dreamland — is invariably the first of these."[47] This is especially relevant to literature composed after the first destruction of Jerusalem by the Babylonians and after the second destruction by the Romans. Scott Appleby, who is much less sympathetic to apocalypticism than Schüssler Fiorenza, grants that "apocalyptic or millenarian fervor takes on a decidedly therapeutic role in the lives and imagination of the 'modern antimodernists.' The anticipated reversal of 'ordinary history' is a source of great comfort for millions of true believers living in conditions of squalor, relative deprivation, or moral decadence."[48] Again, the therapeutic effect is not negated by the fact that the deprivation may be relative, and not necessarily objectively factual.

Eschatological visions are a way of maintaining hope in desperate situations. The violence of destruction is never an end in itself. There is always a new beginning to follow, whether in this world or in the next. The visionary, and his sympathetic readers, can experience an "apocalyptic cure" from the traumas of the present by taking refuge in fantasies of a future where things turn out quite differently from historical experience. To be sure, this may not be the ideal solution to social and economic crises. It might be better to find more practical ways of addressing material and social problems. But apocalypses are written for times when humankind cannot bear very much reality, in the phrase of T. S. Eliot.[49] Even a hope that many might regard as illusory may be better than having no hope at all.

---

45. See especially Dereck Daschke, *City of Ruins: Mourning the Destruction of Jerusalem through Jewish Apocalypse* (Leiden: Brill, 2010), especially his discussion of "the apocalyptic cure," pp. 187-97.

46. Wolfgang Schivelbusch, *The Culture of Defeat: On National Trauma, Mourning and Recovery* (New York: Metropolitan, 2001) 5; Daschke, *City of Ruins*, 16.

47. Schivelbusch, *The Culture of Defeat*, 10.

48. Appleby, "The Unholy Uses," 75.

49. T. S. Eliot, *Four Quartets*, in the first quartet.

Conclusion

Whatever the merits of an apocalyptic solution to historical crises, these fantasies of judgment, violent though they often are, lend little substance to the charge that monotheism is conducive to violence. On the one hand, many of these fantasies are more dualistic than monotheistic, even though they inevitably affirm the ultimate triumph of one supreme God. On the other hand, they often function as a means of avoiding violence rather than of fomenting it. This is not to deny that they may be conducive to violence on occasion, in fostering an attitude of antagonism. Vengeance, even on the level of fantasy, is not the noblest of human desires. Apocalyptic visions cannot be said to provide an ethic for all seasons. Nonetheless, they have proven remarkably durable in western history, and they should not be too readily dismissed as mere fanaticism. They can serve a therapeutic function in times of distress and alienation, and they provide a means of maintaining resistance to oppressive structures that they lack the ability to change.

CHAPTER 19

Radical Religion and the Ethical Dilemmas of Apocalyptic Millenarianism

Radical religion is often associated with apocalypticism, more specifically with apocalyptic millenarianism — the anticipation of "an imminent and radical overturning of the existing social order, with history reaching its penultimate conclusion."[1] Such "radical" religion has a long and illustrious history in the Christian west, as Christopher Rowland has especially shown.[2] In contemporary society, however, it has acquired a negative reputation. On the one hand, it is often associated with militant fringe groups, Christian, Jewish, or Muslim, and often thought to carry an implicit threat of terrorism. On the other hand, apocalyptic millenarianism is exemplified by the writings of Hal Lindsey[3] and the *Left Behind* series,[4] which combine a simplistic dualism of the saved and the damned with a right-wing political ideology.[5] While this strand of apocalypticism does not directly incite violent action, it is widely perceived as promoting polarization and intolerance.

All this is something of an embarrassment for Christianity. Ernst

---

1. Michael Barkun, "Foreword," in Jeffrey Kaplan, *Radical Religion in America: Millenarian Movements from the Far Right to the Children of Noah* (Syracuse: Syracuse University Press, 1997) vii.

2. Christopher C. Rowland, *Radical Christianity: A Reading of Recovery* (Maryknoll, NY: Orbis, 1988); Andrew Bradstock and Christopher Rowland, *Radical Christian Writings: A Reader* (Oxford: Blackwell, 2002).

3. Hal Lindsey, with C. C. Carlson, *The Late Great Planet Earth* (Grand Rapids: Zondervan, 1970).

4. Tim LaHaye and Jerry Jenkins, *Left Behind: A Novel of Earth's Last Days* (Wheaton, IL: Tyndale House, 1995).

5. Amy Johnson Frykholm, *Rapture Culture: Left Behind in Evangelical America* (Oxford: Oxford University Press, 2004).

Käsemann's famous dictum that "apocalyptic is the mother of Christian theology"[6] may not have had Hal Lindsey in mind, but some of the same texts that nourished early Christianity provide language and a conceptual framework for apocalyptic millenarians in the modern world. It is not surprising, then, that revulsion with modern millenarianism should lead to renewed critical scrutiny of its ancient sources. So, in a recent essay, David Frankfurter looks "to identify *sources* for violence and combative self-definition in texts that have been — conveniently or inconveniently — determinative of Christian identity for two thousand years."[7] He finds one such source in the Book of Revelation. He dismisses arguments that the violence in Revelation was "directed either to spark revolutionary justice for the subaltern or to rail against a tyrannical Roman empire — reading the text in either case as advocating justice, equality, and hope rather than brutality, misogyny and vengeance" as attempts to "rationalize" it, and as "canonical special pleading for a very problematic text."[8] Such a sweeping condemnation is not without basis: brutality, misogyny, and vengeance can be found in the Book of Revelation, but Revelation is also a vision of hope and a protest against tyranny. Like any classic text, Revelation lends itself to more than one kind of interpretation.

My purpose in this chapter is not an apologetic one. Apocalyptic literature is indeed problematic and has been recognized as such throughout the history of Christianity.[9] My purpose is, rather, to dwell on the ambiguities of the genre and to warn against some of the pitfalls of oversimplified interpretation.

Reductionist Interpretation

At the outset, we should be clear that the kind of interpretation of apocalyptic literature associated with dispensationalism and its latter-day

---

6. Ernst Käsemann, "The Beginnings of Christian Theology," *Journal for Theology and the Church* 6 (1969) 17-46.

7. David Frankfurter, "The Legacy of Sectarian Rage: Vengeance Fantasies in the New Testament," in David A. Bernat and Jonathan Klawans, eds., *Religion and Violence: The Biblical Heritage* (Sheffield: Sheffield Phoenix, 2007) 114-28.

8. Frankfurter, "The Legacy of Sectarian Rage," 121.

9. Adela Yarbro Collins, *Crisis and Catharsis: The Power of the Apocalypse* (Philadelphia: Westminster, 1984); John J. Collins, "Apocalyptic Literature," in Leo Perdue, ed., *The Blackwell Companion to the Hebrew Bible* (Oxford: Blackwell, 2001) 432-47.

mutations is highly reductionistic. It is not so much an interpretation of apocalyptic literature as a synthetic and harmonized reading of all biblical prophecy from an apocalyptic perspective. Hal Lindsey finds predictions of war in the Middle East, even specifically nuclear war, in Revelation. The European Union takes the place of ancient Rome (Lindsey originally cast the Soviet Union in this role), the rise of the state of Israel is taken as a sign that history is moving to its climax, and so on. This kind of decoding interpretation, which "involves presenting the meaning of the text in another, less allusive form, showing what the text *really* means, with great attention to the details,"[10] has a long history, dating back to the *pesharim* in the Dead Sea Scrolls. It has proven impervious to falsification over the centuries. On the contrary, it is a boon for publishers, as the predictions are always in need of updating. The phenomenon of updating can be found already in the Book of Daniel, where the number of days from the desecration of the temple to the "end" is recalculated at the end of the book, presumably because the first number predicted had passed.[11]

The inadequacy of this kind of interpretation, even apart from repeated falsification, should be obvious. The apocalypses, certainly the canonical apocalypses of Daniel and Revelation, are rich in symbolism, often drawn from ancient myths. Indeed, it is the symbolic character of the language that lends the revelations their multivalent character and facilitates their constant reapplication to various historical scenarios. The lure of simple, one-to-one decoding is ancient and deep-rooted, but it strips the text of the aura of mystery that gives it both literary and religious power. It should be noted that this kind of reductive view of apocalyptic symbolism is not confined to fundamentalists and dispensationalists. The distinguished New Testament scholar Norman Perrin, in a presidential address to the Society of Biblical Literature, argued that "apocalyptic" entails

> a view of myth as allegory and . . . the treatment of symbols as steno-symbols. Typically the apocalyptic seer told the story of the history of his people in symbols where each symbol bore a one-to-one relationship to that which it depicted. This thing was Antiochus Epiphanes, that thing was Judas Maccabeus, the other thing was the coming

10. Judith Kovacs and Christopher Rowland, *Revelation* (Blackwell Bible Commentaries; Oxford: Blackwell, 2004) 8.

11. John J. Collins, *Daniel: A Commentary on the Book of Daniel* (Hermeneia; Minneapolis: Fortress, 1993) 400-401.

of the Romans, and so on. . . . Once the symbols have been correctly identified, the allegory itself can be abandoned and the story retold in steno-language.[12]

But this is to miss completely the allusive power of the mythic symbolism. Daniel 7 may decode the symbolism of the beasts from the sea by saying, "as for these four great beasts, four kings shall arise out of the earth," but the meaning of Daniel's dream vision is not thereby exhausted or rendered dispensable.[13]

Decoding the text in terms of historical and political events is also reductive in another way. It focuses inordinately on one episode in the drama of the end-time: the time of woes and tribulations that precedes the end, the period of the "end of days" as we find it in the Dead Sea Scrolls. This period is certainly important in one type of apocalypses, the so-called "historical apocalypses" (as opposed to the sub-genre of otherworldly ascents, which most often do not engage in such historical reviews). In Daniel, the chief description is found in chapter 11, which lends itself easily to decoding down to the death of the wicked king, Antiochus Epiphanes. But this is only one phase in the drama. Modern adaptions of the end-time drama find more fertile material in Ezekiel 38–39 (Gog), which is admittedly taken up in Revelation 20. In the apocalypses this period is framed vertically by the agency of angelic and demonic forces and horizontally by the imminent judgment.[14] Modern millenarianism also affirms supernatural agency, even to ludicrous degrees in the *Left Behind* series, and it certainly assumes a judgment with reward and punishment after death. "How many times," asks Hal Lindsey, "have we wondered what heaven will be like? . . . [H]eaven is a real and breath-taking place."[15] But much more attention is given to the coming violent judgment and the upheavals that precede it. No doubt all this is reassuring to those who are confident

---

12. Norman Perrin, "Eschatology and Hermeneutics: Reflections on Method in the Interpretation of the New Testament," *JBL* 93 (1974) 11.

13. John J. Collins, *The Apocalyptic Vision of the Book of Daniel* (HSM 16; Missoula, MT: Scholars Press, 1977) 110-15.

14. John J. Collins, "Genre, Ideology and Social Movements in Jewish Apocalypticism," in John J. Collins and James H. Charlesworth, eds., *Mysteries and Revelations: Apocalyptic Studies since the Uppsala Colloquium* (JSPSup 9; Sheffield: Sheffield Academic Press, 1991) 11-32; and in the same volume, George W. Nickelsburg, "The Apocalyptic Construction of Reality in *1 Enoch*," 51-64.

15. Lindsey, *The Late Great Planet Earth*, 167.

of their own salvation, but it also involves a goodly element of scare tactics: "Imagine, cities like London, Paris, Tokyo, New York, Los Angeles, Chicago — obliterated!"[16]

Fantasies of Vengeance

The accounts of the turmoils of the last days in the ancient apocalypses were indebted to Jewish biblical prophecy in the Second Temple period. Typical examples are provided by Ezekiel 38–39 and Joel 3. In the latter passage, the Lord says,

> when I restore the fortunes of Judah and Jerusalem, I will gather all the nations and bring them down to the valley of Jehoshaphat, and I will enter into judgment with them there, on account of my people and my heritage Israel. (Joel 3:1-2a)

There are specific grievances that warrant the judgment: "they have divided my land, and cast lots for my people, and traded boys for prostitutes, and sold girls for wine, and drunk it down" (Joel 3:2b-3). Now, in retribution, "I will turn your deeds back upon your own heads. I will sell your sons and your daughters into the hand of the people of Judah, and they will sell them to the Sabeans, to a nation far away" (Joel 3:7b-8). There is no doubt that the people of Judah suffered many injustices at the hands of foreign peoples in the period after the Babylonian exile. The desire for vengeance is entirely understandable. It goes beyond the retribution of an "eye for an eye":

> Put in the sickle
>   for the harvest is ripe;
> go in, tread,
>   for the wine press is full.
> The vats overflow,
>   for their wickedness is great. (Joel 3:13)

Moreover, the Gentiles are condemned indiscriminately, regardless of whether they had any dealings with Judah. Similarly in Ezekiel 38–39, the

16. Lindsey, *The Late Great Planet Earth*, 155.

name Gog brings to mind Gyges of Lydia, a famous Gentile king who had no dealings whatsoever with Judah.[17] So, while the desire for vengeance in these texts is understandable, it seems more than a little paranoid. The world is against us, and the whole world must pay. This attitude is also typical of modern millenarian movements, whose grievances are often more difficult to document.

Judgments of the vengefulness of post-exilic prophecy must be mitigated by the powerlessness of the people of Judah in this period. In the same way, statements in *4 Ezra* that the nations are like spittle (2 Esdras 6:56) are less offensive than they might otherwise be because of the historical circumstances in the wake of the destruction of Jerusalem.[18] This is not to say that the desire for vengeance is admirable, but to recognize that love of one's enemies is an ideal that is not always within human capabilities.

The situation with Revelation is essentially similar. D. H. Lawrence famously saw the vision of the whore of Babylon in Revelation 17–18 as an expression of the envy and resentment of the weak against the strong:

> How the late apocalyptists love mouthing out all about the silver and cinnamon of evil Babylon! How they *want* them all! How they *envy* Babylon her splendour, envy, envy! How they love destroying it all! The harlot sits magnificent with her golden cup of wine of sensual pleasure in her hand. How the apocalyptists would have loved to drink out of her cup! And since they couldn't: how they loved smashing it.[19]

But Lawrence was a scion of the British empire, with little sympathy for conquered peoples. As Schüssler Fiorenza has argued, the author of Revelation was "clearly on the side of the poor and oppressed."[20] She charges that those who are critical of the violence in the Apocalypse "do not suffer unbearable oppression and are not driven by the quest for justice."[21] Even

17. Walther Zimmerli, *Ezekiel 2: A Commentary on the Book of the Prophet Ezekiel chapters 25–48* (Hermeneia; Philadelphia: Fortress, 1983) 301.

18. John J. Collins, "The Idea of Election in 4 Ezra," *Jewish Studies Quarterly* 16 (2009) 83-96.

19. D. H. Lawrence, *Apocalypse* (New York: Viking, 1932; repr. London/New York: Penguin, 1974) 87-88.

20. Elisabeth Schüssler Fiorenza, *Invitation to the Book of Revelation* (New York: Doubleday, 1981) 173; eadem, *The Book of Revelation: Justice and Judgment* (Philadelphia: Fortress, 1985).

21. Schüssler Fiorenza, *Invitation*, 84-85.

a critic like Scott Appleby, who is much less sympathetic toward apocalypticism than Schüssler Fiorenza, grants that

> apocalyptic or millenarian fervor takes on a decidedly therapeutic role in the lives and imagination of the "modern anti-modernists." The anticipated reversal of "ordinary history" is a source of great comfort for millions of true believers living in conditions of squalor, relative deprivation, or moral decadence. The fundamentalists' present suffering is but a prelude to a profoundly satisfying reward for their perseverance, whether they live in the putrid refugee camps of Gaza or southern Lebanon, or amid the relative affluence of the spiritually sterile suburbs of Dallas.[22]

In many cases, apocalyptic visions that affirm a radical reversal of the present order give hope to people who otherwise would have no hope at all. If these visions are violent, they are at least honest in bringing to expression feelings that are almost inevitable for people who have suffered at the hands of a conquering power. Anger and fantasies of violence may be life-giving for the powerless, and even actual violence may be justified if it serves to relieve oppression.

To be sure, we have learned much since the time of Lawrence about the ambivalence of colonialism, from the viewpoint of both the colonizer and the colonized.[23] The apocalypses are not immune to *mimicry*, to taking the dominating power and wealth of the empire as an ideal to be dreamed of. But the oppression of which they complain was all too real. The late John A. T. Robinson argued that Revelation must have been written out of "an intense experience of Christian suffering at the hands of the imperial authorities," or else it was "the product of a perfervid and psychotic imagination."[24] There does not seem to have been intense persecution in the reign of Domitian, which remains the most likely date for the composition of the book.[25] But

---

22. Scott Appleby, "The Unholy Uses of Apocalyptic Imagination: Twentieth Century Patterns," in Abbas Amanat and John J. Collins, eds., *Apocalypse and Violence* (New Haven: The Yale Center for International and Area Studies and The Council on Middle East Studies, 2002) 69-87.

23. Homi K. Bhabha, *The Location of Culture* (London: Routledge, 1994); Stephen D. Moore, *Empire and Apocalypse: Postcolonialism and the New Testament* (Sheffield: Sheffield Phoenix, 2006).

24. John A. T. Robinson, *Redating the New Testament* (Philadelphia: Westminster, 1976) 230-31.

25. Yarbro Collins, *Crisis and Catharsis*, 54-83; Leonard L. Thompson, *The Book of*

the issue here is not whether there was active persecution of the followers of Jesus in the cities of Asia Minor when Revelation was written. The major trauma that overshadows the book is the destruction of Jerusalem, an event that reverberates in Jewish apocalyptic writings from the end of the first century CE: *4 Ezra, 2 Baruch, 3 Baruch, Sibylline Oracles 5*.[26] Rome had destroyed the sacred center of the Jewish universe and made itself as God in the eastern Mediterranean world. As with many modern millenarians, the basic complaint is about humiliation and loss of respect. Some apocalypses, such as Daniel, seem to have been written in time of persecution, but even there the crucial event was the desecration of the temple and the installation of the "abomination of desolation." Both the Seleucids and Rome were brutal and rapacious in dealing with resistance. One need only recall the indictment of Rome attributed to the Briton Calgacus by the Roman historian Tacitus: "These plunderers of the world . . . To ravage, to slaughter, to usurp under false titles, they call empire; and when they make a desert, they call it peace."[27] Yet the events that provoked the bulk of apocalyptic writings were the disruptions of the cult and the violations of the temple, first by the Seleucids and then definitively by the Romans. The break-up of the symbolic universe structured around the temple was more devastating and called forth a stronger response than any economic or material oppression.[28] The call for vengeance on Babylon is a direct response to the destruction of Jerusalem.

Violence and Catharsis

Even Frankfurter admits that "we have not a whit of evidence for actual physical violence in the immediate milieux of these texts."[29] The violence

---

Revelation: Apocalypse and Empire (Oxford and New York: Oxford University Press, 1990) 95-115; David Aune, *Revelation*, vol. 1 (Word Biblical Commentary 52A; Dallas: Word, 1997) lvi-lxx; pace John W. Marshall, *Parables of War: Reading John's Apocalypse* (Waterloo, ON: Wilfrid Laurier, 2001) 88-97.

26. Derek Daschke, *City of Ruins: Mourning the Destruction of Jerusalem through Jewish Apocalypse* (Leiden: Brill, 2010).

27. Tacitus, *Agricola* 30. On Seleucid state terror, see Anathea Portier-Young, *Apocalypse against Empire* (Grand Rapids: Eerdmans, 2010) 140-75.

28. Pace Richard A. Horsley, *Scribes, Visionaries and the Politics of Second Temple Judea* (Louisville: Westminster John Knox, 2007); idem, *Revolt of the Scribes: Resistance and Apocalyptic Origins* (Minneapolis: Fortress, 2010). See further John J. Collins, "Apocalypse and Empire," *Svensk Exegetisk Årsbok* 76 (2011) 1-19.

29. Frankfurter, "The Legacy of Sectarian Rage," 125.

of the Maccabees cannot be attributed to the "wise teachers" of Daniel, who regarded it as at most "a little help" (Dan. 11:34), and more probably regarded it as counter-productive. Revelation is explicitly a call for endurance: "if you are to be taken captive, into captivity you go; if you kill with the sword, with the sword you must be killed."[30] One of the main things that distinguishes Revelation from the Jewish apocalypses is the example of the death of Jesus and the insistence that it is by "the blood of the Lamb" that Satan is defeated.[31] This quietistic tone is typical of apocalypses, with only rare exceptions (e.g., the *Animal Apocalypse* of *1 Enoch*). There have been scattered examples throughout history of people such as Thomas Müntzer and John of Leiden in the sixteenth century who resorted to violence in pursuit of the millennium,[32] but they have been exceptional. Even modern millenarianists are often resigned to wait. Jeffrey Kaplan writes about the Christian Identity movement in the twentieth-century United States: "Quite simply, as with other historical cases of millenarianism, Identity Christians resist the call to violence for the simple reason that, given the imminent coming of Jesus, what could a premature confrontation with secular authorities accomplish?"[33] The same logic is found already in the ancient Jewish *Testament* (or *Assumption*) *of Moses*, where a man named Taxo takes his sons into a cave in the field to purify themselves and die, in confidence that "the Lord will avenge the blood of his servants," as promised in Deuteronomy 32:43. Equally, the people of the Dead Sea Scrolls vowed to avoid conflict with "the men of the Pit" until the day of wrath, although they made provision for that day in a detailed Rule for the eschatological war, for "to God belongs the judgement" (1QS 10:18). "Vengeance is mine," says the Lord (Deut. 32:35; cf. Rom. 12:19). It is precisely the belief that the Lord will exact vengeance with ultimate ferocity that enables such groups to refrain from violent action in the present.

The psychology of violent fantasies in apocalyptic literature has been helpfully described as a kind of *catharsis*, analogous to the purgation of

---

30. Revelation 13:10; Adela Yarbro Collins, "The Political Perspective of the Revelation to John," in eadem, *Cosmology and Eschatology in Jewish and Christian Apocalypticism* (JSJSup 50; Leiden: Brill, 1996) 198-217.

31. John J. Collins, "The Christian Adaptation of the Apocalyptic Genre," in idem, *Seers, Sibyls and Sages in Hellenistic-Roman Judaism* (JSJSup 54; Leiden: Brill, 1997) 115-27.

32. Norman Cohn, *The Pursuit of the Millennium* (New York: Oxford University Press, 1970); Christopher C. Rowland, "The Evidence from the Reception History of the Book of Revelation," in Amanat and Collins, eds., *Apocalypse and Violence*, 2-4.

33. Kaplan, *Radical Religion*, 167-68.

fear in Greek tragedy.[34] The portrayal of danger and conflict in apocalyptic visions (Daniel's dream of the four beasts rising from the sea; the visions of the dragon and the beasts in Revelation) actually intensifies the terror induced by actual historical events, but then releases that terror by the assurance of ultimate victory. The use of mythic patterns, often drawn from the combat myths of the ancient Near East, facilitates this release, since the reader knows how such stories inevitably end. In both Daniel and Revelation, the moment of victory is portrayed as a judgment rather than a battle, emphasizing that justice rather than raw power is the principle at issue.[35] It is a mistake, however, to think that the motif of judgment removes the drama from the context of the combat myth. In the end, the beast must be slain. This is especially clear in Revelation 19, where the judgment is executed by a heavenly rider on a white horse wading through blood, a classic depiction of the Divine Warrior of ancient mythology. Violence is not rejected, only deferred. It is precisely the assurance of imminent divine violence that enables human forbearance in the present.

The demand for justice and the tendency toward quietism go some way toward rebutting the charge that fantasies of eschatological violence are conducive to terrorism, but the issues are more complicated still. Brutal oppression has always been a fact of life for a significant proportion of the world's population, but this does not mean that fantasies of vengeance are always justified or excusable. What is deemed to constitute "intolerable oppression" can vary greatly from one situation to another. We know from the letters of Pliny something about Roman policy toward Christianity in Asia Minor when the Apocalypse of John was written. It was not benevolent, but it stopped well short of systematic persecution.[36] John found it intolerable because it exalted Rome and its emperor above the God of Jews and Christians. Analogously, American influence in the Arab world may be ambiguous, but whether the United States qualifies as the Great Satan and warrants calls for jihad is open to dispute. As Appleby notes, apocalypticism thrives not only in the slums of Gaza, but also in the suburbs of

---

34. Yarbro Collins, *Crisis and Catharsis*, 141-63; Tina Pippin, *Death and Desire: The Rhetoric of Gender in the Apocalypse of John* (Louisville: Westminster John Knox, 1992) 167-68.

35. Schüssler Fiorenza, *The Book of Revelation*, 169; Barbara R. Rossing, *The Choice between Two Cities: Whore, Bride, and Empire in the Apocalypse* (Harrisburg, PA: Trinity Press International, 1999) 118.

36. Yarbro Collins, *Crisis and Catharsis*, 69-73; Thompson, *The Book of Revelation*, 95-132.

Dallas and Chicago. People embrace apocalyptic fantasies not only because of political oppression, but also because they feel culturally marginalized and feel that their cherished beliefs are not respected or accepted in public discourse. The grievance of fundamentalist Islam against the west is concerned as much with the hegemony of secularism as it is with economic exploitation. In American Christianity, the issues are entirely cultural, but people feel marginalized and aggrieved. Apocalyptic fantasies can serve to create a sense of crisis where it is not generally perceived.[37] This is not to deny that extreme oppression exists, or even is relatively commonplace, but only to point out that the apocalyptic view of the world is not necessarily an objective one, and that it is not necessarily justified by oppression in all cases.

Conducive to Violence?

Nonetheless, the suspicion remains that violent fantasies are conducive to violent action. Mark Juergensmeyer, in his study of religion and terrorism in the contemporary world, argues that many activists who have turned to terror are driven by an image of cosmic war:[38]

> What makes religious violence particularly savage and relentless is that its perpetrators have placed such religious images of divine struggle — cosmic war — in the service of worldly political battles. For this reason, acts of religious terror serve not only as tactics in a political strategy but also as evocations of a much larger spiritual confrontation.

It is a matter of debate whether messianic hopes were a factor in the first Jewish revolt against Rome. Josephus assigns a measure of responsibility to a series of figures whom we might describe as apocalyptic prophets. After describing the activities of these *sicarii*, or daggermen, he goes on:

> Besides these there arose another body of villains, with purer hands but more impious intentions, who no less than the assassins ruined

37. Yarbro Collins, *Crisis and Catharsis;* Paul B. Duff, *Who Rides the Beast? Prophetic Rivalry and the Rhetoric of Crisis in the Churches of the Apocalypse* (New York and Oxford: Oxford University Press, 2001).

38. Mark Juergensmeyer, *Terror in the Mind of God: The Global Rise of Religious Violence* (Berkeley: University of California Press, 2003) 148-49.

the peace of the city. Deceivers and impostors, under the pretence of divine inspiration fostering revolutionary changes, they persuaded the multitude to act like madmen, and led them out into the desert under the belief that God would give them tokens of deliverance. Against them, Felix, regarding them as but the preliminary insurrection, sent a body of cavalry and heavy-armed infantry, and put a large number to the sword. (*Jewish War* 2.259-60)

There was a succession of such sign prophets in the first century CE.[39] Josephus admits that the movements they led were not violent, but were inspired by the hope of miraculous divine intervention. Nonetheless, he blames them for disturbing the peace of the city and creating an atmosphere congenial to rebellion. He also claims that the rebels were inspired by an "ambiguous oracle, which was found in the sacred texts" (*Jewish War* 6.312-15), more than by any other one thing. We do not know which oracle that was. Possibilities include Daniel 7 (the "one like a son of man") or Balaam's prophecy of the scepter and the star in Numbers 24:17. Josephus gives an unsympathetic account of the revolt, but he must be credited with insight into the workings of prophecy, ambiguous or otherwise. If people are told to expect a heavenly deliverer on a white horse who will annihilate their enemies, it may be difficult for them to restrain themselves from giving him a helping hand.

There are examples in both Jewish and Christian history of people who took it upon themselves to "force the end" in defiance of religious authorities and the weight of tradition. While the Christian Identity movement has not preached violence, it has been implicated in the thinking of Timothy McVeigh, the Oklahoma City bomber.[40] In the not too distant past, there was a plot to blow up the Temple Mount in Jerusalem in hopes of accelerating Armageddon.[41] Appleby writes of the "complex sensation of dread mixed with rapturous joy" experienced by dispensationalists at the outbreak of the Gulf War, since reports of Saddam Hussein lobbing Scud missiles at Israel seemed to augur that the final battle was at hand. While that conflict would be bloody, it would hasten the day of salvation.

39. Richard A. Horsley and John S. Hanson, *Bandits, Prophets, and Messiahs* (Minneapolis: Winston, 1985); Rebecca Gray, *Prophetic Figures in Late Second Temple Jewish Palestine* (Oxford: Oxford University Press, 1993); John J. Collins, *The Scepter and the Star: Messianism in Light of the Dead Sea Scrolls* (2nd ed.; Grand Rapids: Eerdmans, 2010) 216-19.

40. Juergensmeyer, *Terror in the Mind of God*, 30-36.

41. Juergensmeyer, *Terror in the Mind of God*, 47.

The first volume of the popular *Left Behind* series imagines a Russian attack on Israel on the model of Ezekiel's prophecy about Gog (which is often taken to symbolize Russia in fundamentalist prophecy interpretation). The planes and missiles fall harmlessly from the sky. While this is described in a novel — and in a film based on the novel — and thus might be considered harmless entertainment, it helps mold opinion on the relation between God and Israel and the justification or condemnation of violence in that part of the world.

Appleby continues, "Fundamentalists, who seek to create an alternative social and political order 'for the long run' are in the impossible situation of wanting to constrain apocalyptic violence after they have set loose its agents and unleashed its dynamics!" Consequently,

> a hallmark of the discourse of religious extremists is the calculated ambiguity of their leaders' rhetoric about violence. An extremist preacher's standard repertoire — the constant use of metaphor and veiled allusion, apocalyptic imagery, and heated rhetoric not always meant to be taken literally or obeyed as a concrete set of directions — allows the preacher to evade accountability.[42]

This is as true of Christian fundamentalists such as Ian Paisley — whose anti-Catholic rhetoric, drawn heavily from the Book of Revelation, has stoked sectarian violence in Northern Ireland for a generation — as for the Islamic clerics who issue the latter-day calls for jihad. It would not be fair to conclude that every apocalyptic-minded preacher is guilty of inciting violence, but the genre has potential to do so, even when the preacher is not consciously trying to exploit it. The fantasized violence of Revelation and other apocalypses gives this literature "a tremendous potential for real psychological and social evil."[43]

One of the reasons why apocalyptic rhetoric is conducive to violence is that it tends toward dualism. When the world is divided between good and evil, sons of light and sons of darkness, then there is little room for compromise, and without compromise there is little alternative to violence. This kind of dualism, of course, can also exist outside of an apoca-

---

42. Appleby, "The Unholy Uses," 77.
43. Adela Yarbro Collins, "Persecution and Vengeance in the Book of Revelation," in D. Hellholm, ed., *Apocalypticism in the Mediterranean World and Near East* (Tübingen: Mohr Siebeck, 1983) 747.

lyptic context, as Bruce Lincoln has shown in the cases of both Osama bin Laden and George Bush.[44] But it is especially characteristic of apocalyptic and eschatological language, in ancient Persia as well as in the Bible, and in Islam as well as in Judaism and Christianity. Associated with this dualism is the certainty associated with apocalyptic revelation, which carries with it the conviction that the believer is absolutely right and the enemy absolutely wrong.

Apocalyptic millenarianism, then, is a complex phenomenon. On the one hand, it can indeed give hope to the oppressed and even provide a way for them to vent their anger and frustration without resort to violent action. On the other hand, it is not conducive to compromise or conciliation but tends to divide the world into camps of light and darkness and to harden attitudes into mutual hatred. The "radicalness" of this religious stance lies in its refusal to compromise, its desire to vomit out those who are neither hot nor cold. It encourages an ethic that may be justified in desperate times, but only as the lesser evil.

Radical Religion as the Pursuit of Equality

When Christopher Rowland writes about "radical Christianity," however, this is not the kind of radicalness he has in mind:

> Throughout Christian history — and particularly at times of crisis and social upheaval — there have emerged writings which, reflecting the values of the Kingdom, have engaged in searching critiques of the political order and promoted change in social and economic relations, most commonly by advocating or enacting equality of wealth, power, gender, or status.[45]

This, too, is part of the effective history of biblical apocalypticism, as exemplified by Gerrard Winstanley and the Diggers.[46] It is easy enough to

---

44. Bruce Lincoln, "Symmetric Dualisms: Bush and Bin Laden on Oct. 7, 2001," in Amanat and Collins, eds., *Apocalypse and Violence*, 89-112; republished as chapter 2 of Lincoln, *Holy Terrors: Thinking about Religion After September 11* (Chicago: University of Chicago Press, 2003).

45. Bradstock and Rowland, *Radical Christian Writings*, xvi; compare Rowland, *Radical Christianity*.

46. Rowland, *Radical Christianity*, 102-14.

see why the expectation of an imminent end of this world should inspire a view of radical equality. Consider the so-called "Apocalypse of Isaiah," one of the late prophetic texts that anticipates the themes of cosmic destruction in the apocalypses:

> Now the Lord is about to lay waste the earth and make it desolate,
> and he will twist its surface and scatter its inhabitants.
> And it shall be, as with the people, so with the priest;
> as with the slave, so with his master;
> as with the buyer, so with the seller;
> as with the lender, so with the borrower;
> as with the creditor, so with the debtor.
> The earth shall be utterly laid waste and utterly despoiled.
>
> (Isa. 24:1-3)

Or the advice of Paul to the Corinthians:

> The appointed time has grown short; from now on, let even those who have wives be as though they had none, and those who mourn as though they were not mourning, and those who rejoice as though they were not rejoicing, and those who buy as though they had no possessions, and those who deal with the world as though they had no dealings with it. For the present form of this world is passing away. (1 Cor. 7:29-31)

If the world as we know it is passing away, then the social distinctions of the present order lose their significance. In fact, however, belief in an imminent eschaton has not always led to the abolition of earthly distinctions. The community described in the Acts of the Apostles seems to have been an exception in this regard. We are told that those who believed that Jesus had been raised up as messiah and that the great and terrible day of the Lord was at hand "were together and had all things in common; they would sell their possessions and goods and distribute the proceeds to all as any had need" (Acts 2:44-45). The underlying assumption was evidently that no one had need of possessions because the world was passing away. The community known from the Dead Sea Scrolls also lived in anticipation of divine intervention and also famously had possessions in common. Nonetheless, that community was hardly a model of egalitarianism. On the contrary, it was thoroughly hierarchical, assigning a rank to every individual, with the priests firmly at the head. In fact, millenarian expectation does not entail a commitment to any form of social organization. Rather, the belief is that the coming judgment will confirm the superiority of whatever form of organization the elect group has adopted. If the group is dominated by priests and greatly concerned with purity, these are the values that will be affirmed at the judgment. If, on the other hand, the group is motivated by protest against social inequality, then egalitarianism is likely to be the value affirmed.

Judgment and Values

Equally, the expectation of an apocalyptic judgment does not necessarily commit one to intolerance and antagonism. The Gospel of Matthew offers a remarkable adaptation of the traditional apocalyptic judgment scene. It begins with the Son of Man taking his seat on his throne of glory, ostensibly to judge the nations. The criteria for judgment, however, are not what we find in Daniel or Revelation. They do not provide for vengeance for the oppressed by throwing oppressive beasts into the fire or casting down the whore of Babylon. Instead, we are told that the separation of the sheep from the goats is determined by whether people fed the hungry, clothed the naked, and gave drink to the thirsty. The scene can be read as a radical deconstruction of typical apocalyptic expectations, but it is nonetheless a classic apocalyptic judgment scene, although it is perhaps more typical of the otherworldly journey type of apocalypse, with its emphasis on the judgment of individuals, rather than of the public scenarios of millenarianism. As Lautaro Lanzillotto has argued with reference to the *Apocalypse of Peter,* "the scenario of the Last Judgement . . . displays before the eyes of the righteous a complete inversion of the unjust state of things according to a system of values implicitly defended by the text."[47] The fact that there is a judgment scene, however, does not predetermine the values. Rather, the scene can be imagined in accordance with whatever the values of the author happen to be.

47. Lautaro Roig Lanzilatto, "Does Punishment Reward the Righteous? The Justice Pattern Underlying the Apocalypse of Peter," in Jan N. Bremmer and István Czachesz, eds., *The Apocalypse of Peter* (Leuven: Peeters, 2003) 127-57.

Conclusion

Apocalyptic eschatology, then, can be related to radical religion in various ways. The contemporary view of radical religion as intolerant devotion to militant fantasies has a basis in the ancient texts, but it is by no means the only way the apocalyptic heritage can be or has been understood. The exclusive focus on the fanatical and intolerant aspects of the tradition, on the part of both the adherents of radical religion and their critics, is unfortunate.

Christopher Rowland has made many important contributions to the understanding of apocalypticism, beginning with his groundbreaking book *The Open Heaven*, which emphasized the vertical, revelatory, and mystical aspects of this literature,[48] and continuing with his work on the history of interpretation.[49] Perhaps his most important contribution, however, lies in his retrieval of the radical social aspects of the apocalyptic tradition, which have all too often been eclipsed by the fantasies of eschatological violence. Biblical texts do not interpret themselves, and the power of apocalyptic images can be harnessed either for evil or for good. In an age when the word "apocalypse" is too often associated with the threat of cosmic catastrophe, we need to be reminded that the transience of this world can also give rise to the vision of radical equality, which the Gospels associate with the kingdom of God.

48. Rowland, *The Open Heaven: A Study of Apocalyptic in Judaism and Early Christianity* (New York: Crossroad, 1982).

49. Rowland, "The Book of Revelation," in Leander E. Keck, ed., *The New Interpreter's Bible*, vol. 12 (Nashville: Abingdon, 1998) 503-736; Kovacs and Rowland, *Revelation*.

Bibliography

Abusch, T. "Ascent to the Stars in a Mesopotamian Ritual: Social Metaphor and Religious Experience." Pages 15-39 in *Death, Ecstasy and Otherworldly Journeys.* Edited by J. J. Collins and M. Fishbane. Albany: SUNY Press, 1995.

Adamik, Tamás. "The Description of Paradise." Pages 78-90 in *The Apocalypse of Peter.* Edited by Jan N. Bremmer and István Czachesz. Leuven: Peters, 2003.

Adams, Samuel. *Wisdom in Transition: Act and Consequence in Second Temple Instructions.* JSJSup 125. Leiden: Brill, 2008.

Albani, Matthias. *Astronomie und Schöpfungsglaube. Untersuchungen zum astronomischen Henochbuch.* Neukirchen-Vluyn: Neukirchener Verlag, 1994.

―――. " 'Zadokite Judaism,' 'Enochic Judaism' und Qumran. Zur aktuellen Diskussion um G. Boccaccinis 'Beyond the Essene Hypothesis'." Pages 85-101 in *Apokalyptik und Qumran.* Edited by Jörg Frey and Michael Becker. Einblicke 10. Paderborn: Bonifatius, 2007.

Albertz, Rainer. *A History of Israelite Religion in the Old Testament Period.* Volume 2: *From the Exile to the Maccabees.* Translated by John Bowden. Louisville: Westminster John Knox, 1994.

Alexander, P. S. "3 (Hebrew Apocalypse of) Enoch." *OTP* 1.223-315.

―――. "Retelling the Old Testament." Pages 99-121 in *It Is Written: Scripture Citing Scripture: Essays in Honour of Barnabas Lindars, SSF.* Edited by D. Carson and H. G. M. Williamson. Cambridge: Cambridge University Press, 1987.

―――. "The Enochic Literature and the Bible: Intertextuality and Its Implications." Pages 57-69 in *The Bible as Book: The Hebrew Bible and the Judaean Desert Discoveries.* Edited by E. D. Herbert and E. Tov. London: The British Library and Oak Knoll Press, in association with The Scriptorium: Center for Christian Antiquities, 2002.

―――. *The Mystical Texts: Songs of the Sabbath Sacrifice and Related Manuscripts.* London and New York: T&T Clark International, 2006.

Alter, Robert. *The Art of Biblical Poetry.* New York: Basic Books, 1985.

Amsler, S. "Zacharie et l'origine de l'apocalyptique." Pages 227-31 in *Congress Volume, Uppsala 1971.* VTSup 22. Leiden: Brill, 1972.

Andersen, F. "2 Enoch." Pages 91-221 in volume 1 of *The Old Testament Pseudepigrapha.* Edited by J. H. Charlesworth. 2 vols. Garden City, NY: Doubleday, 1983.

Anderson, B. W. "The Slaying of the Fleeing, Twisting Serpent: Isaiah 27:1 in Context." Pages 3-15 in *Uncovering Ancient Stones: Essays in Memory of H. Neil Richardson.* Edited by L. M. Hopfe. Winona Lake, IN: Eisenbrauns, 1994.

Anklesaria, B. T. *Zand-i Vohuman Yasn.* Bombay: Camay Oriental Institute, 1967.

Appleby, Scott. "The Unholy Uses of Apocalyptic Imagination: Twentieth Century Patterns." Pages 69-87 in *Apocalypse and Violence.* Edited by Abbas Amanat and John J. Collins. New Haven: Yale Center for International and Area Studies and the Council on Middle East Studies, 2007.

Assefa, Daniel. *L'Apocalypse des animaux (1 Hen 85–90). Une propagande militaire.* JSJSup 120. Leiden: Brill, 2007.

Assmann, Jan. *Moses the Egyptian: The Memory of Egypt in Western Monotheism.* Cambridge, MA: Harvard University Press, 1997.

Atkinson, Kenneth. *I Cried to the Lord: A Study of the Psalms of Solomon's Historical Background and Social Setting.* JSJSup 84. Leiden: Brill, 2004.

Aune, David. "The Apocalypse of John and the Problem of Genre." *Semeia* 36 (1986) 65-96.

———. *Revelation.* Word Biblical Commentary 52A. Dallas: Word, 1997.

Bar-Asher, Moshe. "On the Language of 'The Vision of Gabriel'." *RevQ* 23 (2008) 491-524.

Barclay, John M. G. *Jews in the Mediterranean Diaspora: From Alexander to Trajan (323 BCE–117 CE).* Edinburgh: T&T Clark, 1998.

Barkun, Michael. "Foreword." Pages vii-ix in Jeffrey Kaplan, *Radical Religion in America: Millenarian Movements from the Far Right to the Children of Noah.* Syracuse: Syracuse University, 1997.

Barton, John. *Oracles of God: Perceptions of Ancient Prophecy in Israel after the Exile.* Oxford and New York: Oxford University Press, 1986.

———. *Reading the Old Testament: Method in Biblical Study.* Revised ed. Louisville: Westminster John Knox, 1996.

———. "Theological Ethics in the Book of Daniel." Pages 661-70 in *The Book of Daniel: Composition and Reception.* Edited by J. J. Collins and P. W. Flint. Leiden: Brill, 2001.

Baumgarten, A. I. *The Flourishing of Jewish Sects in the Maccabean Era: An Interpretation.* JSJSup 55. Leiden: Brill, 1997.

Baumgarten, J. M. "The Qumran-Essene Restraints on Marriage." Pages 13-24 in *Archaeology and History in the Dead Sea Scrolls.* Edited by L. H. Schiffman. Sheffield: Sheffield Academic Press, 1990.

Bautch, Kelley Coblentz. *A Study of the Geography of 1 Enoch 17–19: "No One Has Seen What I Have Seen."* JSJSup 81. Leiden: Brill, 2003.

Bibliography

Bedenbender, Andreas. *Der Gott der Welt tritt auf den Sinai. Entstehung, Entwicklung und Funktionsweise der frühjüdischen Apokalyptik.* Berlin: Institut Kirche und Judentum, 2000.

———. "The Place of the Torah in the Early Enoch Literature." Pages 65-79 in *The Early Enoch Literature.* Edited by G. Boccaccini and J. J. Collins. JSJSup 121. Leiden: Brill, 2007.

Begg, C. "Josephus's Portrayal of the Disappearances of Enoch, Elijah and Moses: Some Observations." *JBL* 109 (1990) 691-93.

Bergren, Theodore A. "Ezra and Nehemiah Square Off in the Apocrypha and Pseudepigrapha." Pages 340-63 in *Biblical Figures Outside the Bible.* Edited by Michael E. Stone and Theodore A. Bergren. Harrisburg, PA: Trinity Press International, 1998.

Bergsma, John S. "The Relationship between *Jubilees* and the Early Enochic Books." Pages 36-51 in *Enoch and the Mosaic Torah: The Evidence of Jubilees.* Edited by Gabriele Boccaccini and Giovanni Ibba. Grand Rapids: Eerdmans, 2009.

Berrigan, Daniel. *Daniel Under the Siege of the Divine.* Farmington, PA: The Plough Publishing House, 1998.

Berlin, A. *Zephaniah.* AB25. New York: Doubleday, 1994.

Bernstein, A. E. *The Formation of Hell: Death and Retribution in the Ancient and Early Christian Worlds.* Ithaca, NY: Cornell University Press, 1993.

Bernstein, Moshe. "Rewritten Bible? A Generic Category Which Has Outlived Its Usefulness?" *Textus* 22 (2005) 169-96.

Beyerle, Stefan. " 'Du bist kein Richter über dem Herrn'. Zur Konzeption von Gesetz und Gericht im 4. Esrabuch." Pages 315-37 in *Recht und Ethos im Alten Testament.* Edited by S. Beyerle, G. Mayer, and H. Strauss. Neukirchen: Neukirchener Verlag, 1999.

———. "Daniel and Its Social Setting." Pages 205-28 in volume 1 of *The Book of Daniel: Composition and Reception.* Edited by John J. Collins and Peter W. Flint. 2 vols. VTSup 83. Leiden: Brill, 2001.

Bhabha, Homi K. *The Location of Culture.* London: Routledge, 1994.

Bhayro, Siam. *The Shemihazah and Asael Narrative of 1 Enoch 6–11.* AOAT 322. Münster: Ugarit-Verlag, 2005.

Bietenhard, H. *Die himmlische Welt im Urchristentum und Spätjudentum.* WUNT 2. Tübingen: Mohr, 1951.

Blenkinsopp, J. "Interpretation and the Tendency to Sectarianism: An Aspect of Second Temple History." Pages 1-26 in *Jewish and Christian Self-definition: Aspects of Judaism in the Graeco-Roman Period.* Edited by E. P. Sanders. Philadelphia: Fortress, 1981.

———. *A History of Prophecy in Israel.* Revised ed. Louisville: Westminster, 1996.

———. *Isaiah 1–39.* AB 19. New York: Doubleday, 2000.

———. *Opening the Sealed Book: Interpretations of the Book of Isaiah in Late Antiquity.* Grand Rapids: Eerdmans, 2006.

Boccaccini, Gabriele. *Beyond the Essene Hypothesis: The Parting of the Ways between Qumran and Enochic Judaism.* Grand Rapids: Eerdmans, 1998.

———. *Roots of Rabbinic Judaism: An Intellectual History, from Ezekiel to Daniel.* Grand Rapids: Eerdmans, 2002.

———, ed. *The Origins of Enochic Judaism: Proceedings of the First Enoch Seminar, University of Michigan, Sesto Fiorentino, Italy, June 19-23, 2001,* = Henoch 24/1-2 (2002).

———, ed. *Enoch and Qumran Origins: New Light on a Forgotten Connection.* Grand Rapids: Eerdmans, 2005.

———, ed. *Enoch and the Messiah Son of Man: Revisiting the Book of Parables.* Grand Rapids: Eerdmans, 2007.

———. "Enochians, Urban Essenes, Qumranites: Three Social Groups, One Intellectual Movement." Pages 301-27 in *The Early Enoch Literature.* Edited by G. Boccaccini and J. J. Collins. JSJSup 121. Leiden: Brill, 2007.

Boccaccini, Gabrielle, and Giovanni Ibba, eds. *Enoch and the Mosaic Torah: The Evidence of Jubilees.* Grand Rapids: Eerdmans, 2009.

Boccaccini, Gabriele, and John J. Collins, eds. *The Early Enoch Literature.* JSJSup 121. Leiden: Brill, 2007.

Boda, M. J. "Oil, Crowns and Thrones: Prophet, Priest and King in Zechariah 1:7–6:15." *JHS* 3 (2001) Article 10.

Borger, R. "Die Beschwörungsserie *bīt mēseri* und die Himmelfahrt Henochs." *JNES* 33 (1974) 183-96.

Böttrich, C. *Weltweisheit, Menschheitsethik, Urkult. Studien zum slavischen Henochbuch.* Tübingen: Mohr Siebeck, 1992.

Bousset, W. "Die Himmelsreise der Seele." *Archiv für Religionswissenschaft* 4 (1901) 136-69, 229-73.

Boyarin, Daniel. *A Radical Jew: Paul and the Politics of Identity.* Berkeley: University of California Press, 1994.

Boyce, Mary. "The Poems of the Persian Sibyl and the Zand I Vahman Yasht." Pages 59-77 in *Études Irano-Aryennes Offertes à Gilbert Lazard.* Edited by C. H. de Fouchécour and Ph. Gignoux. Cahiers de Studia Iranica 7. Paris: Association pour l'Avancement des Études Iraniennes, 1989.

Boyer, Paul. *When Time Shall Be No More: Prophecy Belief in Modern American Culture.* Cambridge, MA: Harvard University Press, 1992.

Bradstock, Andrew, and Christopher Rowland. *Radical Christian Writings: A Reader.* Oxford: Blackwell, 2002.

Brandenburger, E. *Die Verborgenheit Gottes im Weltgeschehen.* Zürich: Theologischer Verlag, 1981.

Braude, W. G. *Pesikta Rabbati.* 2 vols. New Haven: Yale University Press, 1968.

Bremmer, Jan N. *The Rise and Fall of the Afterlife.* London: Routledge, 2002.

Brett, Mark. "The Ethics of Postcolonial Criticism." *Semeia* 75 (1996) 219-28.

Brooke, George J. "Rewritten Bible." Pages 777-81 in volume 2 of *Encyclopedia of the*

Dead Sea Scrolls. Edited by Lawrence H. Schiffman and James C. VanderKam. 2 vols. New York: Oxford University Press, 2000.

―――. "4Q158: Reworked Pentateuchᵃ or Reworked Pentateuch A?" *Dead Sea Discoveries* 8 (2001) 219-41.

Broshi, M. "The Gigantic Dimensions of the Visionary Temple in the Temple Scroll." *BAR* 13 (1987) 36-37.

Brox, N., ed. *Pseudepigraphie in der heidnischen und jüdisch-christlichen Antike*. Wege der Forschung 484. Darmstadt: Wissenschaftliche Buchgesellschaft, 1977.

Bruce, F. F. *Biblical Exegesis in the Qumran Texts*. Grand Rapids: Eerdmans, 1959.

Bryan, David. *Cosmos, Chaos and the Kosher Mentality*. Sheffield: Sheffield Academic Press, 1995.

Buitenwerf, Rieuwerd. *Book III of the Sibylline Oracles and Its Social Setting*. SVTP 17. Leiden: Brill, 2003.

Caird, G. B. *The Language and Imagery of the Bible*. Philadelphia: Westminster, 1980.

Campbell, Jonathan G. "'Rewritten Bible' and 'Parabiblical Texts': A Terminological and Ideological Critique." Pages 43-68 in *New Directions in Qumran Studies: Proceedings of the Bristol Colloquium on the Dead Sea Scrolls, 8-10 September 2003*. Edited by J. G. Campbell et al. London: T&T Clark, 2005.

Cancik, Hubert. "Libri Fatales. Römische Offenbarungliteratur und Geschichtstheologie." Pages 549-76 in *Apocalypticism in the Mediterranean World and the Near East*. Edited by David Hellholm. Tübingen: Mohr Siebeck, 1983.

Carey, Greg, and L. Gregory Bloomquist, eds. *Vision and Persuasion: Rhetorical Dimensions of Apocalyptic Discourse*. St. Louis: Chalice, 1999.

Carmignac, Jean. "Qu'est-ce que l'Apocalyptique? Son emploi à Qumrân." *RevQ* 10 (1979) 3-33.

―――. "Description du phénomène de l'Apocalyptique." Pages 163-70 in *Apocalypticism in the Mediterranean World and the Near East: Proceedings of the International Colloquium on Apocalypticism, Uppsala, August 12-17, 1979*. Edited by D. Hellholm. Tübingen: Mohr-Siebeck, 1983.

Casey, M. "The Use of the Term 'Son of Man' in the Similitudes of Enoch." *JSJ* 7 (1976) 11-29.

―――. *Son of Man: The Interpretation and Influence of Daniel 7*. London: SPCK, 1979.

Cavallin, H. C. *Life After Death: Paul's Argument for the Resurrection of the Dead in 1 Cor 15*. Lund: Gleerup, 1974.

Cervelli, Innocenzo. "Questioni Sibilline." *Studi Storici* 34.4 (1993) 895-1001.

Charles, R. H. "The Testaments of the Twelve Patriarchs." *APOT* 2:282-367.

Chester, Andrew. *Future Hope and Present Reality*. Volume 1: *Eschatology and Transformation in the Hebrew Bible*. WUNT 293. Tübingen: Mohr Siebeck, 2012.

Childs, B. S. *Isaiah*. OTL. Louisville: Westminster, 2001.

Chyutin, M. "The New Jerusalem: Ideal City." *DSD* 1 (1994) 71-97.

Clausen, W. "Virgil's Messianic Eclogue." Pages 65-74 in *Poetry and Prophecy: The*

Beginnings of a Literary Tradition. Edited by J. L. Kugel. Ithaca, NY: Cornell University Press, 1990.

Clements, Ronald E. *Old Testament Prophecy: From Oracles to Canon.* Louisville: Westminster, 1996.

Clifford, R. J., S.J. "The Roots of Apocalypticism in Near Eastern Myth." Pages 3-38 in *The Encyclopedia of Apocalypticism,* volume 1: *The Origins of Apocalypticism in Judaism and Christianity.* Edited by J. J. Collins. New York: Continuum, 1998.

Cohen, Ralph. "History and Genre." *New Literary History* 17 (1986) 203-18.

Cohn, Norman. *The Pursuit of the Millennium.* New York: Oxford University Press, 1970.

Collins, John J. "The Place of the Fourth Sibyl in the Development of the Jewish Sibyllina." *JJS* 25 (1974) 365-80.

———. *The Sibylline Oracles of Egyptian Judaism.* SBLDS 13. Missoula: Scholars Press, 1974.

———. *The Apocalyptic Vision of the Book of Daniel.* HSM 16. Missoula, MT: Scholars Press, 1977.

———, ed. *Apocalypse: The Morphology of a Genre.* Semeia 14. Chico, CA: Scholars Press, 1979.

———. "Introduction: Towards the Morphology of a Genre." *Semeia* 14 (1979).

———. "The Jewish Apocalypses." *Semeia* 14 (1979).

———. "The Sibylline Oracles." Pages 317-472 in volume 1 of *The Old Testament Pseudepigrapha.* Edited by J. H. Charlesworth. 2 vols. Garden City, NY: Doubleday, 1983.

———. "The Development of the Sibylline Tradition." Pages 421-59 in *Aufstieg und Niedergang der Römischen Welt* 20.1. Edited by W. Haase and H. Temporini. Berlin: de Gruyter, 1987.

———. "Genre, Ideology and Social Movements in Jewish Apocalypticism." Pages 11-32 in *Mysteries and Revelations: Apocalyptic Studies since the Uppsala Colloquium.* Edited by J. J. Collins and J. H. Charlesworth. Sheffield: Sheffield Academic Press, 1991.

———. "The Son of Man in First Century Judaism." *NTS* 38 (1992) 448-66.

———. *Daniel.* Hermeneia. Minneapolis: Fortress, 1993.

———. "A Throne in the Heavens: Apotheosis in Pre-Christian Judaism." Pages 43-58 in *Death, Ecstasy and Otherworldly Journeys.* Edited by J. J. Collins and M. Fishbane. Albany: SUNY Press, 1995.

———. *The Scepter and the Star.* New York: Doubleday, 1995. Rev. ed., Grand Rapids: Eerdmans, 2010.

———. "Pseudo-Daniel Revisited." *RevQ* 17 (1996) 111-35.

———. *Apocalypticism in the Dead Sea Scrolls.* London: Routledge, 1997.

———. "Jewish Monotheism and Christian Theology." Pages 81-105 in *Aspects of Monotheism: How God Is One.* Edited by Hershel Shanks and Jack Meinhardt. Washington, DC: Biblical Archaeology Society, 1997.

———. *Jewish Wisdom in the Hellenistic Age.* OTL. Louisville: Westminster, 1997.

————. *Seers, Sibyls and Sages in Hellenistic-Roman Judaism.* JSJSup 54. Leiden: Brill, 1997.

————. *The Apocalyptic Imagination.* New York: Crossroad, 1984. Rev. ed., Grand Rapids: Eerdmans, 1998. Third edition: Grand Rapids: Eerdmans, 2016.

————. "Pseudepigraphy and Group Formation in Second Temple Judaism." Pages 44-48 in *Pseudepigraphic Perspectives: The Apocrypha and Pseudepigrapha in Light of the Dead Sea Scrolls.* Edited by Esther G. Chazon and Michael E. Stone. STDJ 31. Leiden: Brill, 1999.

————. "Apocalyptic Literature." Pages 432-47 in *The Blackwell Companion to the Hebrew Bible.* Edited by Leo Perdue. Oxford: Blackwell, 2001.

————. "Temporality and Politics in Jewish Apocalyptic Literature." Pages 26-43 in *Apocalyptic in History and Tradition.* Edited by Christopher Rowland and John Barton. JSPSup 43. Sheffield: Sheffield Academic Press, 2002.

————. "Forms of Community in the Dead Sea Scrolls." Pages 97-111 in *Emanuel: Studies in Hebrew Bible, Septuagint, and Dead Sea Scrolls in Honor of Emanuel Tov.* Edited by S. M. Paul et al. Leiden: Brill, 2003.

————. "Prophecy, Apocalypse and Eschatology: Reflections on the Proposals of Lester Grabbe." Pages 44-52 in *Knowing the End from the Beginning: The Prophetic, the Apocalyptic and Their Relationships.* Edited by Lester L. Grabbe and Robert D. Haak. London and New York: T&T Clark, 2003.

————. "Before the Fall: The Earliest Interpretations of Adam and Eve." Pages 293-308 in *The Idea of Biblical Interpretation: Essays in Honor of James L. Kugel.* Edited by H. Najman and J. H. Newman. Leiden: Brill, 2004.

————. "The Eschatologizing of Wisdom in the Dead Sea Scrolls." Pages 49-65 in *Sapiential Perspectives: Wisdom Literature in Light of the Dead Sea Scrolls.* Edited by John J. Collins, Gregory E. Sterling, and Ruth A. Clements. STDJ 51. Leiden: Brill, 2004.

————. *Encounters with Biblical Theology.* Minneapolis: Fortress, 2005.

————. "Enoch, the Dead Sea Scrolls, and the Essene Groups and Movements in Judaism in the Early Second Century BCE." Pages 345-50 in *Enoch and Qumran Origins. New Light on a Forgotten Connection.* Edited by G. Boccaccini. Grand Rapids: Eerdmans, 2005.

————. *Jewish Cult and Hellenistic Culture.* JSJSup 100. Leiden: Brill, 2005.

————. "An Essene Messiah? Comments on Israel Knohl, *The Messiah before Jesus.*" Pages 37-44 in *Christian Beginnings and the Dead Sea Scrolls.* Edited by John J. Collins and Craig Evans. Grand Rapids: Baker, 2006.

————. "The Yaḥad and 'The Qumran Community'." Pages 81-96 in *Biblical Traditions in Transmission: Essays in Honour of Michael A. Knibb.* Edited by Charlotte Hempel and Judith Lieu. JSJSup 111. Leiden: Brill, 2006.

————. "'Enochic Judaism' and the Sect of the Dead Sea Scrolls." Pages 283-99 in *The Early Enoch Literature.* Edited by G. Boccaccini and J. J. Collins. JSJSup 121. Leiden: Brill, 2007.

————. "How Distinctive Was Enochic Judaism?" Pages 17-34 in *A Festschrift for Devorah Dimant*. Edited by Moshe Bar-Asher and Emanuel Tov = *Meghillot* V-VI (2007).

————. "The Nature and Aims of the Sect Known from the Dead Sea Scrolls." Pages 31-52 in *Flores Florentino: Dead Sea Scrolls and Other Early Jewish Studies in Honour of Florentino García Martínez*. Edited by A. Hilhorst, É. Puech, and E. Tigchelaar. JSJSup 122. Leiden: Brill, 2007.

————. "The Vision of Gabriel." *Yale Alumni Magazine* (September/October 2008) 26-27.

————. "The Beginning of the End of the World in the Hebrew Bible." Pages 137-55 in *Thus Says the Lord: Essays on the Former and Latter Prophets in Honor of Robert R. Wilson*. Edited by John J. Ahn and Stephen L. Cook. New York and London: T&T Clark, 2009.

————. "The Idea of Election in 4 Ezra." *JSQ* 16 (2009) 83-96.

————. "The Interpretation of Psalm 2." Pages 49-66 in *Echoes from the Caves: Qumran and the New Testament*. Edited by Florentino García Martínez. STDJ 85. Leiden: Brill, 2009.

————. "The Life Angelic." Pages 291-310 in *Metamorphoses: Resurrection, Body and Transformative Practices in Early Christianity*. Edited by Turid Karlsen Seim and Jorunn Økland. Ekstasis 1. Berlin: de Gruyter, 2009.

————. *Beyond the Qumran Community: The Sectarian Movement of the Dead Sea Scrolls*. Grand Rapids: Eerdmans, 2010.

————. "Enochic Judaism: An Assessment." Pages 219-34 in *The Dead Sea Scrolls and Contemporary Culture*. Edited by Adolfo Roitman. Leiden: Brill, 2010.

————. "Apocalypse and Empire." *Svensk Exegetisk Årsbok* 76 (2011) 1-19.

————. "The Genre of the Book of *Jubilees*." Pages 737-55 in volume 2 of *A Teacher for All Generations: Essays in Honor of James C. VanderKam*. Edited by Eric F. Mason et al. 2 vols. JSJSup 153. Leiden: Brill, 2011.

————. "The Sibyl and the Apocalypses." Pages 185-202 in *Greco-Roman Culture and the New Testament: Studies Commemorating the Centennial of the Pontifical Biblical Institute*. Edited by David Aune and Frederick E. Brenk. NTSup 143. Leiden: Brill, 2012.

Collins, J. J., and P. W. Flint. "Pseudo-Daniel." Pages 95-164 in *Qumran Cave 4. XVII. Parabiblical Texts, Part 3*. Edited by G. Brooke et al. DJD 22. Oxford: Clarendon, 1996.

Collins, John J., Gregory E. Sterling, and Ruth A. Clements, eds. *Sapiential Perspectives: Wisdom Literature in Light of the Dead Sea Scrolls*. STDJ 51. Leiden: Brill, 2004.

Coogan, M. D. *Stories from Ancient Canaan*. Philadelphia: Westminster, 1978.

Cook, S. L. *Prophecy and Apocalypticism: The Postexilic Social Setting*. Minneapolis: Fortress, 1995.

————. "Apocalyptic Prophecy." Pages 19-35 in *The Oxford Handbook of Apocalyptic Literature*. Edited by John J. Collins. New York: Oxford, 2014.

Cott, Jeremy. "The Biblical Problem of Election." *Journal of Ecumenical Studies* 21 (1984) 199-228.

Crane, R. S. *Critical and Historical Principles of Literary Criticism.* Chicago: University of Chicago Press, 1971.

Crawford, Sidnie White. *Rewriting Scripture in Second Temple Times.* Grand Rapids: Eerdmans, 2008.

Cross, F. M. *Canaanite Myth and Hebrew Epic.* Cambridge, MA: Harvard University Press, 1973.

Culianu, I. P. *Psychanodia I.* Leiden: Brill, 1983.

Culler, Jonathan. *Structuralist Poetics: Structuralism, Linguistics, and the Study of Literature.* Ithaca, NY: Cornell University Press, 1975.

Cullmann, O. "Immortality of the Soul or Resurrection of the Dead." Pages 9-35 in *Immortality and Resurrection.* Edited by K. Stendahl. New York: Macmillan, 1971.

Cumont, F. *Lux Perpetua.* Paris: Geuthner, 1949.

Dalley, S. *Myths from Mesopotamia.* New York: Oxford University Press, 1989.

Dan, Joseph. "Armilus: The Jewish Antichrist and the Origins and Dating of the *Sefer Zerubbavel.*" Pages 73-104 in *Toward the Millennium: Messianic Expectations from the Bible to Waco.* Edited by Peter Schäfer and Mark Cohen. Leiden: Brill, 1998.

Daschke, Dereck. *City of Ruins: Mourning the Destruction of Jerusalem through Jewish Apocalypse.* Leiden: Brill, 2010.

Davies, P. R. "Hasidim in the Maccabean Period." *JJS* 28 (1977) 127-40.

———. *The Damascus Covenant.* Sheffield: JSOT, 1982.

———. *Behind the Essenes: History and Ideology in the Dead Sea Scrolls.* BJS 94. Atlanta: Scholars Press, 1987.

———. "Reading Daniel Sociologically." Pages 345-61 in *The Book of Daniel in the Light of New Findings.* Edited by A. S. van der Woude. Leuven: Leuven University Press, 1993.

———. "The Scribal School of Daniel." Pages 247-65 in volume 1 of *The Book of Daniel: Composition and Reception.* Edited by John J. Collins and Peter W. Flint. 2 vols. VTSup 83. Leiden: Brill, 2001.

Davila, J. R. "Of Methodology, Monotheism and Metatron." Pages 3-18 in *The Jewish Roots of Christological Monotheism.* Edited by C. C. Newman, J. R. Davila, and G. S. Lewis. Leiden: Brill, 1999.

———. *The Provenance of the Pseudepigrapha: Jewish, Christian, or Other?* JSJSup 105. Leiden: Brill, 2005.

Day, J. "Baal (Deity)." *ABD* 1.545-49.

———. *God's Conflict with the Dragon and the Sea: Echoes of a Canaanite Myth in the Old Testament.* Cambridge: Cambridge University Press, 1985.

———. "Resurrection Imagery from Baal to the Book of Daniel." Pages 125-34 in *Congress Volume 1995.* Edited by J. A. Emerton. VTSup 66. Leiden: Brill, 1997.

Dean-Otting, M. *Heavenly Journeys: A Study of the Motif in Hellenistic Jewish Literature.* Frankfurt: Lang, 1984.

de Jong, Albert. *Traditions of the Magi: Zoroastrianism in Greek and Latin Literature.* Leiden: Brill, 1997.

———. "Iranian Connections in the Dead Sea Scrolls." Pages 479-500 in *The Oxford Handbook of the Dead Sea Scrolls.* Edited by T. H. Lim and J. J. Collins. Oxford: Oxford University Press, 2010.

de Jonge, H. J. "Die Textüberlieferung der Testamente der zwölf Patriarchen." Pages 45-62 in *Studies on the Testaments of the Twelve Patriarchs: Text and Interpretation.* Edited by M. de Jonge. Leiden: Brill, 1975.

de Jonge, M., and H. Hollander. *The Testaments of the Twelve Patriarchs: A Commentary.* Leiden: Brill, 1985.

Derrida, Jacques. "The Law of Genre." Pages 219-31 in *Modern Genre Theory.* Edited by David Duff. Harlow, Essex: Longman, 2000.

Devitt, Amy J. *Writing Genres.* Carbondale: Southern Illinois University Press, 2004.

Diels, Hermann. *Sibyllinischer Blätter.* Berlin: Reiner, 1890.

Dieterich, A. *Nekyia. Beiträge zur Erklärung der neuentdeckten Petrusapokalypse.* Leipzig: Teubner, 1893.

Dimant, D. "Qumran Sectarian Literature." Pages 483-550 in *Jewish Writings from the Second Temple Period.* Edited by M. E. Stone. CRINT 2.2. Philadelphia: Fortress, 1984.

———. "4QFlorilegium and the Idea of the Community as Temple." Pages 165-89 in *Hellenica et Judaica. Hommage à Valentin Nikiprowetzky.* Edited by A. Caquot et al. Paris/Leuven: Peeters, 1986.

———. "New Light from Qumran on the Jewish Pseudepigrapha — 4Q390." Pages 405-47 in volume 2 of *The Madrid Qumran Congress: Proceedings of the International Congress on the Dead Sea Scrolls.* Edited by J. Trebolle Barrera and L. Vegas Montaner. 2 vols. STDJ 2. Leiden: Brill, 1992.

DiTommaso, Lorenzo. *The Dead Sea New Jerusalem Text: Contents and Contexts.* Tübingen: Mohr Siebeck, 2005.

Dobroruka, Vicente. *Second Temple Pseudepigraphy: A Cross-Cultural Comparison of Apocalyptic Texts and Related Jewish Literature.* Ekstasis 4. Berlin: de Gruyter, 2014.

Doran, R. "The Non-dating of Jubilees: Jub 34-38; 23:14-32 in Narrative Context." *JSJ* 20 (1989) 1-11.

Doria, Luisa Breglia Pulci. *Oracoli Sibillini tra Rituali e Propaganda (Studi su Flegonte di Tralles).* Naples: Liguori, 1983.

Doty, William G. "The Concept of Genre in Literary Analysis." Pages 413-48 in volume 2 of *Society of Biblical Literature Proceedings 1972.* Edited by Lane C. McGaughey. Atlanta: SBL, 1972.

Doyle, B. *The Apocalypse of Isaiah, Metaphorically Speaking.* BETL 151. Leuven: Peeters, 2000.

Bibliography

Drawnel, H. *An Aramaic Levi Text from Qumran.* JSJSup 86. Leiden: Brill, 2004.

Duff, David. *Modern Genre Theory.* Harlow, UK: Longman, 2000.

Duff, Paul B. *Who Rides the Beast? Prophetic Rivalry and the Rhetoric of Crisis in the Churches of the Apocalypse.* New York and Oxford: Oxford University Press, 2001.

Duhm, B. *Das Buch Jesaia.* 5th ed. Göttingen: Vandenhoeck & Ruprecht, 1968.

Eddy, S. K. *The King Is Dead: Studies in Near Eastern Resistance to Hellenism.* Lincoln: University of Nebraska, 1961.

Ehrman, Bart D. *Forged: Writing in the Name of God — Why the Bible's Authors Are Not Who We Think They Are.* New York: HarperCollins, 2011.

Elgvin, Torleif. "An Analysis of 4QInstruction." Ph.D. dissertation. Hebrew University, 1998.

————. "Wisdom and Apocalypticism in the Early Second Century BCE — The Evidence of 4QInstruction." Pages 226-47 in *The Dead Sea Scrolls Fifty Years after Their Discovery.* Edited by L. H. Schiffman, E. Tov, and J. C. VanderKam. Jerusalem: Israel Exploration Society in cooperation with the Shrine of the Book, Israel Museum, 2000.

————. "The Yahad Is More Than Qumran." Pages 273-79 in *Enoch and Qumran Origins: New Light on a Forgotten Connection.* Edited by G. Boccaccini. Grand Rapids: Eerdmans, 2005.

Elliott, Mark. *The Survivors of Israel: A Reconsideration of the Theology of Pre-Christian Judaism.* Grand Rapids: Eerdmans, 2000.

————. "Covenant and Cosmology in the Book of the Watchers and the Astronomical Book." Pages 23-38 in *The Origins of Enochic Judaism: Proceedings of the First Enoch Seminar, University of Michigan, Sesto Fiorentino, Italy, June 19-23, 2001 = Henoch 24/1-2 (2002).* Edited by G. Boccaccini.

————. "Sealing Some Cracks in the Groningen Foundation." Pages 263-72 in *Enoch and Qumran Origins: New Light on a Forgotten Connection.* Edited by G. Boccaccini. Grand Rapids: Eerdmans, 2005.

Falk, Daniel K. *The Parabiblical Texts: Strategies for Extending the Scriptures in the Dead Sea Scrolls.* London and New York: T&T Clark, 2007.

Festinger, Leon. *A Theory of Cognitive Dissonance.* Stanford, CA: Stanford University Press, 1957.

Festinger, Leon, Henry Riecken, and Stanley Schachter. *When Prophecy Fails: A Social and Psychological Study of a Modern Group That Predicted the Destruction of the World.* Minneapolis: University of Minnesota, 1956.

Fewel, Danna Nolan. *Circle of Sovereignty: Plotting Politics in the Book of Daniel.* Nashville: Abingdon, 1991.

Finitsis, Antonios. *Visions and Eschatology: A Socio-Historical Analysis of Zechariah 1–6.* LSTS 79. London: T&T Clark, 2011.

Fishbane, M. *Biblical Interpretation in Ancient Israel.* Oxford: Oxford University Press, 1985.

————. "Midrash and Messianism: Some Theologies of Suffering and Salvation." Pages

57-71 in *Toward the Millennium: Messianic Expectations from the Bible to Waco*. Edited by Peter Schäfer and Mark Cohen. Leiden: Brill, 1998.

Fishelov, David. *Metaphors of Genre: The Role of Analogies in Genre Theory*. University Park: The Pennsylvania State University Press, 1993.

Flannery-Dailey, Frances. *Dreamers, Scribes, and Priests: Jewish Dreams in the Hellenistic and Roman Eras*. JSJSup 90. Leiden: Brill, 2004.

Fletcher-Louis, Crispin. "Apocalypticism." Pages 1569-1607 in volume 2 of *The Handbook of the Study of the Historical Jesus*. Edited by S. E. Porter and T. Holmén. 4 vols. Leiden: Brill, 2011.

Flint, P. W. "4Qpseudo-Daniel ar^c and the Restoration of the Priesthood." *RevQ* 17 (1996) 137-50.

Flusser, David. "The Four Empires in the Fourth Sibyl and in the Book of Daniel." *Israel Oriental Studies* 2 (1972) 148-75.

———. *Judaism and the Origins of Christianity*. Jerusalem: Magnes, 1988.

Foster, B. R. *From Distant Days: Myths, Tales and Poetry of Ancient Mesopotamia*. Bethesda, MD: BDL, 1995.

Fowler, Alastair. "The Life and Death of Literary Forms." *New Literary History* 2 (1971) 199-216.

———. *Kinds of Literature: An Introduction to the Theory of Genres and Modes*. Cambridge, MA: Harvard University Press, 1982.

Fraade, Steven. "To Whom It May Concern: 4QMMT and Its Addressee(s)." *RevQ* 19 (2000) 507-26.

Frankfurter, David. "The Legacy of Sectarian Rage: Vengeance Fantasies in the New Testament." Pages 114-28 in *Religion and Violence: The Biblical Heritage*. Edited by David A. Bernat and Jonathan Klawans. Sheffield: Sheffield Phoenix, 2007.

Frey, Jörg, Jens Herzer, Martina Janssen, and Clare K. Rothschild, with Michaela Engelmann, eds. *Pseudepigraphie und Verfasserfiktion in frühchristlichen Briefen*. WUNT 246. Tübingen: Mohr Siebeck, 2009.

Frow, John. *Genre*. London: Routledge, 2006.

Frykholm, Amy Johnson. *Rapture Culture: Left Behind in Evangelical America*. Oxford: Oxford University Press, 2004.

García Martínez, F. "Qumran Origins and Early History: A Groningen Hypothesis." *Folia Orientalia* 25 (1989) 113-36.

———. "A Groningen Hypothesis of Qumran Origins." *RevQ* 14 (1990) 521-41.

———. "The 'New Jerusalem' and the Future Temple of the Manuscripts from Qumran." Pages 180-213 in *Qumran and Apocalyptic*. Edited by F. García Martínez. Leiden: Brill, 1992.

———. "The Heavenly Tablets in the Book of Jubilees." Pages 243-60 in *Studies in the Book of Jubilees*. Edited by Matthias Albani, Jörg Frey, and Armin Lange. Tübingen: Mohr Siebeck, 1997.

———. "Response: The Groningen Hypothesis Revisited." Pages 310-16 in *Enoch and*

Bibliography

Qumran Origins: New Light on a Forgotten Connection. Edited by G. Boccaccini. Grand Rapids: Eerdmans, 2005.

García Martínez, F., and E. J. C. Tigchelaar. *The Dead Sea Scrolls Study Edition.* 2 vols. Leiden: Brill, 1997.

George, A. R. *Epic of Gilgamesh: The Babylonian Epic Poem and Other Texts in Akkadian and Sumerian. Translated and with an Introduction.* London: Penguin, 1999.

Gerstenberger, Erhard S. *Psalms: Part One, with an Introduction to Cultic Poetry.* FOTL XIV. Grand Rapids: Eerdmans, 1988.

Gese, H. "Anfang und Ende der Apokalyptik dargestellt am Sacharjabuch." *ZTK* 70 (1973) 20-49.

Ginsberg, H. L. "The Oldest Interpretation of the Suffering Servant." *VT* 3 (1953) 400-404.

Gladigow, B. "Aetas, aevum und saeclorum ordo. Zur struktur zeitlicher Deutungssysteme." Pages 255-71 in *Apocalypticism in the Mediterranean World and the Near East.* Edited by D. Hellholm. Tübingen: Mohr Siebeck, 1983.

Glasson, T. F. *Greek Influence on Jewish Eschatology.* London: SPCK, 1961.

Goff, Matthew J. *The Worldly and Heavenly Wisdom of 4QInstruction.* STDJ 50. Leiden: Brill, 2003.

Goodman, Martin. "Jewish Writings under Gentile Pseudonyms." Pages 617-94 in Emil Schürer, *The History of the Jewish People in the Age of Jesus Christ,* vol. III.1. Revised and edited by Geza Vermes, Fergus Millar, and Martin Goodman. Edinburgh: Clark, 1986.

Goren, Yuval. "Micromorphologic Examination of the 'Gabriel Revelation' Stone." *IEJ* 58 (2008) 220-29.

Grabbe, L. L. "The Social Setting of Early Jewish Apocalypticism." *JSP* 4 (1999) 27-47.

————. "Introduction and Overview." Pages 2-43 in *Knowing the End from the Beginning: The Prophetic, the Apocalyptic and Their Relationships.* Edited by Lester L. Grabbe and Robert D. Haak. London and New York: T&T Clark, 2003.

————. "Prophetic and Apocalyptic: Time for New Definitions and New Thinking." Pages 107-33 in *Knowing the End from the Beginning: The Prophetic, the Apocalyptic and Their Relationships.* Edited by Lester L. Grabbe and Robert D. Haak. London and New York: T&T Clark, 2003.

Graf, F. "Dionysian and Orphic Eschatology: New Texts and Old Questions." Pages 239-58 in *Masks of Dionysus.* Edited by T. H. Carpenter and C. A. Faraone. Ithaca, NY: Cornell University Press, 1993.

Graf, F., and S. Iles Johnston. *Ritual Texts for the Afterlife: Orpheus and the Bacchic Gold Tablets.* London: Routledge, 2007.

Gray, Rebecca. *Prophetic Figures in Late Second Temple Jewish Palestine.* Oxford: Oxford University Press, 1993.

Grayson, A. K. *Babylonian Historical-Literary Texts.* Toronto: University of Toronto, 1975.

Griffiths, J. G. *The Divine Verdict: A Study of Divine Judgement in the Ancient Religions.* Leiden: Brill, 1991.

Gruen, Erich. *Heritage and Hellenism: The Reinvention of Jewish Tradition.* Berkeley: University of California Press, 1998.

Gruenwald, I. *Apocalyptic and Merkavah Mysticism.* Leiden: Brill, 1980.

Gunkel, H. *Creation and Chaos in the Primeval Era and the Eschaton: A Religio-Historical Study of Genesis 1 and Revelation 12.* Trans. W. Whitney. Grand Rapids: Eerdmans, 2006.

Han, Jin Hee. *Daniel's Spiel: Apocalyptic Literacy in the Book of Daniel.* Lanham, MD: University Press of America, 2008.

Hanneken, Todd R. *The Subversion of the Apocalypses in the Book of Jubilees.* SBLEJL 34. Atlanta: SBL, 2012.

Hanson, Paul D. *The Dawn of Apocalyptic.* Philadelphia: Fortress, 1975.

———. "Apocalypse, Genre"; "Apocalypticism." *IDBSup* (1976) 27-34.

———. *Old Testament Apocalyptic.* Nashville: Abingdon, 1987.

Harlow, D. C. *The Greek Apocalypse of Baruch (3 Baruch) in Hellenistic Judaism and Early Christianity.* Leiden: Brill, 1996.

Harnisch, W. *Verhängnis und Verheissung der Geschichte.* Göttingen: Vandenhoeck & Ruprecht, 1969.

———. "Der Prophet als Widerpart und Zeuge der Offenbarung. Erwägungen zur Interdependenz von Form und Sache im 4. Buch Esra." Pages 461-93 in *Apocalypticism in the Mediterranean World and the Near East.* Edited by D. E. Hellholm. Tübingen: Mohr, 1983.

Harrington, Daniel J., S.J. "Palestinian Adaptations of Biblical Narratives and Prophecies." Pages 239-53 in *Early Judaism and Its Modern Interpreters.* Edited by Robert A. Kraft and George W. E. Nickelsburg. Atlanta: Scholars Press, 1986.

———. *Wisdom at Qumran.* London: Routledge, 1996.

Hartman, Lars. *Asking for a Meaning: A Study of 1 Enoch 1–5.* ConBNT 12. Lund: Gleerup, 1979.

Hasel, G. F. "Resurrection in the Theology of Old Testament Apocalyptic." *ZAW* 92 (1980) 267-84.

Hays, Christopher B. *Death in the Iron Age II and in First Isaiah.* FAT 79. Tübingen: Mohr Siebeck, 2011.

Heinemann, Joseph. "The Messiah of Ephraim and the Premature Exodus of the Tribe of Ephraim." *HTR* 68 (1975) 1-15.

Hellholm, David. "The Problem of Apocalyptic Genre." Pages 13-64 in *Early Christian Apocalypticism: Genre and Social Setting.* Edited by Adela Yarbro Collins. *Semeia* 36 (1986).

Hempel, Charlotte. "The Treatise on the Two Spirits and the Literary History of the Rule of the Community." Pages 102-20 in *Dualism in Qumran.* Edited by Géza G. Xeravits. London and New York: T&T Clark, 2010.

Hendel, Ronald. "Isaiah and the Transition from Prophecy to Apocalyptic." Pages 261-

79 in *Birkat Shalom: Studies in the Bible, Ancient Near Eastern Literature and Postbiblical Judaism Presented to Shalom M. Paul on the Occasion of His Seventieth Birthday.* Edited by Chaim Cohen et al. Winona Lake, IN: Eisenbrauns, 2008.

———. "The Messiah Son of Joseph: Simply 'Sign'." *BAR* 35 (2009) 8.

Hengel, M. *Judaism and Hellenism.* Philadelphia: Fortress, 1974.

———. "Setze dich zu meiner Rechten! Die Inthronisation Christi zur Rechten Gottes und Psalm 110,1." Pages 108-94 in *Le Trône de Dieu.* Edited by M. Philonenko. Tübingen: Mohr, 1993.

Henze, Matthias. *Jewish Apocalypticism in Late First Century Israel.* TSAJ 142. Tübingen: Mohr Siebeck, 2011.

Herrero de Jáuregui, Miguel. "Orphic Ideas of Immortality: Traditional Greek Images and a New Eschatological Thought." Pages 289-313 in *Lebendige Hoffnung — Ewiger Tod?! Jenseitsvorstellungen im Hellenismus, Judentum und Christentum.* Edited by M. Labahn and M. Lang. Leipzig: Evangelische Verlagsanstalt, 2007.

Hiebert, T. *God of My Victory: The Ancient Hymn in Habakkuk 3.* Atlanta: Scholars Press, 1986.

Hiers, R. H. "Day of the Lord." *ABD* 2.82-83.

Himmelfarb, Martha. *Tours of Hell: An Apocalyptic Form in Jewish and Christian Literature.* Philadelphia: University of Pennsylvania Press, 1983.

———. *Ascent to Heaven in Jewish and Christian Apocalypses.* New York: Oxford University Press, 1993.

———. "Torah, Testimony, and Heavenly Tablets: The Claim to Authority in the Book of Jubilees." Pages 19-29 in *A Multiform Heritage: Studies on Early Judaism and Christianity in Honor of Robert A. Kraft.* Edited by Benjamin G. Wright III. Atlanta: Scholars Press, 1999.

———. *A Kingdom of Priests: Ancestry and Merit in Ancient Judaism.* Philadelphia: University of Pennsylvania, 2006.

Hinnells, John R. "The Zoroastrian Doctrine of Salvation in the Roman World: A Study of the Oracle of Hystaspes." Pages 125-48 in *Man and His Salvation: Studies in Memory of S. G. F. Brandon.* Edited by E. J. Sharpe and J. R. Hinnells. Manchester: Manchester University Press, 1973.

Hirsch, E. D. *Validity in Interpretation.* New Haven: Yale University Press, 1967.

Hogan, Karina M. *Theologies in Conflict in 4 Ezra: Wisdom Debate and Apocalyptic Solution.* JSJSup 130. Leiden: Brill, 2008.

———. "Pseudepigraphy and the Periodization of History." Pages 61-83 in *Pseudepigraphie und Verfasserfiktion in frühchristlichen Briefen.* Edited by Jörg Frey, Jens Herzer, Martina Janssen, and Clare K. Rothschild, with Michaela Engelmann. WUNT 246. Tübingen: Mohr Siebeck, 2009.

Holladay, Carl R. *Fragments from Hellenistic Jewish Authors.* Volume 2: *Poets.* Atlanta: Scholars Press, 1989.

Horgan, Maurya P. *Pesharim: Qumran Interpretations of Biblical Books.* CBQMS 8. Washington, DC: Catholic Biblical Association, 1979.

Horsley, Richard A. *Scribes, Visionaries and the Politics of Second Temple Judea*. Louisville: Westminster John Knox, 2007.

———. *Revolt of the Scribes: Resistance and Apocalyptic Origins*. Minneapolis: Fortress, 2010.

Horsley, R. A., and J. S. Hanson. *Bandits, Prophets and Messiahs: Popular Movements at the Time of Jesus*. Minneapolis: Winston, 1985.

Hultgård, Anders. "Bahman Yasht: A Persian Apocalypse." Pages 114-34 in *Mysteries and Revelations: Apocalyptic Studies since the Uppsala Colloquium*. Edited by John J. Collins and James H. Charlesworth. JSPSup 9. Sheffield: Sheffield Academic Press, 1991.

———. "Myth et Histoire dans l'Iran Ancien. Etude de quelques themes dans le Bahman Yasht." Pages 63-162 in *Apocalyptique Iranienne et Dualisme Qoumrânien*. Edited by Geo Widengren, Anders Hultgård, and Marc Philonenko. Paris: Maisonneuve, 1995.

———. "Persian Apocalypticism." Pages 56-60 in *Encyclopedia of Apocalypticism*, volume 1: *The Origins of Apocalypticism in Judaism and Christianity*. Edited by J. J. Collins. New York: Continuum, 1998.

Hultgren, S. *From the Damascus Covenant to the Covenant of the Community: Literary, Historical and Theological Studies in the Dead Sea Scrolls*. STDJ 66. Leiden: Brill, 2007.

Humphrey, E. M. *The Ladies and the Cities: Transformation and Apocalyptic Identity in Joseph and Aseneth, 4 Ezra, and the Apocalypse of the Shepherd of Hermas*. Sheffield: Sheffield Academic Press, 1995.

———. *Joseph and Aseneth*. Sheffield: Sheffield Academic Press, 2000.

Humphreys, W. Lee. "A Life-Style for the Diaspora: A Study of the Tales of Esther and Daniel." *JBL* 92 (1973) 211-23.

Jachmann, G. "Die Vierte Ekloge Vergils." *Annali della Scuola Normale Superiore di Pisa* 21 (1953) 13-62.

Jackson, David R. *Enochic Judaism*. LSTS 49. London and New York: Continuum, 2004.

Jacobsen, T. *The Treasures of Darkness: A History of Mesopotamian Religion*. New Haven: Yale University Press, 1976.

Jassen, Alex P. *Mediating the Divine: Prophecy and Revelation in the Dead Sea Scrolls and Second Temple Judaism*. STDJ 68. Leiden: Brill, 2007.

Jenks, G. C. *The Origins and Early Development of the Antichrist Myth*. Berlin: de Gruyter, 1991.

Jervell, Jacob. *Imago Dei*. Göttingen: Vandenhoeck & Ruprecht, 1960.

Johnson, D. G. *From Chaos to Restoration: An Integrative Reading of Isaiah 24–27*. JSOTSup 61. Sheffield: Sheffield Academic Press, 1988.

Juergensmeyer, Mark. *Terror in the Mind of God: The Global Rise of Religious Violence*. Berkeley: University of California Press, 2003.

Kaibel, G., ed. *Epigrammata graeca ex lapidibus conlecta*. Berlin: Reimer, 1978.

Kaiser, O. *Isaiah 13–39*. OTL. Philadelphia: Westminster, 1974.

Kaminsky, Joel. "Did Election Imply the Mistreatment of Non-Israelites?" *HTR* 96 (2003) 397-425.

————. *Yet I Loved Jacob: Reclaiming the Biblical Concept of Election*. Nashville: Abingdon, 2007.

Kampen, J. *The Hasideans and the Origin of Pharisaism*. Atlanta: Scholars Press, 1988.

Käsemann, Ernst. "The Beginnings of Christian Theology." *Journal for Theology and the Church* 6 (1969) 17-46.

Kinnier-Wilson, J. V. *The Legend of Etana*. Warminster, UK: Aris & Phillips, 1985.

Kirkpatrick, Shane. *Competing for Honor: A Social-Scientific Reading of Daniel 1–6*. Leiden: Brill, 2005.

Knibb, Michael A. "2 Esdras." Pages 76-307 in *The First and Second Books of Esdras*. Edited by R. J. Coggins and M. Knibb. The Cambridge Bible Commentary. Cambridge: Cambridge University Press, 1979.

————. "Apocalyptic and Wisdom in 4 Ezra." *JJS* 13 (1983) 56-74.

————. "1 Enoch." Pages 169-319 in *The Apocryphal Old Testament*. Edited by H. F. D. Sparks. Oxford: Clarendon, 1984.

————. *The Qumran Community*. Cambridge: Cambridge University Press, 1987.

————. "The Structure and Composition of the Parables of Enoch." Pages 48-64 in *Enoch and the Messiah Son of Man: Revisiting the Book of Parables*. Edited by G. Boccaccini. Grand Rapids: Eerdmans, 2007.

Knohl, Israel. "On 'the Son of God,' Armilus and Messiah Son of Joseph." *Tarbiz* 68 (1998) 13-38 [Heb.].

————. *The Messiah before Jesus*. Berkeley: University of California Press, 2000.

————. "'By Three Days Live': Messiahs, Resurrection and Ascent to Heaven in *Hazon Gabriel*." *Journal of Religion* 88 (2008) 147-58.

————. "The Messiah Son of Joseph." *Biblical Archeology Review* 34.5 (2008) 58-62.

————. *Messiahs and Resurrection in 'The Gabriel Revelation'*. The Kogod Library of Judaic Studies. London/New York: Continuum, 2009.

Koch, Klaus. *The Rediscovery of Apocalyptic*. Naperville, IL: Allenson, 1972.

————. "Von profetischen zum apokalyptischen Visionsbericht." Pages 413-46 in *Apocalypticism in the Mediterranean World and the Near East*. Edited by David Hellholm. Tübingen: Mohr Siebeck, 1983.

————. "Is Daniel Also among the Prophets?" *Interpretation* 39 (1985) 117-30.

————. *Europa, Rom und der Kaiser vor dem Hintergrund von zwei Jahrtausenden Rezeption des Buches Daniel*. Göttingen: Vandenhoeck & Ruprecht, 1997.

Kovacs, Judith, and Christopher Rowland. *Revelation*. Blackwell Bible Commentaries. Oxford: Blackwell, 2004.

Kratz, R. G. *Translatio Imperii. Untersuchungen zu den aramäischen Danielerzählungen und ihrem theologiegeschichtlichen Umfeld*. Göttingen: Vandenhoeck & Ruprecht, 1991.

Kraus, H.-J. *Psalms 60–150*. Augsburg: Minneapolis, 1989.

Kugel, James L. "The *Jubilees* Apocalypse." *DSD* 1 (1994) 322-37.

———. *Traditions of the Bible*. Cambridge, MA: Harvard University Press, 1998.

———. "On the Interpolations in the Book of Jubilees." *RevQ* 24 (2009) 215-72.

Kuhn, K. H. "The Apocalypse of Zephaniah and an Anonymous Apocalypse." Pages 915-25 in *The Apocryphal Old Testament*. Edited by H. F. D. Sparks. Oxford: Clarendon, 1984.

Kurfess, A. "Oracula Sibylina I/II." *ZNW* 40 (1941) 151-65.

———. "Vergils vierte Ekloge und die Oracula Sibyllina." *Historisches Jahrbuch der Gorres Gesellschaft* 73 (1956) 120-27.

Kvanvig, H. S. *Roots of Apocalyptic: The Mesopotamian Background of the Enoch Figure and of the Son of Man*. WUNT 61. Neukirchen-Vluyn: Neukirchener Verlag, 1988.

Labahn, M., and M. Lang, eds. *Lebendige Hoffnung — Ewiger Tod?! Jenseitsvorstellungen im Hellenismus, Judentum und Christentum*. Leipzig: Evangelische Verlagsanstalt, 2007.

LaHaye, Tim, and Jerry Jenkins. *Left Behind: A Novel of Earth's Last Days*. Wheaton, IL: Tyndale House, 1995.

Lakoff, George. *Women, Fire, and Dangerous Things: What Categories Reveal about the Mind*. Chicago: University of Chicago Press, 1987.

Lambert, W. G. "Enmeduranki and Related Matters." *JCS* 21 (1967) 126-38.

———. *The Background of Jewish Apocalyptic*. London: Athlone, 1978.

Lang, B. "Street Theater, Raising the Dead, and the Zoroastrian Connection in Ezekiel's Preaching." Pages 297-316 in *Ezekiel and His Book*. Edited by J. Lust. Leuven: Leuven University Press, 1986.

Lange, Armin. *Weisheit und Prädestination. Weisheitliche Urordnung und Prädestination in den Textfunden von Qumran*. Leiden: Brill, 1995.

———. "Divinatorische Träume und Apokalyptik im Jubiläenbuch." Pages 25-38 in *Studies in the Book of Jubilees*. Edited by M. Albani, J. Frey, and A. Lange. Tübingen: Mohr Siebeck, 1997.

Lanzilatto, Lautaro Roig. "Does Punishment Reward the Righteous? The Justice Pattern Underlying the Apocalypse of Peter." Pages 127-57 in *The Apocalypse of Peter*. Edited by Jan N. Bremmer and István Czachesz. Leuven: Peeters, 2003.

Lawrence, D. H. *Apocalypse*. New York: Viking, 1931.

Lebram, J. C. H. "Die Weltreiche in der jüdischen Apokalyptik. Bemerkungen zu Tob. 14:4-7." *ZAW* 76 (1964) 328-31.

Lemaire, A. "Zorobabel et la Judée à la lumière de l'épigraphie (fin du VIᵉ S. av. J.-C.)." *RB* 103 (1996) 48-57.

Levenson, J. D. *The Theology of the Program of Restoration of Ezekiel 40–48*. Missoula, MT: Scholars Press, 1976.

———. *Creation and the Persistence of Evil: The Jewish Drama of Divine Omnipotence*. San Francisco: Harper, 1988.

———. *Resurrection and the Restoration of Israel: The Ultimate Victory of the God of Life*. New Haven: Yale University Press, 2006.

Bibliography

Licht, J. "Taxo, or the Apocalyptic Doctrine of Vengeance." *JJS* 12 (1961) 95-103.

Lightfoot, J. L. *The Sibylline Oracles, with Introduction, Translation, and Commentary on the First and Second Books.* Oxford: Oxford University Press, 2007.

Lincoln, Bruce. "Symmetric Dualisms: Bush and Bin Laden on Oct. 7 2001." Pages 89-112 in *Apocalypse and Violence.* Edited by Abbas Amanat and John J. Collins. New Haven: Yale Center for International and Area Studies and the Council on Middle East Studies, 2007.

Lindblom, J. *Die Jesaja Apokalypse. Jesaja 24–27.* Lund: Gleerup, 1938.

Lindsey, Hal, with C. C. Carlson, *The Late Great Planet Earth.* Grand Rapids: Zondervan, 1970.

Linton, Gregory L. "Reading the Apocalypse as Apocalypse: The Limits of Genre." Pages 9-41 in *The Reality of Apocalypse: Rhetoric and Politics in the Book of Revelation.* Edited by David L. Barr. SBL Symposium Series 39. Atlanta: SBL/Leiden: Brill, 2006.

Longenecker, B. W. *Eschatology and the Covenant: A Comparison of 4 Ezra and Romans 1–11.* JSNTSup 57. Sheffield: JSOT, 1991.

Maier, J. *The Temple Scroll: An Introduction, Translation and Commentary.* Sheffield: JSOT, 1985.

———. "The Temple Scroll and Tendencies in the Cultic Architecture of the Second Commonwealth." Pages 53-82 in *Archaeology and History in the Dead Sea Scrolls.* Edited by L. H. Schiffman. Sheffield: JSOT, 1990.

Marshall, John W. *Parables of War: Reading John's Apocalypse.* Waterloo, ON: Wilfrid Laurier, 2001.

McCarter, P. Kyle. "Dualism in Antiquity." Pages 19-35 in *Light against Darkness.* Edited by Armin Lange, Eric M. Meyers, Bennie H. Reynolds, and Randall Styers. Göttingen: Vandenhoeck & Ruprecht, 2011.

McGinn, B. *Visions of the End.* New York: Columbia University Press, 1979.

———. "Love, Knowledge, and Mystical Union in Western Christianity: Twelfth to Sixteenth Centuries." *Church History* 56 (1987) 7-24.

———. *The Foundations of Mysticism.* New York: Crossroad, 1991.

———. *Antichrist: Two Thousand Years of the Human Fascination with Evil.* San Francisco: Harper, 1994.

Meade, D. G. *Pseudonymity and Canon.* Tübingen: Mohr, 1986.

Meeks, W. "Moses as God and King." Pages 354-71 in *Religions in Antiquity: Essays in Memory of Erwin Ramsdell Goodenough.* Edited by J. Neusner. Leiden: Brill, 1968.

Metzger, Bruce M. "Literary Forgeries and Canonical Pseudepigrapha." *JBL* 91 (1972) 3-24.

Meyers, C. L., and E. M. Meyers. *Haggai, Zechariah 1–8.* AB 25. New York: Doubleday, 1987.

Milik, J. T. " 'Prière de Nabonide' et autres écrits d'un cycle de Daniel." *RB* 63 (1956) 407-15.

————. *The Books of Enoch: Aramaic Fragments of Qumrân Cave 4*. Oxford: Clarendon, 1976.

Millar, W. R. *Isaiah 24–27 and the Origin of Apocalyptic*. HSM 11. Cambridge, MA: Harvard University Press, 1976.

Miller, Carolyn R. "Genre as Social Action." *Quarterly Journal of Speech* 70 (May 1984) 151-67.

————. "Rhetorical Community: The Cultural Basis of Genre." Pages 67-78 in *Genre and the New Rhetoric*. Edited by Aviva Freedman and Peter Medway. London: Taylor, 1994.

Mitchell, Christine. "Power, *Eros,* and Biblical Genres." Pages 31-43 in *Bakhtin and Genre Theory in Biblical Studies*. Edited by Roland Boer. Semeia Studies 63. Atlanta: Society of Biblical Literature, 2007.

Momigliano, Arnaldo. "From the Pagan to the Christian Sibyl." Pages 725-44 in *Nono Contributo alla Storia degli Studi Classici e del Mondo antico*. Edited by R. DiDonato. Rome: Edizioni di Storia e Letteratura, 1992.

Moore, G. F. *Judaism*. New York: Schocken, 1971.

Moore, Stephen D. *Empire and Apocalypse: Postcolonialism and the New Testament*. Sheffield: Sheffield Phoenix, 2006.

Mowinckel, S. *He That Cometh*. Nashville: Abingdon, 1954.

————. *The Psalms in Israel's Worship*. Oxford: Blackwell, 1962. Repr. Grand Rapids: Eerdmans, 2004.

Müller, H.-P. *Ursprünge und Strukturen Alttestamentlicher Eschatologie*. BZAW 109. Berlin: Töpelmann, 1969.

Murphy, F. J. "The Temple in the Syriac Apocalypse of Baruch." *JBL* 106 (1987) 671-83.

Najman, Hindy. *Seconding Sinai: The Development of Mosaic Discourse in Second Temple Judaism*. JSJSup 77. Leiden: Brill, 2003.

————. *Past Renewals: Interpretative Authority, Renewed Revelation and the Quest for Perfection in Jewish Antiquity*. JSJSup 53. Leiden: Brill, 2010.

————. "The Inheritance of Prophecy in Apocalypse." Pages 36-51 in *The Oxford Handbook of Apocalyptic Literature*. Edited by John J. Collins. New York: Oxford University Press, 2014.

Najman, H., D. T. Runia, and G. E. Sterling, eds. *Laws Stamped with the Seals of Nature: Law and Nature in Hellenistic Philosophy and Philo of Alexandria*. The Studia Philonica Annual 15. BJSSup 337. Providence: Brown University Press, 2003.

Neujahr, Matthew. *Predicting the Past in the Ancient Near East: Mantic Historiography in Ancient Mesopotamia, Judah, and the Mediterranean World*. Brown Judaic Studies 354. Providence: Brown University, 2012.

Newsom, Carol A. *Songs of the Sabbath Sacrifice: A Critical Edition*. Atlanta: Scholars Press, 1985.

————. " 'He Has Established for Himself Priests': Human and Angelic Priesthood in the Qumran Sabbath Shirot." Pages 101-20 in *Archaeology and History in the*

Dead Sea Scrolls. Edited by L. H. Schiffman. Sheffield: Journal for the Study of the Old Testament, 1990.

———. *The Self as Symbolic Space: Constructing Identity and Community at Qumran.* STDJ 52. Leiden: Brill, 2004.

———. "Spying Out the Land: A Report from Genology." Pages 437-50 in *Seeking Out the Wisdom of the Ancients: Essays Offered to Honor Michael V. Fox on the Occasion of His Sixty-Fifth Birthday.* Edited by R. L. Troxel, K. G. Friebel, and D. R. Magary. Winona Lake, IN: Eisenbrauns, 2005.

———. "Rhetorical Criticism and the Reading of the Qumran Scrolls." Pages 683-708 in *The Oxford Handbook of the Dead Sea Scrolls.* Edited by Timothy H. Lim and John J. Collins. Oxford: Oxford University Press, 2010.

Nickelsburg, George W. E. "Eschatology in the Testament of Abraham: A Study of the Judgement Scenes in the Two Recensions." Pages 23-64 in *Studies on the Testament of Abraham.* Edited by G. W. Nickelsburg. Missoula, MT: Scholars Press, 1976.

———. "Apocalyptic and Myth in 1 Enoch 6–11." *JBL* 96 (1977) 383-405.

———. "Riches, the Rich and God's Judgment in 1 Enoch 92–105 and the Gospel according to Luke." *NTS* 25 (1979) 324-44.

———. "Enoch, Levi, and Peter: Recipients of Revelation in Upper Galilee." *JBL* 100 (1981) 575-600.

———. "The Bible Rewritten and Expanded." Pages 89-156 in *Jewish Writings of the Second Temple Period.* Edited by Michael E. Stone. CRINT 2.2. Assen: van Gorcum/Philadelphia: Fortress, 1984.

———. "The Apocalyptic Construction of Reality in 1 Enoch." Pages 51-64 in *Mysteries and Revelations: Apocalyptic Studies since the Uppsala Colloquium.* Edited by John J. Collins and James H. Charlesworth. JSPSup 9. Sheffield: Sheffield Academic Press, 1991.

———. "Enochic Wisdom: An Alternative to the Mosaic Torah?" Pages 123-32 in *Ḥesed Ve-Emet: Studies in Honor of Ernest S. Frerichs.* Edited by Jodi Magness and Seymour Gitin. BJS 320. Atlanta: Scholars Press, 1998.

———. *1 Enoch 1: A Commentary on the Book of 1 Enoch, Chapters 1–36; 81–108.* Hermeneia. Minneapolis: Fortress, 2001.

———. *Jewish Literature between the Bible and the Mishnah.* 2nd ed. Minneapolis: Fortress, 2005.

———. *Resurrection, Immortality, and Eternal Life in Intertestamental Judaism and Early Christianity.* HTS 56. Expanded edition. Cambridge, MA: Harvard University Press, 2006.

———. "Discerning the Structure(s) of the Enochic Book of Parables." Pages 23-47 in *Enoch and the Messiah Son of Man: Revisiting the Book of Parables.* Edited by G. Boccaccini. Grand Rapids: Eerdmans, 2007.

———. "Enochic Wisdom and Its Relationship to the Mosaic Torah." Pages 81-94 in

The Early Enoch Literature. Edited by G. Boccaccini and J. J. Collins. JSJSup 121. Leiden: Brill, 2007.

Nickelsburg, George W. E., and James C. VanderKam. *1 Enoch: A New Translation.* Minneapolis: Fortress, 2004.

———. *1 Enoch 2.* Hermeneia. Minneapolis: Fortress, 2012.

Niditch, Susan. *The Symbolic Vision in Biblical Tradition.* HSM 30. Chico, CA: Scholars Press, 1983.

Nilsson, M. P. *Geschichte der griechischen Religion.* 3rd ed. Munich: Beck, 1974.

Nisbet, R. G. M. "Virgil's Fourth Eclogue: Easterners and Westerners." *Bulletin of the Institute for Classical Studies* 25 (1978) 59-78.

Novak, D. *Natural Law in Judaism.* Cambridge: Cambridge University Press, 1998.

Oppenheim, A. L. "Nabonidus and the Clergy of Babylon." *ANET* 314.

Orlov, A. A. *The Enoch-Metatron Tradition.* TSAJ 107. Tübingen: Mohr Siebeck, 2005.

Otto, Eckart. "Psalm 2 in neuassyrischer Zeit. Assyrische Motive in der judäischen Königsideologie." Pages 335-49 in *Textarbeit. Studien zu Texten und ihrer Rezeption aus dem Alten Testament und der Umwelt Israels. Festschrift für Peter Weimar.* Edited by Klaus Kiesow and Thomas Meurer. AOAT 294. Münster: Ugarit-Verlag, 2003.

Parke, H. W. *Sibyls and Sibylline Prophecy in Classical Antiquity.* Edited by B. McGing. London: Routledge, 1998.

Peerbolte, B. J. Lietaert. *The Antecedents of Antichrist: A Traditio-Historical Study of the Earliest Christian Views on Eschatological Opponents.* Leiden: Brill, 1996.

Perdue, Leo G. *Wisdom and Creation: The Theology of Wisdom Literature.* Nashville: Abingdon, 1994.

Perrin, Norman. "Eschatology and Hermeneutics: Reflections on Method in the Interpretation of the New Testament." *JBL* 93 (1974) 3-14.

Petersen, Anders Klostergaard. "Rewritten Bible as a Borderline Phenomenon — Genre, Textual Strategy or Canonical Anachronism?" Pages 284-306 in *Flores Florentino: Dead Sea Scrolls and Other Early Jewish Studies in Honour of Florentino García Martínez.* Edited by A. Hilhorst, É. Puech, and E. Tigchelaar. JSJSup 122. Leiden: Brill, 2007.

Petersen, D. L. *Haggai and Zechariah 1–8.* OTL. Philadelphia: Westminster, 1984.

Pippin, Tina. *Death and Desire: The Rhetoric of Gender in the Apocalypse of John.* Louisville: Westminster John Knox, 1992.

Plöger, Otto. *Theocracy and Eschatology.* Richmond: John Knox, 1968.

Polaski, D. C. "Destruction, Construction, Argumentation: A Rhetorical Reading of Isaiah 24–27." Pages 19-39 in *Vision and Persuasion: Rhetorical Dimensions of Apocalyptic Discourse.* Edited by G. Carey and L. G. Bloomquist. St. Louis: Chalice, 1999.

———. *Authorizing an End: The Isaiah Apocalypse and Intertextuality.* Bib Int 50. Leiden: Brill, 2001.

Pomykala, K. E. *The Davidic Dynasty Tradition in Early Judaism.* SBLEJL 7. Atlanta: Scholars Press, 1995.

Portier-Young, Anathea. *Apocalypse against Empire: Theologies of Resistance in Early Judaism.* Grand Rapids: Eerdmans, 2010.

—. "Languages of Identity and Obligation: Daniel as Bilingual Book." *VT* 60 (2010) 98-115.

Puech, E. *La Croyance des Esséniens en la Vie Future. Immortalité, Résurrection, Vie Éternelle?* EB 21. Paris: Gabalda, 1993.

—. "A propos de la Jerusalem nouvelle d'après les manuscrits de la Mer Morte." *Semitica* 43-44 (1995) 64-73.

Qimron, E. *The Temple Scroll: A Critical Edition with Extensive Reconstructions.* Jerusalem: Israel Exploration Society, 1996.

Redditt, P. L. "Zerubbabel, Joshua, and the Night Visions of Zechariah." *CBQ* 54 (1992) 249-59.

—. *Haggai, Zechariah, Malachi.* NCB. Grand Rapids: Eerdmans, 1995.

Reed, Annette Yoshiko. "Interrogating Enochic Judaism: 1 Enoch as Evidence for Intellectual History, Social Realities, and Literary Tradition." Pages 336-44 in *Enoch and Qumran Origins: New Light on a Forgotten Connection.* Edited by G. Boccaccini. Grand Rapids: Eerdmans, 2005.

Rendsburg, G. A. "Linguistic and Stylistic Notes to the Hazon Gabriel Inscription." *DSD* 16 (2009) 107-16.

Reynolds, Bennie H., III. *Between Symbolism and Realism: The Use of Symbolic and Non-Symbolic Language in Ancient Jewish Apocalypses 333-63 B.C.E.* JAJSup 8. Göttingen: Vandenhoeck & Ruprecht, 2011.

Roberts, J. J. M. *Nahum, Habakkuk, and Zephaniah.* OTL. Louisville: Westminster, 1991.

Robinson, John A. T. *Redating the New Testament.* Philadelphia: Westminster, 1976.

Rochberg-Halton, F. "Mesopotamian Cosmology." Pages 398-407 in *Encyclopedia of Cosmology: Historical, Philosophical, and Scientific Foundations of Modern Cosmology.* Edited by N. S. Hetherington. New York: Garland, 1993.

Rohde, E. *Psyche: The Cult of Souls and Belief in Immortality among the Greeks.* New York, 1925.

Rosch, Eleanor. "Cognitive Representations of Semantic Categories." *Journal of Experimental Psychology (General)* 104 (1975) 192-233.

—. "Principles of Categorization." Pages 27-48 in *Cognition and Categorization.* Edited E. Rosch and B. Lloyd. Hillsdale, NJ: Erlbaum, 1978.

Rose, W. *Zemah and Zerubbabel: Messianic Expectations in the Early Postexilic Period.* JSOTSup 34. Sheffield: Sheffield Academic Press, 2000.

Rosmarin, Adena. *The Power of Genre.* Minneapolis: University of Minnesota, 1985.

Rossing, Barbara R. *The Choice between Two Cities: Whore, Bride, and Empire in the Apocalypse.* Harrisburg, PA: Trinity Press International, 1999.

Rowland, Christopher. *The Open Heaven: A Study of Apocalyptic in Judaism and Early Christianity.* New York: Crossroad, 1982.

———. *Radical Christianity: A Reading of Recovery.* Maryknoll, NY: Orbis, 1988.

———. "The Book of Revelation." Pages 503-736 in volume 12 of *The New Interpreter's Bible.* Edited by Leander E. Keck. Nashville: Abingdon, 1998.

———. "The Evidence from the Reception History of the Book of Revelation." Pages 1-18 in *Apocalypse and Violence.* Edited by Abbas Amanat and John J. Collins. New Haven: Yale Center for International and Area Studies and the Council on Middle East Studies, 2007.

Rowley, H. H. *The Servant of the Lord and Other Essays on the Old Testament.* London: Lutterworth, 1952.

Rubinkiewicz, R. "Apocalypse of Abraham." *OTP* 1.681-705.

Rudolph, W. *Jesaja 24–27.* BWANT 4/10. Stuttgart: Kohlhammer, 1933.

Ryle, H. E., and M. R. James. *Psalms of the Pharisees: Commonly Called the Psalms of Solomon.* Cambridge: Cambridge University Press, 1891.

Sacchi, Paolo. *Jewish Apocalyptic and Its History.* Sheffield: Sheffield Academic Press, 1997.

Samely, Alexander, in collaboration with Philip Alexander, Rocco Bernasconi, and Robert Hayward. *Profiling Jewish Literature in Antiquity: An Inventory from Second Temple Texts to the Talmud.* Oxford: Oxford University Press, 2013.

Sanders, E. P. *Paul and Palestinian Judaism.* Philadelphia: Fortress, 1977.

———. "The Genre of Palestinian Jewish Apocalypses." Pages 447-59 in *Apocalypticism in the Mediterranean World and the Near East: Proceedings of the International Colloquium on Apocalypticism, Uppsala, August 12-17, 1979.* Edited by D. Hellholm. Tübingen: Mohr-Siebeck, 1983.

———. "The Testament of Abraham." Pages 882-902 in volume 1 of *The Old Testament Pseudepigrapha.* Edited by J. H. Charlesworth. 2 vols. Garden City, NY: Doubleday, 1983.

Santoso, Agus. *Die Apokalyptik als jüdische Denkbewegung. Eine literarkritische Untersuchung zum Buch Daniel.* Marburg: Tectum, 2007.

Sasson, Victor. "The Vision of Gabriel and Messiah in Mainstream Judaism and in Christianity: Textual, Philological, and Theological Comments." http://victorsasson .blogspot.com/2009/09/vision-of-gabriel-and-messiah-in.html.

Schiffman, Lawrence H. *Sectarian Law in the Dead Sea Scrolls.* Chico, CA: Scholars Press, 1983.

———. "Sacred Space: The Land of Israel in the Temple Scroll." Pages 398-410 in *Biblical Archaeology Today, 1990: Proceedings of the Second International Congress on Biblical Archaeology.* Edited by A. Biran and J. Aviram. Jerusalem: Israel Exploration Society, 1993.

———. "Jerusalem in the Dead Sea Scrolls." Pages 73-88 in *The Centrality of Jerusalem: Historical Perspectives.* Edited by M. Poorthuis and C. Safrai. Kampen: Kok/ Pharos, 1996.

————. "Halakhic Elements in the Sapiential Texts from Qumran." Pages 89-100 in *Sapiential Perspectives: Wisdom Literature in Light of the Dead Sea Scrolls*. Edited by J. J. Collins, G. E. Sterling, and R. A. Clements. STDJ 51. Leiden: Brill, 2004.

————. "The Book of Jubilees and the Temple Scroll." Pages 99-115 in *Enoch and the Mosaic Torah: The Evidence of Jubilees*. Edited by G. Boccaccini and G. Ibba. Grand Rapids: Eerdmans, 2009.

Schivelbusch, Wolfgang. *The Culture of Defeat: On National Trauma, Mourning and Recovery*. New York: Metropolitan, 2001.

Schmidt, F. *La Pensée du Temple. De Jerusalem à Qoumrân*. Paris: Seuil, 1994.

Schniedewind, W. M. *Society and the Promise to David: The Reception History of 2 Samuel 1–17*. New York: Oxford University Press, 1999.

Schultz, Brian. "The Qumran Cemetery: 150 Years of Research." *DSD* 13.2 (2006) 194-228.

Schüssler Fiorenza, Elisabeth. *Invitation to the Book of Revelation*. New York: Doubleday, 1981.

————. *The Book of Revelation: Justice and Judgment*. Philadelphia: Fortress, 1985.

Schwartz, Regina. *The Curse of Cain: The Violent Legacy of Monotheism*. Chicago: University of Chicago Press, 1997.

Scott, James C. *Domination and the Arts of Resistance: Hidden Transcripts*. New Haven: Yale University Press, 1990.

Segal, A. F. "Heavenly Ascent in Hellenistic Judaism, Early Christianity and Their Environment." *ANRW* II.23.2 (1980) 1352-68.

————. *Life after Death: A History of the Afterlife in the Religions of the West*. New York: Doubleday, 2004.

Segal, Michael. "4QReworked Pentateuch or 4QPentateuch?" Pages 391-99 in *The Dead Sea Scrolls: Fifty Years after Their Discovery*. Edited by L. Schiffman, E. Tov, and J. VanderKam. Jerusalem: Israel Exploration Society/Shrine of the Book, Israel Museum, 2000.

————. "Between Bible and Rewritten Bible." Pages 10-28 in *Biblical Interpretation at Qumran*. Edited by Matthias Henze. Grand Rapids: Eerdmans, 2005.

————. *The Book of Jubilees: Rewritten Bible, Redaction, Ideology and Theology*. JSJSup 117. Leiden: Brill, 2007.

Seow, C.-L. *Ecclesiastes*. AB 18. New York: Doubleday, 1997.

Sharp, Carolyn J. *Irony and Meaning in the Hebrew Bible*. Bloomington: Indiana University Press, 2009.

Sievers, J. *The Hasmoneans and Their Supporters*. Atlanta: Scholars Press, 1990.

Sim, D. C. "The Social Setting of Ancient Apocalypticism: A Question of Method." *JSP* 13 (1995) 5-16.

Sinding, Michael. "After Definitions: Genre, Categories, and Cognitive Science." *Genre* 35 (2002) 181-220.

Smith, J. Z. "Native Cults in the Hellenistic Period." *History of Religions* 11 (1971) 236-49.

Smith, Morton. "On the History of *Apokalypto* and *Apokalypsis*." Pages 9-20 in *Apoc-*

alypticism in the Mediterranean World and the Near East: Proceedings of the International Colloquium on Apocalypticism, Uppsala, August 12-17, 1979. Edited by D. Hellholm. Tübingen: Mohr-Siebeck, 1983.

————. "Ascent to the Heavens and Deification in 4QMᵃ." Pages 181-88 in *Archaeology and History in the Dead Sea Scrolls.* Edited by L. H. Schiffman. Sheffield: Journal for the Study of the Old Testament, 1990.

Smith-Christopher, Daniel. "The Book of Daniel." Pages 17-194 in *The New Interpreter's Bible.* Nashville: Abingdon, 1996.

Speiser, E. A. "A Vision of the Nether World." *ANET* 109-10.

Speyer, Wolfgang. *Die Literarische Falschung im Heidenischen und Christlichen Altertum. Ein Versuch Ihrer Deutung.* Munich: Beck, 1971.

————. *Frühes Christentum im antiken Strahlungsfeld.* Tübingen: Mohr, 1989.

Steck, O. H. *Israel und das gewaltsame Geschick der Propheten.* Neukirchen-Vluyn: Neukirchener Verlag, 1967.

Stegemann, Hartmut. *Die Entstehung der Qumrangemeinde.* Bonn: published privately, 1971.

————. "Die Bedeutung der Qumranfund für die Erforschung der Apokalyptik." Pages 495-530 in *Apocalypticism in the Mediterranean World and the Near East: Proceedings of the International Colloquium on Apocalypticism, Uppsala, August 12-17, 1979.* Edited by D. Hellholm. Tübingen: Mohr-Siebeck, 1983.

————. "Some Remarks to *1QSa,* to *1QSb* and to Qumran Messianism." *RevQ* 17 (1996) 479-505.

Stemberger, G. *Der Leib der Auferstehung. Studien zur Anthropologie und Eschatologie des palästinischen Judentums im neutestamentlichen Zeitalter.* Rome: Pontifical Biblical Institute, 1972.

Stendahl, Krister. "Hate, Non-Retaliation, and Love: 1QS X, 17-20 and Rom 12:19-21." *Harvard Theological Review* 55 (1962) 343-55.

Steudel, Annette. "Psalm 2 im antiken Judentum." Pages 189-97 in *Gottessohn und Menschensohn. Exegetische Paradigmen biblischer Intertextualität.* Edited by Dieter Sänger. Neukirchen-Vluyn: Neukirchener Verlag, 2004.

Stone, Michael E. "Lists of Revealed Things in Apocalyptic Literature." Pages 414-54 in *Magnalia Dei: The Mighty Acts of God.* Edited by F. M. Cross et al. Garden City: Doubleday, 1976.

————. "The Book of Enoch and Judaism in the Third Century B.C.E." *CBQ* 40 (1978) 479-92.

————. *Scriptures, Sects and Visions: A Profile of Judaism from Ezra to the Jewish Revolts.* Philadelphia: Fortress, 1980.

————. *Fourth Ezra: A Commentary on the Book of Fourth Ezra.* Hermeneia. Minneapolis: Fortress, 1990.

————. "On Reading an Apocalypse." Pages 65-78 in *Mysteries and Revelations: Apocalyptic Studies since the Uppsala Colloquium.* Edited by John J. Collins and James H. Charlesworth. JSPSup 9. Sheffield: Sheffield Academic Press, 1991.

Stone, M. E., and J. C. Greenfield. "Aramaic Levi Document." Pages 1-72 in *Qumran Cave 4. XVII. Parabiblical Texts, Part 3*. Edited by G. Brooke et al. DJD 22. Oxford: Clarendon, 1996.

Strugnell, J., and D. J. Harrington. *Qumran Cave 4. XXIV. Sapiential Texts, Part 2. 4QInstruction (Musar le Mevin)*. DJD 24. Oxford: Clarendon, 1999.

Stuckenbruck, L. T. "4QInstruction and the Possible Influence of Early Enochic Traditions: An Evaluation." Pages 245-61 in *The Wisdom Texts from Qumran and the Development of Sapiential Thought*. Edited by C. Hempel, A. Lange, and H. Lichtenberger. BETL 159. Leuven: Peeters, 2002.

————. "The Early Traditions Related to 1 Enoch from the Dead Sea Scrolls: An Overview and Assessment." Pages 41-63 in *The Early Enoch Literature*. Edited by G. Boccaccini and J. J. Collins. JSJSup 121. Leiden: Brill, 2007.

Suter, D. W. "Fallen Angel, Fallen Priest: The Problem of Family Purity in 1 Enoch 6–16." *HUCA* 50 (1979) 115-35.

Swain, J. W. "The Theory of the Four Monarchies: Opposition History under the Roman Empire." *Classical Philology* 35 (1940) 1-21.

Swales, John. *Genre Analysis: English in Academic and Research Settings*. Cambridge: Cambridge University Press, 1990.

Sweeney, M. A. *Isaiah 1–39, with an Introduction to Prophetic Literature*. FOTL XVI. Grand Rapids: Eerdmans, 1996.

————. "The End of Eschatology in Daniel." *Bib Int* 9 (2001) 123-40.

Tabor, J. D. *Things Unutterable: Paul's Ascent to Paradise in Its Greco-Roman, Judaic, and Early Christian Contexts*. Lanham, MD: University Press of America, 1986.

————. " 'Returning to the Divinity': Josephus's Portrayal of the Disappearances of Enoch, Elijah and Moses." *JBL* 108 (1989) 225-38.

————. "Heaven, Ascent to." *ABD* 3.91-94.

Tcherikover, Victor. "Jewish Apologetic Literature Reconsidered." *Eos* 48 (1956) 169-93.

————. *Hellenistic Civilization and the Jews*. New York: Atheneum, 1970.

Thilo, G., ed. *Servii Grammatici qui feruntur in Vergilii Bucolica et Georgica Commentarii*. Leipzig: Teubner, 1887.

Thompson, Alden Lloyd. *Responsibility for Evil in the Theodicy of 4 Ezra*. SBLDS 29. Missoula, MT: Scholars Press, 1977.

Thompson, Leonard L. *The Book of Revelation: Apocalypse and Empire*. Oxford and New York: Oxford University Press, 1990.

Tigchelaar, E. J. *Prophets of Old and the Day of the End: Zechariah, the Book of the Watchers and Apocalyptic*. Leiden: Brill, 1997.

Tiller, P. A. *A Commentary on the Animal Apocalypse of 1 Enoch*. Atlanta: Scholars Press, 1993.

————. "The 'Eternal Planting' in the Dead Sea Scrolls." *DSD* 4 (1997) 312-35.

Tov, Emanuel, and Sidnie White. "Reworked Pentateuch." Pages 187-351 in *Qumran Cave 4, VIII*. Edited by Harold Attridge et al. DJD 13. Oxford: Clarendon, 1994.

Tuell, S. S. "Ezekiel 40–42 as Verbal Icon." *CBQ* 58 (1996) 649-64.

Valeta, David. *Lions and Ovens and Visions: A Satirical Reading of Daniel 1–6.* Sheffield: Sheffield Phoenix, 2006.

van der Horst, P. W. "Moses' Throne Vision in Ezekiel the Dramatist." *JJS* 34 (1983) 21-29.

VanderKam, James C. "The Putative Author of the Book of *Jubilees.*" *Journal of Semitic Studies* 26 (1981) 209-17.

———. *Enoch and the Growth of an Apocalyptic Tradition.* CBQMS 16. Washington, DC: The Catholic Biblical Association, 1984.

———. *The Book of Jubilees.* Leuven: Peeters, 1989.

———. "The Temple Scroll and the Book of Jubilees." Pages 211-36 in *Temple Scroll Studies.* Edited by G. Brooke. Sheffield: JSOT, 1989.

———. "Biblical Interpretation in 1 Enoch and Jubilees." Pages 96-125 in *The Pseudepigrapha and Early Biblical Interpretation.* Edited by James H. Charlesworth and Craig A. Evans. JSPSup 14. Sheffield: Sheffield Academic Press, 1993.

———. *Enoch: A Man for All Generations.* Columbia: University of South Carolina Press, 1995.

———. "The Angel of the Presence in the Book of *Jubilees.*" *DSD* 7 (2000) 378-93.

———. *The Book of Jubilees.* Guides to Apocrypha and Pseudepigrapha. Sheffield: Sheffield Academic Press, 2001.

———. "The Interpretation of Genesis in 1 Enoch." Pages 129-48 in *The Bible at Qumran: Text, Shape, and Interpretation.* Edited by Peter W. Flint. Grand Rapids: Eerdmans, 2001.

———. "Too Far beyond the Essene Hypothesis?" Pages 388-93 in *Enoch and Qumran Origins: New Light on a Forgotten Connection.* Edited by G. Boccaccini. Grand Rapids: Eerdmans, 2005.

———. "Mapping Second Temple Judaism." Pages 1-20 in *The Early Enoch Literature.* Edited by G. Boccaccini and J. J. Collins. JSJSup 121. Leiden: Brill, 2007.

———. "Moses Trumping Moses: Making the Book of Jubilees." Pages 25-44 in *The Dead Sea Scrolls: Transmission of Traditions and Production of Texts.* Edited by S. Metso, H. Najman, and E. Schuller. STDJ 92. Leiden: Brill, 2010.

———. "The Book of Enoch and the Qumran Scrolls." Pages 254-77 in *The Oxford Handbook of the Dead Sea Scrolls.* Edited by T. H. Lim and J. J. Collins. Oxford: Oxford University Press, 2010.

van der Kooij, Arie. "The Concept of Covenant *(Berît)* in the Book of Daniel." Pages 495-501 in *The Book of Daniel in the Light of New Findings.* Edited by A. S. van der Woude. BETL 106. Leuven: Peeters, 1993.

van der Toorn, Karel. "Scholars at the Oriental Court: The Figure of Daniel against Its Mesopotamian Background." Pages 37-54 in volume 1 of *The Book of Daniel: Composition and Reception.* Edited by John J. Collins and Peter W. Flint. 2 vols. VTSup 83. Leiden: Brill, 2001.

Vermes, Geza. *Scripture and Tradition in Judaism: Haggadic Studies.* 2nd ed. Studia Post-Biblica 4. Leiden: Brill, 1973.

————. *The Complete Dead Sea Scrolls in English.* Revised edition. London: Penguin, 2004.

Vermes, G., and M. Goodman, eds. *The Essenes according to the Classical Sources.* Sheffield: JSOT, 1989.

Vermeylen, J. "La composition littéraire de l'apocalypse d'Isaïe (Is. XXIV–XXVII)." *ETL* 50 (1974) 5-38.

————. *Du prophète Isaïe à l'apocalyptique.* Paris: Gabalda, 1977.

Vielhauer, Phillipp. "Apocalypses and Related Subjects." Pages 581-607 in *New Testament Apocrypha II.* Edited by E. Hennecke and W. Schneemelcher. Translated and edited by R. McL. Wilson. Philadelphia: Westminster, 1965.

Vines, Michael E. "The Apocalyptic Chronotope." Pages 109-17 in *Bakhtin and Genre Theory in Biblical Studies.* Edited by Roland Boer. Semeia Studies 63. Atlanta: Society of Biblical Literature, 2007.

von Rad, Gerhard. *Theologie des Alten Testaments.* 2 vols. 4th ed. Munich: Kaiser, 1965.

Wacker, M. T. *Weltordnung und Gericht. Studien zu 1 Henoch 22.* Würzburg: Echter, 1982.

Wassmuth, Olaf. *Sibyllinische Orakel 1–2. Studien und Kommentar.* Leiden: Brill, 2011.

Watley, Gordon Lyn. "Sibylline Identities: The Jewish and Christian Editions of Sibylline Oracles 1–2." Ph.D. diss., University of Virginia, 2010.

Wellek, René, and Austin Warren. *Theory of Literature.* New York: Harcourt, Brace and World, 1956.

Wellhausen, J. *Die kleinen Propheten.* Berlin: Reimer, 1893.

————. "Zechariah, Book of." Pages 5390-95 in *Encyclopaedia Biblica.* Edited by T. Cheyne. New York: Macmillan, 1903.

Werman, Cana. "'The תורה and the תעודה Engraved on the Tablets." *DSD* 9 (2002) 75-103.

Widengren, G. *The Ascension of the Apostle and the Heavenly Book.* Uppsala: Lundequist, 1950.

Widengren, G., M. Philonenko, and A. Hultgård, eds. *Apocalyptique Iranienne et Dualisme Qoumrânien.* Paris: Maisonneuve, 1995.

Wiesehöfer, Joseph. "Vom 'oberen Asien' zur gesamten bewohnten Welt'. Die hellenistische-römische Weltreiche-Theorie." Pages 66-83 in *Europa, Tausendjähriges Reich und Neue Welt. Zwei Jahrtausende Geschichte und Utopie in der Rezeption des Danielbuches.* Edited by Mariano Delgado, Klaus Koch, and Edgar Marsch. Freiburg Schweiz: Universitätsverlag, 2003.

————. "Daniel, Herodot und 'Darius der Meder'. Auch ein Beitrag zur Idee der Abfolge von Weltreichen." Pages 647-53 in *Von Sumer bis Homer. Festschrift für Manfred Schretter zum 60. Geburtstag.* Edited by R. Rolliger. AOAT 325. Münster: Ugarit-Verlag, 2005.

Wildberger, H. *Isaiah 1–12.* CC. Minneapolis: Fortress, 1991.

————. *Isaiah 13–27*. CC. Minneapolis: Fortress, 1997.

Williams, G. *Tradition and Originality in Roman Poetry*. Oxford: Oxford University Press, 1968.

Wills, Lawrence M. *The Jew in the Court of the Foreign King: Ancient Jewish Court Legends*. Minneapolis: Fortress, 1990.

Wilson, Robert R. "From Prophecy to Apocalyptic: Reflections on the Shape of Israelite Religion." *Semeia* 21 (1981) 79-95.

Wise, Michael O. "4QFlorilegium and the Temple of Adam." *RevQ* 15 (1991) 103-32.

Wittgenstein, Ludwig. *Philosophical Investigations*. Oxford: Blackwell, 1958.

Wright, B. G. "Putting the Puzzle Together: Some Suggestions concerning the Social Location of the Wisdom of Ben Sira." Pages 133-49 in *SBL Seminar Papers*. Atlanta: Scholars Press, 1996.

Wright, J. E. *The Early History of Heaven*. New York: Oxford University Press, 2000.

Wright, M. R. *Cosmology in Antiquity*. London: Routledge, 1995.

Yadin, Y. "Le Rouleau du Temple." Pages 115-19 in *Qoumrân. Sa Piété, sa théologie et son milieu*. Edited by M. Delcor. Leuven: Leuven University Press, 1978.

Yarbro Collins, Adela. *The Combat Myth in the Book of Revelation*. HDR 9. Missoula: Scholars Press, 1976.

————. "Persecution and Vengeance in the Book of Revelation." Pages 729-49 in *Apocalypticism in the Mediterranean World and the Near East*. Edited by David Hellholm. Tübingen: Mohr, 1983.

————. *Crisis and Catharsis: The Power of the Apocalypse*. Philadelphia: Westminster, 1984.

————. "Introduction." *Semeia* 36 (1986) 1-11.

————. *Cosmology and Eschatology in Jewish and Early Christian Apocalypticism*. JSJSup 50. Leiden: Brill, 1996.

————. "The Dream of a New Jerusalem at Qumran." Pages 231-54 in *The Bible and the Dead Sea Scrolls*, volume 3: *The Scrolls and Christian Origins*. Edited by J. H. Charlesworth. Waco, TX: Baylor University Press, 2006.

Yarbro Collins, Adela, and John J. Collins. *King and Messiah as Son of God*. Grand Rapids: Eerdmans, 2009.

Yardeni, A. "A New Dead Sea Scroll on Stone?" *Biblical Archaeology Review* 34.1 (2008) 60-61.

Yardeni, A., and B. Elitzur. "Document: A First-Century BCE Prophetic Text Written on Stone: First Publication." *Cathedra* 123 (2007) 55-66 [Heb.].

Yuditsky, Alexey, and Elisha Qimron. "Notes on the Inscription, 'The Vision of Gabriel." *Cathedra* 133 (2009) 133-44 [Heb.].

Zaehner, R. C. *The Dawn and Twilight of Zoroastrianism*. London: Weidenfeld & Nicholson, 1961.

Zahn, Molly M. "The Problem of Characterizing the 4QReworked Pentateuch Manuscripts: Bible, Rewritten Bible, or None of the Above?" *Dead Sea Discoveries* 15 (2008) 315-39.

———. "Rewritten Scripture." Pages 323-36 in *The Oxford Handbook of the Dead Sea Scrolls*. Edited by Timothy Lim and John J. Collins. Oxford: Oxford University Press, 2010.

———. *Rethinking Rewritten Scripture: Composition and Exegesis in the 4QReworked Pentateuch Manuscripts*. STDJ 95. Leiden: Brill, 2011.

Zangenberg, J. "The 'Final Farewell,' a Necessary Paradigm Shift in the Interpretation of the Qumran Cemetery." *Qumran Chronicle* 8 (1999) 273-78.

Zimmerli, Walther. *Ezekiel 2: A Commentary on the Book of the Prophet Ezekiel chapters 25–48*. Hermeneia. Philadelphia: Fortress, 1983.

Index of Modern Authors

Index of Ancient Sources